The Law of the Sea and Maritime Boundary Disputes in Areas of Hydrocarbon Potential

The United Nations Convention on the Law of Sea (UNCLOS) is hailed as one of the most significant multilateral legal agreements executed in the past few decades. However, its shortcomings are neither trivial nor inconsequential, especially regarding maritime boundary disputes involving hydrocarbon resources. This monograph examines the relationship between UNCLOS and maritime boundaries in five non-polar regions, encompassing almost 90% of global unresolved disputes involving offshore hydrocarbon development. The regions, which include the eastern Mediterranean, the Caspian Sea, the Persian Gulf, northeast Asia, and the South China Sea, were chosen for their oil and gas resources potential, and recent military skirmishes have the potential to lead to wider regional confrontations. The book addresses each region's maritime boundary status in the context of specific articles within UNCLOS that have been exploited by disputing states to justify their overlapping claims. The history and future applicability of multilateral Joint Development Area agreements for each region are evaluated for their potential to provide a cooperative solution to resolve ongoing tensions. Highlighting the limitations of current 'gunboat' diplomacy, the monograph makes practical suggestions for new paradigms for resolving outstanding disputes, promoting lasting peace, and generating economic benefits resulting from resource development.

Vivek Chandra is a natural gas and liquefied natural gas (LNG) entrepreneur with over 30 years of global petroleum-industry technical, commercial, financial, and project development experience. Dr Chandra is the author of *Fundamentals of Natural Gas: An International Perspective*, a book currently in its second edition, and has degrees in Geophysical Engineering (Colorado School of Mines), Energy Management (University of Pennsylvania), Petroleum Economics (IFP, France), Commercial Law (Deakin University, Australia), and a PhD in International Law with a dissertation on disputed international maritime boundaries (Deakin University, Australia). Vivek Chandra can be reached at vchandra@natgas.info.

Routledge Research on the Law of the Sea

Available titles in this series include:

The International Court of Justice in Maritime Disputes
The Case of Chile and Peru
Julio Faundez

Freedoms of Navigation in the Asia-Pacific Region
Strategic, Political and Legal Factors
Sam Bateman

Maritime Claims and Boundary Delimitation
Tensions and Trends in the Eastern Mediterranean Sea
Nicholas A. Ioannides

Freedom of Navigation and the Law of the Sea
Warships, States and the Use of Force
Cameron Moore

Due Diligence and the High Seas
Tony Cabus

The Law of the Sea
Normative Context and Interactions with other Legal Regimes
Edited by Nele Matz-Lück, Øystein Jensen and Elise Johansen

Law of the Sea and Maritime Delimitation
State Practice and Case Law in Latin America and the Caribbean
Angel Horna

Maritime Salvage Operations and Environmental Protection
Durand M Cupido

Peaceful Management of Maritime Disputes
James Kraska and Hee Cheol Yang

The Law of the Sea and Maritime Boundary Disputes in Areas of Hydrocarbon Potential
A Review of Global Hot Spots
Vivek Chandra

The Law of the Sea and Maritime Boundary Disputes in Areas of Hydrocarbon Potential

A Review of Global Hot Spots

Vivek Chandra

Routledge
Taylor & Francis Group
LONDON AND NEW YORK

First published 2024
by Routledge
4 Park Square, Milton Park, Abingdon, Oxon OX14 4RN

and by Routledge
605 Third Avenue, New York, NY 10158

Routledge is an imprint of the Taylor & Francis Group, an informa business

British Library Cataloguing-in-Publication Data
A catalogue record for this book is available from the British Library

ISBN: 978-1-032-34616-8 (hbk)
ISBN: 978-1-032-34617-5 (pbk)
ISBN: 978-1-003-32305-1 (ebk)

DOI: 10.4324/9781003323051

Typeset in Times New Roman
by Deanta Global Publishing Services, Chennai, India

Contents

Figures

Acknowledgements

I would like to express my sincere gratitude to my friends and family who have provided me with enormous support as I pursue my varied interests.

I also would like to specifically acknowledge Dr John Morss, my PhD Advisor, who provided me with an optimal balance of suggestions and encouragement during much of the research period. I would also like to recognise my father, Vinod Chandra, for his tireless proofreading of the drafts, and my sister, Vinita Chandra Domier, for her assistance with the graphics. I also appreciate the support of my wife, Anamica Roy, her son, Shay Nazareth, my son, Kiran Chandra, and my mother, Pushpa Chandra, for their patience during this enjoyable, but prolonged, journey.

Dr Vivek Chandra
vchandra@natgas.info

Abbreviations

ACG	Azeri–Chirag–Gunashli fields, offshore Azerbaijan, Caspian
ADIZ	Air Defence Identification Zone (declared by China and others in northeast Asia)
AGP	Arab Gas Pipeline
ASEAN	Association of South East Asian Nations
Bbls	Barrels (of oil)
Bcf	Billion cubic feet (of natural gas)
Bcm	Billion cubic metres (of natural gas)
BP	Formerly British Petroleum (British multinational energy company)
CIS	Commonwealth of Independent States (former USSR States)
CIL	Customary International Law
CLCS	Commission on the Limits of the Continental Shelf
CNOOC	Chinese National Offshore Oil Company
CPC	Chinese Petroleum Company (Taiwan)
DoC	(ASEAN–China) Declaration on the Conduct of Parties in the South China Sea
EIA	US Energy Information Agency
EEZ	Exclusive Economic Zone
ENI	Ente Nazionale Idrocarburi (Italian multinational energy company)
GCC	Gulf Cooperation Council
EU	European Union
ICJ	International Court of Justice
IEC	Israel Electricity Company
ITLOS	International Tribunal for the Law of the Sea
JDA	Joint Development Area
JMSU	Joint Marine Seismic Undertaking (between China, the Philippines, and Vietnam)
KNOC	Korean National Oil Company
LNG	Liquefied Natural Gas
nm	Nautical mile (1 nm = 1.85 km)
PCA	Permanent Court of Arbitration
PLA	Peoples Liberation Army, China

PLAN	Peoples Liberation Army Navy, China
PNOC	Philippines National Oil Company
PRC	People's Republic of China
ROC	Republic of China (Taiwan)
ROK	Republic of Korea (South Korea)
SSR	Soviet Socialist Republic
Tcf	Trillion cubic feet (of natural gas)
TRNC	Turkish Republic of Northern Cyprus
UAE	United Arab Emirates
UK	United Kingdom
UN	United Nations
UNECAFE	United Nations Economic Commission for Asia and the Far East
UNCLCS	UN Commission on the Limits of the Continental Shelf
UNCLOS	United Nations Convention on the Law of the Sea
UNIFIL	UN Interim Force in Lebanon
US	United States of America
USGS	United States Geological Survey
USSR	Union of Soviet Socialist Republics
WW I & WW II	World War I & World War II

1 Introduction

1.1 Introduction and Monograph Focus

> Recognizing the desirability of establishing through this Convention, with due regard for the sovereignty of all states, a *legal order for the seas and oceans* which will facilitate international communication, and will *promote the peaceful uses of the seas and oceans*, the *equitable and efficient utilization of their resources*, the conservation of their living resources, and the study, protection and preservation of the marine environment.[1]

The text above, from the Preamble of the United Nations Convention on the Law of Sea (UNCLOS, or the 'Convention'), demonstrates the lofty ambitions of the drafters of this monumental Convention. Though UNCLOS has been described as 'a landmark in the history of the politico-diplomatic negotiating system … the most innovative international law-making project ever undertaken,'[2] and has been ratified by 168 parties,[3] praise for UNCLOS has been widespread with relatively few questioning if the Convention has, in fact, lived up to its expectations.[4] Because UNCLOS was, like other multilateral agreements, a 'political bargain' which aspired to be universal, it is 'undoubtedly an imperfect and incomplete instrument.'[5]

This monograph critically examines the impact of UNCLOS on offshore oil and gas exploitation and reviews global hotspot regions where bilateral and regional maritime boundary tensions remain high. The regions, which include the eastern Mediterranean, the Caspian Sea, the Persian Gulf, northeast Asia, and the South China Sea, were highlighted because of their offshore oil and gas resources potential, recent military skirmishes which have the potential to lead to wider regional confrontations, and because they represent over 80% of resolved and unresolved hydrocarbon resource-related global maritime boundary disputes. Each region's maritime boundary and hydrocarbon activity history is examined against the backdrop of specific articles within UNCLOS that have been exploited by disputing States to justify their claims. The history and future applicability of multilateral cooperative Joint Development Area (JDA) agreements, which allow hydrocarbon activities to proceed with or without prior boundary delimitation, is reviewed for each of the regions.

Though UNCLOS granted rights to coastal States to explore and exploit seabed resources by establishing distinct maritime zones, there are no specific provisions

DOI: 10.4324/9781003323051-1

for oil and gas exploration or production within the Convention. In fact, UNCLOS does not mention the terms 'hydrocarbon,' 'petroleum,' 'oil,' or 'gas' anywhere within the Convention.[6] This is surprising as UNCLOS III negotiations convened shortly after the 1973 war in the Middle East which led to a period of rising oil prices and a growing recognition of the need for States to define their offshore maritime boundaries to facilitate the legal framework for offshore oil and gas production.[7] At the time of the final draft of UNCLOS in 1982, the global petroleum industry had ventured deep offshore, discovering many of the largest offshore oil and gas fields in the North Sea, Middle East, Southeast Asia, US, and elsewhere. The lack of legal clarity and guidance in relation to these valuable natural resources is an omission that has undoubtedly contributed to some of the unresolved maritime boundary disputes that will be highlighted in this book.

Hydrocarbon resources are different from other maritime resources such as fisheries. Hydrocarbon exploration and production activities, more than other minerals and mineral nodules found on the seabed, require large amounts of capital, are often undertaken in partnership with international private companies who take most of the risks under exclusive licence of the national government, can be a major contributor to a State's economy and employment, and, because many years (sometime decades) transpire between initial discovery and production, require high degrees of boundary, fiscal, commercial, and political certainty. Uniquely, oil and gas resources are migratory which can move across maritime boundaries via subsurface rock strata. Thus, an action of one State acting within its territory can impact the production of a cross border field shared with an adjoining State.

The exploitation of hydrocarbons is a key motivation for States to define their maritime zones. As most of the global offshore hydrocarbon resources lie within the economic areas of coastal States,[8] the urgency of border delimitation becomes relevant when States realise the value in exploitation of their resources. Unfortunately, once hydrocarbon resource potential is established, negotiations and agreements to delimit maritime boundaries between adjoining or opposite-facing coastal States often become more contentious because of this perceived resource value.

An unresolved maritime boundary dispute adds an additional 'above-ground' risk factor that energy companies may not have the power or ability to mitigate.[9] Energy companies are usually granted concessions by a State for a specific geographic area where the company would have exclusive rights to explore and produce hydrocarbons for a defined term. The concession-granting State is assumed to have complete jurisdiction and rights over the construction of infrastructure for the development of oil and gas resources. If the geographic area is claimed by more than one State, the rights granted to the energy company by one of these States are put at risk and may lead to diplomatic, and in some cases, military confrontations between the disputing States, sometimes placing the energy company in the 'firing line.' This has been the case in many regions of the world, including recently in the eastern Mediterranean, the Caspian Sea, the Persian Gulf, and the South China Sea. On a macro level, as global economies transition away from fossil fuels, there is an urgency for peaceful resolution of outstanding boundary issues to hasten monetisation of disputed hydrocarbon resources for the economic benefit of their citizens.

The highlighted maritime border disputes were examined in their regional context and the role, if any, UNCLOS has played in either its resolution or its continued disputed status. Out of the 108 total identified disputes, the subset of 81 resolved disputes were studied to determine their resolution methodology and to determine if the pace of resolution has changed in the past few decades. The remaining 27 unresolved disputes were examined for their common characteristics and potential for resolution under the framework of UNCLOS. The compiled dataset includes the overwhelming majority of all significant international maritime borders involving hydrocarbon resource potential.[10]

This book evaluates the effect that UNCLOS's arguably ambiguous articles have had on this economically valuable subset of maritime boundary disputes. UNCLOS articles associated with the overlapping maritime claim zones, status of islands and rocks, provisional solutions, and dispute resolution procedures are highlighted as they relate to specific disputes.

The highlighted disputes also share other characteristics, including the presence of a large regional player that is involved in many of the individual disputes (such as China in northeast Asia and the South China Sea, Iran in the Persian Gulf and Caspian Sea, and Turkey in the eastern Mediterranean), restricted oil and gas exploration activities, and the liberal use of historical justifications to support claims. The potential for serious conflict, beyond the regular military skirmishes (though there has not been an overt war in recent history directly relating to maritime delimitations), and the use of nationalistic fervour by politicians (such as those in China, Japan, Vietnam, Iran, and Turkey) is also a common theme in the chosen regions.

All five selected regions are in the Eastern Hemisphere. Though the Western Hemisphere accounts for a relatively large number of resolved disputes (15%), it only has two unresolved geographically dispersed maritime boundaries in the dataset and was thus not included as a case study. Notably, Western Europe, which is a region with 16% of the resolved disputes, does not have any remaining unresolved hydrocarbon-related maritime disputes, and thus did not warrant its own detailed case study chapter. However, the importance of precedents derived from European maritime border disputes cannot be overstated. Seminal cases, such as the *North Sea Continental Shelf Cases*[11] and the *Maritime Delimitation in the Area between Greenland and Jan Mayen case*[12] have greatly influenced subsequent cases, arbitrations, and treaties. Though the first JDAs were in the Persian Gulf, the landmark framework agreements between the UK and Norway, and UK and Netherlands were the models used for many negotiated JDAs studied in this book.

1.2 Maritime Jurisdiction Zones

One of the key purported achievements of UNCLOS was the establishment of 'a clear framework for the limits of coastal States' claims to maritime jurisdiction.'[13]

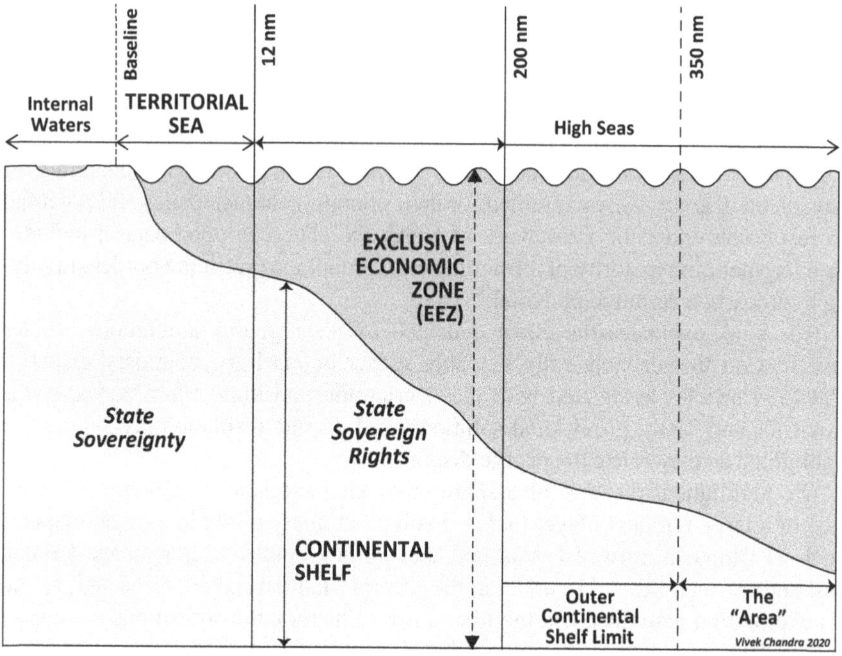

Figure 1.1 Maritime zones

Prior to UNCLOS, the situation was dominated by unilateral claims and an 'incongruous legal state of affairs for offshore rights'[14] some of which were based on the 1958 *Convention on the Continental Shelf*[15] and others on coastal States' self-serving proclamations.

1.2.1 Territorial Sea and Continental Shelf

The basic premise governing the law of the sea is that 'the land dominates the sea.'[16] If a coastal State does not have sovereignty over the land, it cannot claim sovereignty over the maritime zones extending from the land.[17] Thus, the sovereign status of the land is the starting point for the rights of the adjacent seas.[18]

The maritime zone with the clearest rights and obligations is the territorial sea. The International Court of Justice (ICJ) has confirmed that all coastal States have an entitlement to a territorial sea and a coastal State has sovereignty and extensive jurisdictional control over its territorial seas.[19]

The width of the territorial sea has been the subject of much debate and discrepancy. In the late 1800s, the standard was based on standard 'cannon-shot' range of three nautical miles (nm).[20] In 1911, Russia extended its claim to 6 nm of territorial sea plus additional 6 nm of exclusive fishing rights, followed by similar proclamations by European powers such as France, Italy, Spain, and others.

In the post-WW II period, the trend accelerated with more ambitious claims made by both the victorious as well as newly independent States. The President of the US, Harry S. Truman, is credited with beginning the process of unilateral proclamations on 28 September 1945 with his *Continental Shelf Proclamation* and *Fisheries Proclamation.*[21] These twin proclamations extended the claimed rights of the US beyond the 3-nm limit, and were followed by numerous States following suit, many with larger and often differing unilateral claims into maritime areas that had previously been considered *res nullius.*[22]

The Truman *Continental Shelf Proclamation* legitimised the US claim of an exclusive 250 nm contiguous 'continental shelf' from the US east coast and 50 nm from the US west coast. The Truman Proclamations were driven in part by the recognition of offshore oil resources as an increasingly important strategic and economic advantage.[23] It should be noted that the Truman Proclamations specifically stated that waters were to remain 'high seas' and that certain freedoms, such as navigation and overflight were not to be affected.[24] As a result of these proclamations, the US became the first nation to assert control and rights over the natural resources of its continental shelf.

The ensuing period presented lawyers with the problem of reconciling zones of maritime jurisdiction with each other. The resulting inconsistency of claims and definitions encouraged the International Law Commission to include the regime of territorial waters and of high seas as topics for codification in its 1956 report.[25] Subsequently, the UN General Assembly adopted Resolution 1105 (XI) of 21 February 1957, which convened the first United Nations Conference on the Law of the Sea (often referred to as 'UNCLOS I') in Geneva in 1958.[26] As a result of this Conference, four landmark agreements, including the *Convention on the Continental Shelf* and 1958 *Convention on the Territorial Sea and the Contiguous Zone* were drafted.[27]

Article 1(a) of the *Convention on the Continental Shelf* defined 'continental shelf' as

> the seabed and subsoil of the submarine areas adjacent to the coast but outside the area of the territorial sea, to a depth of 200 meters or, beyond that limit, to where the depth of the superjacent waters admits of the exploitation of the natural resources of the said areas.[28]

The *Convention on the Continental Shelf* effectively codified the rights coastal States enjoy over their claimed continental shelf by giving States the exclusive right to explore and exploit the resources of the seabed and subsoil of the submarine areas.[29] However, the inclusion of the clause, 'admits to the exploitation of natural resources' in Article 1(a), was considered 'most problematic,' and not surprisingly, led to further confusion.[30]

Defining the width of the territorial sea and the inconsistent interpretation of the limits of the continental shelf were some of the difficulties the first UNCLOS conference (UNCLOS I) had in attracting a majority of States to accept the agreement. Ambassador Arvid Pardo, one of the leading advocates for UNCLOS, feared that the exploitability criteria would allow any coastal State, 'as its technical capability develops … [to] extend its jurisdiction across the deep-sea floor up to the midway point between it and the coastal state opposite' resulting in a 'scramble for sovereign rights over the land underlying the world's seas and ocean,' and appealed at the 1967 UN General Assembly to convene another conference on the law of the sea.[31]

The subsequent 1960 UNCLOS II conference was called to specifically address the unresolved issues of the breadth of the territorial sea and fisheries limits. The US and Canada proposed 6 nm of territorial sea coupled with an exclusive fisheries zone for a further 6 nm.[32] The conference failed to reach agreement and ended with deferral of outstanding issues to a later convention.

The third UNCLOS conference, UNCLOS III, stretched over 11 separate sessions between 1973 and 1982. The resulting *Law of the Sea Convention*, commonly referred to as simply the *United Nations Convention on the Law of the Sea* ('UNCLOS'), opened for signatures on 10 December 1982 after 14 years of negotiations involving more than 150 States. All four Convention landmark agreements, including the *Convention on the Continental Shelf,* from UNCLOS I were superseded by UNCLOS, which had incorporated 'traditional rules for the uses of the oceans and at the same time introduced new legal concepts and regimes and addressed new concerns.'[33] UNCLOS entered into force in accordance with its Article 308 on 16 November 1994, 12 months after the date of its 60th State ratification.[34]

UNCLOS Article 76 defines the continental shelf as:

> [T]he seabed and subsoil of the submarine areas that extend beyond [coastal State's] territorial sea throughout the natural prolongation of its land territory to the outer edge of the continental margin, or to a distance of 200 nautical miles from the baselines from which the breadth of the territorial sea is measured where the outer edge of the continental margin does not extend up to that distance.[35]

On the continental shelf, coastal States have sovereign rights to explore and exploit the natural resources, rights to construct artificial islands, installations and structures, and exclusive rights to permit drilling.[36]

The definition of the continental shelf no longer includes the problematic exploitability criterion – the critical factor that caused uncertainty in the previous *Convention on the Continental Shelf.* Also, in contrast to previous definitions, such as the one used by the ICJ in the *North Sea Continental Shelf Cases*, there was no longer any role for geologic characteristics to play in defining the continental shelf.[37] The new definition also went beyond the linkage of the continental shelf to the natural prolongation of coastal State territorial landmasses suggested in the *North Sea Continental Shelf Cases* by also entitling coastal States up to 200 nm of the continental shelf, even if the sea floor did not 'conform to a geographic definition of a continental shelf.'[38] The extension of the continental shelf to 200 nm, even if the 'geologic' continental shelf did not extend as far, provided certainty for subsea resource control and exploitation, but has also attracted criticism for setting a generous minimum limit.[39] Geographic and seabed geometry factors only matter if the coastal State applies to extend its continental shelf up to a maximum of 350 nm from baselines.

1.2.1.1 Extension of Outer Limits of Continental Shelf

States can submit scientific and technical data evidence to extend the outer limits of their continental shelf beyond the 200-nm limit, up to a jurisdiction of 350 nm from the baseline or 100 nm from the 2,500-m depth line. There have been over 70 submissions to the special committee for extension of the outer continental shelf beyond 200 nm.[40] Under UNCLOS, any exploitation of non-living resources beyond 200 nm would require payments or contributions in kind to be made to the International Seabed Authority which will organise and regulate activities in the deep seabed beyond national jurisdiction and distribute the receipts in 'an equitable manner to all States.'[41] The 2023 passing of the High Seas Treaty, which establishes marine protection areas in the High Seas (generally considered as beyond the 200-nm limit), will further define activities in this area.

1.2.2 Exclusive Economic Zone

Arguably, one of the most revolutionary aspects of UNCLOS is the granting of an Exclusive Economic Zone (EEZ) to all coastal States.[42] Scholars credit UNCLOS with the introduction of the EEZ defined by a 200-nm jurisdictional zone. However, the concept of an exclusive economic maritime area, though not the defined 200-nm breadth, was already an accepted concept in customary law, predating UNCLOS by many decades.[43]

Similar to the continental shelf regime, EEZs are not subject to a State's sovereignty, but are maritime zones where a coastal State claims certain sovereign rights.[44] These 'exploration and exploitation' rights extend to the management of both living and non-living natural resources in the water column, the seabed, and its subsoil, and include the production of energy from water, current, and winds.[45] All States, whether coastal or landlocked, have certain rights and freedoms within the declared EEZs of other States.[46] These universal rights include freedom of navigation and overflight, laying of submarine cables and pipelines, and other 'internationally lawful uses of the seas' related to these freedoms.[47] UNCLOS stresses that 'rights enjoyed by all States' have to be balanced against the 'due regard to the rights and duties of the coastal State.'[48]

This complex nature of the legal status of the EEZ has been a subject to much debate and was one of the prolonged negotiation topics during the drafting of UNCLOS. As noted by Koh:

> One of the most difficult questions relating to the EEZ is its legal status. Is the EEZ a zone of national jurisdiction? Is it part of the high seas? Is it a *sui generis* zone? The negotiations over this question at the conference took several years … First, it was agreed that the EEZ was neither territorial sea

nor part of the high seas but was *sui generis* ... Second, it was agreed that no State could subject the EEZ to its sovereignty.[49]

This book examines a number of instances where the conduct of some States in their EEZ more closely resembles zones of 'sovereignty' as traditionally understood rather than 'sovereign rights.'[50] In these cases, the coastal States treat their EEZ as part of their national territory with the same degree of control as they would any other part of its jurisdiction, in contradiction to what was 'agreed' by UNCLOS negotiators as observed by Koh.[51]

Confusingly, the EEZ covers the same 200-nm belt extending from a State's baseline that was used to define the continental shelf. In contrast to the continental shelf regime, which deals with the seabed and subsoil, the EEZ regime also includes the water column, and as stated above, cannot be wider than 200 nm.

The diminished role of historical rights in defining the EEZs has caused tensions in many parts of the world, including the South China Sea, northeast Asia, the Persian Gulf, and the Caspian Sea, where States continue to claim access to fisheries and hydrocarbon resources based on purported historical and traditional rights. Court rulings, including the 2016 *South China Sea Arbitration* Tribunal's conclusion that the text of UNCLOS supersedes any historical rights a State may claim in the EEZ or continental shelf, have confirmed the diminished role of historical rights.[52] However, as is discussed extensively in this book, the tensions between claimed historical rights and UNCLOS-granted EEZ rights continue to be prevalent in most of the disputes discussed.

The global area covered under the EEZ definition is significant. By some estimates, the EEZ regime embraces about a third of the marine environment and 87% of the known and potential hydrocarbon resources.[53] In its own report published in 1998, the UN admits that the EEZs are a 'generous endowment.'[54] The lack of guidance regarding exploitation of trans-border hydrocarbon deposits and rights of States to build trans-border pipelines crossing the EEZ of other States will be shown to be a weakness of UNCLOS present in many of the disputes examined in this book.

1.2.3 Overlapping Zones and Maritime Border Delimitation

UNCLOS mandates that delimitation of the EEZ and the continental shelf between States with opposite or adjacent coasts shall be 'effected by agreement based on international law, as referred to in Article 38 of the Statute of the International Court of Justice, in order to achieve an equitable solution.'[55]

However, UNCLOS does not prescribe methods to reach an 'equitable solution.' Unsurprisingly, coastal States have made claims that maximise their own individual rights – and these claims often overlap, especially where opposite coastlines are less than 400 nm apart. This is a common situation in smaller semi-enclosed seas, including the South China Sea, the Persian Gulf, and the Mediterranean Sea. There is limited guidance within UNCLOS on how to resolve the overlapping continental shelf or EEZ claims, and how to exploit resources in disputed zones.[56] Arguably, the ambiguous text allows 'much room for radically differing interpretations as to which factors and methods of delimitation are appropriate to a particular case, and therefore the potential for dispute and deadlock in delimitation negotiations.'[57] A prominent ICJ judge, Bernardo Sepúlveda-Amor, has called this aspect of UNCLOS language as 'deliberately ambiguous' and others have called it 'vague.'[58]

Prior to the establishment of UNCLOS's 'equitable principles,' maritime boundaries relied on notions of equality and proportionality, typically resolving to a median line boundary.[59] Both the 1958 *Convention on the Continental Shelf* and the 1958 *Convention on the Territorial Sea and Contiguous Zone* recommended the principle of equidistance to resolve maritime delimitation disputes.[60] The landmark 1969 *North Sea Continental Shelf Cases*[61] established State rights over their continental shelf and, for the first time, described the 'equitable principles' for maritime boundary delimitation which were adopted by UNCLOS and referenced in a number of ICJ and International Tribunal for the Law of the Sea (ITLOS) cases thereafter.[62] During the 1973 UNCLOS III negotiations, States were divided between pro-equidistance and pro-equity groups. This became a 'hard issue' on the agenda of UNCLOS III.[63] After much negotiation, and intervention by the UNCLOS III President Koh, the compromise language that appears in Articles 74 and 83 was adopted.

With these articles, UNCLOS established 'the principle that sea boundary definitions are to be effected by agreement between the parties, rather than dictating substantive rules that must be followed when determining such boundaries.'[64] UNCLOS also confirmed ICJ jurisprudence for its concept of 'equitable principles' which, as Sepúlveda-Amor stated, 'found reflection in the deliberately ambiguous provisions of Articles 74 and 83 of UNCLOS.'[65]

The issue with including equity criteria is its lack of uniformity and precision. Recognising the 'unicum' in the meaning of 'equitable principles,' the ICJ declared, in the 1984 *Gulf of Maine Area* (*Canada/United States of America*) case,

> [t]hat each specific case is in the final analysis, different from all the others, that it is monotypic and that, more often than not, the most appropriate criteria, and the method or combination of methods most likely to yield a result consonant with what the law indicates, can only be determined in relation to each particular case and its specific characteristics.[66]

The ICJ, which has adjudicated 11 of the maritime boundaries in the dataset, has continued to evolve its delimitation guidelines. In the 2001 *Maritime Delimitation and Territorial Questions between Qatar and Bahrain* and in the 2002 *Land and Maritime Boundary between Cameroon and Nigeria (Cameroon v. Nigeria: Equatorial Guinea intervening*) [2002], the court used a two-stage process to delimit maritime boundaries.[67] In the 2009 *Maritime Delimitation in the Black Sea (Romania v. Ukraine)*[68] the court was requested by the disputing parties to delimit a single boundary for both the continental shelf and EEZ between Romania and Ukraine in the Black Sea. In the February 2009 *Summary of Judgment*, the ICJ clarified a three-stage 'delimitation methodology.'[69]

The three-stage delimitation method, considered as the ICJ's preferred method since the 2009 Black Sea case,[70] consists of the following steps: (1) establish the provisional delimitation line equidistant between the States, (2) consider any relevant circumstances that may require the adjustment of that provisional equidistance line, and lastly (3) verify that the line does not lead to an inequitable result 'disproportionality test.'[71] This formula, or variations thereof, has been referenced in subsequent decisions by the ICJ and other tribunals and termed as the 'equidistance/relevant circumstances method.'[72]

The evolution from equidistance to equitable, and now, equidistance/relevant circumstances, represents the continued evolution of the principles of marine boundary delimitation. However, the continued existence of a relatively large number of unresolved boundaries, especially those that involve hydrocarbon activities where the economic stakes are perceived to be high, may be a testament to either the inefficiency or inadequacy of these principles.

1.2.4 Maritime Zone Baselines

The breadth of a coastal State's territorial sea, continental shelf, and EEZ are all measured from delimited baselines. UNCLOS defines the 'normal' baseline as the 'low-water line along the coast.'[73] This is an accepted principle of international law codified in Article 3 of the 1958 *Convention on the Territorial Sea and the Contiguous Zone*.[74] UNCLOS allows straight baselines where the coastline is 'deeply indented and cut into, or if there is a fringe of islands along the coast,' but does not further define the meaning of terms such as 'deeply indented' or 'fringe of islands.'[75] By some estimates, more than 80 States have adopted straight baselines to their maximum advantage, encompassing thousands of square kilometres of maritime space as internal waters and thus within the State's sovereignty.[76] Not surprisingly, the use of straight baselines is controversial and open to abuse, especially when near-shore oil and gas fields have been identified. The lack of consistency in defining baselines, and the fact that so many States continue to assert excessive baseline claims, undermines the authority of the Convention to enforce its own rules.[77]

1.3 Islands and Rocks

Ambiguous language used in definitions of maritime zones and baselines has arguably contributed to some of the ongoing maritime boundary disputes. According to some observers, the distinction of 'islands' versus 'rocks' is an uncertainty that has 'probably given rise to more controversy between States than any other aspect of the Convention.'[78]

An 'island,' as defined in Article 121(1), is 'a naturally formed area of land, surrounded by water, which is above water at high tide.'[79] The importance of islands becomes evident in Article 121(2), which grants 'islands' identical rights bestowed to coastlines of land territory including the full suite of maritime zones. An 'island' with open seas of 400 nm in any direction could generate 125,664 nm^2 (431,014 km^2) of territorial sea, EEZ, and continental shelf rights.[80] Thus, the maritime space associated with an island, especially a remote island, can be more valuable and strategic than the island itself.[81]

By contrast, a 'rock' does not have an equivalent definition, and thus has vastly different economic and marine territorial implications. As per Article 121(3), 'rocks which cannot sustain human habitation or economic life of their own shall have no exclusive economic zone or continental shelf.'[82] In this case, a 'rock' feature with no immediate neighbours would generate a territorial sea of only 452 nm^2 (1,550 km^2), less than 0.3% of the entitlement of an 'island.'[83] During maritime negotiations, States have been 'extremely reluctant to admit that any of their insular features are in fact (at least in legal terms) rocks, which only generate a relatively small area of territorial sea.'[84]

These definitions are examples where UNCLOS seems to be 'drafted in a deliberately ambiguous fashion, and that a definitive, authoritative interpretation of what constitutes an "island" or a "rock" is currently out of reach.'[85] The distinction between the two features is a 'legal grey area.'[86] If a feature is uninhabited, but otherwise meets the definition of island, including its capability to support life, does the feature deserve an EEZ and continental shelf? In some cases, the legal status of the feature is not in dispute, but there remains disagreement over the influence that the feature should have on the boundary.[87]

The distinction between 'island' and 'rock' is an underlying issue in many of the highlighted maritime border disputes – not only because of the value or sovereignty of the island (or rock) feature itself, but because of the known and potential hydrocarbon resources in the surrounding maritime zones. This is especially the case in the South China Sea, in northeast Asia, and the Persian Gulf, where certain States justify their maritime claims based on the ability of disputed maritime features, some of which are artificial constructions on submerged reefs, to sustain human habitation to meet UNCLOS's island definition.[88]

1.4 Provisional Arrangements

Although UNCLOS suggests that coastal States involved in boundary disputes should formulate provisional solutions pending the final EEZ and continental shelf boundary delimitations, there is no elaboration on the nature or structure of these provisional settlements. Article 74 (and in almost identical language, Article 83) discusses the delimitation of EEZ and continental shelf between States with opposite or adjacent coasts:

> [p]ending agreement ... the States concerned, in a spirit of understanding and cooperation, shall make every effort to enter into provisional arrangements of a practical nature and, during this transitional period, not to jeopardize or hamper the reaching of the final agreement. Such arrangements shall be without prejudice to the final delimitation.[89]

JDA agreements are a relatively common example of a provisional agreement for the development of oil and gas. In the context of this book, JDA agreements include both unitisation agreements to development of hydrocarbon deposits straddling delimited as well as non-delimited overlapping maritime boundary claim areas.

Beyond the indirect references in the text of Articles 74 and 83, UNCLOS does not provide any further clarifications or details on the JDA cooperative solution. Articles 74 and 83 have been interpreted to imply an obligation for the affected States to enter into agreements that will not jeopardise or hamper a permanent delimitation treaty. Thus, the agreements have to both promote joint development as well as not prejudice a permanent boundary solution.

The landmark ICJ 1969 *North Sea Continental Shelf* cases introduced joint exploitation agreements as those that 'provide for joint exploitation or profit sharing in areas of considerable extent where the national boundaries were undetermined.'[90] The ICJ's favourable disposition towards joint development was further confirmed in the 1982 *Continental Shelf (Tunisia/Libya) case*.[91] The concept of joint development was contained in the 1974 UN *Charter of Economic Rights*, predating UNCLOS by almost a decade, which stated,

> [i]n the exploitation of natural resources shared by two or more countries, each state must co-operate on the basis of a system of information and prior consultations in order to achieve optimum use of such resources without causing damage to the legitimate interest of others.[92]

Though JDAs give disputing States a 'face-saving' alternative, allowing for creative solutions to solve otherwise intractable differences, they can be difficult to negotiate. The process can take years of cooperative effort and requires a high degree of trust between disputing States. As evidenced by multiple North Sea joint field development agreements signed prior to UNCLOS, the JDA concept would have been understood and accepted as a border delimitation resolution solution prior to UNCLOS.[93] Hypothetically, if UNCLOS had provided further guidance or even terms of a model JDA agreement, the negotiation process for each could have been expedited and JDAs may have proliferated more widely.

This book suggests, with maps, potential multilateral and bilateral JDAs that could be implemented to break the impasse present in many unresolved disputes. Though the approach taken is simplistic, its purpose is to provide a 'straw man' that could form the basis of initial negotiations. By adopting model agreements from successful JDAs, such as those in Southeast Asia and elsewhere, the long negotiation cycle could be accelerated, and development of disputed resources could be expedited.

As discussed above, among UNCLOS's most notable achievements is its allowance for States to claim maritime zones. However, when adjacent or opposite coastal States are less than 400 nm apart, or islands and other features complicate sovereignty, it is not surprising that overlapping claims will exist, and, unless States can negotiate a mutually agreeable maritime boundary, delimitation disputes could arise.

Provisional arrangements, such as JDA agreements, are a viable solution for disputing States to develop hydrocarbon resources. If the parties are unable or unwilling to negotiate a JDA agreement, UNCLOS offers comprehensive dispute resolution procedures.

1.5 Dispute Resolution

As with other sections of UNCLOS, the Convention's dispute resolution articles have been hailed as major achievements of the Convention. Compulsory dispute resolution articles within UNCLOS were a deviation from previous international treaties and agreements which had relied on dispute resolution via diplomatic efforts or negotiated settlement rather than obligatory prescribed mechanisms.[94] UNCLOS requires State parties to be bound by dispute resolution clauses integrated into the Convention, and, in another departure from the norm, once a State has ratified UNCLOS, the State is deemed to give consent and jurisdiction for any related disputes to the provisions within the Convention.[95]

In accordance with principles of the UN Charter, UNCLOS prioritises peaceful negotiations to resolve their disputes.[96] However, if negotiations do not reach an acceptable resolution, UNCLOS, adopting an innovative scheme, gives disputing States a choice among four resolution procedures.[97] All four of these procedures involve binding third-party settlement that the disputing parties have committed, in advance, to respect.

Though dispute resolution provisions are distributed throughout UNCLOS, detailed dispute resolution rules are found in Part XV of the Convention. Section 1 of Part XV deals with conventional international dispute resolution procedures, such as negotiations and mediations, based on UN Charter principles. Section 2 of Part XV includes the most important dispute resolution articles within UNCLOS. Subject to the exceptions and limitations contained in Section 3, any dispute where no settlement has been reached by Section 1 procedures shall be 'submitted at the request of any party to the dispute to the court or tribunal having jurisdiction' under Section 2.[98] Lastly, Section 3 covers limitations and exceptions to the compulsory procedures outlined in Section 2.

Dispute settlements resulting from Section 2 procedures are binding upon the parties and are final.[99] The most important article in this section is Article 287, offering States a choice of dispute resolution procedure between two judicial tribunals and two arbitrations tribunals. There are two permanent judicial tribunals (ITLOS and the ICJ) and two arbitrations tribunals, a general jurisdiction arbitral tribunal constituted in accordance with Annex VII, and special arbitral tribunal constituted in accordance with Annex VIII for resolving disputes falling within the categories specified in the Annex. States can make a formal Article 287 declaration to choose their preferred dispute resolution procedure not only when they sign, ratify, or accede to the Convention, but also at any time thereafter.[100]

The drafters of UNCLOS debated choosing the ICJ, which was established under the Charter of the United Nations, as the sole judicial forum to resolve UNCLOS disputes. During UNCLOS negotiations, proponents advocated giving all responsibility to the ICJ, arguing that the court had already successfully dealt with several relevant cases, such as the North Sea cases, and that multiple tribunals would hinder the development of a uniform jurisprudence on law of the sea issues.[101] Opponents to sole jurisdiction recognised that the ICJ, due to its jurisdictional restrictions, only allowed States to appear before it, and thus is unable to adjudicate

UNCLOS disputes that involve non-State parties such as international organisations, corporations, and individuals.[102] To provide flexibility and specific jurisprudence for UNCLOS cases, the Convention, via statute integrated into Annex VI of UNCLOS, created the 'international maritime court' which changed its name to the 'Law of the Sea Court/Tribunal' eventually becoming the 'International Tribunal for the Law of the Sea' (ITLOS) to supplement the role of the ICJ.

During UNCLOS drafting meetings, some States completely opposed adjudication – both that of the ICJ and ITLOS – and were only willing to accept arbitration procedures to resolve disputes.[103] These States felt that arbitration would be quicker to resolve disputes and better suited because of 'the technical nature of many law of the sea disputes.'[104] This group, which included States under the Soviet sphere of influence, were unwilling to accept international tribunals which they perceived as biased towards Western States.[105] Some States also favoured arbitration because they could influence the dispute settlement process by being able to select members of an arbitral panel.[106]

For the approximately 70% of the 168 signatories of UNCLOS that have not made an Article 287 declaration, general arbitration would be the default procedure for their disputes, unless alternative procedures have been agreed by the disputing parties.[107] Thus, arbitration plays a dual role within Part XV: It is one of the optional procedures listed in Article 287(1), and, if there is no declaration in place or different procedures have been declared between disputing States, arbitration becomes the default procedure.

Section 3 of Part XV imposes limitations and lists exceptions to the compulsory binding procedures outlined in Section 2. Importantly, Article 298 in Section 3 allows a State to opt out of Section 2 compulsory procedures for maritime boundary delimitation disputes, among other listed exemptions.[108]

Article 298(1)(a)(i), optional exceptions to applicability of Section 2, states:

> 1. When signing, ratifying or acceding to this Convention or at any time thereafter, a State may … declare in writing that it does not accept any one or more of the procedures provided for in Section 2 with respect to one or more of the following categories of disputes:
>
> (a) (i) *disputes concerning the interpretation or application of articles 15, 74 and 83 relating to sea boundary delimitations*, or those involving historic bays or titles, provided that a State having made such a declaration shall … accept submission of the matter to conciliation under Annex V, Section 2.[109]

At present, 36 States have made Article 298 declarations opting out of some or all of the Section 2 compulsory binding procedures for disputes related to maritime boundary disputes.[110] Interestingly, these 'declaration' States make up a disproportionate share of States involved in unresolved disputes, with 11 (out of 36 declaration States) involved in more than half of all unresolved disputes highlighted in this study.[111] The timing of when a State makes its Article 298(1)(a) declaration is also important and will be shown to be a factor in the eventual resolution, or in the case of the unresolved disputes, continued tensions for maritime boundary disputes involving hydrocarbon resources.

Though the declaration exempts the application of compulsory procedures, States are still expected to resolve disputes peacefully. If an agreement is not reached, 'within a reasonable time,'[112] the dispute may be submitted to conciliation.[113] This conciliation process may be started unilaterally by a party to a dispute and produces a non-binding recommendations report.[114] If, within three months, the disputing States are unable to agree on settlement, the process terminates and the dispute will likely remain unresolved with any hydrocarbon resources remaining unexploited.[115]

Defining maritime zones is one of the most revolutionary aspects of the Convention,[116] and UNCLOS grants coastal States considerable rights – including rights to hydrocarbon resource exploitation, in these zones. The inclusion of maritime boundaries delimitation to the list of disputes that can be excluded from compulsory binding resolution may have made the Convention more palatable to the majority of States but are shown in this study as a common factor in a majority of unresolved maritime boundary disputes involving hydrocarbons, thus weakening the overall dispute settlement regime of the Convention.

1.6 Book Relevance

UNCLOS is a much broader agreement covering a wide range of topics, is a result of many years of negotiation and compromise, and that its acceptance by a vast majority of the States and referral in subsequent judgments and bilateral agreements is a testament to its important role in international law. Though this book offers suggestions for future amendments, the author is under no illusion that these can be implemented easily or will be accepted by many States who have exploited the inherent ambiguities in the Convention.

The identified crucial 'gaps' could have a large impact on economics and tensions in regions that have witnessed the increased importance of hydrocarbon resources in their maritime zones.[117] Unlocking these benefits by understanding the impediments to resolution of disputes is invaluable. At the risk of stating the obvious, undeveloped resources in disputed maritime boundary areas offer no benefits to the citizens of these littoral States.

Notes

1 *United Nations Convention on the Law of the Sea*, opened for signature 10 December 1982, 1833 UNTS 3 (entered into force 16 November 1994) Preamble ('*UNCLOS*'). Emphasis added.

2 Nugzar Dundua, *Delimitation of maritime boundaries between adjacent states*, United Nations – The Nippon Foundation (2006–2007) 10.

3 Chronological lists of ratifications of accessions and successions to the Convention and the related Agreements, *United Nations Oceans & Law of the Seas* (Web Page, 10 March 2020) including accessions and successions. <https://www.un.org/depts/los/reference_files/chronological_lists_of_ratifications.htm>. The 168th State to ratify the convention was Azerbaijan which did so in June 2016.

4 David Freestone, 'The Law of the Sea Convention at 30: Successes, Challenges and New Agendas' (2012) 27(4) *International Journal of Marine & Coastal Law*, 675.; Alan Boyle, 'Dispute Settlement and the Law of the Sea Convention: Problems of

Fragmentation and Jurisdiction' (1997) 46(1) *International and Comparative Law Quarterly* 37, 38.; Robin Churchill, 'The Persisting Problem of Non-compliance with the Law of the Sea Convention: Disorder in the Oceans' (2012) 27(4) *International Journal of Marine & Coastal Law* 813, 813.; Vaughan Lowe, 'Was it Worth the Effort?' (2012) 27(4) *International Journal of Marine & Coastal Law* 875; Peter Prows, 'Tough Love: The Dramatic Birth and Looming Demise of UNCLOS Property Law (and What Is to Be Done About It)' (2007) 42(2) *Texas International Law Journal* 241, 248. Phillipe Gautier, 'Some Reflections on the "New Law of the Sea"' (2022) 99 *International Law Studies* 1051 and others.

5 Prows (n 4) 245.

6 In the EEZ regime, the term refers to living and non-living resources. For articles referring to the continental shelf, the term refers to mineral and other non-living resources of the seabed and subsoil. In the high seas regime, natural resources refer to living resources, including fish and marine mammals. And, lastly, in the 'Area,' the deeper seabed beyond the limits of natural jurisdiction, the term includes all solid, liquid, and gaseous minerals and polymetallic nodules, but does not include living resources. The indirect mentions of hydrocarbons are in Article 124, which discusses 'gas lines' in rights of access for land-locked States and Article 133 which mentions 'gaseous mineral resources' in its definition of resources for the Area. Even the term 'natural resources' has separate and distinctive meanings in its articles.

7 Martin Pratt and Derek Smith, 'How to Deal with Maritime Boundary Uncertainty in Oil and Gas Exploration and Production Areas' (Research Paper prepared for Association of International Petroleum Negotiators, IBRU Durham University & Dewey & LeBoeuf, December 2007), note 3, 15.

8 The UN claims that '[a]bout 87 per cent of all known and estimated hydrocarbon reserves under the sea fall under some national jurisdiction as a result of the EEZ Endowment.' See United Nations Oceans & Law of the Seas, Division for Ocean Affairs and the Law of the Sea, United Nations Office of Legal Affairs, The United Nations Convention on the Law of the Sea (A historical perspective) at http://www.un.org/Depts/los/convention_agreements/convention_historical_perspective.htm. ('UNCLOS historical perspective').

9 Examples of 'below-ground' risks include geologic and reservoir risks. Other 'above-ground' risks include regulations, environmental constraints, political uncertainties, and fiscal/tax regime changes.

10 The dataset does not include disputes in the Artic or Antarctic regions due to complexity with other issues. The list of disputes can be found in the appendix of this book. The dataset is believed to be current as of date of publishing (mid-2023). The terms 'boundary' and 'borders' are used interchangeably throughout this book.

11 *North Sea Continental Shelf Cases* (*Ger. v. Den.; Ger. v. Neth.*) [1969] ICJ Rep 3 [96].

12 *Case concerning Maritime Delimitation in the Area between Greenland and Jan Mayen* [1993] ICJ Rep 38.

13 Clive Schofield, 'Departures from the Coast: Trends in the Application of Territorial Sea Baselines under the Law of the Sea Convention' (2012) 27(4) *International Journal of Marine & Coastal Law* 723, 723.

14 Prows (n 4) 253 quoting William Wertenbaker.

15 *Convention on the Continental Shelf*, opened for signature 29 April 1958, 499 UNTS 311 (entered into force 10 June 1964).

16 *North Sea Continental Shelf Cases* (*Ger. v. Den.; Ger. v. Neth.*) (Judgment) [1969] ICJ Rep 3 [96]. Article 96 states '… the principle is applied that the land dominates the sea.'; *Aegean Sea Continental Shelf Case, (Greece/Turkey)* (Judgment) [1978] ICJ Reports 62 [86]. Article 86 states, '[t]he reason is that legally a coastal State's rights over the continental shelf are both appurtenant to and directly derived from the State's sovereignty over the territory abutting on that continental shelf.'

17 *North Sea Continental Shelf Cases (Ger. v. Den.; Ger. v. Neth.)* (Summaries of Judgment) [1969] ICJ Rep 3, 19 ILR 29, 8 ILM 340 (1969). 'The rights of the coastal State in respect of the area of continental shelf constituting a natural prolongation of its land territory under the sea existed ipso facto and ab initio, by virtue of its sovereignty over the land.'

18 Malcolm Shaw, International Law (Cambridge University Press, 6th edn, 2008) 554.

19 *Territorial and Maritime Dispute between Nicaragua and Honduras in the Caribbean Sea (Nicaragua v. Honduras) (Judgment)* [2007] ICJ Rep 659 [234]. Paragraph 234 states, 'The Court further observes that Nicaragua and Honduras as new independent States were entitled by virtue of the *uti possidetis* juris principle to such mainland and insular territories and territorial seas which constituted their provinces at independence.'; *UNCLOS* (n 1) art 2(1). The article states, 'The sovereignty of a coastal State extends, beyond its land territory and internal waters and, in the case of an archipelagic State, its archipelagic waters, to an adjacent belt of sea, described as the territorial sea.

20 James Crawford, *Brownlie's Principles of Public International Law* (Oxford University Press, 9th edn, 2019) 245; The Florida Senate, 'Legal Issues and State Authority Related to Territorial Water' (Interim Project Report 2008-142, October 2007). In some States, such as the US, individual States have defined the limit of their territorial sea. For instance, in Florida, the width of the territorial sea is 3 nm or to the edge of the Gulf Stream, whichever is farther on a particular day.

21 *US Proclamation No. 2667 Policy of the United States with Respect to the Natural Resources of the Subsoil and Sea-Bed of the Continental Shelf*, 10 Fed. Reg. 12305 (28 September 1945).

22 Prows (n 4) 253.

23 Crawford (n 20) 255.

24 *US Proclamation No. 2667* (n 21). The Truman Proclamation states, 'The character as high seas of the waters above the continental shelf and the right to their free and unimpeded navigation are in no way thus affected.'

25 *Report of the International Law Commission on the work of its eighth session*, UN GAOR, 11th sess., Supp No 9, UN Doc A/CN.4/104 (4 July 1956) pt 1 art 3 Territorial Sea. This Article states, '1. The Commission recognises that international practice is not uniform as regards the delimitation of the territorial sea. 2. The Commission considers that international law does not permit an extension of the territorial sea beyond twelve miles. 3. The Commission, without taking any decision as to the breadth of the territorial sea up to that limit, notes, on the one hand, that many States have fixed a breadth greater than three miles and, on the other hand, that many States do not recognise such a breadth when that of their own territorial sea is less. 4. The Commission considers that the breadth of the territorial sea should be fixed by an international conference.'

26 *International conference of plenipotentiaries to examine the law of the sea*, UN GAOR, 11th sess., 658th plen. mtg, GA Res 1105 (XI) (21 Feb 1957).

27 *Convention on the Continental Shelf* (n 15) and *Convention on the Territorial Sea and the Contiguous Zone,* opened for signature 29 April 1958, 516 UNTS 205 (entered into force 10 September 1964).

28 *Convention on the Continental Shelf* (n 15) art 1.

29 *Convention on the Continental Shelf* (n 15) art 2(1). This Article states, 'The coastal States exercise over the continental shelf exclusive rights for the purpose of exploring it and exploiting its natural resources.' Article 2(2) states, 'The rights referred to in paragraph 1 of this article are exclusive in the sense that if the coastal State does not explore the continental shelf or exploit its natural resources, no one may undertake these activities, or make a claim to the continental shelf, without the express consent of the coastal State.'

30 Prows (n 4) 256.

31 UN GAOR, 22nd sess., 1515th mtg, Agenda Item 92 [67]–[91].

32 Tommy TB Koh, 'The Origins of the 1982 Convention on the Law of the Sea' (1987) 29(1) *Malaya Law Review* 1, 14.
33 United Nations Convention on the Law of the Sea of 10 December 1982 Overview, *United Nations Oceans & Law of the Seas*, (Web Page, updated 12 February 2020) <http://www.un.org/Depts/los/convention_agreements/convention_overview_convention.htm> ('UNCLOS Overview').
34 United Nations Oceans & Law of the Seas, 'UNCLOS historical perspective' (n 8) 4. Guyana was the 60th State to ratify the Convention on 16 November 1993.
35 *UNCLOS* (n 1) art 76 (1).
36 *UNCLOS* (n 1) arts 79–81.
37 *North Sea Continental Shelf Cases* (n 11). The judgment states that factors that needed to be taken in account included, 'the physical and geological structure, and natural resources,' of the continental shelf areas involved.
38 J Van Dyke, 'Disputes Over Islands and Maritime Boundaries in East Asia' in Seoung-Yong Hong and Jon Van Dyke (eds), *Maritime Boundary Disputes, Settlement Processes, and the Law of the Sea* (Martinus Nijhoff Publishers, 2009) 74; *North Sea Continental Shelf Cases* (n 11). Preamble of the ICJ Decision states, 'Fundamental character of the principle of the continental shelf as being the natural prolongation of. the land territory.'
39 Richard McLaughlin, 'Maritime Boundary Delimitation and Cooperative Management of Transboundary Hydrocarbons in the Ultra-Deepwaters of the Gulf of Mexico' in Seoung-Yong Hong and Jon Van Dyke (eds), *Maritime Boundary Disputes, Settlement Processes, and the Law of the Sea* Martinus Nijhoff Publishers, 2009) 231.; The 'dual' definition of the continental shelf, distance and natural prolongation, is discussed in Chapter 2 (eastern Mediterranean), Chapter 4 (northeast Asia), and Chapter 5 (South China Sea).
40 United Nations Oceans & Law of the Seas, *Submissions, through the Secretary-General of the United Nations, to the Commission on the Limits of the Continental Shelf, pursuant to article 76, paragraph 8, of the United Nations Convention on the Law of the Sea of 10 December 1982* (Web Page updated 12 December 2019) <http://www.un.org/depts/los/clcs_new/commission_submissions.htm>.
41 Shaw (n 18) 590.
42 United Nations Oceans & Law of the Seas, 'UNCLOS historical perspective' (n 8).
43 Stuart Kaye, 'The use of multiple boundaries in maritime boundary delimitation: law and practice' (1998) 19 *Australian Year Book of International Law* 49. 'The EEZ has been asserted by states, in one form or the another, for up to half a century.'; Robert Beckman, 'International Law, UNCLOS and the South China Sea' in Robert Beckman, et al. (ed.), *Beyond Territorial Disputes in the South China Sea* (Edward Elgar Publishing, 2003) 54. 'UNCLOS made a revolutionary change in the law of the sea by establishing a new resource zone … EEZ.'; Tim Stephens and Donald R Rothwell, 'The LOSC Framework for Maritime Jurisdiction and Enforcement 30 Years On' (2012) 27(4) *International Journal of Marine & Coastal Law* 701, 704. Stephens and Rothwell credit UNCLOS for its innovation in creating the EEZ 'specific legal regime.'
44 Ayla Gürel, Fiona Mullen, and Harry Tzimitras, '*The Cyprus hydrocarbons issue: Context, positions and future scenarios*' (PCC Report 1/2013, PRIO Cyprus Center, 2013) 11.
45 *UNCLOS* (n 1) art 56. The Article States '(1) In the exclusive economic zone, the coastal State has: (a) sovereign rights for the purpose of exploring and exploiting, conserving and managing the natural resources, whether living or non-living, of the waters superjacent to the seabed and of the seabed and its subsoil, and with regard to other activities for the economic exploitation and exploration of the zone, such as the production of energy from the water, currents and winds.' Article 56(b) provides the

Coastal State rights to establish and use artificial islands, marine scientific research, and protection and preservation of marine environment.

46 *UNCLOS* (n 1) art 58.

47 *UNCLOS* (n 1).

48 *UNCLOS* (n 1).

49 Tommy T. B. Koh, 'The Exclusive Economic Zone '(1988) 30(1) *Malaya Law Review* 1, 32 ('Exclusive Economic Zone').

50 This book highlights instances where States have prevented other States from laying pipelines in their EEZ (in the eastern Mediterranean and Caspian Sea), where States have prevented other States from navigation in their EEZ (in the South China Sea) and have used military forces to defend their EEZs (in northeast Asia, South China Sea, eastern Mediterranean, and Caspian Sea).

51 Crawford (n 20) 432. Crawford refers to sovereignty as a 'collection of rights held by a State, first in its capacity as entity entitled to exercise control over its territory and, secondly, in its capacity to act on the international plane, representing that territory and its people.'

52 *South China Sea Arbitration (The Republic of Philippines v. The People's Republic of China)* (2016) PCA Case 2013-19, 170 ILR 1 [247]. Article 247 states, 'The Tribunal considers the text and context of the Convention to be clear in superseding any historic rights that a State may once have had in the areas that now form part of the exclusive economic zone and continental shelf of another State. There is no ambiguity here that would call for the Tribunal to have recourse to the supplementary means of interpretation.'

53 United Nations Oceans & Law of the Seas, 'UNCLOS historical perspective' (n 8) 7.

54 United Nations Oceans & Law of the Seas, 'UNCLOS historical perspective' (n 8) 7.

55 *UNCLOS* (n 1) art 74 & art 83.

56 Kaye (n 43) 50.

57 Victor Prescott and Clive Schofield, *The Maritime Political Boundaries of the World* (Martinus Nijhoff Publishers, 2nd edn, 2005) 246.

58 Bernard Sepulveda-Amor, 'Contribution of the International Court of Justice to the development of the international law of the sea' (2010)1(6) *Aegean Review of the Law of the Sea and Maritime Law* 5, 6. 'The concept of equitable principles established by the Court found reflection in the deliberately ambiguous provisions of Articles 74 and 83 of UNCLOS.'; Beckman (n 53) 73. Beckman observes that 'The end result was a compromise on a text which is vague.'

59 Natalie Klein, *Dispute Settlement in the UN Convention on the Law of the Sea* (Cambridge University Press, 2005) 230.

60 *Convention on the Continental Shelf* (n 15) art 6(2) and *Convention on the Territorial Sea and the Contiguous Zone* (n 27) art 12.

61 *North Sea Continental Shelf Cases* (n 11).

62 Bernardo Sepúlveda-Amor, 'The International Court of Justice and the Law of the Sea' (2011) *Anuario Mexicano de Derecho, International Universidad Nacional Autonoma de Mexico – Insituto de Investigaciones Juridicas* 511. Most subsequent ICJ and ITLOS dealing with maritime delimitation have referenced the North Sea Cases.

63 Dundua (n 2) 11.

64 Anne Sheehan, 'Dispute Settlement under UNCLOS: The Exclusion of Maritime Delimitation Disputes' (2005) 7 *University of Queensland Law Journal* 175, 166.

65 Sepúlveda-Amor 'The International Court of Justice and the Law of the Sea' (n 62) 9.

66 *Delimitation of the Maritime Boundary in the Gulf of Maine Area* (*Canada/United States of America*) (Judgment) [1984] ICJ Rep 246 [81].

67 2001 *Maritime Delimitation and Territorial Questions between Qatar and Bahrain* (n 119); *Land and Maritime Boundary between Cameroon and Nigeria (Cameroon v. Nigeria: Equatorial Guinea interven*ing) [2002] ICJ Rep 303, [288].

68 *Maritime Delimitation in the Black Sea (Romania v. Ukraine)* (Judgment) [2009] ICJ Rep 61.
69 *Romania v. Ukraine* (n 70); Lowell Bautista, 'The Implications of Recent Decisions on the Territorial and Maritime Boundary Disputes in East and Southeast Asia' in Schofield, C, (ed.) *Maritime Energy Resources in Asia – Legal Regimes and Cooperation* (The National Bureau of Asian Research, February 2012) 105, 116. 'Although not wholly novel, is a clarification and clear articulation not seen in previous cases.'
70 *Maritime Delimitation in the Black Sea (Romania v. Ukraine)* (Overview of Case) [2009] ICJ Rep 61. In its own statement, the ICJ Stated, 'On the basis of established State practice and of its own jurisprudence, the Court declared itself bound by the three-step approach laid down by maritime delimitation law.'
71 *Romania v. Ukraine* (n 70) Section 7–11 [115–216].
72 Fayokemi Olorundami, 'Objectivity versus Subjectivity in the Context of the ICJ's Three-stage Methodology of Maritime Boundary Delimitation' (2017) 32(1) International Journal of Marine & Coastal Law 36, 37.
73 *UNCLOS* (n 1) art 5.
74 *Convention on the Territorial Sea and the Contiguous Zone* (n 27) art 3. This article states, 'the normal baseline for measuring the breadth of the territorial sea is the low-water line along the coast as marked on large-scale charts.'
75 *UNCLOS* (n 1) art 7.
76 Pratt and Smith (n 7) 8.
77 J. Ashley Roach and Robert W. Smith, *Excessive Maritime Claims* (Martins Nijhoff, 2012) 254. Roach and Smith State, 'Unless these excessive claims are actively opposed, the challenged rights will be effectively lost.'
78 Pratt and Smith (n 7) 8. This may be a debatable statement. Almost all the unresolved disputes in the dataset include status of rocks vs islands.
79 *UNCLOS* (n 1) art 121.
80 Clive Schofield, 'The Trouble with Islands: The Definition and Role of Islands and Rocks in Maritime Boundary delimitation' in Seoung-Yong Hong and Jon Van Dyke (eds), *Maritime Boundary Disputes, Settlement Processes, and the Law of the Sea* (Martinus Nijhoff Publishers, 2009) 19, 21.
81 Pratt and Smith (n 7) 18.
82 *UNCLOS* (n 1) art 121(3).
83 Schofield (n 80) 21.
84 Schofield (n 80).
85 Schofield (n 80).
86 Song Yann-Huei and N. Elias Blood-Patterson, 'Likelihood of U.S. Becoming a Party to the Law of the Sea Convention During the 112th Congress' (2012) 43(4) *Journal of Maritime Law & Commerce* 447, 451.
87 Pratt and Smith (n 7) 8.
88 Sarah Raine and Christian Le Mière, *Regional Disorder: the South China Sea Disputes* (Routledge, 2013) 221.
89 UNCLOS, art 74. Article 83 discusses the delimitation of the continental shelf between States with opposite or adjacent coasts in almost identical language.
90 *North Sea Continental Shelf Cases (Ger. v. Den.; Ger. v. Neth.)* (Sep. Op. Jessup) [1969] ICJ Rep 3, [82].
91 *Continental Shelf (Tunisia/Libya)* (Diss. Op. Evensen) [1982] ICJ Rep 18 [320].
92 *Charter of Economic Rights and Duties of States*, GA Res 3281(XXIX) UN GAOR, 29th Sess., Supp. No. 31 (12 December 1974) 50, Art 3.
93 These include the *Agreement between the Government of the United Kingdom of Great Britain and Northern Ireland and the Government of the Kingdom of Norway Relating to the Delimitation of the Continental Shelf between the Two Countries* (10 March 1965, in force 29 June 1965) 551 *UNTS* 213 and the *Agreement between the*

Government of the Kingdom of the Netherlands and the Government of the United Kingdom of Great Britain and Northern Ireland relating to the exploitation of single geological structures extending across the dividing line on the continental shelf under the North Sea (6 October 1965, in force 23 December 1966) 595 *UNTS* 105.

94 Klein (n 59) 2; John Noyes, 'The International Tribunal for the Law of the Sea' (1999) 32(1) *Cornell Int'l Law Journal* 110, 114. As stated by Noyes, 'Most treaties relating to the international law of the sea have not provided for obligatory binding third-party dispute settlement. Informal dispute settlement mechanisms have been more common.'

95 Anne Sheehan, 'Dispute Settlement under UNCLOS: The Exclusion of Maritime Delimitation Disputes' (2005) 7 *University of Queensland Law Journal* 175, 188.

96 United Nations Convention on the Law of the Sea, opened for signature 10 December 1982, 1833 UNTS 3 (entered into force 16 November 1994) art 279 ('UNCLOS'). Article 279 states, 'States Parties shall settle any dispute between them concerning the interpretation or application of this Convention by peaceful means in accordance with Article 2, paragraph 3, of the Charter of the United Nations and, to this end, shall seek a solution by the means indicated in Article 33, paragraph 1, of the Charter.'

97 *UNCLOS* (n 1) art 287. The four options are submission of the dispute to the International Tribunal for the Law of the Sea (ITLOS), adjudication by the International Court of Justice (ICJ), submission to binding international arbitration procedures, or submission to special arbitration tribunals (to be chosen from lists prepared by United Nations specialised agencies or separate programmes dealing, respectively, with navigation, fisheries, marine environment, or marine scientific research).

98 *UNCLOS* (n 1) art 286. 'Subject to Section 3, any dispute concerning the interpretation or application of this Convention shall, where no settlement has been reached by recourse to Section 1, be submitted at the request of any party to the dispute to the court or tribunal having jurisdiction under this section.'

99 *UNCLOS* (n 1) art 296. 'Any decision rendered by a court or tribunal having jurisdiction under this section shall be final and shall be complied with by all the parties to the dispute.'

100 *UNCLOS* (n 1) art 287(1).

101 Noyes (n 94) 119.

102 International Court of Justice, 'How the Court Works' (Web Page) <https://www.icj-cij.org/en/how-the-court-works>. 'Only States (States Members of the United Nations and other States which have become parties to the Statute of the Court or which have accepted its jurisdiction under certain conditions) may be parties to contentious cases.'

103 Igor V. Karaman, *Dispute Resolution in the Law of the Sea* (Martinus Nijhoff Publishers, 2012) 4. States in this group included France, Madagascar, and 'Soviet bloc states.'

104 Noyes (n 94) 119.

105 Karaman (n 103) 4. Karaman states, 'Moreover, the need for arbitration in the Convention was also dictated by the reluctance of the Soviet bloc States to accept the western "bourgeois" international tribunals. Instead, they favoured arbitration, where they could have a significant influence on the dispute settlement process.'

106 Karaman (n 103) 4–5.

107 *UNCLOS* (n 1) art 287(3).

108 *UNCLOS* (n 1) art 298. Exceptions include military activities and UN Security Council matters.

109 *UNCLOS* (n 1) art 298(1). Emphasis added.

110 UN, 'Chapter XXI: Law of the Sea,' *United Nations Treaty Collection* (Web Page, 5 October 2020) <https://treaties.un.org/Pages/ViewDetailsIII.aspx?src=TREATY&mtdsg_no=XXI-6&chapter=21&Temp=mtdsg3&clang=_en#EndDec>. ('UNCLOS Declarations'). Based on author analysis of declarations.

111 States involved in the unresolved disputes that have made 298(1)(a) declarations include China, Egypt, Gabon, Greece, Kenya, Republic of Korea, Malaysia, Nicaragua,

Philippines, Thailand, and Trinidad & Tobago (11 states). Some States involved in multiple unresolved disputes, such as China, Republic of Korea, and Malaysia have made Article 298 declarations. China is involved in seven unresolved disputes (out of 27 identified unresolved disputes) in the database. Malaysia is involved in three unresolved disputes.

112 *UNCLOS* (n 1) art 298(1)(a)(i).

113 *UNCLOS* (n 1) art 298(1)(a)(i) and Annex V, Article 7 (2). Annex V of UNCLOS details conciliation procedures to be followed by disputing parties. A five-member conciliation commission is assembled consisting of two conciliators chosen by each party. The fifth member is nominated by these four members. Once the conciliation commission has presented its report (to be completed within 12 months), the parties 'shall negotiate an agreement.' Unfortunately, as clearly stated in Annex V, 'The report of the commission, including its conclusions or recommendations, shall not be binding upon the parties.' If the post-conciliation report negotiations do not result in an agreement, only by consent of both parties, not unilaterally by a single party, the dispute can be referred to a Section 2 compulsory procedure. Some States felt that the compromise in Article 298 was unacceptable, and that parties should have right to request a final and binding determination by an international tribunal if conciliation fails. However, UNCLOS does not offer any such binding procedure. If both parties do not agree to compulsory dispute resolution after conciliation fails, their maritime border may remain undelimited and any hydrocarbon or other resources remain unexploited.

114 *UNCLOS* (n 1) art 298(1)(a)(ii). Annex V Article 7(2). The report of the commission, including its conclusions or recommendations shall not be binding upon the parties.

115 *UNCLOS* (n 1) art Annex V Article 8. 'The conciliation proceedings are terminated when a settlement has been reached, when the parties have accepted or one party has rejected the recommendations of the report by written notification addressed to the Secretary-General of the United Nations, or when a period of three months has expired from the date of transmission of the report to the parties.'; Sheehan (n 8) 186. Sheehan states that 'The report of the commission, including its conclusions and recommendations, is not binding upon the parties. However, such as report would carry with it significant political pressure.'

116 United Nations Oceans & Law of the Seas, 'UNCLOS historical perspective' (n 8).

117 The background and education of the author of the book, which includes advanced degrees in petroleum exploration, geophysical engineering, economics, commercial law, international law, and over three decades of experience working in the international oil and gas industry – including working offshore in the South China Sea, is well suited to tackle this important topic.

2 Maritime Borders

Eastern Mediterranean

2.1 Introduction

The eastern Mediterranean offshore region consists of seas around Egypt, Israel, Palestine, Lebanon, Cyprus, Syria, Turkey, and Greece.[1] The region is beset with bilateral and multilateral conflicts, religious tension, and pseudo-State entities with contested status. Until few decades ago, the region was not considered a hydrocarbon-rich basin. In fact, Golda Meir, the Prime Minister of Israel in the 1970s, is quoted as having said 'the only thing the Jews have against Moses is that he led his people to the only place in the Middle East without oil.'[2]

Since the 1990s, the hydrocarbon potential in the eastern Mediterranean region has gradually increased. The US Geological Survey estimates that the basin may have potential gas resource volumes of over 120 Tcf, and over 1.5 billion bbls of oil,[3] a world-class resource that could be a source of energy for not only the region, but potentially, for export to Europe and beyond. Though a large part of this potential volume remains to be discovered in the future, over 35 Tcf of gas have been confirmed since 2009.[4] It seems that Golda Meir was wrong about Moses.

The discovery of large gas resources has added complexity to the politics and stability in the region. States and resource companies operating under their licence continue to debate export options for discovered gas resources. The discoveries could be the enablers for increased wealth and prosperity for the region, allowing transition from energy importing to energy exporting economies thereby increasing energy security. They could also contribute to increasing regional cooperation and trust. Unfortunately, some of the recent discoveries have provoked new fault lines leading to provocative maritime zone declarations, military muscle flexing, and delayed investments, and, unfortunately for regional economies, delayed economic benefits.

Discoveries have been made over multiple geologic areas spread over Egyptian, Israeli, Palestinian, and Cypriot offshore waters. There has been limited drilling success in Lebanese, Syrian, Turkish and Greek zones, though these countries remain optimistic that they will also discover commercial volume resources in the future. Eastern Mediterranean States are not in competition over one large reservoir, but rather, an unknown number of distinct, mostly natural gas, deposits spread over a relatively large area.

DOI: 10.4324/9781003323051-2

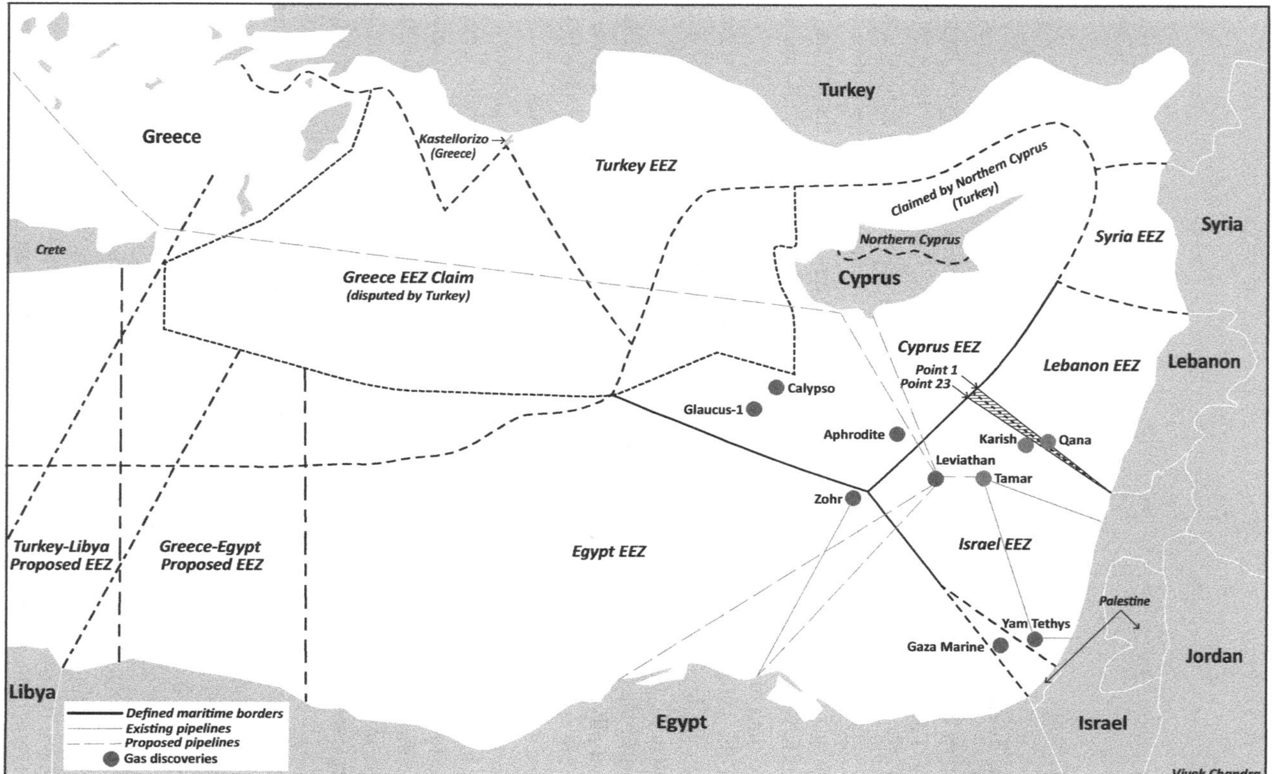

Figure 2.1 Schematic of conflicting EEZ claims and natural gas discoveries in the eastern Mediterranean[5]

Due in part to the oil and gas discoveries and the promise for additional success in the future, the entire Mediterranean Sea is now fully covered by EEZ claims, leaving no unclaimed zones.[6] EEZ declarations by Israel, Cyprus, and Turkey have prompted counter claims by their neighbours, and encouraged the contested pseudo-State entities[7] of Palestine and the Turkish Republic of Northern Cyprus (TRNC) to also claim their own EEZ rights.

Though its own hydrocarbon resources are limited, Turkey has a significant economic and political role in the region. Turkey is a large oil and gas importer, a major transit hub for energy into southern Europe, and a crucial player in any pipeline export project for Israeli or Cypriot gas. The current regime in Turkey opposes any cooperation between Cyprus and Israel, has pressured Lebanon not to ratify its maritime border agreement with Cyprus, has protested the EEZ delimitation agreement between Cyprus and Egypt, and has used force to assert exploration rights, for itself and the TRNC, in all offshore regions surrounding Cyprus.

Historical considerations make cooperation to jointly develop hydrocarbons challenging. Until the Palestinian issue is settled, it is unlikely that Israel will allow the development of offshore Gaza discoveries. Lebanon and Israel are engaged in sporadic skirmishes and have only in late 2022 agreed to a permanent maritime boundary. The ongoing Cyprus impasse precludes Turkey's recognition of Cyprus's EEZ, and thus restricts the export of Cypriot gas via Turkey or through Turkish-claimed maritime zones en route to Europe. As long as these conflicts persist, cross-border gas development and pipeline transport options in the region will be constrained.

2.2 Applicability of UNCLOS

The Mediterranean Sea would fall under the UNCLOS definition of an 'enclosed or semi-enclosed sea.'[8] Along with other semi-enclosed seas in the region, such as the Black and Adriatic Seas, UNCLOS requires States that border enclosed or semi-enclosed seas to cooperate with each other in the 'exercise of their rights and in performance of their duties under the Convention.'[9] Article 123 also suggests that normal definitions and terms to delimit EEZ and Continental Shelf present in other coastal regions should remain unchanged in enclosed or semi-enclosed seas.[10]

A number of States in the region are not State parties to UNCLOS, including Turkey, Israel, Syria, and the two pseudo-States of Palestine[11] and the TRNC. Turkey is one of the four States that voted against the adoption of UNCLOS in 1982. Turkey's main objection is the Convention's handling of maritime zones within the Aegean Sea, including the granting of maritime zones to Greek islands located close to the Turkish mainland.[12] Turkey continues to assert that the mostly Greek Aegean islands are located on Turkey's continental shelf and should not be entitled to their own maritime zones.[13] Both the ICJ and UNCLOS have rejected geologic considerations in preference to distance criteria for 'delimitation of overlapping entitlements within 200 nautical miles.'[14] Turkey disputes this distance-defined entitlement, as well as 'island' definitions within the Convention, which grant the Greek islands large EEZ areas which block Turkey's unhindered access to the sea and potential offshore resources.[15]

The two pseudo-State entities in the region, the TRNC and Palestine, have had different experiences within UNCLOS. The TRNC is not an internationally recognised State, does not have any UN status and is not a UNCLOS signatory. In contrast, Palestine was granted non-member Observer State status in the United Nations in 2012[16] and, in 2015, deposited its instrument of accession to UNCLOS.[17]

The rights of individual States to develop (and to prevent) undersea pipelines in other State's EEZs is an important matter in the region. Under UNCLOS Article 58(1), a coastal State may not prevent other States from laying cables or pipelines in its EEZ.[18] However, UNCLOS Article 79(3) qualified this by stating that '[t]he delineation of the course for the laying of such pipelines on the continental shelf is subject to the consent of the coastal State.'[19] Turkey, with its 2019 EEZ agreement with Libya, has effectively blocked Cyprus and Israel from exporting their gas to Europe via subsea pipelines. Other potential pipeline export routes, such as Israel to Turkey, would also require crossing of disputed EEZ zones (in this case, the disputed zone between Cyprus and Turkey) are also difficult to progress. The ability of transit States to block third-party pipeline developments is an example of flaunting UNCLOS and leveraging its confusing articles without any obvious repercussions to the offending State.

2.3 Oil and Gas Activities and Historical Background

Prior to the turn of the century, the region's offshore oil and gas activities were limited to Egypt. A series of successful exploration wells in Palestine (offshore Gaza), Israel, and Cyprus in the early 2000s sparked new enthusiasm for the southeastern portion of the eastern Mediterranean basin. More recently, 'world-class' deep-water discoveries in offshore Egypt and Cyprus have renewed interest in the region. The northern and eastern portions of the basin are beset with political turmoil and long-term conflicts (in Syria, Lebanon, the TRNC, and Turkey) and have attracted limited ongoing or near-term oil and gas investment.

Until two decades ago, Israel had relied almost entirely on importing fossil fuels to meet its growing energy requirements. Israel's fortunes turned in 1999 with the first commercial offshore natural gas discoveries at the Noa and Mari-B fields (collectively called Yam Tethys) off the coastline near Ashkelon. The fields were used for power generation in Israel and are now largely depleted.

Soon after the Yam Tethys discoveries in 1999, Israel, in a gesture of peace and recognition of Palestine, granted British Gas (later rebranded as 'BG') permission to drill exploration wells off the coast of Gaza in 2000. The wells were declared commercial discoveries with reserves of more than 1 Tcf. To finance the investment, BG sought long-term gas purchase agreements from Palestinian entities. However, once it was clear that the market in Gaza was not large enough to support the investment, BG also sought commitments from Israeli buyers. Under political pressure from Israel's prime minister Ariel Sharon, Israeli customers refused to commit to purchasing the gas.[20] Ultimately, BG, unable to find a viable market for the gas, was forced to walk away from its discoveries. Israel's naval blockade of Gaza since 2009 and deteriorating relations between Israel and the Palestinian authorities has effectively stopped any further oil and gas activities in offshore Gaza.

The Yam Tethys and Gaza exploration successes encouraged further drilling in Israeli waters. In 2009, Noble Energy, an American company, in a joint venture with local Israeli partners, discovered Tamar, a deep-water gas field located off the coast of northern Israel. In 2010, Noble Energy and its partners continued their list of discoveries with the massive Leviathan gas field, located 47 km from Tamar. At 22 Tcf of potential gas volume, Leviathan is one of the largest offshore gas fields in the world and could satisfy Israel's domestic gas requirements for 100 years.[21] Leviathan was brought into production at the end of 2019, and in 2021, more than a decade after its discovery, Israel and Egypt agreed to pipe Leviathan gas to export terminals in Egypt for export as liquefied natural gas (LNG) to global markets. Israel and the owners of the field have expressed interest, if economic, legal, and political obstacles could be overcome, for its gas to be piped to Europe.[22]

The discovery of Leviathan was followed by Noble Energy's discovery of the Aphrodite gas field in Block 12 of Cyprus's EEZ. Though not as large as Leviathan, Aphrodite is still a significant resource with 4–5 Tcf of gas. The distance from Leviathan, in Israel's EEZ, to Aphrodite, in Cyprus's EEZ, is estimated to be just 34 km. The relative locations of these fields are shown in Figure 2.1.

In September 2011, immediately prior to the Block 12 exploration well drilling campaign, the Republic of Cyprus signed the EEZ delimitation agreement with Israel.[23] This was a precondition by the private company drilling the well which insisted on jurisdictional certainty and EEZ boundary delimitation. Development of the discovery has been complicated because a portion of Aphrodite may be within Israel's EEZ, and Israel has insisted on a unitisation agreement prior to commencement of development. Since the 2011 discovery of Aphrodite, a number of smaller discoveries have been made by international companies in the Cyprus EEZ. None of the discoveries in Cyprus's EEZ have been developed as yet.

Cyprus has a complicated history involving many outside forces, including Greece, Turkey, and the United Kingdom. In 1974, in response to a coup by Greek Cypriots to reunify the island, Turkey occupied the northern territory of the island. The island remains divided with the southern Greek-speaking section, ('Republic of Cyprus'), claiming itself as the 'sole internationally recognized state on the island.'[24] Turkey does not recognise the Republic of Cyprus and supports only the TRNC.

Turkey has argued that the Republic of Cyprus has no rights to conduct or authorise offshore hydrocarbon activities without the explicit consent of the TRNC.[25] The Republic of Cyprus government has maintained that as the internationally recognised Cypriot representative, only it has the sovereign right to explore for and exploit the natural resources in the Cyprus EEZ. It has maintained that joint management of offshore resources and sharing of revenue will only be acceptable within the framework of a united Cyprus.[26] Some have questioned why the TRNC, which insists that the Republic of Cyprus does not have sovereignty rights in the northern part of Cyprus, should be able to demand that it (TRNC) should have rights in the south, especially in the southern extremity of Cyprus' EEZ where the Aphrodite and more recent gas discoveries are located.[27]

The TRNC, with the backing of Turkey, has objected to all three EEZ delimitation agreements signed by the Republic of Cyprus (with Egypt in 2003, with Lebanon in 2007, and with Israel in 2010, signed prior to the Aphrodite discovery). The TRNC's official position is that all hydrocarbon exploration activities should be suspended until both sides 'cooperate to bring them under the authority of a provisional joint (i.e., bicommunal) body which the two sides will specifically establish together for this purpose, and which will also decide how the two sides will share the revenues.'[28] This could be the basis of a future JDA where territorial and unification claims can be set aside while revenue and regulatory framework is developed for joint development.

In 2011 Turkey and the TRNC signed an agreement to delimit the continental shelf between the coasts of the southern Turkey and northern Cyprus. Soon thereafter, the TRNC issued licences to the Turkish State-owned oil company to explore for oil and gas in TRNC-designated offshore blocks, some of which overlap with the Republic of Cyprus blocks southeast of the island.[29] At the same time, Turkey also claimed several other Cypriot offshore exploration blocks in the southwest as being a part of its own continental shelf ('extended EEZ'), promising to stop any Cyprus-authorised exploration activities, and to blacklist companies that participated in Cyprus's initiatives.[30]

In a show of strength, in 2018, the Turkish navy blocked the Italian company, ENI, from drilling a second well near their 'Calypso' discovery in Cyprus's EEZ. This action temporarily deterred ENI from further activities in the region. This action was followed, in May 2019, by Operation Seawolf, with over 130 Turkish naval vessels deployed in the Cyprus EEZ to assert Turkish claims over the area. The is no current production from any offshore Cyprus discoveries, and in order to alleviate its energy shortage, Cyprus is constructing an LNG import facility on the island.

In 2019, Turkey sent a drilling ship escorted by navy vessels to drill an unsuccessful exploration well off the western coast of Cyprus. Since then, in 2021 and more recently, Turkey has drilled additional unsuccessful wells in both the TRNC's and Turkey's EEZ claims, some of which overlap Cyprus's EEZ. These efforts have provoked protests by the Republic of Cyprus and the European Union. To date, no commercial discoveries have been made by Turkey in the Mediterranean.

In contrast, offshore Egypt has made numerous gas discoveries over many decades. In August 2015, ENI, discovered the giant Zohr field inside the Egyptian EEZ, close to the intersection of delimited EEZ boundaries of Israel, Cyprus, and Egypt and within a relatively short distance from Leviathan and Aphrodite. Zohr is estimated to contain 75 Tcf of natural gas. It is the largest gas discovery in the Mediterranean and has been producing since 2018. Gas produced from Zohr has allowed Egypt to resume exports of LNG from its two previously underutilised export facilities.

2.3.1 Historic JDA Proposals

As a way to ensure that it shares in the benefits from Cyprus's discoveries, the TRNC has taken the lead in proposing to cooperate with Cyprus to jointly develop the offshore resources of Cyprus. In 2019, the TRNC submitted a proposal to the Republic of Cyprus via the UN.[31] The proposal called for the establishment of a joint committee under the supervision of the UN and suggested that the TRNC, as 'equal partners' should have equal rights and income sharing from the offshore resources.[32] Cyprus has ignored all the TRNC joint development proposals, reiterating that it has the sole right to exploit its natural resources and recognising the proposals would elevate the unrecognised TRNC on 'equal footing.'[33]

Cyprus has been in discussions with Egypt for cooperation for hydrocarbon activities since 2006.[34] In 2013, Cyprus and Egypt were reported to have signed a unitisation agreement on the joint exploitation of offshore resources.[35] This agreement may become relevant if the giant Zohr gas resource producing from the Egyptian EEZ is shown to extend into Cyprus's EEZ, and thus be eligible for joint development under the agreement.[36] Cyprus and Israel have also been in discussion about joint development of Aphrodite but these negotiations have had limited success to date.[37]

2.4 Maritime Boundaries

The region's EEZ declarations have come under increased scrutiny since natural gas discoveries were made in offshore regions of Gaza, Israel, Cyprus, and in eastern Egypt. The prospect of further discoveries has encouraged littoral States to delineate their EEZs.

Cyprus has been the leader in executing maritime boundary agreements in the region. Out of the six States that have maritime borders with Cyprus (Egypt, Greece, Israel, Lebanon, Syria, and Turkey), Cyprus has signed EEZ boundary agreements with three of them (Egypt, Israel, and Lebanon). In 2004, Cyprus declared its 200 nm EEZ in a proclamation law explicitly for exploring subsea natural resources.[38] The EEZ proclamation law, which was hailed as 'one of the most important events in the fifty-year history of the Republic of Cyprus'[39] recognised that any overlapping EEZ claims would be delimited by agreement between the States and would be settled in accordance with the median line unless otherwise negotiated.[40]

As discussed earlier, Cyprus's agreement with Lebanon has not been ratified by the Lebanese parliament, its maritime border with Turkey remains undefined due to the TRNC issue, and Syrian discussions have been suspended since the Syrian civil war.[41]

Though the maritime border between Cyprus and Greece's maritime border remains undefined, there is a close friendly relationship between the two Greek-speaking States. The delimitation of the Cyprus–Greece maritime border would be dependent on the validity of Turkey's EEZ agreement with Libya. If Turkey's maritime border claim with Libya was accepted by Greece, an unlikely case given regional dynamics, a Cyprus–Greece maritime boundary would not exist, and Cyprus would border Turkish EEZs off its northern and western coasts.

2.4.1 Israel–Palestine (Unresolved)

When exploration activities began off Gaza in 2000, drilling was limited to an area between Egypt's eastern maritime boundary and Israel's exploration blocks. When Palestine acceded to UNCLOS in 2015, a Palestinian official stated that

> our maritime boundaries would have to be negotiated not only with Israel, but also with other nearby coastal States. These talks would have to address issues pertaining to shared resources in various maritime zones. We seek the full array of maritime rights under international [law] as a coastal state.[42]

As Israel–Palestine peace talks, have stalled over the past few years, the boundaries of a future Palestinian EEZ remain undelimited. Some have speculated that Israel's long-term goal is to keep the maritime boundaries undefined, preventing Palestinian gas production and ultimately, to integrate the Gaza gas fields into its own offshore developments.[43]

2.4.2 Israel–Lebanon (Resolved)

Israel and Lebanon have been technically at war for decades. Not surprisingly, onshore tensions have evolved to offshore disputed borders, especially since the discovery of Israeli gas resources, which Lebanon claims, extend into Lebanese EEZ waters.[44] The discovery of Israeli gas has resulted in the most 'serious threats'[45] between these countries since the last war in 2006, becoming 'a catalyst for a new source of conflict between the States.'[46]

Since the 2010 Cyprus–Israel agreement which overlapped Lebanon's claimed borders, Lebanon has insisted that the equidistance point between the three countries should determine the intersect of their respective EEZ claims.[47] A few months before the Cyprus–Israel agreement announcement, Lebanon deposited its proposed EEZ boundary coordinates with the United Nations, extending southward the 2007 Cyprus–Lebanon EEZ to a new intersection point. In 2011, Israel similarly deposited with the UN its own proposed coordinates which extended the maritime border to the north of the equidistant Point 23.

The disputed points define a triangular area of 860 km^2 where the claimed EEZs of Lebanon and Israel overlap. This area is relatively small compared to the total EEZ of both countries (48,000 km^2) and overlaps Israel's Karish gas field. Lebanon's Hizbullah party had previously threatened gas exploration efforts of a private companies developing the Karish field, and the Lebanese parliament had warned Israel against 'looting' the country's wealth.[48]

In October 2022, facilitated by mediation from the US, and accelerated by Lebanon's energy and economic crisis, the two States announced an agreement to resolve the maritime border impasse. Israel would accept the extending of the border from Point 23 as a permanent boundary, but in return, if any gas discovery is made in the disputed triangular area, Israel would receive a share of the proceeds.[49] The negotiated settlement has elements of joint development and could become a model for other unresolved disputes in the region and beyond.

2.4.3 Cyprus–Egypt (Resolved)

The Cyprus–Egypt EEZ agreement was signed in March 2003, and entered into force more than a decade later, in March 2014.[50] Turkey refused to recognise the Cyprus–Egypt EEZ agreement and simultaneously made claims on the delineated area, though Turkey does not have a recognised maritime border with Egypt.[51]

Turkey objects to Cyprus's westward EEZ boundary with Egypt that extends to the intersection of the Greece–Egypt EEZ. Because Turkey disputes the capacity of the Greek island of Megisti/Kastelorizo to generate its own EEZ, it maintains that the island should be considered to be 'enclaved' within the Turkish continental shelf. This would justify Turkey's extension of its own EEZ southward towards Egypt and then westward to a point south of Rhodes. Under this scenario, Turkey could claim a EEZ maritime boundary with Egypt.

2.4.4 Cyprus–Israel (Resolved)

Israel and Cyprus signed their EEZ delimitation agreement in 2010. Immediately after the signing of the Cyprus–Israel EEZ agreement, Turkey criticised the agreement, calling it 'null and void' because it did not take into account the rights and jurisdiction of the TRNC over Cyprus's maritime areas.[52] This may be an overstretch for Turkey, since unlike the Cyprus–Egypt agreement, where Turkey has made an overlapping EEZ claim, Turkey has no direct claim to the area delimited by the Cyprus–Israel EEZ agreement.[53]

2.4.5 Cyprus–Lebanon (EEZ Treaty Not Ratified – Unresolved)

Prompted by estimates of large gas reserves in the region, Lebanon and Cyprus started EEZ negotiations as early as 2002, and an agreement between the two countries was signed in 2007.

Though the Agreement has been ratified by Cyprus, there is a number of possible reasons why the agreement has not been ratified by the Lebanese parliament. Turkey has formally requested Lebanon not to ratify the agreement, alleging 'that Lebanon should ask for Turkey's opinion before signing any agreement with Cyprus, since it should contain "a Turkish part."'[54] The 2022 resolution of the Israel–Lebanon maritime dispute may prompt Lebanon to put aside any Turkish concerns and resolve its border with Cyprus.

2.4.6 Greece–Turkey (Unresolved)

Greece has yet to declare any EEZ coordinates, either in the Aegean or Mediterranean Seas. The Greece–Turkey dispute in the Aegean Sea has been ongoing for decades. In 1975, Turkey sent a seismic exploration ship to an area west of the Greek island of Lesbos. This led to a military confrontation that required the UK to mediate. In 1976, Greece submitted its continental shelf maritime boundary dispute with Turkey to the ICJ.[55] In the case, Greece alleged that Turkish granting of petroleum exploration permits constituted infringement of its exclusive sovereign rights to the exploration and exploitation of its continental shelf. Turkey refused to recognise the Court's jurisdiction and subsequently, the ICJ declared itself incompetent and dropped the case.[56] Turkey has maintained that Greek islands closest to the Turkish mainland are a 'natural prolongation of the Anatolian land mass' and therefore are not entitled to a continental shelf.[57]

2.4.7 Cyprus–Turkey (Unresolved)

Turkey does not recognise the Republic of Cyprus as the island's legitimate authority and the two governments have not had diplomatic relations since 1974. Turkey has objected to the EEZ delineation treaties that Cyprus had concluded with Egypt, Israel, and Lebanon, and has pressured the Lebanese parliament not to ratify the Cyprus–Lebanon EEZ agreement.[58] Turkey has also argued that the Republic of Cyprus has no right to authorise hydrocarbon exploration activities without the permission of the TRNC.[59] It is estimated that Turkey claims 44% of Cyprus's EEZ as part of its own EEZ claims.[60]

The TRNC has declared its own 12 nm territorial sea and 200 nm EEZ.[61] In 2011, the TRNC signed a marine boundary delimitation treaty with Turkey, drawing a boundary between the northern coast of Cyprus and the southern coast of Turkey, a line that was 'declared to be not a median/equidistance line but a line determined on the basis of international law and equitable principles.'[62] The agreement has been declared illegal by both Republic of Cyprus and Greece.

Turkey has refused to negotiate with the Republic of Cyprus government until the northern and southern Cypriot communities are reunited. Without peace on the island, the maritime border between Cyprus and Turkey is likely to remain unresolved.

2.4.8 Egypt–Greece and Libya–Turkey (Unresolved – Disputed)

Cyprus signed an EEZ agreement with Egypt in 2003 based on equidistance principles.[63] Turkey has disputed this agreement because its own continental shelf claims in the region extend from Cyprus in the east, to the Greek island of Rhodes in the west.

Turkey asserts that it shares maritime boundaries with Egypt and Libya, effectively blocking Greece from having a maritime border with Cyprus or with Egypt.[64] Turkey's claims overlap with Cyprus's western exploration blocks announced in 2007 and 2012 bid rounds.[65]

Turkey's 2019 agreement with Libya's Government of National Accord 'ignore[d] the proximity of the Greek island of Crete'[66] and was opposed by Greece, Cyprus, Israel, Syria, and Egypt, among others.[67] The action prompted Syria, a State not party to UNCLOS, to lodge a protest letter to the UN Secretary-General referencing violation of UNCLOS maritime zones. The letter asserted that there

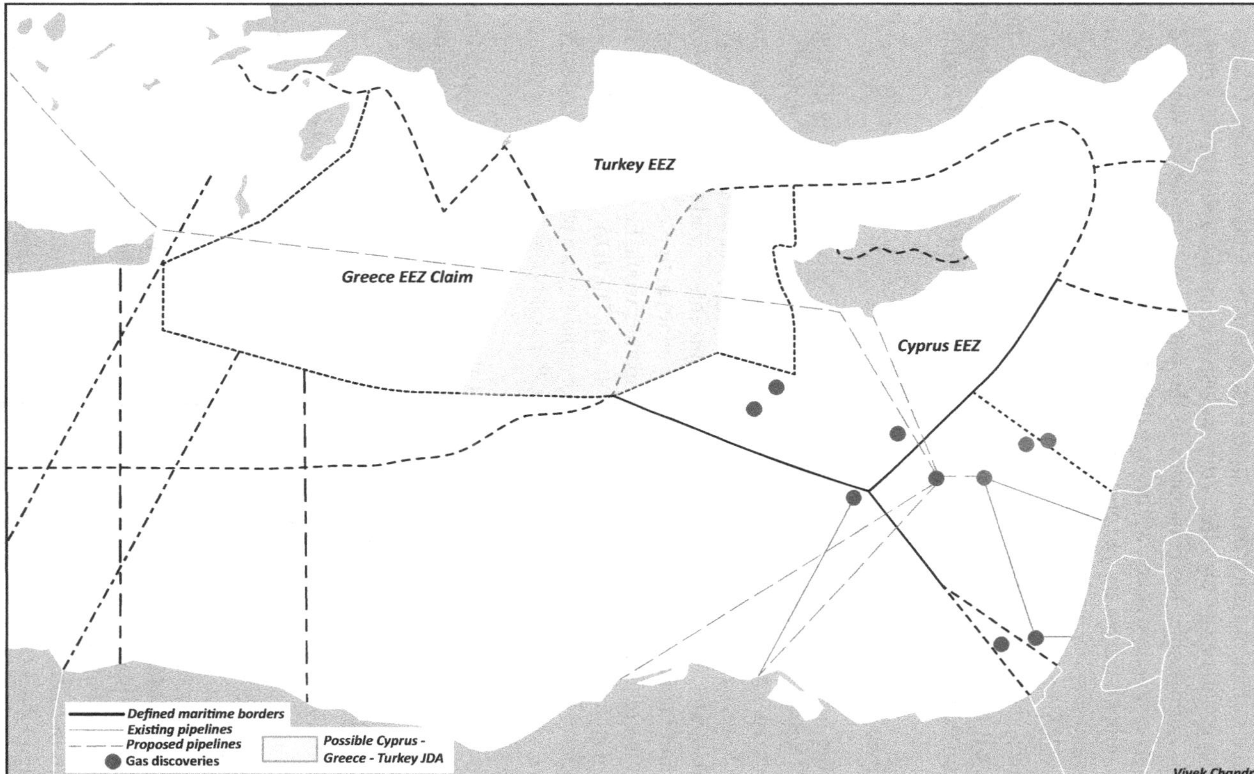

Figure 2.2 Proposed Cyprus–Greece–Turkey trilateral JDA

are no overlapping maritime borders between Turkey and Libya, and Turkey's declaration

> represents a blatant assault on the sovereign economic rights of Greece, Cyprus and Egypt and negatively affects the exclusive economic zone between these States. Furthermore, the boundaries of the purported 'continental shelf and exclusive economic zone', as they are defined in this memorandum, are fictitious, unlawful, arbitrary and provocative, thus seriously endangering regional peace and stability, and risking the Mediterranean becoming a conflict zone.[68]

In contrast, Turkey proclaimed the agreement 'a new regional partnership that includes all actors, rather than trying to isolate Turkey and TRNC, and prevent them from their legitimate rights in accessing their share of the region's wealth.'[69]

2.5 Proposed JDA: Cyprus–Greece–Turkey

One of the most contentious portions of the eastern Mediterranean is the region west of Cyprus, south of the Turkish mainland and southeast of the majority of the Greek islands. This is also strategically located on the future pipeline route between known discoveries in Israel, Cyprus, and Egypt and mainland Europe.

A trilateral Cyprus–Greece–Turkey JDA agreement could alleviate regional tension and facilitate joint exploration (and pipeline) activities to the benefit of all States in the region. International energy companies would be attracted to the JDA if its legal status was undisputed by regional States. The JDA could also diffuse the contentious overlapping EEZ claims of Turkey and Greece which have effectively reduced Cyprus's eastern EEZ by over 50%. Potential boundaries of this trilateral JDA are shown in Figure 2.2.

Turkey (and possibly, even Cyprus) could also offer to share any revenues from this JDA with its TRNC partners in return for resuming reunification discussions.

2.6 Gas Export Options and Conclusions

Apart from Egypt and more recently, Israel, the region has been, and continues to be, a net importer of energy.[70] There has been much excitement about the prospects of exporting the discovered gas resources of Israel, Palestine, and Cyprus, as well as resuming Egyptian exports, much of it sold to Europe. However, the complicated geopolitics of the region, as well as disputed and undefined EEZ boundaries in the eastern Mediterranean, have so far thwarted any attempts at developing a realistic export plan (other than via the existing LNG facilities in Egypt), to the detriment of the regional economies and individual companies that would otherwise benefit from such earnings.

Though UNCLOS explicitly gives the right to all States to lay submarine pipelines in the EEZ of other States,[71] potential transit States in the region, especially Turkey and Lebanon, have so far prevented recent transnational pipelines to export gas to Europe from being built.

As tensions in the region become 'chronic,'[72] it seems that only a multilateral cooperation agreement, possibly in the form of a JDA involving multiple States, will allow the hydrocarbon resources to be developed and exported. In a mid-2020 article, *The Economist* summarised the situation by stating, '[t]he longer that the eastern Mediterranean's leaders bicker, the greater the chance that gas riches beneath the seabed will remain there.'[73] The Russian invasion of Ukraine in 2022 has encouraged European States to look at alternative sources of natural gas for their energy security. The resources in the eastern Mediterranean are a tempting option. A gentle nudge by the Europeans, and the 2022 maritime boundary agreement between Israel and Lebanon, may prompt others to also resolve their long-standing disputes and allow natural gas to be the 'catalyst for peace in the region.'[74]

Notes

1 US Geological Survey, *Fact Sheet: Assessment of Undiscovered Oil and Gas Reserves of the Levant Basin Province, Eastern Mediterranean* (World Petroleum Resources Project Fact Sheet 2010-3014, March 2010) 1. The US Geological Survey (USGS) defines the eastern Mediterranean basin as an 83,000 km^2 area that their map indicates stretches from the Sinai Peninsula to the northern border of Syria, and from the Northern Sinai coast into the Mediterranean Sea to the western side of Cyprus. Turkey has changed its official name to Türkiye. This book will continue to use its common name, 'Turkey.'

2 Agdemir, A. Murat, 'Israel and The Gas Resources of the Levant Basin' (2015) 6(2) Ortadoğu Etütleri Turkmen Cooperation & Cultural Foundation Center for Middle Eastern Strategic Studies (ORSAM) 136, 139.

3 US Geological Survey (n 1) 2. Please refer to the Abbreviations section in the beginning of this book for definition of these resource volume measurements.

4 Peter E. Paraschos, 'Offshore Energy in the Levant Basin: Leaders, Laggards, and Spoilers' (2013) 24(1) *Mediterranean Quarterly* 38, 39.

5 Schematic map created by author based on various sources, including Ayla Gürel, Fiona Mullen, and Harry Tzimitras, *The Cyprus hydrocarbons issue: Context, positions and future scenarios* (PCC Report 1/2013) VII; Athanasios Dagoumas and Flouros Floros, 'Energy Policy Formulation in Israel Following its Recent Gas Discoveries' (2017) 7(1) *International Journal of Energy Economics and Policy* 19, 19; George Al Darazy, 'The Impact of Levant Basin Oil and Natural Gas Discoveries on Lebanese-Israeli Relations' (Master of Military Art and Science Thesis, US Army Command and General Staff College, 2014) 3.; Tareq Baconi, *Pipelines and Pipedreams. How the EU can support a regional gas hub in the Eastern Mediterranean* (European Council on Foreign Relations Policy Brief (April 2017); Daniel Meier, 'Lebanon's Maritime Boundaries – Between Economic Opportunities and Military Confrontation' (Research Paper, Center of Lebanese Studies – Papers on Lebanon, June 2013) 4.; 'A row between Turkey and Greece over gas is raising tension in the eastern Mediterranean,' *The Economist* (UK, 22 August 2020).

6 James Stocker, 'No EEZ Solution: The Politics of Oil and Gas in the Eastern Mediterranean' (2012)(4) *The Middle East Journal* 579. 584.; Tullio Scovazzi, 'Implications of the new law of the sea for the Mediterranean' (1981) 5(4) *Marine Policy* 302, 305.

7 The status of these contested entities is beyond the scope of this book and is widely debated. Jamshid Farshidi, *Palestine-Israel A Just Plan for Permanent Peace* (Xlibris US, 2009) 30. Farshidi defines Palestine as a pseudo-State as 'without independence in any of the characteristics: economy, politics, military or determined borders.'; Nikolaos Ioannidis, 'The Continental Shelf Delimitation Agreement Between Turkey and "TRNC"' (May 2014) *EJIL: Talk! Blog of the European Journal of International Law*.

The TRNC is 'not valid under international law, as the latter party is not a legitimate state entity.'; *Case of Cyprus v. Turkey* (Judgment) [2001] European Court of Human Rights Application no. 25781/94, 77. Turkey has 'effective overall control over northern Cyprus.'

8 *United Nations Convention on the Law of the Sea*, opened for signature 10 December 1982, 1833 UNTS 3 (entered into force 16 November 1994) art 122. ('*UNCLOS*'). 'For the purposes of this Convention, "enclosed or semi-enclosed sea" means a gulf, basin or sea surrounded by two or more States and connected to another sea or the ocean by a narrow outlet or consisting entirely or primarily of the territorial seas and exclusive economic zones of two or more coastal States.'

9 *UNCLOS* (n 8) art 123. Article 123 obliges littoral States to 'coordinate the management, conservation, exploration and exploitation of the living resources of the sea' and 'to coordinate the implementation of their rights and duties with respect to the protection and preservation of the marine environment.'

10 Andrew Filis and Rafael Leal-Arcas, 'Legal Aspects of Inter-State Maritime Delimitation in the Eastern Mediterranean Basin' (2013) 11(3) *Oil, Gas & Energy Law Intelligence* 1,9.

11 Palestine is a non-member observer to the United Nations and though it has deposited its instrument of accession to UNCLOS and will not be considered as a State party to UNCLOS for this book's analysis. The status of these contested entities is beyond the scope of this book and remains widely debated.

12 Nilufer Oral, 'Non-Ratification of the 1982 LOS Convention: An Aegean Dilemma of Environmental and Global Consequence' (March 2009) *Publicist – an online Publication of Berkeley Journal of International Law* 1. The other States that voted against the adoption of UNCLOS were US, Venezuela, and Israel. All four States have still not ratified the Convention.

13 Petros Siousiouras and Chrysochou Georgios, 'The Aegean Dispute in the Context of Contemporary Judicial Decisions on Maritime Delimitation' (2014) 3(1) *Laws* 12, 38. Greece has a total of 3,100 islands, of which 2,463 are in the Aegean. Turkey has only three islands in the Aegean.; Ioannidis (n 7); Gürel, Mullen and Tzimitras (n 5) 20. There are a number of Greek islands located within a few miles from the Turkish mainland, including Greek island of Kastellorizo (Meyisti) with a population of 500 inhabitants located only 2 km from Turkey.

14 *Territorial and Maritime Dispute (Nicaragua v. Colombia)* (Judgment) [2012] ICJ Rep 624 [214]; *UNCLOS* (n 8) art 76 and 57. UNCLOS defines continental shelf and by EEZ by distance.

15 Nilufer (n 12) 1.

16 UN General Assembly *Status of Palestine in the United Nations*, GA Res 67/19, 67th sess., Agenda item 37, UN Doc A/RES/67/19 (4 December 2012). Palestine is a non-member observer State of the United Nations.

17 UN, 'Chronological lists of ratifications of, accessions and successions to the Convention and the related Agreements,' *United Nations Oceans & Law of the Seas* (Web Page) <https://www.un.org/depts/los/reference_files/chronological_lists_of_ratifications.htm>. The 168th State to ratify the convention was Azerbaijan which did so in June 2016.

18 *UNCLOS* (n 8) art 58(1). 'In the exclusive economic zone, all States, whether coastal or land-locked, enjoy, subject to the relevant provisions of this Convention, the freedoms referred to in Article 87 of navigation and overflight and of the laying of submarine cables and pipelines, and other internationally lawful uses of the sea related to these freedoms.'

19 *UNCLOS* (n 8) art 79(3). Article 79(3) effectively requires the consent of the coastal State for the route of any pipelines that cross their EEZ.

20 Anaïs Antreasyan, 'Gas Finds in the Eastern Mediterranean Gaza, Israel, and Other Conflicts' (2013) 42(3) *Journal of Palestine Studies* 29, 32–38.
21 Charles Levinson and Guy Chazan, 'Big Gas Find Sparks a Frenzy in Israel,' *Wall Street Journal* (30 December 2010).
22 Geoffrey Aronson, 'Conflict expands in Eastern Mediterranean over gas riches,' *The Arab Weekly* (UK, 19 January 2020).
23 *Agreement between the Government of the State of Israel and the Government of the Republic of Cyprus on the Delimitation of the Exclusive Economic Zone*, signed on 17 December 2010 (entry into force on 25 February 2011).
24 Ioannis N. Grigoriadis, 'Energy Discoveries in the Eastern Mediterranean: Conflict or Cooperation?' (2014) XXI(3) *Middle East Policy* 124, 127.
25 Grigoriadis (n 24).
26 Ayla Gürel and Laura Le Cornu, 'Can Gas Catalyse Peace in the Eastern Mediterranean?' (2014) 49(2) *International Spectator* 11, 17.
27 Gürel, Mullen and Tzimitras (n 5) 45.
28 Gürel, Mullen and Tzimitras (n 5) 46. The paper quotes TRNC Leader Dervis Eroglu discussion with the UN Secretary General published in the Turkish Cypriot newspapers on 25 September 2011.
29 Nicholas Emilou, Permanent Representative of Cyprus, *Letter dated 15 June 2012 from the Permanent Representative of Cyprus to the United Nations addressed to the Secretary-General*, UNGA 66th sess., Agenda item 76, UN Doc A/66/851 (19 June 2012). The letter named the TRNC licences were in areas 'which fall either partly or wholly within the exclusive economic zone (EEZ) and continental shelf of the Republic of Cyprus.'
30 Gürel and Le Cornu (n 26) 18.
31 BRTK, 'New proposal on hydrocarbons,' *Bayrak Radio Television Corporation* (TRNC, 13 July 2019).
32 Büşra Nur Bilgiç, 'Turkey will continue its activities in E. Med,' *Andalou Agency* (Ankara, Turkey, 14 July 2019). [D-EM89#]
33 Gürel and Le Cornu (n 26) 18.
34 *The Framework Convention for the sharing of hydrocarbon reservoirs between The Republic of Cyprus and The Arab Republic of Egypt*, signed 27 June 2012 ('*Framework Convention*').
35 Stefanos Evripidou, 'Cyprus and Egypt sign unitisation deal on the joint exploitation' *Cyprus Mail* (Cyprus, 13 December 2013).
36 Middle East Strategic Perspectives, 'Egypt: ENI's Zohr, a boost for political stability' *Oil & Gas in Lebanon and the Eastern Mediterranean* (Web Page) <http://www.mesp.me/2015/09/06/egypt-enis-zohr-a-boost-for-political-stability-in-egypt/>.
37 Evripidou (n 35).
38 *The Exclusive Economic Zone and the Continental Shelf Laws 2004 and 2014* (Cyprus), Laws 64(I)/2004, 97(I)/2014). The laws state that, 'the Republic [of Cyprus] has sovereign rights for the purposes of exploring and exploiting, conserving and managing the natural resources … of the waters superjacent to the seabed and of the seabed and its subsoil.'
39 Theodore C Kariotis, 'Hydrocarbons and the Law of the Sea in the Eastern Mediterranean: Implications for Cyprus, Greece, and Turkey' (Spring 2011) (2) *Mediterranean Quarterly* 45, 45 ('Hydrocarbons and LOS').
40 Gürel, Mullen and Tzimitras (n 5) 14.
41 Stocker (n 6) 584. 'An agreement between Syria and Cyprus was discussed in 2001, but no agreement has been reached.'
42 Nikolaj A Dobronravin and Alexandra Rubtsova, 'Contested States and Maritime Boundaries in the Contemporary Eastern Mediterranean' (2016) 100(3) *Nuova Rivista Storica* 1011, 1022, 1019.

43 Antreasyan (n 20) 35.
44 Al Derazy (n 5) 5.
45 Antreasyan (n 20) 38.
46 Brenda Shaffer, 'Israel—New natural gas producer in the Mediterranean' (2011) 39 *Energy Policy* 5379, 5381.
47 Minster for Foreign Affairs and Emigrants, Lebanon letter to the Secretary-General of the United Nations, 3 September 2011 *UN Doc.* 3372.11D.
48 Antreasyan (n 20) 39; Colby Connelly, 'Eastern Mediterranean gas discoveries, progress, and what to watch in 2023' (Jan 2023), Middle East Institute.
49 Yuval Shany, 'International Law of the Sea Meets Israeli Constitutional Law: The New Israeli-Lebanese Maritime Border Agreement' (2023) Lawfare (January 9 2023).
50 *Agreement between the Republic of Cyprus and the Arab Republic of Egypt on the Delimitation of the Exclusive Economic Zone*, signed 17 February 2003.
51 Kariotis, 'Hydrocarbons and LOS' (n 39) 51.
52 Antreasyan (n 20) 41.
53 Kariotis, 'Hydrocarbons and LOS' (n 39) 47.
54 Kariotis, 'Hydrocarbons and LOS' (n 39) 47.
55 *Aegean Sea Continental Shelf Case, (Greece/Turkey)* (Overview of the Case) [1978] ICJ Reports 62.
56 *Aegean Sea Continental Shelf Case, (Greece/Turkey)* (Reports of Judgments, Advisory Opinions and Orders) [1978] ICJ Reports 62, par 108. Article 108 states, 'In so finding, the Court emphasizes that the sole question for decision in the present proceedings is whether it does, or does not, have jurisdiction to entertain the Application filed by Greece on 10 August 1976. Having concluded that the Joint Communiqué issued in Brussels on 31 May 1975 does not furnish a basis for establishing the Court's jurisdiction in the present proceedings, the Court is not concerned, nor is it competent, to pronounce upon any other implications which that Communiqué may have in the context of the present dispute.'
57 Siousiouras and Georgios (n 13) 17.
58 Grigoriadis (n 24) 129.
59 Grigoriadis (n 24).
60 Nick Squires, 'High stakes in Cyprus as Turkish north bids to turn Bardot's beloved resort into new Las Vegas,' *The Telegraph* (London, 6 October 2019).
61 Gürel, Mullen and Tzimitras (n 5). Referencing TRNC Maritime Jurisdiction Areas Law, No. 63/2005.
62 Gürel, Mullen and Tzimitras (n 5). Referencing a 2011 Turkish Ministry of Foreign Affairs announcement.
63 *Agreement between the Republic of Cyprus and the Arab Republic of Egypt on the Delimitation of the Exclusive Economic Zone* (n 50).
64 Siousiouras and Georgios (n 13) 17; Kariotis, 'Hydrocarbons and LOS' (n 39) 51. Figure 2.1 shows the relative positions of each EEZ claim.
65 Gürel, Mullen, and Tzimitras (n 5) 53.
66 Robin Mills, 'Why offshore gas in the Eastern Mediterranean has a complicated road ahead,' *The National* (UAE, 15 June 2020).
67 Gerald Butt, 'Turkey pushes East Mediterranean boundaries' (4 December 2019) *Petroleum Economist*; Scott Carpenter, 'New Pipeline Deal Gives Europe Access To Eastern Mediterranean Gas Reserves, Angering Turkey' (2 January 2020) *Forbes*. Cyprus has stated that the 'MOU has no validity, while Greece decries it a distortion of international law. Egypt also says the agreement is illegal.'
68 Permanent Representative of the Syrian Arab Republic, *Letter dated 29 April 2020 from the Permanent Representative of the Syrian Arab Republic to the United Nations addressed to the Secretary-General*, UN General Assembly 74th sess., Agenda Item 74(a) and 83, UN Doc A/74/831 (29 April 2020).

69 Enex Yavuz, 'The Eastern Mediterranean dispute: is there light at the end of the tunnel?' *TRT World* (Turkey, 3 December 2019).
70 Baconi (n 5) 7.
71 *UNCLOS* (n 8) art 58. Article 58 states, 'In the exclusive economic zone, all States, whether coastal or land-locked, enjoy, subject to the relevant provisions of this Convention, the freedoms referred to in Article 87 of navigation and overflight and of the laying of submarine cables and pipelines.'
72 Yavuz (n 69).
73 'Dealing with a dangerous dispute in the eastern Med' *The Economist* (UK, 22 August 2020).
74 Stocker (n 6) 597.

3 Maritime Borders

Caspian Sea

3.1 Introduction

The Caspian Sea is unique and complicated. Straddling both Europe and Asia, the Caspian Sea has been an important trading route linking Russia and Central Asia since the Middle Ages. The Caspian Sea is entirely landlocked, and it is the largest enclosed body of water in the world. Its main sources of water come from three major rivers – the Volga, Ural, and Terek – which all flow through Russia. There are no outlets flowing from the Caspian Sea, making it unique among similar bodies of water, such as the Black Sea, Mediterranean Sea, Persian Gulf, and others.

The Caspian's hydrocarbon endowment was noted 700 years ago by Marco Polo when he observed a natural oil seep in what is now Azerbaijan, as 'a fountain from which oil springs in great abundance.'[1] Prior to WW II, the Azerbaijan Soviet Socialist Republic was the largest producer of oil in the world, accounting for 50% of global oil production, and supplying over 75% of Soviet oil during the war.

Prior to the dissolution of the Soviet Union in 1991, only two countries, the USSR and Iran, bordered its shores. These countries had signed several bilateral treaties governing their roles and rights over the sea's resources, and though the maritime boundary between them was not formally defined, it was relatively non-contentious.

The situation dramatically changed with the end of the USSR and the subsequent birth of the independent States of Kazakhstan, Azerbaijan, and Turkmenistan, plus the Russian Federation which controlled the vital rivers and canals that link the Caspian Sea with other navigable bodies, and Iran, whose territory offers the shortest distance to open seas. All three of the newly created independent States are landlocked, were not parties to previous treaties between the USSR and Iran, and claim significant offshore hydrocarbon resources in the Caspian Sea, unlike Russia and Iran, which have a relatively small share of the basin's resources of oil and gas.[2]

As this chapter discusses, the applicability of UNCLOS in determining and resolving maritime disputes in the Caspian Sea has been much debated and has led to tensions which have escalated to sporadic military confrontations between some of the five littoral States. As the east–west width of the Caspian Sea is less than 250 km, if UNCLOS maritime zone definitions were applied to it, the EEZs of the littoral States would overlap and many of the Caspian oil and gas fields would

DOI: 10.4324/9781003323051-3

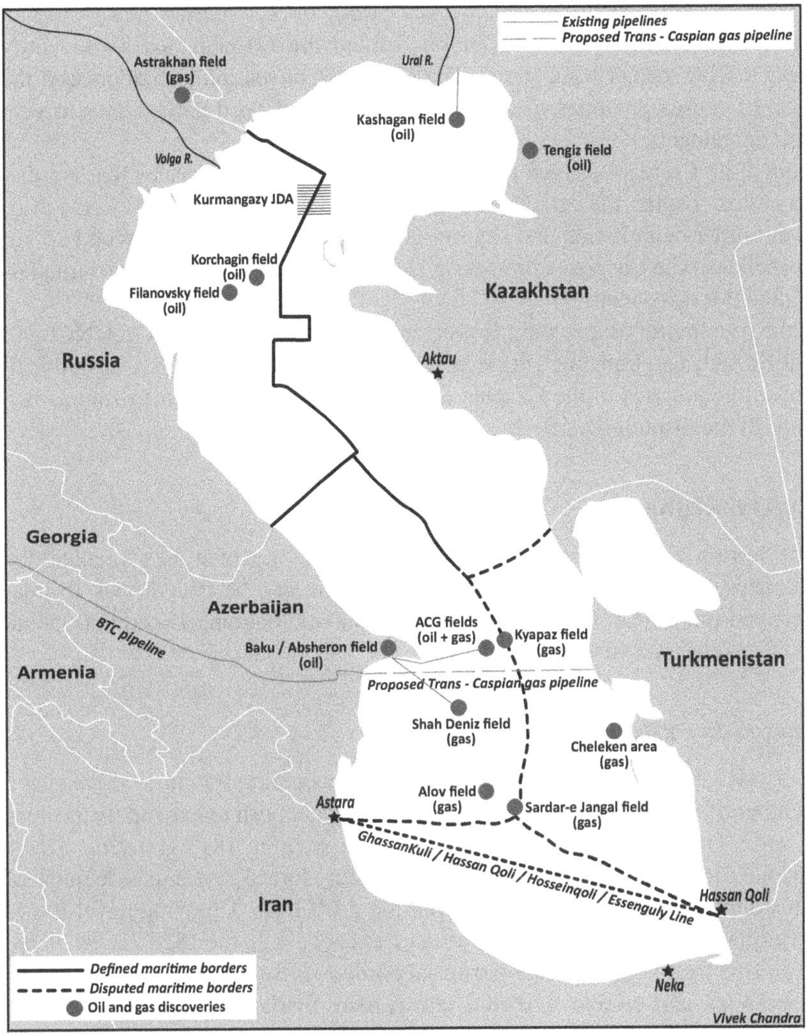

Figure 3.1 Schematic of conflicting EEZ claims and hydrocarbon discoveries in the Caspian Sea.[3]

be in disputed overlapping zones. Four of the littoral States (Russia, Azerbaijan, Kazakhstan, and Turkmenistan) have evolved their positions over the past three decades and are now advocating partition of the sea by defined boundaries based on the UNCLOS median-line equidistance principle. Iran's traditional position, inherited from the Soviet era, is that the Caspian is an enclosed water body that is not under the jurisdiction of UNCLOS,[4] and all its resources should be either jointly developed or sectioned into equal portions between the littoral States.[5]

In 2018, despite 'substantive differences' and 'deep-rooted' disputes, the five States signed the *Convention on the Legal Status of the Caspian Sea* ('Caspian Convention').[6] The Caspian Convention defined the Caspian Sea as an entity *sui generis* with special legal status. The Caspian Convention also addressed the approval of subsea pipelines by removing the rights of third-party States to veto bilateral agreements.

Though the Caspian Convention resolved a number of key issues that are discussed in this chapter, the agreement remains incomplete with regards to the principles of border delimitation and sharing of hydrocarbon resources beyond 15 nm from baselines. The Caspian Convention has not come into force because Iran has not ratified the agreement.

Of the five littoral States, only Russia and Azerbaijan are parties to UNCLOS. Neither Kazakhstan, Iran, nor Turkmenistan are parties of UNCLOS. Currently, all unresolved boundaries in the Caspian Sea involve Iran and Turkmenistan as one (or both) of the disputing parties.[7]

3.2 Legal Background

Current territorial and sovereignty disputes in the Caspian Sea predate the 1991 collapse of the Soviet Union. The issues can also be traced back to treaties between pre-Soviet Tsarist Russia and Persia and ongoing uncertainty about UNCLOS's relevance to the Caspian Sea.

3.2.1 Russia–Iran Relationship

Since the 19th century, Tsarist Russia and Persia (becoming Iran in 1935) engaged in a number of wars and treaties prompted by Russia's push to expand its territory southward.[8] The first major treaty between them was the 1813 *Golestan Treaty* signed after the 1804 Russo–Persian war.[9] The treaty forced Persia to cede much of its Caucasian territories, effectively preventing itself from deploying naval forces in the Caspian.[10] The second Russo–Persian war ended with the 1828 *Turkmenchai Treaty*.[11] This treaty extended the territorial borders of Russia, incorporated northern Azerbaijan and eastern Armenia into Russia, marked the land border with Persia, and established navigation rules for the Caspian Sea. Both treaties gave Russia exclusive rights to sail naval vessels in the Caspian, promising to protect Persia from Turkmen attackers in exchange. The 1828 treaty also effectively converted the Sea into 'Russia's internal body of water'[12] and was the foundation of future Soviet control of the Caspian Sea.[13]

After the Russian revolution in 1917, Russia's colonial attitude towards Persia softened. This resulted in the 1921 *Treaty of Friendship* which restored Iran's rights of free navigation, naval force, and fishing in the Caspian.[14] The treaty barred shipping from other nations but did not address demarcation of the maritime border or the legal regime of the Caspian.[15] The subsequent 1940 *Treaty of Commerce and Navigation* specified an exclusive right to fishing to 10 nm from the coasts of each State but did not mention sharing of other resources, specifically oil which had already begun commercial production in offshore Azerbaijan Soviet Socialist Republic (SSR) waters.[16]

Both the 1921 and 1940 treaties referred to the Caspian Sea as an internal water basin of both countries which gave no right of access or resources to other States. As a result, only Soviet and Iranian vessels were allowed to navigate or fish in the Caspian. The treaties described the Caspian as a '*common sea*' whereby both parties have 'equal access to and equal treatment of its waters, and any decisions affecting the Sea and its resources must be made jointly.'[17] Though the treaties do not define the common ownership regime, subsequently referred to as *res communis* (condominium) principle, that had been the basis of Russian (until 1998) and Iranian positions.[18]

In the late 19th century, offshore commercial hydrocarbon production began in the Azerbaijan SSR. The Soviet government did not offer revenue sharing or involvement of Iran in the production of the resources, contradicting the condominium principles envisioned in their treaties.[19] The USSR also discouraged any offshore or near-shore Iranian exploration efforts.[20]

In 1935, the Soviet interior ministry unilaterally declared a straight-line boundary across the southern Caspian, connecting the eastern coastal village of GhassanKuli[21] in the Turkmen SSR (now Turkmenistan) to Astara in Azerbaijan SSR (now Azerbaijan).[22] This boundary line, shown in Figure 3.1, became known as the GhassanKuli line and became a 'state boundary of the USSR' though it was never officially declared.[23] In 1964, a Soviet–Iranian aerial agreement for determination of flight information zones established the line of demarcation between the two countries using the GhassanKuli line, and subsequent maps showed the line as the international boundary.[24]

The Soviet authorities also divided their portion of the Caspian into symbolic 'national sectors' for administration by the USSR. The sectoral division was first carried out by the Soviet Ministry of Oil Industry in the early 1920 and updated in 1970, when a 'more comprehensive delimitation based on an approximation of the median line separating the four republics' defined *de facto* 'national sectors.'[25]

3.2.2 Post-Soviet Era

Since the 1991 dissolution of the Soviet Union, questions about the validity of Soviet–Iranian treaties and inherited obligations of the newly created States have continued to fuel disputes in the region. Iran and Russia have asserted that the 1921 and 1940 Soviet-Iran treaties obligations should be honoured by the successor States.[26] They cite two factors for their assertion; firstly, under the 1978 *Vienna Convention on Succession of States* in respect of Treaties, newly created independent States are obliged to fulfil Soviet-era obligations.[27] Secondly, under the 1991 *Alma-Ata Declaration*,[28] the former Soviet republics pledged to recognise the validity of Soviet-era treaties.[29] Both States had insisted that future boundary delimitation and resource development agreements should reflect the *common seas* approach as the Caspian's 'historical, geographic, and environmental characteristics warrant such an approach.'[30] Their position implied that 'no wealth extracted from the Caspian could be disposed of without consent from all bordering States.'[31]

Proponents of sectoral division of the Caspian, led by Azerbaijan and Kazakhstan, rejected both the Soviet-era joint development and equal portion approaches.[32] They assert that the delimitation lines by the Soviet Ministry of Oil Industry were *de facto* boundary lines.[33]The Azeris and Kazakhs also suggested that since the Soviet Union 'administratively divided its portion of the Caspian Sea,' the Caspian Sea was not a strict *res communis* regime.[34] These opponents of the *common seas* regime also cite the history of unilateral Soviet development of Azeri oil fields without Iranian approval and participation as evidence against the condominium principle.[35] Russia, prior to its change of stance in 1998, had dismissed the boundary claims by the newly created States. Russia maintained that under Soviet law, the continental shelf and ownership of its resources was the property of the USSR, not the individual Soviet republics, and that the divisions were for administrative purposes, not to define boundaries or grant ownership.

By the early 2000s, Iran realised that its condominium joint development proposal was not going to be ratified by the other littoral States.[36] As a result, Iran developed a 'fallback plan' that accepted the premise of dividing the Caspian into national sectors, with the caveat that the division must be in equal portions, granting each of the five States a 20% share of the Caspian's surface rights and seabed resources.[37] A 20% share in the Caspian would give Iran a larger portion of shared hydrocarbon resources than sectoral division granting each State a share proportional to its shoreline. Under the division based on shoreline length, Iran would have the smallest portion of shared resources.[38]

To the credit of all five States, diplomatic efforts to resolve their diverging interests continued for the ensuing decades. In August 2018, they all signed the landmark *Convention on the Legal Status of the Caspian Sea* ('Caspian Convention').[39] The Caspian Convention has been hailed as 'the cornerstone of a new legal regime.'[40] Once ratified, the Caspian Convention will replace the 1921 and 1940 Soviet–Iranian treaties, validate the Northern Caspian maritime border delimitation treaties previously signed between Azerbaijan, Kazakhstan and Russia, and define the legal status of the Caspian Sea.[41] Because Iran has not ratified the Convention, the agreement has not entered into force.

The Caspian Convention aims to strengthen the sentiment of 'Caspian for the Caspians,' restricting natural resources, transit, security, and common space to the five littoral States only. To appease Iran and Russia, which have had concerns about foreign military access, non-Caspian military vessels would be prohibited from the Caspian.[42] Benefiting Azerbaijan, Kazakhstan, and Turkmenistan, are the rights of all littoral States to build oil and gas export pipelines under the waters of the Caspian. This has long been resisted by Russia which prefers all hydrocarbon resources to be exported using its pipeline system and, in tandem with Iran, has been able to block any cross-border subsea pipeline development.[43]

The Caspian Convention differentiates the division of the water column versus the seabed and subsurface resources.[44] The water column, including surface waters, is divided into internal waters, territorial waters, fishery zones, and common maritime space – all concepts 'inspired' by UNCLOS.[45] Article 8 grants each State exclusive rights for the exploitation of seabed resources and all other associated economic activities in maritime sectors extending to 15 nm. Resources in more distant areas from baselines are to be shared according to future agreements.[46] Other than stating that 'delimitation should be carried out by agreement between States with adjacent and opposite coasts, with due regard to the generally recognised principles and norms of international law' there is no further guidance on specific principles of maritime border delimitation or joint development.

Iran has been consistent in rejecting any bilateral agreements that delimit maritime boundaries in the Caspian. Though Iran was a signatory to the Caspian Convention, there remains public opposition against the 'unfair' allocation of the seabed.[47] Until Iran's Majlis (parliament) completes the ratification process, the Convention will not take effect or be binding on the signatories.[48]

3.3 Applicability of UNCLOS

The question of whether UNCLOS is applicable to the Caspian Sea is the subject of much debate within public international law. The 'threshold' question is actually whether the Caspian Sea is a sea or a lake. If recognised as a 'sea,' it would be an UNCLOS-defined 'semi-enclosed sea.'[49]

The Caspian has been called a 'sea' since it was first mentioned in ancient texts, and all littoral States call it a 'sea' in their respective languages. The Intergovernmental Oceanographic Commission of the United Nations Educational Scientific and Cultural Organization has asserted that, 'from an oceanographic point of view (composition of water, fauna, flora) the Caspian Sea should be considered as a sea. In fact, the Caspian Sea is a relict marine basin.'[50] Geographically, the Caspian Sea resembles many other 'seas' because it is large and deep, contains saltwater, and is bordered by independent States.

However, the Caspian Sea is landlocked and only connected 'to another sea or the ocean' (in this case, Black Sea) via a series of fresh-water man-made canals in the Volga delta. In this regard, the Caspian resembles the geography of other international lakes, such as the Great Lakes (between the US and Canada), Lake Tanganyika (Tanzania, D.R. Congo, Burundi and Zambia), Lake Chad (Nigeria, Chad, Niger, and Cameroon), Lake Titicaca (Bolivia and Peru), Lake Geneva (Switzerland and France), and Lake Constance (Germany, Switzerland and Austria), rather than a semi-enclosed sea like the Persian Gulf or the Black Sea with natural outlets to larger oceans.

Uniquely, the canals and rivers that connect the Caspian to the Black Sea flow in the opposite direction – they flow *into* the Caspian instead of out of the Caspian – thereby the 'outlet' is going in the wrong direction and the definition used by Article 122 may not be valid.[51] Other proponents of the lake classification for the Caspian have noted that, because of its unique geography, navigation by international shipping requires Russia to grant passage through its internal Volga–Don canal system.

If the Caspian Sea is recognised as a 'lake,' UNCLOS would not apply, and littoral States would not be obliged to follow international sea norms in boundary delimitation. The surface waters and resources of international lakes can be designated to be used exclusively by the littoral States, unlike those of 'seas' where freedom of navigation is granted to all States.[52] International maritime boundaries in lakes are usually based on the median line without consideration of other factors (such as islands) or equity principles.

Under the 'sea' definition, as an UNCLOS applicable regime, each littoral State would be granted territorial sea and EEZ zones. Since the maximum width of the Caspian is 250 nm, conventional 200 nm EEZ zones would overlap requiring opposite States to delimit their EEZ boundaries in accordance with equitable principles, as per Article 74 and other provisions of UNCLOS.[53] The entire surface area of the Caspian would be covered by territorial seas and EEZs.[54]

UNCLOS also requires that all international States be granted freedom of navigation and overflight and be allowed to lay cables and pipelines in an EEZ area of another State.[55] Caspian States, especially Iran and Russia, have resisted granting navigation rights to non-Caspian States or allowing third-party trans-border subsea pipelines.

Of the five littoral States, only Russia and Azerbaijan are parties to UNCLOS.[56] Azerbaijan has actively promoted UNCLOS subdivisions of the Caspian – the reasons for this position are clear. A delimitation median line adjusted for equity principles under UNCLOS would locate many of the largest hydrocarbon fields within Azeri maritime zones. Because these deposits are located in relatively shallow portions of the Caspian, they can be easily developed.

Though Iran is an original 1982 signatory of UNCLOS, Iran's government never ratified the Convention.[57] The two reasons that this is important for Iran are firstly, that Iran opposes foreign ships, especially navy ships, sailing in the Caspian under UNCLOS freedom of navigation rules.[58] Secondly, if the Caspian was divided under UNCLOS boundary delimitation principles based on median line adjusted for equity, Iran's sector could be approximately 14%, significantly less than the 20% Iran has been insisting on under an equal sectoral division method.

3.4 Oil and Gas Activities

For centuries, the primary resources of interest in the Caspian Sea were its rich fish stocks, especially the sturgeon and its valuable caviar. Overfishing, and production of large volumes of oil and gas have 'eclipsed fisheries and made oil and gas exploitation the paramount economic driver' in the region.[59] The Caspian Sea is considered one of the world's first energy provinces and played an important role in both world wars. In fact, historians have identified that Germany's failure to secure access to the Caspian's oil resources was a major reason for its defeats in 1918 and in 1945.[60] The control of oil and gas resources remain 'at the heart of the controversies in the Caspian.'[61]

At the end of the 19th century, more than half of the world's oil production was produced from what is now Azerbaijan's Baku region. Until 1960, when the hydrocarbon focus of the Soviet Union moved to Siberia, Azeri offshore and near-shore fields remained the most productive in the entire USSR.[62] During the past 30 years, the region has experienced a resurgence in hydrocarbon activities, and production has mainly risen due to large offshore and near-shore developments in Kazakhstan, Turkmenistan, and Azerbaijan involving international energy companies.

In the late 1980s, the offshore 'ACG' fields (the Azeri, Chirag, and Guneshli oil fields), located 80 miles off Azerbaijan's coastline, initiated the current era of renewed hydrocarbon activities in the Caspian. In 1994, the Azerbaijan International Operating Company (AIOC), a consortium led by BP, won the 'Contract of the Century' – the rights to develop the ACG.[63] This was the first major contract between a former Soviet republic and a Western-led consortium.

Originally, the AIOC consortium, which included British, American, Japanese, Turkish, and other international energy companies, did not include participation from any Iranian or Russian entities. This prompted a stern response from the Russian Foreign Ministry which sent diplomatic notes to Azerbaijan, Kazakhstan, and Turkmenistan.[64]

At the time, Russia disputed the right of any Caspian nation to make unilateral developments in the region, claiming that 'all mineral resources of the Caspian outside of a narrow twelve-mile limit should be the joint property of all littoral States.'[65] As an appeasement to Russia, the AIOC consortium ultimately allocated a 10% share to the Russian oil company Lukoil, ensuring that Russia would not block Azerbaijan's development of the Caspian resources.

Kazakhstan is also well endowed with hydrocarbons, having the second largest hydrocarbon reserves in the former USSR after Russia. Though many of the known fields are onshore (such as the giant Tengiz field), the offshore Caspian fields of Kashagan are considered some of the largest fields in the world. Large international companies are involved in the Kazakh petroleum sector.

Though the Iranian economy is heavily dependent on oil and gas production, all its reserves are found in the southwest Persian Gulf region. The Iranian Caspian coast, where the water is relatively deeper, is 'regarded as relatively unpromising'[66] and has had no commercial oil or gas discoveries. Iran has claimed that its offshore resources in the Caspian have high potential but there is no oil or gas production and limited exploration efforts over the past few decades to substantiate this claim. Drilling in Iranian waters has been limited because prospects are in water too deep for conventional Caspian rigs designed for the shallower waters of Azerbaijan, Kazakhstan, and Turkmenistan.

The region's vast natural gas resources, which could be larger than its oil resources, are mainly found in the southern Caspian where territorial disputes hinder development and undersea export pipeline investment.[67]

Complicating any oil and gas development in the Caspian region are the limited export routes. Due to maritime border delimitation uncertainties and opposition by Russia and Iran, no subsea pipelines currently traverse the Caspian Sea. Of the five littoral States, only Russia and Iran have access to the open seas. Thus, any development in Azerbaijan, Kazakhstan, or Turkmenistan would require transit via a neighbouring country. Since Russia has the most extensive pipeline network in the region, though much is obsolete and dated, most of Kazakhstan's and, to a lesser extent, Turkmenistan's hydrocarbon exports are dependent on the Russian system.

In 2005, a 2,000-km pipeline from Kazakhstan's Caspian coast to China was completed. The pipeline is China's first direct oil import pipeline, and it has allowed Kazakhstan to reduce its dependence on the Russian pipeline system. Until 2009, all of Turkmenistan's natural gas exports depended on Russian pipelines. The completion of the Central Asia–China gas pipeline provided an alternative route to the market and gave Turkmenistan the leverage it required to renegotiate the purchase price paid for exports via the Russian system.[68] Turkmenistan also exports gas (and electricity) to north-eastern regions of Iran in a swap arrangement whereby equivalent volumes of Iranian gas are exported to southern Azerbaijan.

Azerbaijan has chosen to export via its own export system called the Baku–Tbilisi–Ceyhan (BTC) pipeline, bypassing the Russian network entirely and exporting to Turkey via Georgia. A parallel oil pipeline this route was completed in 2005 and was followed by a parallel gas pipeline in 2007.

A future subsea Trans-Caspian Pipeline (TCP) connecting Turkmenistan and Azerbaijan under the Caspian, and onto Turkey in a parallel route or expanded BTC pipeline, is seen as a major beneficiary of the Caspian Convention once the agreement is ratified by Iran. The project – the most expensive of all proposed Caspian export projects – has attracted official protests from Iran and Russia, ostensibly based primarily on environmental grounds, the logistics of constructing an underwater pipeline across the Caspian and ongoing maritime border disputes and sectoral divisions in the Caspian.[69] Because the Caspian Convention effectively eliminates the ability of Iran and Russia to obstruct subsea pipelines such as the TCP pipeline, further hydrocarbon development in the Caspian basin may become more attractive.[70]

Iran also promotes itself to other Caspian States as an export route via oil 'swaps.' Iran would benefit from imported oil (by tankers crossing the Caspian) to be used for consumption in northern Iran, far from its own resources in the Persian Gulf. In return, an equivalent volume of oil would be exported via Persian Gulf ports. Iran claims that this exchange would facilitate easier access to Asian economies and realise higher commodity prices than competing pipelines to Black Sea and Mediterranean ports.[71] In 1995, Iran offered the Azerbaijan consortium an opportunity to swap up to 100,000 bbls of oil per day from the ACG fields. Because of deterioration in their relationship due to maritime border disputes and Iranian claims to Azeri fields, no Azeri crude oil has been exported via Iran, though limited quantities of Turkmen oil have taken advantage of the swap arrangement.[72]

3.5 JDA Status – Operational and Proposed

Iran and Russia have been the main proponents of joint development of hydrocarbon resources in the Caspian Sea. Their common position (until Russia changed its stance in the late 1990s) is that all resources outside territorial sea zones should be jointly developed in arrangements involving all five littoral States.[73] Energy companies from outside the region would only be allowed to participate if the five national energy companies either decline to participate or they jointly agree to invite the foreign entity.[74] Caspian-wide joint development proposals have been rejected by Azerbaijan and Kazakhstan, which will have the most to lose under any revenue sharing scheme.

In 2006, eight years after Russia and Kazakhstan delimited their maritime boundary, they agreed to jointly explore and develop the Kurmangazy field which straddles their maritime boundary.[75] The development is owned, on an equal basis, by State-owned oil companies in Russia and Kazakhstan, and became the first jointly developed project in the Caspian.[76] However, the development of the field remains uncertain because of disappointing well results.[77]

As discussed in the next section of this chapter, Azerbaijan and Turkmenistan have long disputed the ownership of several fields, including the producing ACG cluster and the undeveloped Kyapaz/Serdar field. In 2009, there were statements by the Azerbaijan national energy company that the two States had agreed to start 'joint work' on the Kyapaz/Serdar field, continuing 'Soviet-era geologic cooperation in the Caspian Sea.'[78] Subsequent hostilities ended these discussions, but, in the wake of the Caspian Convention, they are motivated to not only jointly develop the Kaypaz/Serdar field, but also to construct the subsea TCP pipeline to further facilitate Turkmenistan's exports.

Azerbaijan also has a disputed maritime border with Iran. This has largely been prompted by Iranian claims over a number of discovered but yet undeveloped gas fields.[79] Encouraged by the Caspian Convention, as well as the precedent of the Russia–Kazakhstan JDA, representatives from Azerbaijan and Iran signed a JDA Memorandum of Understanding in 2018.[80] The *Joint Development of Relevant Blocks of the Caspian Sea* called for equal sharing of fields in 'common area' of the Caspian under a joint oil company, owned by respective national energy companies to be established to develop the Sardar-e Jangal and Alov fields.[81] There seems to be no recent progress on the JDA since the signing of this agreement.

3.6 Maritime Boundaries

In the absence of a binding agreement among the five countries on the legal status of the Caspian,[82] only the northern States have negotiated bilateral and trilateral agreements to clarify their maritime border positions while the southern boundaries remain undelimited.

3.6.1 Kazakhstan–Azerbaijan (Resolved)
3.6.2 Kazakhstan–Russia (Resolved)
3.6.3 Russia–Azerbaijan (Resolved)
3.6.4 Kazakhstan–Turkmenistan (Resolved)

In defiance of Russia and Iran, Azerbaijan and Kazakhstan have been aggressively pursuing the development of offshore reserves under sectoral division. Their position is that all littoral States should be entitled to UNCLOS-determined maritime zones, and for all maritime boundaries to be determined using median lines. Each State would have an exclusive entitlement to explore mineral resources in its territorial waters and EEZ, and landlocked Caspian States should have open access to the Caspian through Russian waterways.

In 1997, as international energy companies increased their interest in Kazakhstan's offshore fields, Kazakhstan declared the Caspian as an 'enclosed sea,' arguing for UNCLOS delimitation principles (though it is not a signatory to the Convention), specifically Articles 122 and 123, should be applied to the Caspian.[83]

In the same year, Kazakhstan and Turkmenistan issued a Joint Statement to the UN General Assembly. This declaration explicitly stated that '[u]ntil the Caspian States reach an agreement on the status of the Caspian Sea, the parties will adhere to the delimitation of administrative and territorial borders along a line running through the middle of the Sea.'[84] The declaration accepted the sectoral division between Kazakhstan and Turkmenistan delimited on equidistant lines.[85] In 2014, Kazakhstan and Turkmenistan signed the *Agreement on the delimitation of the bottom of the Caspian Sea* finalising their maritime borders.

Faced with conflicting positions within the Russian government, loss of hydrocarbon profits, and the success of Azerbaijan and Kazakhstan in attracting foreign energy companies into the offshore oil and gas sector, Russia was compelled to adopt a new strategy in the Caspian.[86] In February 1998, Russia made a 'surprising announcement' that it was ready for a 'fair division of the Caspian seabed.'[87] In 1998, Russia signed an agreement with Kazakhstan dividing the northern part of the Caspian.[88] In accordance with the 1997 Kazakhstan–Turkmenistan Joint Statement and UNCLOS principles, the median line was also used to define the respective Russian and Kazakh EEZ boundaries.[89]

In July 1998, Russia and Azerbaijan signed a protocol on the legal status of the Caspian. In this document, Russia accepted sectoral division along the median line for subsea resources. In November 2001, Kazakhstan and Azerbaijan signed the *Delimitation of the Caspian Seabed between the Republic of Kazakhstan and the Azerbaijan Republic* agreement.[90] The document stipulated that the seabed be divided along the median line, 'on the basis of equal distance from the original base points on the coastline and the islands.'[91]

In May 2003, Russia, Azerbaijan, and Kazakhstan entered into a trilateral agreement accepting the 'modified median line' method of subsea delimitation while maintaining joint use of surface waters.[92] The width of each State's EEZ was based on the median line adjusted for the length of the territorial coast, with an identified junction point where all three maritime boundaries meet.[93] At the insistence of Russia, the trilateral agreement stated that surface waters (beyond each State's territorial seas) will remain subject to joint use, managed by the three States as a 'common space.'[94]

3.6.1 Azerbaijan–Turkmenistan (Unresolved)

Of the five Caspian States, the position of Turkmenistan has been the least consistent.[95] Turkmenistan initially considered the Caspian Sea to be an 'interior body of water-lake, to which neither the categories of marine law nor the separation into national sectors applied,' in accordance with the 1921 and 1940 Soviet–Iranian treaties.[96] In October 1993, Turkmenistan became the first Caspian State to declare its 12-nm territorial sea and a maritime economic zone extending to the Soviet-era GhassanKuli line.[97] More recently, Turkmenistan has ratified the Caspian Convention, which advocates a common sea and divided seabed.

Though both Turkmenistan and Azerbaijan have been negotiating their maritime boundary since 1994, and have agreed to use the median line as the basis of the negotiations, they have been unable to agree on the location of the median line.[98] Turkmenistan's position is that the median line proposed by Azerbaijan should not consider the Azeri Absheron peninsula, which extends into the Caspian, or Zhilov island, both of which could lead to 'significant deviation of the median line.'[99] Turkmenistan insists on the median line in the geographic middle of the sea, instead of bending eastward to account for the peninsula. The Azerbaijan median line, which they claim is in accordance with UNCLOS practice adjusted for geographic features, gives Azerbaijan a larger share of the southern Caspian EEZ areas. Their proposed line places a number of fields, including the prized ACG Azeri and Chirag fields, within Azerbaijan's EEZ.

In February 1998, Turkmenistan and Azerbaijan reiterated their intention to delimit the boundary along a median line. However, Turkmenistan also added the Kyapaz/Serdar field to the list of disputed fields even though the field was discovered by Azerbaijan and is on the Azeri side of both the Soviet 1970 ministerial border and the median line.[100] In 2000, the Ministry of Foreign Affairs of Turkmenistan sent a memorandum to foreign embassies that Turkmenistan is in 'absolute disagreement with Azerbaijan's unilateral behaviour' regarding the development of deposits and threatened to appeal the 'wrongful activity of certain oil companies in the Caspian' to the ICJ.[101] Both also threatened military action, accusing each other of violating territorial waters and illegal exploration and development activities.[102]

In 1999, the Azerbaijan foreign ministry announced that Kyapaz/Serdar would be developed jointly by State energy companies of Azerbaijan, Turkmenistan, and Russia's Lukoil.[103] Turkmenistan also demanded that Azerbaijan suspend work at all disputed fields, including the ACG fields. Azerbaijan rejected the warning. In response, Turkmenistan closed its embassy in Azerbaijan, which remained closed until 2006. In 2012, Turkmenistan began seismic exploration work in the area, in defiance of a 2008 agreement by the two countries not to conduct any work on the disputed field until the maritime border is delimited.

The maritime border between the two States remains disputed, preventing any development of the Kyapaz/Serdar field, and halting plans to build the TCP pipeline. The dispute has also limited exploration of Turkmenistan's offshore reserves because international companies have been reluctant to explore in disputed waters.[104] It remains to be seen if the Caspian Convention agreement, once ratified by all States, will remove this impasse.

3.6.2 Azerbaijan–Iran (Unresolved)

Unlike other littoral States, Iran has not entered into bilateral agreements with its Caspian neighbours. This is not surprising as no other State currently shares its view of equal division of the Caspian Sea – a position most 'advantageous' for Iran because of having the shortest coastline of any Caspian State.[105] Iran has condemned the treaties signed between Russia, and Azerbaijan, and Kazakhstan, and has repeatedly suggested that the other States should cease all oil and gas activities until a treaty with all five States is signed.[106]

In 1998, Iran invited an international company to explore in Iran's claimed sector of the Caspian prompting Azerbaijan to issue a statement claiming that this was illegal, and the exploration area was in an Azeri-claimed area.[107] Iran rejected Azeri objections and continued the exploration work. The activity ended in 2000 because identified prospects were in deepwater and there were no drilling rigs available in the Caspian capable of drilling in water depths of 900 metres.[108] In the same year, Iranian ships attempted to remove Azeri buoys that had been placed to mark the GhassanKuli line promoted by Azerbaijan.[109] Azerbaijan replaced the buoys, prompting a warning by Iran that the markers would be removed again.

In 2001, BP-operated survey vessels, under contract from Azerbaijan, were drilling in the Alov field. The Alov field was discovered by the Soviet Union and is within the Azeri sector of Soviet-era division.[110] The vessels were intercepted by Iranian gunboats and aircraft which forced the drilling ships to leave the disputed area and was followed by flights of Iranian military aircraft into Azerbaijan-claimed airspace.[111]

The military incident was the first of its kind in the Caspian Sea. Azerbaijan urged Iran to stop increasing tensions and to resolve issues through bilateral negotiations.[112] Iran responded by stating that it would bear no responsibility for 'what might follow' if oil activities in the disputed area continued, and began massing troops on its land border with Azerbaijan.[113] Iran also officially warned the British government that all BP activity in the disputed area was illegal, and that any company that operated in the area would be excluded from working in other regions of Iran, including in the prolific Persian Gulf.[114]

The 2001 standoff was followed by a similar incident in 2004, when Iran sent warships to intercept Azerbaijani seismic vessels in the disputed zone. The incidents are seen as an indication that Iran will not make any further concessions on its demand for an equal share of the Caspian.[115]

3.6.3 Iran–Turkmenistan (Unresolved)

Iran has also not confirmed its maritime border with Turkmenistan, though there is more consensus between Iran and Turkmenistan than between Iran and Azerbaijan. In 1998, in a joint Iran–Turkmenistan letter to the UN Secretary-General, the two

States reiterated the validity of the Soviet-era treaties, and stated their preference for 'a condominium arrangement for the common use of the Caspian Sea' and that in the case of division, there should be equal shares for all littoral States and equitable exploitation of the resources of the Caspian Sea.[116]

In the absence of a multilateral solution involving all five States, and Iran's position against bilateral agreements in the Caspian, Iran's maritime border with Turkmenistan remains undefined.[117]

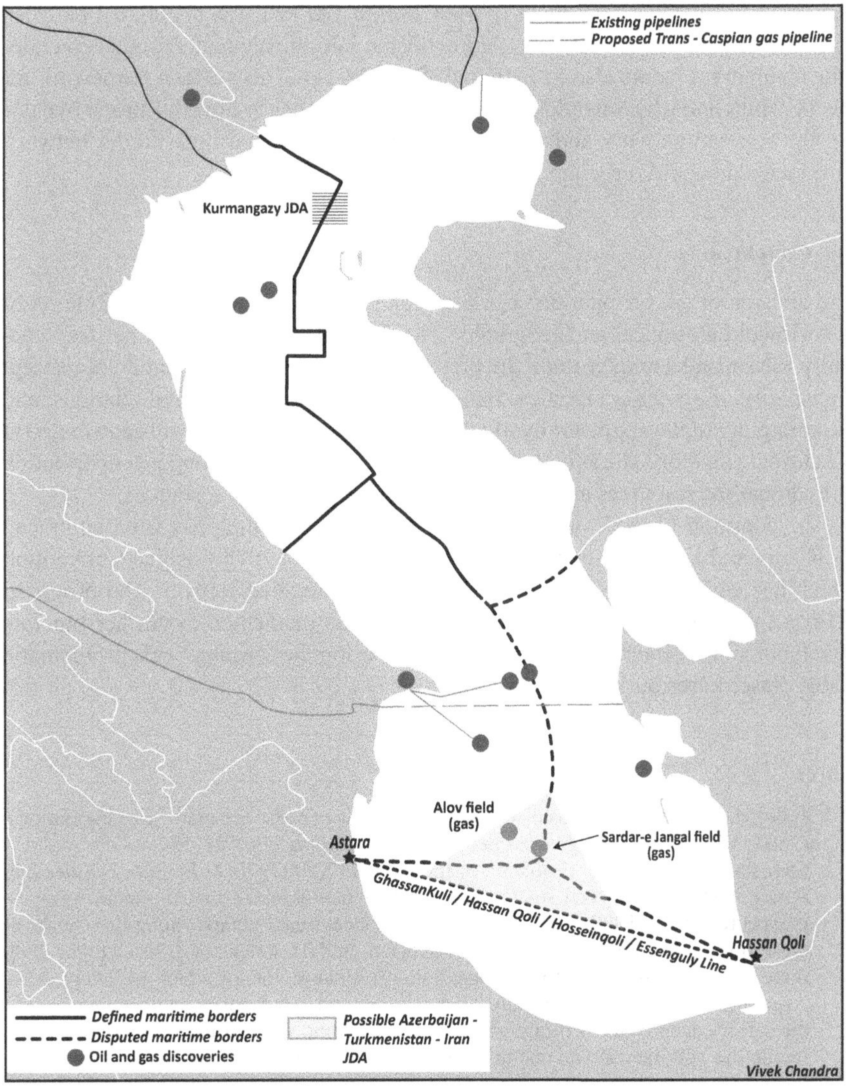

Figure 3.2 Proposed trilateral JDA in the Caspian Sea

3.7 Proposed JDA: Azerbaijan–Turkmenistan–Iran

One of the most contentious areas of the Caspian Sea is the southern region at the confluence of Azerbaijan, Turkmenistan, and Iran. This is the region where most military confrontations have occurred, and where all the unresolved maritime boundaries exist.

The trilateral agreement, as shown in Figure 3.2, could be bounded by the GhassanKuli line in the south and cover the overlapping claims over the contested Alov and Sardar-e Jangal fields. The JDA would revive the dormant 2018 *Joint Development of Relevant Blocks of the Caspian Sea* that was negotiated between Iran and Azerbaijan. By inviting Turkmenistan into the agreement, other overlapping claim areas would also be included. The JDA could also offer a framework for the TCP pipeline which would allow Turkmenistan's gas to flow to Europe bypassing the Russian network and resolution of the disputed maritime border between Turkmenistan and Azerbaijan.

3.8 Conclusions

The division of the Caspian Sea is a complex problem arising from a unique set of historical circumstances and geography. The changing positions of the parties, especially Russia and Turkmenistan, the presence of successor States that do not accept the validity of Soviet-era treaties, Iranian domestic and international relations, and the ambiguity of the applicability of UNCLOS in the Caspian have all contributed to the current situation. The situation is further complicated by the unequal distribution of hydrocarbon resources and the geopolitics in exporting the resources.

The adoption of the concept of joint development, which has been embraced by Russia and Kazakhstan, and the unratified (by Iran) 2018 Caspian Convention which has embraced UNCLOS concepts, are encouraging steps.[118] The proposed JDA in this chapter could, especially if it was complemented by further pipeline development agreements, have the potential to bring the Caspian Sea's problematic status closer to resolution.

Notes

1 Julie M. Folger, 'A proposal to end the stalemate in the Caspian Sea negotiations' (2003) 18(2) *Ohio State Journal on Dispute Resolution* 529, 532–533.

2 Stanislav Cherniavskii, 'Problems of the Caspian' (2002) 40(2) *Russian Politics and Law* 85, 86. Cherniavskii states that, '[n]ature has ordained that the main reserves, prospected in the 1970s and the 1980s, are concentrated mainly along the shores of these three countries [Azerbaijan, Kazakhstan, and Turkmenistan]. In October 2000 there were 360 promising formations in the Caspian region, of which 145 were in the Azerbaijani sector of the Caspian. Thirty-six oil and gas deposits had been reached in the sea by deep-water drilling, of which twenty-nine were in the Azerbaijani sector, five in the Turkmen sector, one in the Russian sector, and one in the Kazakh sector.'

3 Schematic map created by author based on various sources, including US Energy Information Agency EIA, 'Caspian Sea Region' (Web page, 26 August 2013) <https://www.eia.gov/international/analysis/regions-of-interest/Caspian_Sea>; Anis H. Bajrektarevic and Petra Posega, 'The Caspian Basin: Territorial and Status- Related

Disputes, Energy Transit Corridors, and Their Implications for EU Energy Security' (2014) 16(1) *Seton Hall Journal of Diplomacy and International Relations* 85, 94, and 103; J. Ashley Roach and Robert W. Smith, 'Caspian Sea Boundaries' in Jonathan Charney, et al. (eds), *International Maritime Boundaries* (M. Nijhoff, 1993) 3549; Klaus W. Grewlich, 'International Regulatory Governance of the Caspian Pipeline Policy Game' (2011) *Journal of Energy & Natural Resources Law*, 29(1), 87, 103; Daniel Müller and Ketevan Betaneli, The new Convention on the Legal Status of the Caspian Sea: New Opportunities and New Challenges (Briefing Report, Freshfields Bruckhaus Deringer LLP, 1 November 2018).)

4 *United Nations Convention on the Law of the Sea*, opened for signature 10 December 1982, 1833 UNTS 3 (entered into force 16 November 1994) art 122. ('*UNCLOS*'). Article 122 states, 'Enclosed or semi-enclosed seas' are defined as 'a gulf, basin or sea surrounded by two or more States and connected to another sea or the ocean by a narrow outlet or consisting entirely or primarily of the territorial seas and exclusive economic zones of two or more coastal States.'

5 Ziyad Ziyadzade, 'Drilling for Black Gold: The Demarcation for Hydrocarbon Resources in the Caspian Sea' (2015) 16 *Chicago Journal of International Law* 312, 326.

6 *Convention on the Legal Status of the Caspian Sea*, Republic of Azerbaijan, the Islamic Republic of Iran, the Republic of Kazakhstan, the Russian Federation and Turkmenistan), signed 12 August 2018 (not yet in force). <http://en.kremlin.ru/supplement/5328>. ('*Caspian Convention*'); Yiqiang Jiao, 'The Signing of the Convention on the Legal Status of the Caspian Sea and Its Implications' (2019) (75) *China International Studies* 178, 184.

7 The borders between Kazakhstan and Russia, Turkmenistan, and Azerbaijan, as well as the maritime border between Azerbaijan and Russia have been resolved. Unresolved borders include those between Iran and Turkmenistan, Iran and Azerbaijan, and Turkmenistan and Azerbaijan.

8 Kamyar Mehdiyoun, 'Ownership of oil and gas resources in the Caspian Sea' (2000) 94(1) *American Journal of International Law* 179, 180.

9 *Treaty of Golestan*, Russia and Persia, signed 12 October 1813, British and Foreign State Papers vol. 5 HMSO.

10 Mehdiyoun (n 8) 180.

11 *Treaty of Turkomanchai*, Persia and Russia, signed 22 February 1828, British and Foreign State Papers vol. 15 HMSO.

12 Sergey Zhiltsov, 'The International Legal Status of the Caspian Sea: Geopolitical Considerations of the Caspian States and Hydrocarbon Resources' (2017) 18(1) *Central Asia & the Caucasus* 50, 52.

13 Zhiltsov (n 12).

14 *Treaty of Friendship between the Russian Socialist Federal Soviet Republic (RSFSR) and Persia*, signed 26 February 1921, 9 LNTS 383.

15 Elena Karataeva, 'The Convention on the Legal Status of the Caspian Sea: The Final Answer or an Interim Solution to the Caspian Question?' (2020) 35(2) *International Journal of Marine & Coastal Law* 232, 249; Elchin Ganjaliyev, 'Building Azerbaijan's Legal Framework for Marine Operations on the Basis of UNCLOS' (Thesis, University of Southampton, 2011–2012).

16 Pierre Thevenin, 'The Caspian Sea Convention: New Status but Old Divisions' (2019) 44(4) *Review of Central and East European Law* 437,439; Christopher C. Joyner and Kelly Zack Walters, 'The Caspian Conundrum: Reflections on the Interplay between Law, the Environment and Geopolitics' (2006) 21 *International Journal of Marine and Coastal Law* 173, 183. All three rivers carry heavy levels of residual chemical pollutants in the Caspian Sea.; Yiqiang (n 5) 179.

17 Ilias Bantekas, 'Bilateral delimitation of the Caspian Sea and the exclusion of third parties,' (2011) 26(1) *The International Journal of Marine and Coastal Law* 47, 51;

Hanna Zimnitskaya and James von Geldern, 'Is the Caspian Sea a sea; and why does it matter?' (2011) 2(1) *Journal of Eurasian Studies*, 1, 7.

18 Seyed Amin Nejat, Davoud H. Bavand, and Parvin Farshchi, 'Formulation of the Caspian Sea's legal regime using a joint zone approach' (2016) 43(3) *Water Resources* 571, 577; Joyner (n 16) 182-183; Zimnitskaya (n 17) 9–11. After Russia signed maritime border delimitation agreements with Kazakhstan and Azerbaijan in 1998, and the trilateral treaty (Russia, Kazakhstan, and Azerbaijan) in 2003, Russia 'effectively abandoned' the common ownership principle. Iran still refuses to recognise any Caspian bilateral delimitation agreement, insisting on equal sectoral division or joint ownership.

19 Bantekas (n 17) 51.

20 Pirouz Mojtahed-Zadeh, Hashem Amiri and Ramtin Salarian, 'Maritime Political Geography: Iran's Legal Dilemma in the Caspian Sea Ends up in Geographical Certainties for All' (2015) 12(1) *International Studies Journal* (ISJ), 67, 69.

21 Also spelled Hassan Qoli, Hosseinqoli, Ghassan-Koli, and Essenguly, among others.

22 Zhiltsov (n 12) 52. See Figure 3.1 for the location of this line.

23 Guenter Weissberg, 'Maps as Evidence in International Boundary Disputes: A Reappraisal' (1963) 57(4) *The American Journal of International Law* 781. The relative importance of maps for the adjudication of boundary disputes can be further analysed by comparing the *Temple of Preah Vihear* case where the maps were considered accepted by the parties and important in the judgment versus the *Island of Palmas* case where the adjudicator did not attach weight to the maps; *Temple of Preah Vihear (Cambodia v. Thailand)* (Judgment) (1961) ICJ Reports 52; *Island of Palmas (or Miangas) (The Netherlands/The United States of America)* (1928) PCA Case 1925-01; Faraz Sanei, 'Caspian Sea Legal Regime, Pipeline Diplomacy, and the Prospects for Iran's Isolation from the Oil and Gas Frenzy' (2001) 34(3) *Vanderbilt Journal of Transnational Law* 681,771; Cherniavskii (n 2) 86.

24 Sanei (n 23) 779.

25 Sanei (n 23) 780 fn 667. The four republics were Russian SFSR, Azerbaijan SSR, Kazakh SSR, and Turkmen SSR.

26 Zimnitskaya (n 17) 7. Zimnitskaya states that 'in the Iranian assessment of treaty law, the break-up of the Soviet Union did not affect the legal or factual reality of the Iran-U.S.S.R. treaties.' This was disputed by the newly created littoral States Azerbaijan, Kazakhstan, and Turkmenistan.

27 *Vienna Convention on Succession of States in respect of Treaties*, signed 23 August 1978, 1946 UNTS. 3, (entered into force on 27 January 1980) ('Vienna Convention'). Under the Vienna Convention, treaties signed by predecessor States bind newly independent States. However, under exception on Article 34(2), the rule does not apply 'if the states concerned otherwise agree; or it appears from the treaty or is otherwise established that the application of the treaty would be incompatible with the object and purpose of the treaty or would radically change the conditions for its operation.'

28 *Alma-Ata Declaration*, the Republic of Armenia, the Republic of Azerbaijan, the Republic of Belarus, the Republic of Kazakhstan, the Republic of Kyrgyzstan, the Republic of Moldova, the Russian Federation, the Republic of Tajikistan, the Republic of Turkmenistan, the Republic of Ukraine, and the Republic of Uzbekistan, signed 21 December 1991.

29 Zimnitskaya (n 17) 6.

30 Sanei (n 23) 804.

31 Folger (n 1) 543.

32 Ziyadzade (n 4) 320–321.

33 *Temple of Preah Vihear* (n 23); *Island of Palmas (or Miangas)* (n 53). In these cases, the role of maps in boundary delimitation was an important consideration; Sanei (n 23) 777.

34 Sanei (n 23) 804.

35 Sanei (n 23) 776.

36 Zhiltsov (n 12) 54.
37 Zhiltsov (n 12) 52. As stated by Zhiltsov, though Iran had a plan, how to actually divide the Caspian in equal 'shares' remained a 'conundrum.'
38 Folger (n 1) 546 fn 79. 'Because sectoral division based upon a median line (under which each state would receive a share of the Caspian proportional to its shoreline) would afford Iran the smallest portion of the Caspian, it has vehemently opposed any type of median division and instead advocates equal division among the littoral states ... It is unlikely that Iran will agree to the current proposals concerning the delimitation of the Caspian Sea because it will receive the smallest share of the resources.' Zimnitskaya (n 17) 10.
39 *Caspian Convention* (n 5) art 5–9.
40 Thevenin (n 16) 438 and 461 'The significance of this instrument resides in the fact that it provides the Caspian Sea with a stable legal framework, which it had lacked since the collapse of the Soviet Union in 1991 and that every actor in the region had sought.'
41 Thevenin (n 16) 438, 454, and 458.
42 'What Does the New Caspian Sea Agreement Mean for the Energy Market?' (Research article, Stratfor Analysis, 17 August 2018) 3.; RFE/RL, 'Russia Ratifies Caspian Convention with Iran Still Holding Out,' Radio Free Europe/Radio Farda, 2 October 2019.; *Caspian Convention* (n 5) art 3; The Caspian Convention regulates the navigation of warships, submarines, and other underwater vessels, prohibiting any non-Caspian military force from accessing the Sea. The implication of this is to prevent NATO or the US from deploying ships or troops to the area, ensuring that Russia remains the dominant military power.
43 Müller (n 7).
44 *Caspian Convention* (n 5) art 5–9.
45 Thevenin (n 16) 456.
46 Karataeva (n 15) 256; Thevenin (n 16) 457; Charles Whitney, 'The Convention on the Legal Status of the Caspian Sea – A sea or not a sea: that is still the question' (Briefing Paper, Norton Rose Fulbright, September 2018).
47 RFE/RL (n 42).
48 Yiqiang (n 5) 195 fn 44.
49 *UNCLOS* (n 3) art 122. The article states, 'A gulf, basin or sea surrounded by two or more States and connected to another sea or the ocean by a narrow outlet or consisting entirely or primarily of the territorial seas and exclusive economic zones of two or more coastal States.'
50 Sergei Vinogradov and Patricia Wouters, 'The Caspian Sea: Quest for a New Legal Regime' (2004) 9(1) *Leiden Journal of International Law* 87, 90 fn 17. The footnote cites the 15 January 1995 *Minutes of the meeting on Cooperation of UN Organizations in the Caspian Sea Initiatives.*
51 Barry Hart Dubner, 'The Caspian: Is It a Lake, a Sea or an Ocean and Does It Matter – The Danger of Utilizing Unilateral Approaches to Resolving Regional/International Issues' (2000) 18(2) *Dickinson Journal of International Law* 253, 278.
52 Farid Shafiyev, 'The Legal Regime of the Caspian Sea: Views of the Littoral States' (2001) 7(6) *Jamestown Prism* 1. In this article, Shafiyev, an official at the Mission of Azerbaijan to the United Nations states that, 'the practice of delimiting lakes between/among littoral states overwhelmingly shows that lakes are divided so that each costal [sic] state has an exclusive sovereignty over the biological and natural resources, water surface and shipping in the national sectors, which are formed by outlining a median line and the external border of the respective sectors.'; Zimnitskaya (n 17) 2; *UNCLOS* (n 3) art 58 states, 'In the exclusive economic zone, all States, whether coastal or land-locked, enjoy, subject to the relevant provisions of this Convention, the freedoms referred to in Article 87 of navigation and overflight and of the laying of submarine cables and pipelines, and other internationally lawful uses of the sea related to these

freedoms, such as those associated with the operation of ships, aircraft and submarine cables and pipelines, and compatible with the other provisions of this Convention.'

53 Zimnitskaya (n 17) 3; *UNCLOS* (n 3) art 74 obliges States to delimit their EEZ 'by agreement on the basis of international law, as referred to in Article 38 of the Statute of the International Court of Justice, in order to achieve an equitable solution.'

54 Zimnitskaya (n 17) 3. As the east–west width of the Caspian is less than 250 km, if UNCLOS maritime zone definitions were applied to the Caspian, the EEZs of the littoral States would overlap.

55 *UNCLOS* (n 3) art 58.

56 Kazakhstan and Turkmenistan are not UNCLOS States parties. Iran is a signatory but never ratified UNCLOS.

57 UN, 'Chapter XXI: Law of the Sea,' *United Nations Treaty Collection* (Web Page, 5 October 2020) <https://treaties.un.org/Pages/ViewDetailsIII.aspx?src=TREATY&mtdsg_no=XXI-6&chapter=21&Temp=mtdsg3&clang=_en#EndDec>. This list indicates other States that have signed but not ratified UNCLOS include Burundi, Cambodia, Central African Republic, Colombia, DR Korea, Libya, Liechtenstein, Rwanda, and the UAE. A number of these are land-locked States.

58 Zimnitskaya (n 17) 13.

59 Zimnitskaya (n 17) 2.

60 Gawdat Bahgat, 'Regional Report – The Caspian Sea: Potentials and Prospects' (2004) 17(1) *Governance*, 116

61 Yusin Lee, 'Toward a New International Regime for the Caspian Sea. Problems of Post-Communism' (2005) 52(3) *Problems of Post-*Communism 37, 40.

62 Sanei (n 23) 711. At its peak, over 70% of Soviet production came from onshore and offshore Azerbaijan.

63 Greg Englefield, 'A Spider's Web: Jurisdictional Problems in the Caspian Sea' (Autumn 1995) *IBRU Boundary and Security Bulletin*, 30, 30; Joyner (n 16) 175.

64 Suha Bolukbasi, 'The controversy over the Caspian Sea mineral resources: conflicting perceptions, clashing interests.' (1998) 50(3) *Europe-Asia Studies*, 397, 400. Russian warned, 'All responsibility for (undesirable) situations, including material damage, will lie with those who have taken unilateral steps, disregarding the Caspian Sea's judicial nature and obligations brought by international agreements. The Russian Federation reserves the right to take the necessary measures to restore order and to eliminate the results of such unilateral moves.'

65 Sanei (n 23) 714 fn 174.

66 Cherniavskii (n 2) 86.

67 US Energy Information Agency EIA, 'Oil and natural gas production is growing in Caspian Sea region' (Web page, 11 September 2013) <https://www.eia.gov/todayinenergy/detail.php?id=12911>; RFE/RL, 'Iran Under Pressure by Russia To Accept A Small Share Of The Caspian' (2017) *Radio Free Europe/Radio Liberty - Radio Farda.*

68 Bolukbasi (n 64) 399; Sanei (n 23) 727; Thevenin (n 16) 451.

69 Sanei (n 23) 721, 746.

70 *Caspian Convention* (n 5) art 12(2) and art 14. Article 12(2) states, 'Each Party shall, within its sector, exercise jurisdiction over the artificial islands, installations, structures, its submarine cables and pipelines.' Article 14 states, 'The Parties may lay submarine cables and pipelines on the bed of the Caspian Sea. The Parties may lay trunk submarine pipelines on the bed of the Caspian Sea, on the condition that their projects comply with environmental standards and requirements embodied in the international agreements to which they are parties, including the Framework Convention for the Protection of the Marine Environment of the Caspian Sea and its relevant protocols.' Thus, States are able to object to a pipeline on environmental grounds; Müller (n 7); Bahgat (n 60) 116 and 119.

71 Bahgat (n 60) 120.

72 Bahgat (n 60). Iran was also importing Turkmenistan gas (via onshore pipeline) but this was stopped in 1996 due to price disputes.
73 Zhiltsov (n 12) 54; Zimnitskaya (n 17) 9.
74 Cherniavskii (n 2) 87.
75 Azamat Batyrov, 'Russia, Kazakhstan Push For Hydrocarbon Expansion With Kurmangazy Project,' *Caspian News* (9 December 2018).
76 Joyner (n 16) 179; Bahgat (n 60) 123; Lee (n 61) 44.
77 Batyrov (n 75).
78 Nijat Mustafayev, 'Azerbaijan and Turkmenistan may start joint development of disputed Kepez Field in the Caspian,' *Azeri-Press Agency,* (Azerbaijan, 27 April 2009).
79 These disputes, mainly over the Sardar-e Jangal and Alov fields have escalated to military confrontations between Azerbaijan and Iran.
80 Rahim Rahimov, 'Azerbaijan, Iran Reach Breakthrough on Disputed Fields in the Caspian Sea' (2018) 15(52) *Eurasia Daily Monitor.*
81 Omid Shokri Kalehsar, 'Iran and Azerbaijan share oil fields, so what's stopping Tehran from drilling?' *The New Arab* (London, 16 November 2018).
82 Yiqiang (n 5) 195. 'The Caspian Convention formally takes effect only after ratification by the five countries' respective legislatures.'
83 Bantekas (n 17) 54; Zhiltsov (n 12) 54.
84 United Nations Permanent Representatives of Kazakstan and Turkmenistan to the United Nations, *Letter dated 14 March 1997 from the Permanent Representatives of Kazakstan and Turkmenistan to the United Nations addressed to the Secretary-General*, 52nd sess., Agenda Items 39, 99, 100 and 101, UN Doc A/52/93 (17 March 1997).
85 Bantekas (n 17) 52.
86 Zimnitskaya (n 17) 10.
87 Sanei (n 23) 762. As per Sanei, 'In February 1998 Russian Foreign Ministry Special Envoy Feliks Kovalev made the surprising announcement that Russia was ready to carry out a "fair division of the Caspian seabed".'
88 *Agreement between the Russian Federation and the Republic of Kazakhstan on the Delimitation of the Seabed of the Northern Part of the Caspian Sea for the Purposes of Exercising Their Sovereign Rights to the Exploitation of its Subsoil,* IMB 4022–4033, signed 6 July 1998.
89 Zimnitskaya (n 17) 10; Cherniavskii (n 2) 87.
90 *Seabed Boundary Agreement between the Republic of Azerbaijan and the Republic of Kazakhstan,* IMB 4048–4054, signed 29 November 2001 <http://www.caspinfo.ru/library/doc/inter/inter_01.htm>.
91 Zhiltsov (n 12) 58.
92 *Agreement 14 May 2003 on the junction point of lines delimiting adjacent zones of the seabed and subsoil of the Caspian Sea between the Republic of Azerbaijan, Republic of Kazakhstan, and the Russian Federation,* signed 14 May 2003, IMB 4056; Joyner (n 16) 191; Zimnitskaya (n 17) 10.
93 Zhiltsov (n 12) 61; Zimnitskaya (n 17) 10.
94 Joyner (n 16) 191.
95 Folger (n 1) 543.
96 Zhiltsov (n 12) 54.
97 Mehdiyoun (n 8) 187.
98 Bantekas (n 17) 57–58.
99 Roach & Smith (n 7) 3546. The Azeris insist that island of Zhilov (Cilov) should influence the median line boundary with Turkmenistan.
100 Bahgat (n 60) 124.
101 Cherniavskii (n 2) 92.
102 Bajrektarevic (n 7) 95; Whitney (n 46).

103 'Turkmenis, Azeris said nearer to resolving Kyapaz dispute' (1999) 77(119) *Platts Oilgram News*.
104 Ziyadzade (n 4) 325.
105 Bantekas (n 17) 53.
106 Zimnitskaya (n 17) 11.
107 Sanei (n 23) 765.
108 'Iran's best Caspian Sea prospects are in deepwater, and rigs are scarce' *Offshore Magazine* (US, 1 September 2000).
109 Cherniavskii (n 2) 92.
110 Vladimir Socor, 'The Guns of Summer: Iran Prowls the Caspian,' *Wall Street Journal* (US, 3 August 2001).
111 Socor (n 110).
112 Lee (n 61) 43.
113 Lee (n 61) 43.
114 Socor (n 110).
115 Lee (n 61) 43.
116 Permanent Representatives of the Islamic Republic of Iran and Turkmenistan, *Letter dated 30 September 1998 from the Permanent Representatives of the Islamic Republic of Iran and Turkmenistan to the United Nations addressed to the Secretary-General*, UN GAOR, 53rd sess., Agenda items 38, 93, and 94, UN DOC A/53/453 (2 October 1998) http://undocs.org/A/53/453.
117 Roach & Smith (n 31) 3546. The Turkmens are insisting Ogorjinsky island should influence any future negotiated maritime border with Iran.
118 Karataeva (n 15) 262 and 236.

4 Maritime Borders

Northeast Asia

4.1 Introduction

Northeast Asia, encompassing the East Sea (also known as Sea of Japan) and the East China Sea, is surrounded by the vibrant economies of China, South Korea, Japan, and Taiwan and, to a lesser extent, Russia.[1] This large area includes two major and one relatively minor sovereignty disputes involving maritime features which have left portions of the region's maritime borders unresolved and potential hydrocarbon resources undeveloped.

The two major disputes, the Senkaku (Diaoyu in Chinese) Islands between Japan and China in the East China Sea, and the Dokdo (Takeshima in Japanese) Islands between South Korea and Japan in the East Sea, have involved nationalistic fervour, periodic military confrontations, and have the potential to attract broader alliance partners, including the US. Both disputes involve interpretation of UNCLOS and questions of island sovereignty that could determine the delimitation of maritime boundaries. The third dispute in the region relates to the maritime areas around Ieodo, a submerged rock in the East China Sea. In this case, both South Korea and China claim rights in the surrounding seas, but do not dispute the sovereignty of the rock itself.

The East China Sea is a semi-closed shallow sea bounded in the north by the Yellow Sea and Taiwan in the south. To the northeast is Japan's main chain of islands and to the west, the Chinese mainland. At its widest axis, the East China Sea is only 360 nm across.[2] In these waters are the eight Senkaku Islands with a total area of just 6.3 km^2 and, as stated above, Ieodo rock which is continuously submerged.[3]

Further north is the East Sea (also called the Sea of Japan) bordered by Japan to the east, and the Korean peninsula and Russia to the west. It is larger and deeper than the East China Sea. Though Japan and South Korea have uncontested islands in the Korean Straits, they are locked in an increasingly tense sovereignty dispute over the tiny Dokdo Islands.[4] Though the Japanese dispute with South Korea over the Dokdo Islands in the East Sea has been less volatile than the Senkaku Islands dispute between Japan and China, there have been dangerous incidents and deployments of warships, with implications on wider Japan–Korea–US defence alignments.

DOI: 10.4324/9781003323051-4

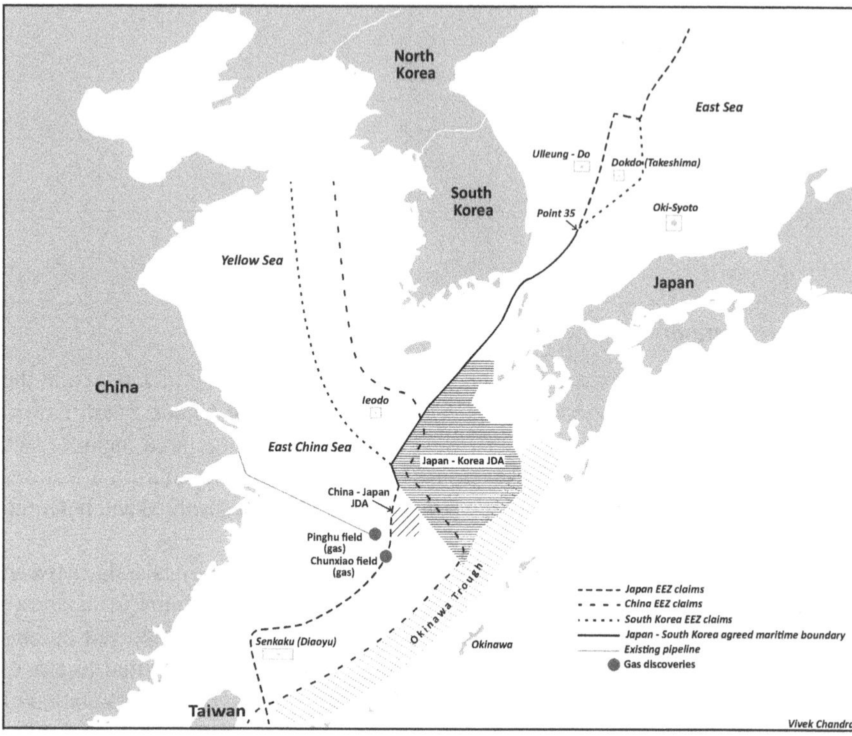

Figure 4.1 Schematic map of conflicting EEZ claims, JDAs, and hydrocarbon discoveries in northeast Asia.[5]

Both the East China Sea and the East Sea are important sea trading routes. Though China has an extensive coastline of 18,000 km in length, its sea lanes depend on passage through the EEZs of neighbouring States in the South China and East China Seas. China's economy is dependent on seaborne trade and on largely imported energy resources. Similarly, much of the trade to North and South Korea, and to Japan, transits via the East China Sea and East Sea. Escalating tensions could lead to one of the disputing States limiting access to vital sea routes for adversaries.

Though the region remains relatively underexplored for oil and gas, with limited production to date, there have been studies, though many are dated, that show potential for abundant offshore hydrocarbon resources, especially natural gas.[6] All the main disputing parties are large energy importers that would benefit from offshore energy production in their maritime zones. Unresolved territorial disputes have made exploration and development of these potential resources difficult.[7]

All three actively involved States are UNCLOS member States. China and South Korea have made Article 298 declarations to opt out of the compulsory dispute resolution procedures for maritime border delimitation disputes.[8]

4.2 Legal Background

Territorial disputes in the northeast Asia region have threatened diplomatic relations between regional States, inflamed nationalistic tensions, and have the potential to lead to Asia's 'most dangerous military conflict.'[9] All three claimants in these disputes cite historical evidence and their interpretation of UNCLOS articles to justify their claims.

4.2.1 East China Sea

The Senkaku island group consists of eight uninhabited islands, five of which are considered to be islets and the remaining three 'barren rocks.'[10] They are situated approximately 120 nm northeast of Taiwan, 200 nm east of China, and 240 nm southwest of the Japanese Okinawa islands. The islands are situated on the Asian continental shelf, separated from the Japanese Ryukyu Islands by the deep Okinawa Trough. They are currently uninhabited, under Japanese control, and have limited anchorage making access difficult.

Despite the strong economic links between China and Japan over the past few decades, the Senkaku Islands dispute continues to foster bilateral tensions and threaten regional security. Both Japan and China have 'collected a range of historical evidence, relied upon a variety of treaties and official declarations, and asserted multiple alternative theories of title, the question [of sovereignty] has an air of complexity.'[11] It should be noted that Taiwan has also presented similar claims to China for the Senkaku Islands.[12] As China has been more vocal and has shown more force than Taiwan in asserting its claims, this chapter emphasises China's position.

The Senkaku Islands have been mentioned in the travel accounts of Chinese envoys representing the Ming Dynasty.[13] Chinese scholars have claimed that, from 1372 to 1895, China had maintained a 'continuous and peaceful display of territorial sovereignty' on the islands.[14] At the conclusion of the 1894–1895 Sino-Japanese War, under the April 1895 *Treaty of Shimonoseki*, the defeated Chinese Qing empire was forced to cede to Japan, '[t]he island of Formosa together with all islands appertaining or belonging to the said island of Formosa.'[15] Though the treaty did not specifically mention the Senkaku Islands, China's position has been that it does cover the Senkaku Islands as the islands are 'appertaining to the said island of Formosa.'[16]

In January 1895, a few months before the *Treaty of Shimonoseki* was executed, the Japanese government incorporated the Senkaku Islands as part of its Okinawa Prefecture. This action has been used by Japan to justify its argument that the islands were not 'war spoils' related to Formosa (Taiwan) exchanged under the terms of the *Treaty of Shimonoseki*.[17] Instead, the Japanese claim that the islands were previously 'discovered' in 1884 by a Japanese merchant, Tatsushiro Koga. A few decades later, Koga started a business collecting albatross feathers and tortoise shells from the islands to be sold in Japan.[18] By 1910, Koga's business employed over 200 people living on the islands, expanding the operations to include catching, drying, processing, and canning fish. In 1950, the business ceased but the Koga family continued to maintain its ownership.[19]

China has argued that Japan used its victory in the Sino-Japanese War to annex the Senkaku Islands by force from China.[20] From the Chinese point of view, Allied declarations, specifically the *Cairo Declaration*[21] at the conclusion of WW II, enabled restoration of Chinese territories taken by Japan through military aggression. China claims that this applies to the Senkaku Islands.[22] Japan has argued that the *Cairo Declaration* does not apply because the islands were unoccupied at the time of Koga's discovery, never 'stolen' from China, and that the incorporation of the islands occurred through prior government decisions unrelated to the Sino-Japanese War and the subsequent Shimonoseki treaty.[23]

After the surrender of Japan in 1945, the US administered the islands as part of the post-war occupation of Okinawa and paid rent to Koga's son for access to the islands being used as firing ranges.[24] When the US returned the islands to Japan in 1972 under the terms of the 1971 *Treaty on Reversion to Japan of the Ryukyu and Daito Islands*,[25] it did so without expressing any position on the sovereignty or competing claims on the islands.[26] At the time when the US and Japan executed the reversion treaty, both China and Taiwan protested the inclusion of the Senkaku Islands in the transfer.[27]

In 1970, China warned the US and Japan to halt their oil exploration activity in the East China Sea.[28] Since then, the intensity of the dispute between China and Japan has increased. There have been multiple incidents of activists from China (and Hong Kong and Taiwan) as well as from Japan attempting to land on the islands. There have also been incidents of collisions between Chinese fishing trawlers and Japanese patrol boats.[29] In 2004, a Chinese nuclear submarine entered the disputed seas, prompting the Japanese military to be on full alert by sending destroyers and aircraft to block the submarine.[30]

In 2012, the dispute further escalated when the Tokyo municipal government announced the purchase of the islands from the Koga family, ostensibly for commercial development. Unsurprisingly, China reacted by reaffirming that Chinese islands cannot be bought or sold unilaterally by Japan. This led to further Chinese attempted landings (as well as arrests of the activists involved) and Chinese armed fishing vessel incursions.

In November 2013, China declared an Air Defence Identification Zone (ADIZ) over large portions of the East China Sea, including the airspace over the Senkaku Islands. The Chinese ADIZ stretched as far north as Ieodo rock, infringing on South Korean claims. The ADIZ required that foreign aircraft, both military and civilian, identify themselves to Chinese authorities when entering the zone. The ADIZ declaration prompted the US government to reiterate support for Japan in case of attack by China as well as continued US patrols in defiance of Chinese declarations.[31]

The situation remains at an impasse. China (and Taiwan) continue to justify their claims to the Senkaku Islands on historical events dating from the 15th-century Ming Dynasty, arguing that the islands were only ceded to Japan after China lost the Sino-Japanese War and should have been returned after WW II.[32] The Japanese, on the other hand, maintain that the islands were *terra nullius*[33] when they were incorporated into Japan in 1895 and that it has maintained 'continuous and effective control' of the islands, except when the islands were under US trusteeship between WW II and 1972. It seems unlikely that either party will surrender or compromise its position, especially since the involvement of civilian nationalistic activists has made compromising difficult.

4.2.2 East Sea

In the East Sea, which lies east of Korea and northwest of Japan, South Korea and Japan dispute the sovereignty of the Dokdo Islands and the seas around the islands. This sovereignty dispute resembles that of the Senkaku Islands as each claimant has justified their position on historical evidence, invoked the concept of *terra nullius* that existed prior to their occupation, and cited post-WW II treaty uncertainties. In both disputes, there is potential for military action and the involvement of other nations such as the US.

The Dokdo Islands consist of a group of rocky islands with a total area of 0.18 km^2 located in the middle of the East Sea. The islands are minimally inhabited and have been controlled by South Korea since 1952. The residents of the main islands are troops from the South Korean military and Coast Guard plus a small group of seasonal fishermen.

South Korea's claim to the Dokdo Islands is based on the discovery of the islands during the Silla Kingdom in the sixth century and 'effective occupation' since then.[34] According to South Korean scholars, the islands' discovery was recorded by the Samguk-Sagi (Chronicles of Three Kingdoms), Korea's oldest history text published in 1145.[35] South Korea also refers to a 1696 decree issued by the Tokugawa Shogunate that banned Japanese fishing in the area, implying recognition by the Japanese royalty of South Korean control of the islands. Japan refutes this interpretation, claiming that the ban only referred to passage to Korea's Ullungdo Island, not specifically fishing near Dokdo.[36] South Korean scholars have also cited 'a number of Korean official maps over the centuries, which have shown Dokdo as Korean territory, have not been challenged.'[37]

Japan's Ministry of Foreign Affairs asserts that the formal incorporation of the Dokdo Islands into Japanese territory was established by a February 1905 cabinet decision of the Shimane Prefecture to integrate the islands to curb the amount of sea lion hunting taking place in the seas around the Islands.[38] Japan has also cited documentary evidence of its knowledge of the Islands, including the 1667 Inshu Shicho Goki text which mentioned the presence of the islands and their rich fish stocks.[39]

Contradictory evidence has been cited as to whether Korea protested Japan's 1905 declaration for the islands to become 'an integral part of Japan.'[40] Complicating the discussion is the relationship between Japan and Korea at the time. In 1904, one year before its declaration on the Dokdo Islands, Japan began to colonise the Korean peninsula. In November 1905, a few months after the Shimane declaration, Korea was 'transformed into a Japanese protectorate' by the *Japan–Korea Protectorate Treaty* of November 1905 (also known as the *Eulsa Restriction Treaty*).[41] Because the *Protectorate Treaty* gave Japan control over Korea's diplomatic relations,

Korea has argued that the Korean government at the time was unable to protest the Japanese integration of the Dokdo Islands.[42]

Japan ruled the Korean peninsula until the end of WW II. As in the case of the Senkaku Islands in the East China Sea, the Dokdo dispute remains unresolved because post-WW II treaties failed to specifically mention the islands. Early drafts of the 1945 *San Francisco Peace Treaty* included references to the Dokdo Islands as a part of Korean territory and called for the return of the Islands to Korea. However, during the period between the draft version and the final treaty, the US changed its position, arguing that 'there were legitimate historical reasons for believing the islets to be considered Japanese territory.'[43] In the final treaty draft, the Dokdo Islands were not mentioned.[44] The deletion of references to the islands from the final version of the *San Francisco Peace Treaty* has been taken by Japan as an international recognition of its sovereignty over the islands.[45]

Because the *San Francisco Peace Treaty* 'incorporated' the *Cairo Declaration* of 1943, which required for territories taken by 'violence or greed' to be returned.[46] South Korea has maintained that the Dokdo Islands, which it claims were taken forcefully, should be included in this category and thus formally returned to South Korea. In circumstances very similar to the Senkaku Islands, Japan has defended the exclusion of the islands from the treaty on the basis that the islands were not acquired by force but by formal incorporation prior to the aggression.[47]

Since 1952, South Korea has maintained a permanent coast guard base and supported fishing families to live on the islands. South Korea continues to promote its claim on the islands by naming navy ships after the islands, as well as in popular culture with songs such as 'Dokdo is Our Land' and a Dokdo video game based on repelling Japanese invaders. South Korean municipal offices are known to be streaming videos of the islands, and there is a Dokdo museum in Seoul that displays Korean documents to contradict Japan's historical claims. South Korean primary schools have to teach Dokdo education programmes, and the government has placed placards in train stations and airports to support its claims.[48]

Japan has also been vocal on its claims. At the Shimane Prefecture governor's offices there is a museum dedicated to the islands. The Dokdo dispute has implications for other island disputes involving Japan – its claims on the Senkaku and the Kuril Islands (disputed with Russia) are based on similar interpretations of *terra nullius* and post-WW II treaties. If Japan renounced its claims to Dokdo, it could weaken its position on the other disputes as well.

4.3 Applicability of UNCLOS

The complicated legal disputes in northeast Asia have, arguably, become more difficult after China, South Korea, and Japan ratified UNCLOS in 1996.[49] Each of the disputing States have relied on various UNCLOS articles to justify their respective positions. These include articles related to definitions of islands versus rocks, the impact of underwater features such as troughs, historical possession, proportionality, and maritime zones definition criteria.

The Dokdo Islands have no source of fresh water and their only inhabitants are a platoon of South Korean military and coast guards, and seasonal fishermen. As per

UNCLOS Article 121, if the maritime feature 'cannot sustain human habitation or economic life of [its] own,' the feature is a 'rock' and not entitled to the complete set of maritime zones, only to the 12-nm territorial sea.

Some scholars have argued that the inclusion of the word 'or' in Article 121 means that the maritime feature does not need *both* 'human habitation' and 'an economic life' to be a rock. Because Dokdo has seasonal fishing activity which provides economic value, Dokdo could be considered an 'island.' On the other hand, a valid argument can be made that Article 121 requires a 'stable' human population that can be sustained with its own supply of fresh water. Lack of fresh water and a population requiring support should not qualify the Dokdo maritime features to be 'islands.'

South Korea would prefer that the ownership of the Dokdo Islands be determined by an equidistance boundary and not by its 'island' status. The disputed islands are located 49 nm from the South Korean island of Ulleung-do and 86 nm from the Japanese island of Oki-syoto.[50] An equidistance maritime boundary between the two undisputed, permanently inhabited islands (Ulleung-Do and Oki-syoto) would place Dokdo, which is closer to Ulleung-Do, on the Korean side of the median-line boundary.[51]

Japan claims that the Dokdo Islands should be deemed to be 'islands' under Article 121. In this case, the sovereignty of the islands becomes critical. If Japan can establish sovereignty over the disputed 'islands', the median maritime boundary could be drawn between the Dokdo Islands and the Korean island of Ulleung-do. This would grant more valuable maritime areas (and the islands themselves) to Japan rather than the Korean alternative of a median-line between Ulleung-Do and Oki-syoto.[52] Thus, Japan stands to benefit from 'vagueness of the terms' in UNCLOS's definition of island versus rock to support its view that Dokdo is an 'island' that is illegally occupied by South Korea.[53]

The main island in the Senkaku archipelago has a forest and known sources of fresh water. Under Article 121, the presence of fresh water and trees could sustain human life (though the islands are unoccupied) and would qualify the Senkaku islands as 'islands' entitled to their own maritime zones. However, neither China nor Japan have formally asserted their claims based on this principle.[54]

Instead, the marine delimitation arguments revolve around the impact of the Okinawa Trough. The East China Sea overlies the Asian continental shelf, extending 450 km eastward from the Asian continent. The relatively shallow (less than 200 m) continental shelf slopes gently until the seabed drops into the Okinawa Trough, where depth reaches 2,300 m. The Okinawa Trough lies more than 200 nm from the Chinese mainland but is less than 100 nm from the main chain of Japanese Islands, significantly east of the equidistant line between Japan and China.[55]

UNCLOS defines the continental shelf zone by two, sometimes conflicting, criteria: Firstly, by natural prolongation of 'land territory to the outer edge of the continental margin' and, secondly, by maximum distance of 200 nm from an accepted baseline.[56] The ICJ, in its 1982 judgment of the *Continental Shelf* (*Tunisia/Libya*) case, ruled that natural prolongation was the 'main' criterion and that the 200-nm distance was to be the basis for delimitation only in 'certain circumstances.'[57] However, in its 1985 judgment of the *Continental Shelf* (*Libya/Malta*) case, the ICJ seemed to have been influenced by UNCLOS (which was drafted in 1982) by ruling that continental shelf limits depend solely on the distance from the coasts, and that 'geological or geomorphological characteristics are immaterial.'[58]

Not surprisingly, China has used the first criterion of Article 76(1) – the 'natural prolongation of land territory' definition – in its claim, which extends beyond both the median line and the 200-nm limit, extending to the edge of the Okinawa Trough. This allows China to claim a boundary based on the continental shelf that extends beyond 200 nm, placing the Senkaku Islands within its maritime zone.[59] On the other hand, Japan asserts that the second criterion of Article 76(1), which defines the width of the continental shelf to be limited by a distance of 200 nm should be used for determining the outer limits of its maritime boundary.[60] Japan asserts that a median / equidistant line from its Okinawa Islands chain and the Chinese mainland should be used to determine the maritime boundary which will grant ownership of the Senkaku Islands to Japan.

The ambiguity of having two, inconsistent, 'equally valid' definitions within UNCLOS Article 76(1) has fuelled the debate about the claim on Senkaku islands.[61] China has repeatedly stated that 'it does not recognise the so-called median line unilaterally claimed by Japan, nor Japan's position of delimiting the East China Sea on the basis of the so-called median line,'[62] Neither State has published maps of their declared EEZ claims. Therefore, the extent of claims overlap in the East China Sea between them is therefore not known.

Japan's position in these two disputes discussed above is not consistent. In the East China Sea, Japan is arguing for the adoption of a single (continental shelf and EEZ) boundary based on an equidistance line without 'island' status for the Senkaku Islands. This approach, when compared to natural prolongation, benefits Japan in the Senkaku dispute.[63]

However, further north, in the East Sea, Japan objects to South Korea using the equidistance line between their respective inhabited islands to define the maritime border around the Dokdo Islands.[64] In this case, Japan claims sovereignty and 'island' status for Dokdo, thereby extending Japan's EEZ claim to include the Islands. This extends the Japanese maritime zone claim beyond an equidistance line between their respective undisputed islands.[65]

The case regarding Ieodo rock located in the northern East China Sea, is different. Ieodo rock is a small permanently submerged maritime feature on the edge of the Yellow Sea in between China and the Korean peninsula. It is located 80 nm from Marado, an inhabited South Korean island and 150 nm from the Chinese island of Yushandao. Both South Korea and China accept that Ieodo does not generate its own EEZ entitlement because it does not qualify as an 'island,' but the submerged rock lies in a region of overlapping EEZ claims that remain unresolved.

All disputants in northeast Asia have invoked historical justification for their claims. For maritime claims, UNCLOS allows for consideration of historic rights only for delimitation of the territorial seas – not for EEZ or continental shelf delimitations.[66] The 2016 *South China Sea Arbitration* made this clear when it stated,

> No article of the Convention expressly provides for or permits the continued existence of historic rights to the living or non-living resources of the exclusive economic zone. Similarly, nothing within UNCLOS expressly provides

for or permits a State to maintain historic rights over the living and non-living resources of the continental shelf, the high seas, or the Area.[67]

The lack of clarity or hierarchy in the UNCLOS definitions of islands (versus rocks), delimitation rules to be used for EEZ and continental shelf, and evolving ICJ maritime boundary criteria,[68] have allowed States in the region to adopt different approaches to the delimitation of the region's maritime boundaries.[69] Disregarding UNCLOS's dismissal of historical justifications defining the continental shelf or EEZ without impunity seems to another hallmark of the region's maritime disputes.

4.4 Oil and Gas Activities

The seas in northern Asia have been called 'one of the last unexplored high potential resource areas' and 'another Persian Gulf, a treasure trove of untapped seabed oil and gas reserves.'[70] However, enthusiasm should be tempered as the region (outside the nearshore Xihu area Chinese fields) remains largely underexplored, no substantial production currently exists, and overlapping claims with ongoing disputes preclude further hydrocarbon development.

The US Energy Information Agency has estimated that the East China Sea has 200 million bbls of proved and probable oil reserves and between 1 and 2 Tcf of proved and probable natural gas reserves.[71] A Japanese government survey following a 1968 UN report estimated that there was approximately 100 bbls of oil trapped in the shallow waters to the northwest and south of the Senkaku Islands.[72] Others have claimed that there could also be up to 7 Tcf of natural gas resources in addition to the oil deposits.[73]

All the countries in the region are large energy importers requiring oil and gas to sustain their economic growth and are motivated to establish domestic production in the surrounding seas.

4.4.1 East China Sea

In 1967, a Japanese government-sponsored report identified the hydrocarbon potential of the East China Sea, proclaiming it to be 'one of the most potentially favourable but little investigated' continental shelves worldwide.[74] Soon thereafter, in 1968, the Committee for Coordination of Joint Prospecting for Mineral Resources in Asian Offshore Areas, in conjunction with the Maritime Bureau of the US Navy and representatives from Taiwan, South Korea, and Japan, sent a research ship to prospect for resources in the entire area, surveying the seas from north of Taiwan to the Yellow and East China Seas. The results of the survey were published in May 1969 under the auspices of the United Nations Economic Commission for Asia and the Far East (UNECAFE).

The UNECAFE report concluded that the continental shelf edges between Taiwan and Japan 'appeared to have great promise as a future oil province of the world … the last remaining, richest, as yet unexploited depository of oil and natural gas,' in the world.[75] The report identified the region surrounding the Senkaku Islands as the highest potential area for oil and gas resources. Soon after the report was published, the regional government of Okinawa Prefecture received 4,000 applications for drilling rights in the area, and by September 1970, the number of applications was up to 25,000.[76] The interest prompted Japan to request to revert sovereignty of the islands from US administration to Japanese control. This resulted in the 1971 *Okinawa Reversion Treaty* and the return of the islands to Japan for 'full responsibility and authority for the exercise of all powers of administration, legislation and jurisdiction.'[77]

Concurrently, in November 1970, the Republic of China (Taiwan) Ministry of Foreign Affairs also claimed sovereignty around the Senkaku islands, declaring that the Chinese Petroleum Corporation (the national oil company of Taiwan) was working with US oil companies to explore around the islands.[78] Taiwan passed the *Maritime Area Petroleum Oil Exploration Act* to facilitate these efforts.[79] This action is likely to have prompted, on 3 December 1970, Radio Peking from China to announce that the Senkaku Islands belonged to the PRC.[80] The next day, on 4 December 1970, the Japanese Minister of Foreign Affairs announced that the Islets were fully Japanese territory.[81] The timing of China's first protestations of sovereignty 'makes it highly implausible that their prime motivation was anything other than a chance at the area's potential hydrocarbon wealth.'[82]

By December 1971, China and Taiwan increased actions to support their sovereignty claims. Taiwan threatened to send patrol vessels to protect its sovereignty while conducting its own hydrocarbon exploration activities. Considering the strong reactions, the Japanese government suspended further exploration efforts around the islands and, by 1971, all Japanese exploration activities throughout the Yellow Sea and the East China Sea were halted.[83]

Meanwhile, Chinese exploration companies working in the Xihu Trough area, an undisputed section of the East China Sea, made a number of mid-sized gas discoveries.[84] The first discovered field in the area was the Pinghu field, located 45 nm on the Chinese side of the Japanese-declared median-line boundary. The field was discovered in 1989 and it began production in 1998.

In 1995, the Chinese Ministry of Geology announced the discovery of the Chunxiao gas field, in the Xihu Trough area, south of Pinghu. Unlike the Pinghu field, the larger 1.6 Tcf Chunxiao field is located only 3 nm inside the Chinese side of the Japanese-declared median-line boundary. In 2003, China invited foreign companies to join Chinese companies to assist in developing the Chunxiao field to be able to supply gas to Shanghai and Zhejiang Provinces.[85] The announcement provoked Japan to demand that all development work should be halted as its own survey indicated that the Chunxiao gas field was connected to 'resources on Japan's side of the median line.'[86] Japan cited UNCLOS Article 74(3) which obliges disputing States to halt activities that may jeopardise resolution, but this argument was rejected by China.[87] In April 2004, the Japanese Foreign Minister visited China, demanding that China share geologic data for the Chunxiao gas field. At the time, Japan again cited UNCLOS Article 74(3) warning China not to take any action that would 'jeopardize or hamper the reaching of a final agreement.'[88] Chinese foreign partners withdrew their participation after receiving Japanese threats, and in 2005, the two state companies, CNOOC and Sinopec, announced that they would continue Chunxiao development work by themselves.[89] Chunxiao has been declared one of China's top gas discoveries.[90]

Tensions continued to rise, and in July 2004, a Chinese naval vessel confronted a Japanese research ship exploring the area.[91] The risk of a clash between China and Japan increased when, in July 2005, Japan granted a local company the rights to drill on the Japanese side of the median line, adjacent to the Chunxiao field.[92] The Chinese embassy in Tokyo responded that any activity would be considered an invasion of Chinese territory and highly provocative. An official in the Chinese foreign ministry stated that, 'it is untenable for Japan, based on its unilateral position on the so-called "middle line," to grant test-drilling rights to Japanese firms in the disputed sea area,' stressing that China has never 'recognized the median line and will never recognize it.'[93]

Chinese naval and air force units were put on alert against any further activities by Japanese oil companies on Chinese-claimed territory.[94] In a reciprocal move, when China announced commencement of production from the Chunxiao gas field in 2006, Japan accused China of conducting an unauthorised survey in Japanese-claimed territory.[95]

To defuse tensions, Japan proposed to China that a JDA agreement encompassing the four discovered gas fields on the Chinese side of the median line, including Chunxiao, should be negotiated. China, which had already begun unilaterally developing the Chunxiao field, and had previously insisted that the field was situated entirely within its EEZ, rejected Japan's JDA proposal as this would be 'tacitly lending validity' to Japan's EEZ claim.[96]

After more than a dozen rounds of negotiations, in May 2008, China and Japan reached a 'Principled Consensus' on joint development of seabed resources.[97] They negotiated a JDA agreement covering a small region in the northern part of the East China Sea, adjacent to the previously established, and much larger, South Korea–Japan JDA. The China–Japan JDA area, shown on Figure 4.1, is north of the Chunxiao field, and east of the Pinghu field area, and excludes both these producing fields as well as disputed areas around the Senkaku Islands further to the south. Since 2008, there has been limited progress on the implementation of this JDA.

4.4.2 East Sea

Though Japan and South Korea were able to agree to establish a JDA in the East China Sea in 1974, the two countries have been unable to do the same in the more contentious East Sea area around the Dokdo Islands. The prize could be substantial as the seas around the Dokdo Islands have been estimated to contain large natural gas and gas hydrate deposits.[98] The Korean Gas company, KOGAS, has estimated that natural gas and gas hydrates in the surrounding waters could, if commercial, meet South Korean gas demand for 30 years.[99]

In 2006, after unsuccessful negotiations with South Korea, Japan began unilateral exploration surveys in the area around the Dokdo Islands. South Korea escalated tensions by sending a fleet of warships. The standoff was diffused with the signing of an agreement to suspend future surveys pending sovereignty resolution.[100] However, in defiance of this agreement, a few months later, South Korea sent its own survey ship to the disputed area. Since then, sporadic exploration efforts by both Japan and South Korea have provoked reciprocal military and diplomatic responses.[101]

4.4.3 JDA Status – Operational and Past Proposals

Encouragingly, all the disputing States seem to have accepted the premise that JDA solutions can allow hydrocarbon activities to proceed without resolution of the maritime boundary dispute. Discussions of JDAs can be traced back to the publication of the 1966 UNECAFE report. At that time, Japan, South Korea, and Taiwan proposed jointly developing yet-to-be-discovered resources in the East China Sea, explicitly 'to avoid boundary issues.'[102] The mainland (PRC) Chinese government protested this arrangement, which excluded them, because it would violate their interests and their rights. Faced with this opposition, Taiwan stopped its participation, and the joint development talks failed.[103]

In 1974, one of the first global JDA agreements was executed between Japan and South Korea for an area in the East China Sea, south of the South Korean Island of Jeju. The large 80,000 km^2 joint development zone, still nominally active today, covers their overlapping maritime claims in the East China Sea.[104] China protested its formation to both South Korea and Japan, declaring that since the agreement was signed without Chinese involvement, it is considered 'an infringement on China's sovereignty.'[105] The Chinese reaction delayed Japanese ratification of the JDA agreement until 1977. Since then, seven non-commercial exploration dry wells have been drilled in this JDA but no hydrocarbon resources have been identified.[106]

Further south in the East China Sea, after decades of discussions, China and Japan reached an understanding for a modest JDA covering an area of 2,000 km^2 straddling the disputed median-line boundary, a quarter of the size of the Japan–South Korea JDA.[107] The 2008 'Principled Consensus' on cooperation, proclaimed the East China Sea a 'sea of peace, cooperation and friendship.'[108] To date, the objectives of the 'JDA agreement have not been achieved' and Japan continues to protest Chinese gas production that can 'siphon off petroleum from the Japanese side.'[109] No recent activity has been reported.

4.5 Maritime Boundaries

The three largest countries in the region (China, South Korea, and Japan) have extensive economic and cultural ties – but large portions of their maritime borders remain disputed and under tension. The maritime borders are made more complicated by legacy historical issues.

4.5.1 China–Japan (Unresolved in the Maritime Area around the Senkaku Islands)

The region around the Senkaku Islands has been called 'one of the most complicated marine areas anywhere in the world in terms of its overlapping claims, sovereign disputes over islands, and boundary delimitation.'[110]

Japan has been publicly campaigning to publicise the 'fairness' of its position, appealing to the 'human sense of equality.'[111] In 2004, the Japanese Embassy in Beijing issued statements explaining that since the distance between the baselines of each country's maritime zones is less than 400 nm, the median line would 'result in fair resolution' and dismissing China's use of prolongation to the Okinawa Trough as an 'outdated theory used in the 1960s' and 'groundless.'[112] In 2004, a statement by the Deputy Chinese Foreign Minister to the Japanese Ambassador called the Japanese position 'provocative' and 'very dangerous.'[113]

Over the years, there have been calls to resolve the impasse by arbitration or ICJ litigation. The chances that the two countries agree to do this are considered low.[114] Cited reasons include the fact that since Japan already controls the islands, it has 'nothing to gain and much to lose through putting them at stake in a contested proceeding.'[115] China, which has had a 'historical reluctance' to settle its maritime boundaries by adjudication by third parties,'[116] may not want to set a precedent in the East China Sea that would open China to similar dispute resolution measures in the South China Sea.

Both States have increased official patrols and threatened to use military force against each other's vessels. China operates naval and paramilitary forces near the islands and has asked Japan to follow 'three noes' – no Japanese persons should land on the islands, no development of resources around the islands, and no construction of buildings on the islands.[117]

The situation in the East China Sea has been further aggravated by military actions of both sides, including the 2010 collision incident between a Chinese fishing vessel and a Japanese Coast Guard ship and the Chinese declaration of an ADIZ over large portions of the East China Sea.[118] It is not unreasonable to assume that an escalated conflict between China and Japan could involve other players, such as the US.[119]

4.5.2 China–South Korea (Unresolved around Ieodo Rock)

In the East China Sea, South Korea has argued for a maritime boundary based on application of an 'equidistance-special circumstances' maritime boundary line, placing Ieodo within South Korea's EEZ.[120] China, in a similar position to its stance in the Senkaku Islands, has argued for its EEZ limits based on an equitable formula based on the length of the coastline and natural prolongation. Using this principle, the Ieodo feature will be in China's maritime zone.[121]

Since the South Korean construction of the marine research platform on Ieodo, China has increased surveillance activities in the region, including a 2011 incident involving three Chinese patrol boats threatening South Korean workers on the platform.

The listing of Ieodo as Chinese territory on an official Chinese Ministry of Foreign Affairs website encouraged South Korea to announce that it will prepare a claim to the UN Commission on the Limits of the Continental Shelf (UNCLCS).[122] At the same time, South Korea asked China to remove the area around Ieodo from its declared ADIZ.

The dispute between South Korea and China for control of the seas surrounding the submerged Ieodo rock could be as 'pivotal' as other higher-profile disputes in the region. They point to Ieodo's strategic location lose to important shipping lanes, and the potential of hydrocarbons in the surrounding seas.[123] There have been multiple rounds of stalled negotiations on the fate of Ieodo between South Korea and China with no tangible progress.

4.5.3 Japan–South Korea (Unresolved in Parts)

South Korea and Japan have delimited their maritime boundaries in the Korean Straits and East China Sea. In the narrow Korean Straits between the Korean peninsula and Japan's main island chain, the two States have established a 260-nm maritime border based on the equidistance principle, using numerous small islands in the Straits as base points. The defined border abruptly stops once the Korean Straits opens to the East Sea, leaving the Sea without defined maritime borders.

The Dokdo Islands are in the middle of the East Sea. As discussed previously in this chapter, if an equidistance median line is measured between inhabited islands, Dokdo would be on the South Korean side of the maritime border. If Japan establishes its sovereignty and 'island' status for Dokdo, Japan could claim an EEZ covering half the seas from Dokdo to Ullung-do (the nearest South Korean island).

In keeping with its position denying the existence of a dispute over the sovereignty of the Dokdo Islands, South Korea has rejected Japan's multiple proposals to take the matter to the ICJ, first proposed in 1954.[124] The issue continues to have important economic, military, and strategic implications for both States.

4.6 Proposed JDAs: China–Japan (Senkaku Islands) and Japan–Korea (Dokdo Islands)

A pragmatic solution to the two most contentious maritime border disputes in the region would be to create JDAs around the Dokdo Islands and the Senkaku Islands, as shown in Figure 4.2.

As discussed in this chapter, there are pre-existing JDAs between these States in the East China Sea. Though these have not been successful in discovering hydrocarbon resources, they could form a framework for similar JDAs over the disputed islands.

Though tension is high, by focusing on the commercial benefits of joint hydrocarbon development and putting aside island sovereignty issues, ruling governments could unlock economic benefits without political fallout. Inviting neutral international private energy companies with superior technical skills, instead of promoting their own national companies, could increase trust and, hopefully, generate superior results. Following international model agreements, such as the successful Malaysia–Thailand JDA, could also facilitate the JDA negotiations.

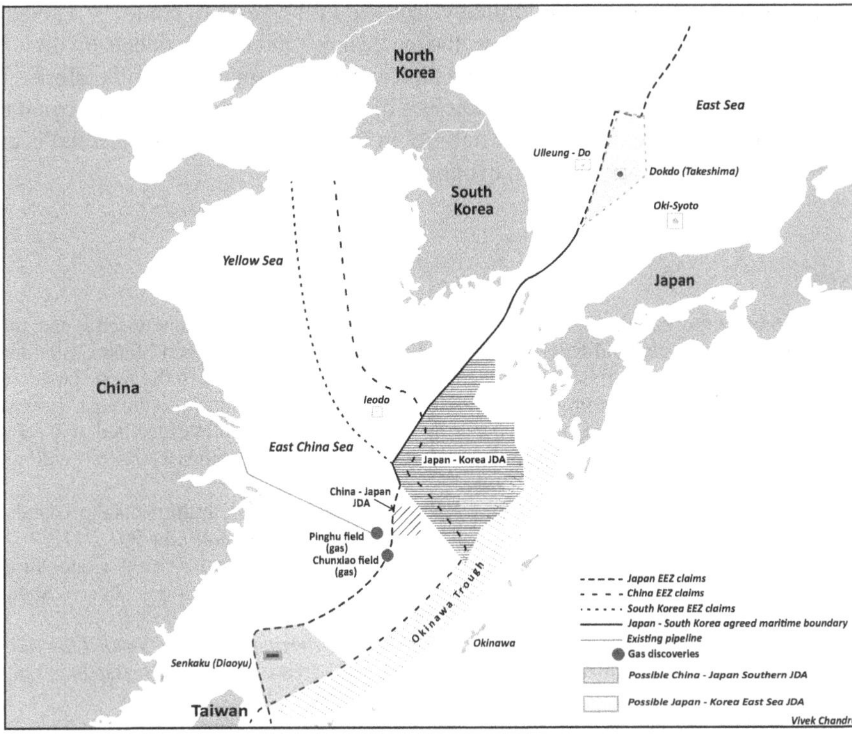

Figure 4.2 Proposed JDAs northeast Asia

4.7 Conclusions

The maritime border disputes in northeast Asia are intractably linked to the questions of territorial sovereignty over the Senkaku and Dokdo Islands, and, to a lesser extent, the Ieodo submerged rock. Establishing sovereignty entitles the islands to generate maritime zones to give access to marine resources such as fisheries and hydrocarbons. The sovereignty disputes are, in turn, linked to 'unresolved historical grievances and the politics of national identity.'[125] The disputes became more complicated after the main claimants declared their maritime claims after ratifying UNCLOS in 1996.

The value of these islands lies in the maritime zones that could be granted under UNCLOS.[126] However, defining these zones is complicated by ambiguities both in UNCLOS and evolving ICJ judgments.

The JDA solution is seen by many as the most feasible solution to break the impasse.[127] To the credit of all three disputing States, the JDA concept has been actively discussed for regional disputes, and in two cases, implemented in the region. As proposed in this chapter, new JDAs could be negotiated to cover the two main disputes in the region. However, in order for this to occur, rising nationalistic sentiments and militarisation of the maritime disputes must be put aside. Undoubtedly, this is an 'unlikely scenario in the years to come.'[128] Though the risk of a regional war may be low, the increasing number of incidents involving both military and civilian vessels and nationals hinder dispute resolution efforts.[129] These disputes, along with the wider issues of Taiwan, North Korea, and regional US military presence, hinder both stability in the region as well as potential economic benefits from hydrocarbon exploitation.

Notes

1 For the purpose of this analysis, 'East Sea' is used to denote the seas between Japan, the Korean peninsula, and Russia. It is also known as the 'Sea of Japan.' East China Sea will refer to the maritime area bordered by the Chinese mainland to the west, Japanese southern islands extending from its main islands through Okinawa to the east, Taiwan to the south, and South Korea to the north. The term 'Korea,' unless specified, will refer to South Korea. North Korea and part of Russia are also in northeast Asia but will not be discussed in this chapter.

2 Carlos Ramos-Mrosovsky, 'International law's unhelpful role in the Senkaku Islands' (2008) 29(4) *University of Pennsylvania Journal of International Law* 903, 911.

3 Seokwoo Lee, 'Territorial Disputes among Japan, China, and Taiwan Concerning the Senkaku Islands' (2002) 3(7) *Boundary and Territory Briefing – International Boundaries Research Unit* 2.

4 Sun Pyo Kim, *Maritime Delimitation and Interim Arrangements in North East Asia* (Brill Academic Publishers, 2004) 203. Total land area of the Dokdo islands is only 0.187 km^2.

5 Schematic map created by author based on various sources, including Kim, S. P. (n 4) 192, 198, 202; Ralf Emmers, *Resource Management and Contested Territories in East Asia* (Palgrave Pivot, London, 2013) 89–90; EIA (n 6); James Manicom, 'Sino-Japanese Cooperation in the East China Sea: Limitations and Prospects' (2008) 30(3) *Contemporary Southeast Asia* 455, 467; Tyler Durden, 'Japan Protests After Discovering Chinese Military Radar In Disputed Waters' *Zero Hedge* (7 August 2018); Constantinos Yiallourides, *Maritime disputes and international law: disputed waters and seabed resources in Asia and Europe* (Routledge, 2019) 101; Masahiro Miyoshi, The Joint Development of Offshore Oil and Gas in Relation to Maritime Boundary Delimitation' (1999) 2(5) *Maritime Briefing International Boundaries Research Unit* 12.

6 Gavan McCormack, 'Much Ado over Small Islands: The Sino-Japanese Confrontation over Senkaku/Diaoyu' in Tim F. Liao, Kimie Hara, and Krista Wiegand (eds), *The China-Japan Border Dispute: Islands of Contention in Multidisciplinary Perspective* (Taylor & Francis Group, 2016)15, 20.

7 US Energy Information Agency EIA, 'Territorial disputes hamper exploration and production of resources in the East China Sea,' *Today in Energy* (Web page, 5 October 2012), < https://www.eia.gov/todayinenergy/detail.php?id=8270>.

8 UN, 'Chapter XXI: Law of the Sea,' *United Nations Treaty Collection* (Web page, 5 October 2020) <https://treaties.un.org/Pages/ViewDetailsIII.aspx?src=TREATY&mtdsg_no=XXI-6&chapter=21&Temp=mtdsg3&clang=_en#EndDec>.

9 Ramos-Mrosovsky (n 2) 904. In this case, Ramos-Mrosovsky refers to the Senkaku Islands and the potential military actions between Japan and China.

10 US Energy Information Agency EIA, 'East China Sea' *Regions of Interest* (Web page, 17 September 2014) <https://www.eia.gov/international/content/analysis/regions_of_interest/East_China_Sea/east_china_sea.pdf>> 4.

11 Ryan M. Scoville, 'Sovereignty over the Senkaku/Diaoyu Islands: A Guide to the Legal Debate' in Tim F. Liao, Kimie Hara, and Krista Wiegand (eds), *The China-Japan Border Dispute: Islands of Contention in Multidisciplinary Perspective* (Taylor & Francis Group, 2016) 85, 86.
12 Lee, S (n 3) 11.
13 Lee, S (n 3) 2.
14 Emmers (n 8) 33 n 6. Emmers quotes K. Hara, *Cold War Frontiers in the Asia-Pacific: Divided Territories in the San Francisco System* (New York: Routledge, 2007) 17.
15 *Treaty of Shimonoseki*, Japan-China, signed 17 April 1895 (entered into force 8 May 1895) art 2(B). Note that Formosa is the former name of Taiwan.
16 Mark E. Manyin, 'The Senkakus (Diaoyu/Diaoyutai) Dispute: U.S. Treaty Obligations' (CRS Report R42761 7-5700, Congressional Research Service, 14 October 2016) 3 n 11. Manyin cites the State Council Information Office, The People's Republic of China, 'White Paper on Diaoyu Dao, an Inherent Territory of China' (September 2012); Emmers (n 8) 34.
17 McCormack (n 5) 24.
18 McCormack (n 5) 19. Koga is credited with giving the name 'Senkaku Islands' (in 1900) as a translation of the name 'Pinnacle Rocks' found on British naval charts. In 1896, he submitted a claim through the newly established Okinawa prefecture to have the islands declared as Japanese territory, allowing his family to formally lease the islands under a 30-year fee-less basis from the Okinawa government. In 1926, the lease was converted to a freehold grant to the Koga family.
19 McCormack (n 5) 18–19.
20 Manyin (n 16) 3.
21 *The Cairo Declaration,* US–China–UK, signed 26 November 1943, Foreign Relations of the United States, Diplomatic Papers, History and Public Policy Program Digital Archive, The Conferences at Cairo and Tehran 448–449.
22 Manyin (n 16) 3 n 12. Manyin cites the Ministry of Foreign Affairs of the Republic of China (Taiwan), 'The Diaoyutai Islands: An Inherent Part of the Territory of the Republic of China (Taiwan).'
23 Scoville (n 11) 102.; Government of Japan Ministry of Foreign Affairs, 'The Senkaku Islands' (Position Paper, March 2013). Emmers (n 8) 34.
24 Mark J. Valencia, 'The East China Sea Dispute: Context, Claims, Issues and Possible Solutions' (2007) 31(1) *Asian Perspective* 127, 153; EIA (n 10) 4; Manyin (n 16) 3.
25 *Treaty on Reversion to Japan of the Ryukyu and Daito Islands*, US–Japan, signed 17 June 1971, 23 U.S.T. 446. The preamble of the treaty called for 'Japan to take full responsibility and authority for the exercise of all powers of administration, legislation and jurisdiction over the territory and inhabitants of the Ryukyu Islands and the Daito Islands.'
26 Robert C Watts, 'Origins of a Ragged Edge U.S. Ambiguity on the Senkakus' Sovereignty' (2019) 72(3) *Naval War College Review* 101. 101; Emmers (n 8) 34. Emmers has stated that the 1971 *Treaty on Reversion* is the only multilateral treaty that explicitly lists the Senkaku Islands; Manyin (n 16) 4. As per Manyin, the general area description ('Nansei Shoto southwestern islands south of 29 degrees north latitude') was referred to by US State department to assert that the treaty included Senkaku Islands.'
27 EIA (n 10) 4; Emmers (n 8) 35.
28 Lee, S (n 3) 12. At the time, Chinese media reported that Chairman Mao Zedong had promised that the Chinese people would defend their territory and not permit 'encroachment' by foreign entities. Taiwan's Foreign Minister asserted Taiwan's sovereignty over the islands, stating that 'we disagree with [the] Japanese Government in [the] latter's claim that they [are] part of Japan ... As to [the] exploration and exploitation of the continental shelf in this maritime area, the natural boundary of our continental

shelf, according to existing principles of international law and convention on continental shelf, should be Okinawa Trough … [w]e, therefore, have full and unrestricted rights in [the] exploration and exploitation of continental shelf in this area.'

29 McCormack (n 5) 21; Scoville (n 11) 117–118.
30 Ramos-Mrosovsky (n 2) 921–922.
31 US concern following China's announcement of air defence zone over disputed islands, *ABC News* (Australia, 25 November 2013).
32 Emmers (n 8) 34.
33 Mark A. Smith, 'Sovereignty Over Unoccupied Territories – The Western Sahara Decision,' (1977) 9(9) *Case Western Reserve Journal of International Law* 135; Relevant landmark cases on *terra nullius* include *Western Sahara* [1975] ICJ Rep 12; *Legal Status of Eastern Greenland* (1933) PCIJ Ser A/B No. 53; *Clipperton Island Arbitration* (France-Mexico) (1931) 2 R. Int'l Arb. Awards 1107.
34 Michael C Davis, 'Can International Law Help Resolve the Conflicts over Uninhibited Islands in the East China Sea?' (2015) 43(2)) *Denver Journal of International Law and Policy* 119, 142.
35 Emmers (n 8) 21.
36 Emmers (n 8) 21.
37 Davis (n 34), 143. *Temple of Preah Vihear (Cambodia v. Thailand)* (Judgment) (1961) ICJ Reports 52; *Island of Palmas (or Miangas)* (n 44). In these cases, the role of maps in boundary delimitation was an important consideration.
38 Emmers (n 8) 22.
39 Seokwoo Lee, 'The Resolution of the Territorial Dispute between Korea and Japan over the Liancourt Rocks' (2002) 3(8) *Boundary and Territory Briefing - International Boundaries Research Unit* 1, 11.
40 Lee, S. (n 38) 12.; Davis (n 34) 142. Davis states that the 1905 Japanese claim was under Korean protest. Lee states, 'the Japanese Government formally reaffirmed its claim to Liancourt Rocks as an integral part of Japan, apparently without protest from Korea.'
41 Emmers (n 8) 22.
42 *The Eulsa Restriction Treaty*, Japan–Korea, signed 17 November 1905. Also known as *Japan–Korea Protectorate Treaty*. Article 1 states, 'The Government of Japan, through the Ministry of Foreign Affairs in Tokyo, will hereafter have control and direction of the external relations and affairs of Korea, and the diplomatic and consular representatives of Japan will have charge of the subjects and interests of Korea in foreign countries.'
43 Emmers (n 8) 23.
44 Emmers (n 8) 23.
45 Emmers (n 8) 22.
46 Davis (n 34) 143; *The Cairo Declaration* (n 21). The declaration states that, 'Japan will also be expelled from all other territories which she has taken by violence and greed.' The San Francisco treaty listed specific territories which Japan had to exit but did not specifically refer to the Dokdo Islands.
47 Akihiro Iwashita, *Japan's Border Issues: Pitfalls and Prospects* (Taylor & Francis Group, 2015) 82.
48 Kyung Moon Hwang, 'A Modest Proposal for Dokdo' in *Past Forward* (Anthem Press, 2019) 167, 167.
49 UN 'Chapter XXI: Law of the Sea' (n 7). Formal confirmation(c), Accession(a), Succession(d), Ratification dates for Republic of Korea (South Korea) is 29 January 1996, China's date is 7 June 1996, and Japan's date is 20 June 1996. North Korea has signed the Convention (on 10 December 1982) but has not ratified it. Taiwan is not a member of the United Nations and not a signatory to UNCLOS.
50 See Figure 4.1 for location of the maritime features discussed in this section.

51 Kim, S. P. (n 4) 202. Even though the Dokdo Islands are closer to the main islands of Japan than the Korean peninsula, they are closer to the South Korean inhabited island of Ullung-do than the Japanese island of Oki-syoto. An equidistance line from the mainland of South Korea and Japan would place Dokdo on the Japanese side of this line. Drawing of an equidistant line between islands of Ullung-do and Oki-syoto would result in the Dokdo Islands on the South Korean side of the equidistant boundary.
52 Kim, S. P. (n 4) 203.
53 Kim, S. P. (n 4).
54 Seokwoo Lee and Young Kil Park, 'Maritime Delimitation and Joint Resource Development in the East China Sea' (Conference Paper, Law of the Sea Institute, UC Berkeley–Korea Institute of Ocean Science and Technology Conference, Seoul, Korea, 21–24 May 2012) 17.
55 Lee and Park (n 54) 14; Emmers (n 8) 35.
56 *United Nations Convention on the Law of the Sea*, opened for signature 10 December 1982, 1833 UNTS 3 (entered into force 16 November 1994) art 76(1). ('*UNCLOS*'). Art 76(1) states, 'The continental shelf of a coastal State comprises the seabed and subsoil of the submarine areas that extend beyond its territorial sea throughout the natural prolongation of its land territory to the outer edge of the continental margin, or to a distance of 200 nautical miles from the baselines from which the breadth of the territorial sea is measured where the outer edge of the continental margin does not extend up to that distance.'
57 *Continental Shelf* (*Tunisia/Libya*) (Judgment of 24 February 1982) [1982] ICJ Rep 18, [47]. 'That definition consists of two parts, employing different criteria. According to the first part of paragraph 1 the natural prolongation of the land territory is the main criterion. In the second part of the paragraph, the distance of 200 nautical miles is, in certain circumstances, the basis of the title of a coastal State.'
58 *Continental Shelf* (*Libya/Malta*) (Judgment) [1985] ICJ Rep 13, [39]. 'The Court however considers that since the development of the law enables a State to claim that the continental shelf appertaining to it extends up to as far as 200 miles from its coast, whatever the geological characteristics of the corresponding sea-bed and subsoil, there is no reason to ascribe any role to geological or geophysical factors within that distance either in verifying the legal title of the States concerned or in proceeding to a delimitation as between their claims … title depends solely on the distance from the coasts of the claimant States of any areas of sea-bed claimed by way of continental shelf, and the geological or geomorphological characteristics of those areas are completely immaterial.
59 Yiallourides (n 8) 100; Lee and Park (n 54) 14–17.
60 Yiallourides (n 8) 100; Lee and Park (n 54) 14–17.
61 Yiallourides (n 8) 100.
62 People's Republic of China, Ministry of Foreign Affairs, 'China's Oil and Gas Exploration in the East China Sea Is Rightful and Legitimate' (Press Release, 24 July 2015).
63 Kim, S. P. (n 4) 211, 217. In the East China Sea, Japan has the largest number of islands and rocks – many of them are not capable of sustaining human populations and thus Japan would like to 'play down' the provisions of Article 121(3) that would reclassify some of these features as rocks, instead of using all the features as basepoints for its equidistance line.
64 Kim, S. P. (n 4) 218.
65 Kim, S. P. (n 4) 203.
66 *UNCLOS* (n 56) art 15. 'Where the coasts of two States are opposite or adjacent to each other, neither of the two States is entitled … to extend its territorial sea beyond the median line. The above provision does not apply, however, where it is necessary by reason of historic title … to delimit the territorial seas of the two States in a way which is at variance therewith.' Historical justifications within UNCLOS are also in Article 10

(historic bays), Article 46 (archipelagic baselines) and for Article 149 (historic objects in the Area).

67 *South China Sea Arbitration (The Republic of Philippines v. The People's Republic of China)* (2016) PCA Case 2013-19, 170 ILR 1 [239].

68 The ICJ, which has adjudicated ten of the maritime boundaries in the database, has changed its own preferred methodology over time. For example, the ICJ used a two-stage process to delimit maritime boundaries in the 2001 *Maritime Delimitation and Territorial Questions between Qatar and Bahrain* (n 119) and in *Land and Maritime Boundary between Cameroon and Nigeria (Cameroon v. Nigeria: Equatorial Guinea interven*ing) [2002] ICJ Rep 303, [288]. However, in the *Maritime Delimitation in the Black Sea (Romania v. Ukraine)* (Judgment) [2009] ICJ Rep 61, [115]–[122], the ICJ has adopted a three-stage process to delimit a single maritime boundary based on the 'equidistance/relevant circumstances' method. The steps, explained in [115]–[122] of the Judgments, are (1) construction of a provisional equidistance line, (2) line is adjusted to achieve equitable result, and (3) court conducts a disproportionality test to the lengths of the relevant coasts, and make adjustments if required.

69 Emmers (n 8) 35.

70 Valencia (n 24) 127; Selig S. Harrison, '*Seabed Petroleum in Northeast Asia: Conflict or Cooperation?*' (Research Report, Woodrow Wilson International Center for Scholars Asia Program, 2005) 3.

71 EIA (n 10) 2–3. Chinese estimates are much higher, with volumes as high as 70 to 160 billion bbls in the entire area, though not all of these have been discovered or likely to be economic. Chinese sources point to multiples of one hundred time higher – as much as 250 Tcf in undiscovered natural gas resources.

72 Harrison (n 70) 6.

73 Kung-wing Au, 'The East China Sea Issue: Japan-China Talks for Oil and Gas' (2008) 25(3) *East Asia: An International Quarterly* 223, 239.

74 Emmers (n 8) 40 n 36. Emmers cites a study by S. S. Harrison, *China, Oil, and Asia: Conflict Ahead? A Study from the Carnegie Endowment for International Peace* (New York, Columbia Press, 1977) 174.

75 McCormack (n 5) 20; K.O Emery et al. 'Geological Structure and Some Water Characteristics of the East China Sea and the Yellow Sea' (1969) 2 (Technical Bulletin, UN Economic Commission for Asia and the Far East Committee for Co-ordinating of Joint Prospecting for Mineral Resources in Asian Offshore Areas (C.C.O.P)) 41.

76 Krista E. Wiegand, 'How Japan Benefits from the Senkaku/Diaoyu Islands Dispute' in Tim F. Liao, Kimie Hara, and Krista Wiegand (eds), *The China-Japan Border Dispute: Islands of Contention in Multidisciplinary Perspective* (Taylor & Francis Group, 2016) 161, 163.

77 Wiegand (n 76) 161.; *Treaty on Reversion to Japan of the Ryukyu and Daito Islands* (n 25).

78 Man-houng Lin, 'US Diplomatic Note on the Diaoyutai Issue: Taiwan's Sovereignty Claim and the US Response' in Tim F. Liao, Kimie Hara, and Krista Wiegand (eds), *The China-Japan Border Dispute: Islands of Contention in Multidisciplinary Perspective* (Taylor & Francis Group, 2016) 57, 67.

79 Lin, M. (n 78) 66.

80 Lin, M. (n 78) 67.

81 Lin, M. (n 78) 67; Valencia (n 24) 132. In the 1970s Taiwan also leased concessions in the area to major oil companies and Taiwan's China Petroleum Corporation apparently still holds blocks there.

82 Ramos-Mrosovsky (n 2) 933; Wiegand (n 76) 163.

83 Emmers (n 8) 41 n 41. Emmers cites Suganuma, *Sovereign Rights and Territorial Sea* (1977) 175.

84 James C. Hsiung, 'Sea Power, Law of the Sea, and China-Japan East China Sea' Resource War' (Conference Paper, Forum on China and the Sea, 9–11 October 2005) 6. Other than the larger Pinghu and Chunxiao, other discoveries included Canxue, Duanqiao, and Tianwaitian covering 22,000 km^2.
85 'Oil giants pull out of East China Sea gas fields project,' *China People's Daily* (30 September 2004).
86 Lee and Park (n 54) 4.
87 *UNCLOS* (n 56) art 74(3).
88 *UNCLOS* (n 56) art 74(3). 'Pending agreement as provided for in paragraph 1, the States concerned, in a spirit of understanding and cooperation, shall make every effort to enter into provisional arrangements of a practical nature and, during this transitional period, not to jeopardize or hamper the reaching of the final agreement.'
89 Au (n 73) 225, Hsiung (n 84) 8.
90 China People's Daily (n 85).
91 Valencia (n 24) 131. In September 2005, five Chinese naval vessels, including a guided missile destroyer, were observed near the gas field, and guns were pointed at Japanese surveillance aircraft.
92 Yusin Lee and Sangjoon Kim, 'Dividing Seabed Hydrocarbon Resources in East Asia: A Comparative Analysis of the East China Sea and the Caspian Sea' (2008) 48(5) *Asian Survey* 794, 802; Valencia (n 24) 132.
93 'Provocative Japanese Test-drilling Condemned' (*China Daily*, 16 July 2005).
94 Hsiung (n 84) 8.
95 Emmers (n 8) 41.
96 Valencia (n 24) 132.
97 Lee and Park (n 54) 18.
98 Emmers (n 8) 27.
99 'Dispute bolsters economic profile of Dokdo Islands,' *Korea Herald* (6 April 2010).
100 Emmers (n 8) 27.
101 Emmers (n 8) 27. In 2006, after Japan sent two ships to survey the waters around Dokdo, Korea sent 20 warships in response.
102 Li Guo Zhao, 'Seabed Petroleum in the East China Sea: Geological Prospects and Search for Hydrocarbons' in Selig S Harrison (ed), *'Seabed Petroleum in Northeast Asia: Conflict or Cooperation?'* (Research Report, Woodrow Wilson International Center for Scholars Asia Program, 2005) 31.
103 Zhao, L. (n 102) 31.
104 Davis (n 34) 154. 24,000 nm^2 is equivalent to 80,000 km^2.
105 Valencia (n 24) 150 n 82. Valencia quotes an article from *Hsinhua Weekly* (11 February 1974) 27.
106 Emmers (n 8) 42; Korea National Oil Corporation (n 235).
107 See Figure 4.1 for location of the two JDAs.
108 Clive Schofield, 'Defining Areas for Joint Development in Disputed Waters' (Conference Paper, Recent Development of the South China Sea Dispute and Prospects of Joint Development Regime, 6–7 December 2012, Haikou, China) 17.
109 Davis (n 34) 157.
110 Zhao (n 102) 37.
111 Au (n 73) 236.
112 Au (n 73) 267.
113 Au (n 73) 239 n 36. Au quotes a 8 July 2004 Chinese Foreign Ministry statement, 'The so-called "median line" is only a unilateral idea from Japan, and China has never recognized it and cannot recognize it. This kind of method of imposing its own idea on others by the Japanese side will not be accepted by the Chinese side. This kind of provocative behaviour is very dangerous, and the Chinese side resolutely opposes it.'

114 Carlos Ramos-Mrosovsky, 'A Constructive Role for International Law in the Senkaku Islands?' in Tim F. Liao, Kimie Hara, and Krista Wiegand (eds), *The China-Japan Border Dispute: Islands of Contention in Multidisciplinary Perspective* (Taylor & Francis Group, 2016) 115.
115 Carlos Ramos-Mrosovsky (n 114) 115.
116 Carlos Ramos-Mrosovsky (n 114) 115. Arbitration and litigation are processes that 'China has consistently refused.' For example, China did not participate in the 2016 *South China Sea Arbitration.*
117 Davis (n 34) 128; Watts (n 26) 101.
118 Emmers (n 8) 45.
119 Davis (n 34) 127; Lindsay Maizland and Beina Xu, 'The U.S.-Japan Security Alliance,' *Council on Foreign Relations* (Web Page, August 22, 2019) <https://www.cfr.org/backgrounder/us-japan-security-alliance>.
120 Kim, S. P. (n 4) 206.
121 Kim, S. P. (n 4) 207. China has also mentioned that the population of the claimant States should also be considered; Jon Van Dyke, 'The Republic of Korea's Maritime Boundaries' (2003) 18(4) *The International Journal of Marine and Coastal Law* 509, 509.
122 Scott W. Harold, 'Ieodo as metaphor? The growing importance of sovereignty disputes in South Korea-China relations and the role of the United States' (2012) 36(2) *Asian Perspective* 287, 300; UN, 'Outer limits of the continental shelf beyond 200 nautical miles from the baselines: Submissions to the Commission: Submission by the Republic of Korea' Oceans and Law of the Sea *Commission on the Limits of the Continental Shelf (CLCS)* (Web Page, 28 August 2013). <https://www.un.org/Depts/los/clcs_new/submissions_files/submission_kor_65_2012.htm.>. However, South Korea's subsequent 2012 submission to UNCLCS covered an area near the Okinawa Trough, not the immediate region around Ieodo.
123 Lily Kuo, 'Will a Tiny, Submerged Rock Spark a New Crisis in the East China Sea?' (9 December 2013) *The Atlantic*; Young-jin Kim, 'Reef vital to protecting Korea's economic zone,' *Korea Times* (18 September 2012).
124 Kim, S. P. (n 4) 195.
125 Valencia (n 24) 157.
126 Ramos-Mrosovsky (n 2) 931.
127 Emmers (n 8) 82.
128 Emmers (n 8) 86.
129 Carlos Ramos-Mrosovsky (n 114) 116; Davis (n 34) 128.

5 Maritime Borders

South China Sea

5.1 Introduction

The region that may have the most complex and volatile maritime disputes in the world is the South China Sea. The region's conflicting sovereignty claims are based on historical justifications, post-WW II treaties, producing nearshore and potentially larger deepwater hydrocarbon resources, and differing interpretations of UNCLOS articles. In contrast to other disputes elsewhere in this book, the South China Sea disputes largely involve the actions of one State, the People's Republic of China ('China' or 'PRC') and, by extension, the Republic of China ('Taiwan' or 'ROC'), in individual disputes with the other protagonists including the Philippines, Vietnam, Malaysia, Brunei Darussalam ('Brunei') and, to a much lesser extent, Indonesia. To add to this cauldron is the larger geopolitical rivalry between China and the United States and the region's importance to global commerce as these two economies account for a quarter of international trade and more than half of the world's shipping.

The South China Sea is a semi-enclosed section of the western Pacific Ocean stretching from Singapore in the southwest, Taiwan in the northeast, Vietnam in the west and to the Philippines in the east. This congested area has almost all of its waters covered with overlapping claims of territorial seas, continental shelves, and EEZs. There are deeply indented bays, archipelagic States, over 200 small maritime features (variously called islands, reefs, and rocks), an abundance of historical claims, and rising nationalism that have resulted in all littoral States pushing for their maximum, sometime unjustified, entitlements.

The South China Sea's disputed maritime features are distributed in three major groups: the Pratas Islands, the Paracel Islands, and the Spratlys.[1] The Pratas Islands are located 200 nm southwest of Hong Kong at the northern reaches of the South China Sea and are claimed both Taiwan and China. The Paracels Islands are located between Vietnam and China's Hainan Island, are controlled by China, and also claimed by Vietnam and Taiwan. The Spratlys, a large, dispersed group of mainly submerged maritime features, are in the central region of the South China Sea and claimed by six countries, including China, Taiwan, and Vietnam (which claim the entire group of features) and the Philippines, Malaysia, and Brunei (which claim sovereignty over certain portions of the Spratlys). With the exception of Brunei, the remaining five claimants have established a military presence in the various maritime features in the Spratlys.

DOI: 10.4324/9781003323051-5

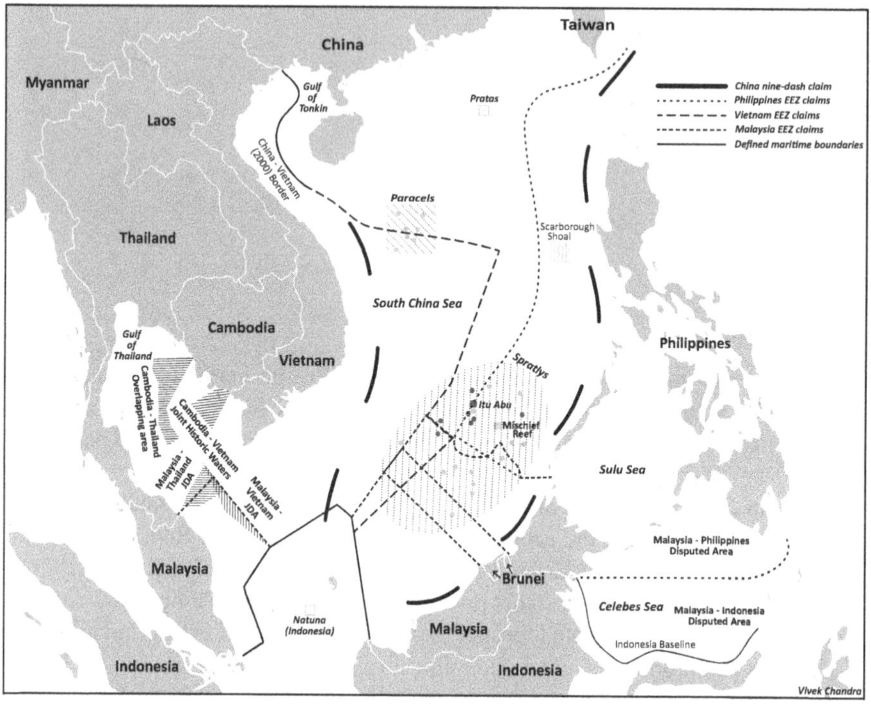

Figure 5.1 Schematic map showing the South China Sea claims, JDAs, and main maritime features.[2]

The waters of the South China Sea, as well as its branches into the Gulf of Thailand, Sulu, and Celebes Seas, are rich in energy resources and fisheries. Over 200 companies, both national and international, are, or have been, engaged in oil and gas exploration and production off the littoral coasts. With the exception of existing production relatively close to the coastlines of China, Vietnam, Malaysia, and Brunei, little substantive hydrocarbon exploitation activity has taken place in the deeper, central (and more contested) waters of the South China Sea, leading some to classify hydrocarbon reserve estimates there as a 'matter of some conjecture.'[3]

The region is also one of the richest fishing areas in the world. Studies have indicated that fisheries, including major species of tuna, mackerel, shrimp, and shellfish, are dwindling as overfishing, destruction of marine ecosystems and pollution is taking its toll. This is forcing both legal and illegal fisherman to venture into further offshore waters, further escalating tensions over overlapping maritime claims.

The regional maritime disputes are multifaceted. The maritime features, many of which are submerged at low tide, are subject to competing sovereignty claims based on historical justifications, much of it derived from their colonial occupiers which independent States have attempted to strengthen through effective occupation. Claims are also complicated by ongoing construction activities, mainly by China, in an attempt to change the status of the features to gain access to resources.

Though not technically in the South China Sea, this chapter also briefly covers two disputes in the Sulu and Celebes Seas, immediately to the southeast of the South China Sea, and two disputes in the Gulf of Thailand, west of the South China Sea. The Sulu Sea disputes involve undefined maritime borders and security concerns in the vicinity of producing oil and gas resources. The Gulf of Thailand disputes involve Cambodia's maritime borders with Vietnam and Thailand.

It should be noted that though the disputes in the South China Sea and its fringes seem to be at an impasse, the wider Southeast Asia region has been remarkably successful in resolving many of its maritime border disputes. Indonesia has defined most of its extensive maritime borders, Malaysia and Thailand have a successful (and producing) JDA in their overlapping claim region, Malaysia and Vietnam have a defined JDA, and China and Vietnam have delimited their northern maritime border in the Gulf of Tonkin. JDAs of various forms have also been proposed for disputed regions of the South China Sea as well as for the disputes in the Sulu Sea and Gulf of Thailand.

5.2 Legal Background

Chinese government sources cite written records indicating that the Spratlys were under the jurisdiction of China from the Yuan (Mongol) dynasty in the 1300s, naming the Hainan garrison of the Ming Dynasty (late 1300s–1600s), as being responsible for 'patrolling as well as exercising jurisdiction' over the Spratlys (Nansha), Macclesfield Bank (Zhongsha), and Paracel (Xisha) Islands.[4]

Chinese ships dominated trade and exploration in the South China Sea from the 12th to the mid-15th centuries. Notably, this marked the only period in Chinese history, except arguably the current period, when China embarked on a quest to become a leading naval power.[5] The era ended when a combination of natural disasters, the threat of Mongols from the north, and internal fragmentation within the Ming Court, led to government prohibition on the construction of double-masted ships. By 1525, the Ming Court had ordered the destruction of all oceangoing ships, dissolving the 'greatest navy in history' which once had 3,500 ships.[6] The ensuing power vacuum in the region was soon exploited by the Ryukyu Kingdom in Okinawa, by Portuguese and Dutch traders and, later, by the Vietnamese Nguyen kings.

The arrival of Europeans brought silver, gold, and opium, as well as concepts of 'sovereignty' and 'freedom of navigation' to the region. Initially, their focus was on establishing colonies and negotiating land boundary treaties. By the end of the 19th century, British, French, Spanish, and American forces had joined the Portuguese and Dutch to establish colonies in areas surrounding the South China Sea. The mix of European and Asian monarchies later began to delineate territorial waters, plant flags and markers on maritime features, and remove markers erected by others.

The first Western-style legal claim on any of the maritime features was made in the Spratlys in 1877 by English guano merchants from northern Borneo operating under a licence granted by the British Crown. In 1925, the French colonial government based in the southern part of French Indochina (Vietnam), apparently without knowledge of the prior British claim, made their own claims on the Spratlys.

The Paracel Islands, strategically located on the shipping route between Singapore and Hong Kong, were first formally claimed by China in 1909. After initially accepting the Chinese claim,[7] the French position changed in 1930 when colonial authorities in Annam (in Central Vietnam) began to agitate for control over the islands. The ensuing Chinese revolution further diminished Chinese control, allowing regular unauthorised guano exploitation visits by Japanese companies based in occupied Taiwan.[8]

Between 1932 and 1935, the Chinese government published a list of 132 names of maritime features in the South China Sea.[9] In the 1930s, the fear of Japanese expansion in the region led France to renew its own claim to the Spratlys and the Paracels, where France had established a permanent presence. In the ensuing period, France, China, and Japan began a rivalry of claims over both the Spratlys and the Paracels, sending expeditions, placing markers, making official declarations and maps, and exchanging diplomatic notes. During the Sino–Japanese war in 1937, Japan occupied Pratas Island, increasing French and British anxieties.

During the early years of WW II, the South China Sea became a 'Japanese lake' with the deployment of Japanese naval forces and fortifications throughout the region.[10] Japan's interest in the region ended with their surrender and loss of Taiwan at the end of WW II. In 1946–1947, General Chiang Kai-shek, the President of the Republic of China (Taiwan) sent an expedition to the Spratlys and occupied Woody Island in the Paracels. In 1947, the legislative body of the Republic of China passed a resolution to delineate its territory.[11] This resolution has been suggested as the background for the issuing of the nine-dash 'U'-shaped claim line that is discussed further in this chapter.[12]

As discussed in the previous chapter, ambiguities within the 1951 *Treaty of Peace with Japan*[13] exacerbated the already complicated resolution of surrendered Japanese territories after WW II. Referring to South China Sea territories, Article 2(f) of the Treaty simply states, 'Japan renounces all right, title and claim to the Spratly Islands and to the Paracel Islands' without specifying their future status.[14] Neither the Communist Chinese on the mainland, nor the Republic of China (which had since retreated to Taiwan), participated in the 1951 conference. France and Vietnam did participate but were apparently unable to include clarity on the sovereignty of the South China Sea maritime features in the Treaty.[15]

In 1956, the Cloma brothers from the Philippines attempted to install *Kalayaan* (translated as 'Freedomland') in the Spratlys by landing on Thitu and Itu Aba Islands. This private expedition was apparently with the backing of the vice-president of the Philippines and was based on the assertion that the islands were *res nullius* after they were abandoned by Japan following WW II.[16] Unsurprisingly, China and Taiwan protested the creation of *Kalayaan*, prompting Taiwan to reoccupy Itu Aba. The *Kalayaan* claim may have also persuaded South Vietnam, which became a republic in 1955, to renew its own claims in the Paracels, and later to the Spratlys, as successor to France's earlier claims.[17]

In 1971, 'clearly motivated by the prospect of finding oil,' the Philippines officially claimed *Kalayaan*, expanding its claims to another five features in the Reed Bank area (northeast of the Spratlys). During the same period, South Vietnam awarded a number of oil exploration contracts in areas west of the Spratlys to international companies and incorporated the Spratlys under the governance of one of its provinces. After the fall of South Vietnam in 1976, the unified Socialist Republic of Vietnam took over these claims.

Malaysia, which had gained its independence from Britain in 1963, passed its own *Continental Shelf Act*, followed by the 1979 publication of a map that gave it an extensive continental shelf extending north of Borneo, including features in the southern Spratlys.[18] In the early 1970s, Malaysia and Brunei began offshore oil production off the northern coast of Borneo, and exploration wells were drilled off South Vietnam and the Philippines.[19]

After the US withdrawal from Vietnam in 1973, China sent additional troops and vessels to the Paracel Islands. The 1974 Battle of the Paracel between China and South Vietnam lasted only a few days as the weakened South Vietnam government was unable to evict the stronger Chinese flotilla. Despite requests for assistance, the US did not provide any military support in the Paracels to their South Vietnam allies.[20]

During the next decade, China reinforced its position in the Paracels. China, Taiwan, Vietnam, and the Philippines occupied various maritime features in the central Spratlys and Malaysia occupied Swallow Reef in the southern sector of the Spratly group. Some claimants issued oil and gas concessions in their claimed zones, and, with the introduction of UNCLOS in 1982, drew baselines to claim their own UNCLOS maritime zone entitlements.

In 1992, China enacted its *Law on the Territorial Sea and Contiguous Zone*.[21] The law specifically referred to Pratas Island (Dongsha), the Paracel Islands (Xisha), Macclesfield Bank (Zhongsha), and the Spratlys (Nansha) as being a part of the territory of China. Importantly, the waters between the Chinese mainland and the claimed islands are referred to as 'internal waters' of China.

5.2.1 ASEAN and South China Sea

Although there were frequent talks between claimant States, there is no substantive progress in resolving conflicting claims. After China occupied Mischief Reef in the Spratlys in the 1990s, the Philippines sought backing from its fellow Association of South East Asian Nations (ASEAN) members to unite to constrain further Chinese encroachment.[22] In 2002, ASEAN issued the *Declaration on the Conduct of Parties* (*DoC*) which was adopted by all members of ASEAN plus China. The document restated a commitment for all parties to undertake 'self-restraint' and to resolve disputes in accordance with universally recognised principles of international law, including the 1982 UN Convention on the Law of the Sea.[23] Though the impact of the *DoC* has been limited, it was the first agreement to include China in a regional framework for South China Sea disputes.[24] Critics of the *DoC* have noted its lack of enforcement mechanisms or defined punitive measures for non-compliance.[25]

In 2009, China, as well as the Philippines, protested Malaysia and Vietnam's joint attempt to define the outer extent of respective continental shelves beyond 200 nm, alleging that their new claims overlapped their sovereignty.[26] This further escalated tensions in the region, prompting China to send military vessels to disputed areas. The action also prompted China to issue a *Note Verbale* which included, for the first time, a map of its 'U'-shaped nine-dash line claim and stating its 'indisputable sovereignty over the islands in the South China Sea and the adjacent waters and enjoys sovereign rights and jurisdiction over the relevant waters as well as the seabed and subsoil thereof.'[27]

Standoffs between the Philippines and China, including a 2012 Scarborough Shoal incident where the Philippine Navy confronted Chinese official vessels protecting their fisherman, have continued over the past decade.[28] The Philippines, invoking its 1951 mutual defence treaty with the US, has requested the US to intervene. The US has, so far, only agreed to conduct Freedom of Navigation patrols and reiterate its ongoing support for the Philippines.[29]

In 2013, after it was clear that China was not going to withdraw from the Scarborough Shoal, the Philippines, frustrated by the lack of diplomatic progress, issued a *Notification and Statement of Claim on the West Philippines Dispute* to begin arbitration under UNCLOS Article 287 at the Permanent Court of Arbitration (PCA).[30] The Philippines sought resolution to questions concerning the role of historic rights, marine entitlements, and the status of maritime features occupied by China, plus other acts by China that the Philippines alleged violated UNCLOS.[31]

The action was rejected by China, which stated that the Philippines was illegally occupying islands over which China held 'indisputable sovereignty,' and was in violation of previous commitments by both countries to settle their disputes through bilateral negotiations, including the 2002 ASEAN *DoC*.[32] China refused to participate in the PCA arbitration process, insisting that the Tribunal lacked jurisdiction.[33] China's absence did not prevent the *South China Sea Arbitration* from moving ahead or the Tribunal from issuing its award in 2016.[34] Hereafter in this chapter, these are referred to as the 'Arbitration' and 'Tribunal.' China has chosen to ignore the Tribunal award, maintaining its 'aggressive South China Sea policies while escaping sanction for its non-compliance.'[35]

Negotiations for a *Code of Conduct*, the successor to the *DoC* between China and ASEAN, have dragged on for decades, in part due to increasing US–China tensions and increasing militarisation of the South China Sea. In mid-2020, tensions again escalated with the US rejecting China's 'expansive maritime claims' and 'campaign of bullying to control offshore resources' as 'completely unlawful.'[36] In response, China fired missiles in the disputed region, 'sending the US a message.'[37] Incidents and increasingly dangerous encounters between Chinese, American, Filipino, Vietnamese, Indonesian, and Malaysian defence forces have continued, and are unlikely to abate in the near future.

5.3 Applicability of UNCLOS

UNCLOS Article 123 obliges littoral States of semi-enclosed seas to 'cooperate with each other in the exercise of their rights and in the performance of their duties under this Convention.'[38] The Convention does not elaborate on how the littoral States should cooperate, especially when dealing with issues of maritime boundary definition. This is especially problematic in the South China Sea where there are six States with overlapping claims of sovereignty over 'hundreds of small islands … uninhabited islets, shoals, reefs, banks, sands, cays, and rocks.'[39]

All the claimant States (with the exception of Taiwan) in the South China Sea disputes are parties to UNCLOS.[40] China and Malaysia are the only two regional States that have made explicit Article 298 declarations opting out of the Convention's dispute resolution procedures for maritime boundary delimitation.[41] The declaration allows China (and Malaysia) to insist that any dispute concerning its sovereignty or other rights over maritime zones would be excluded from the Convention's compulsory dispute resolution clauses, leaving the dispute to be resolved by negotiation instead of adjudication.[42] China and Malaysia are also the two Asian States involved in the largest number of unresolved maritime boundary disputes in the dataset.[43] The declaration of the Philippines in 1984 is not as explicit, but can be interpreted as an equivalent rejection of the dispute resolution procedures and has been counted as such in this book's dataset analysis.[44]

China made its UNCLOS Article 298 declaration in 2006.[45] Because of this declaration, the *South China Sea Arbitration* initiated by the Philippines was unable to adjudicate or delimitate the maritime boundaries between China and the Philippines – instead, the Tribunal had to focus on status of maritime features and their impact on maritime claims.[46]

5.3.1 Historic Rights

In the South China Sea, three claimants, (China, Taiwan and, to a limited extent, Vietnam) have based their continental shelf and EEZ maritime claims on historical rights.[47] China has justified its 'U'-shaped nine-dash claim line on the basis of its historical rights. The Tribunal's conclusion on the usage of historic rights is clear in a number of paragraphs in the Award:

> No article of the Convention expressly provides for or permits the continued existence of historic rights to the living or non-living resources of the exclusive economic zone. Similarly, nothing in the Convention expressly provides for or permits a State to maintain historic rights over the living and non-living resources of the continental shelf, the high seas, or the Area.[48]
>
> Accordingly, in the Tribunal's view, China's ratification of the Convention … relinquished the freedoms of the high seas that it had previously utilized with respect to the living and non-living resources … within the ambit of the exclusive economic zone of other States.[49]

> The Tribunal considers the text and context of the Convention to be clear in superseding any historic rights that a State may once have had in the areas that now form part of the exclusive economic zone and continental shelf of another State. There is no ambiguity here that would call for the Tribunal to have recourse to the supplementary means of interpretation.[50]

In summary, the Tribunal found that even if China had established historic rights for exclusive use of the resources of the South China Sea, they would have been superseded by China's acceptance of UNCLOS and EEZ entitlements granted by UNCLOS.[51]

5.3.2 Baselines

Several littoral States in the South China Sea have adopted straight baselines that do not conform to the UNCLOS guidelines. UNCLOS outlines specific cases for the use of straight baselines, including around certain island groups and indented bays.[52] Largely contrary to these guidelines, Malaysia, the Philippines, Vietnam, and China have drawn straight baselines off their coastlines and, in some cases, around their claimed maritime features. Malaysia has passed a series of laws regulating its continental shelf claim and, in 1979, released a map showing a continental shelf claim north of its eastern states of Sabah and Sarawak using straight baselines.[53] Not coincidently, the offshore waters of Sabah and Sarawak are the locations of the majority of Malaysia's oil and gas fields.

China's 1992 Law on Territorial Sea and Contiguous Zones actually *requires* the use of straight baselines for its coasts.[54] Based on this law, China has drawn straight baselines using coastal mainland and coastal islands, in defiance of UNCLOS's guidelines.

China has also not clarified the legal status of its 'U'-shaped nine-dash claim line and how it co-exists with UNCLOS's baselines but has indicated that its nine-dash line claim marks its 'indisputable sovereignty' over the waters encompassed by the line.[55]

5.3.3 Islands vs Rocks

Hundreds of small maritime features with contested UNCLOS status lie scattered throughout the South China Sea. UNCLOS Article 121, discussed in previous chapters of this book, defines an 'island' as 'a naturally formed area of land, surrounded by water, which is above water at high tide.' The last paragraph in Article 121 clarifies further that 'rocks which cannot sustain human habitation or economic life of their own' are not entitled to an EEZ and a continental shelf.[56]

The meaning of terms used in Article 121, including, 'cannot sustain human habitation or economic life of their own,' 'naturally formed,' 'high tide,' and 'rocks,' are not defined within UNCLOS. These 'deliberately vague' phrases are 'a frequent bugbear in maritime delimitation negotiations and adjudications' and have been subject to inconsistent interpretations.[57] The presence of fresh water, naturally occurring vegetation capable of providing shelter, and minimum number of permanent civilian residents have been proposed as determination criteria for capacity to sustain human habitation, but their usage remains disputed.[58]

The 2016 *South China Sea Arbitration* was specifically asked to adjudicate on the status of the Spratlys' features and their maritime entitlements. Since most of the Spratlys lie within 200 nm of the Philippines archipelago, any maritime entitlement by another State would encroach on the Philippines EEZ. In order to make its decision, the Tribunal ruled that 'human habitation' requires a 'stable community of people for whom the feature constitutes a home and on which they can remain.'[59] Economic life, according to the Tribunal, should 'ordinarily be the life and livelihoods of the human population inhabiting and making its home on a maritime feature or group of features.'[60] The Tribunal made it clear that if economic activity is dependent on external resources or entirely dependent on extracting the natural resources of the feature, the 'economic life' threshold for island classification is not reached.[61] In essence, economic life must be 'oriented around the feature itself and not focused solely on the waters or seabed of the surrounding territorial sea,'[62] and attempts to control an EEZ based on 'artificial economic life supported by a distant population' would not be sufficient.[63]

5.3.4 Artificial Islands

The status of artificial islands is more relevant to the South China Sea dispute than any other region covered in this book. Claimants have built artificial structures of varying degrees of sophistication on disputed maritime features. The Chinese occupation of Subi Reef, Johnson South Reef, and Mischief Reef; the Malaysian occupation of Dallas Reef and Investigator Shoal; and the Vietnamese occupation of Vanguard and Prince of Wales Banks, all include structures that could be called 'artificial islands.' These structures are built to 'reinforce and expand maritime territorial claims.'[64] In the period between the end of 2013, when the *South China Sea Arbitration* began, and mid-2016, when the Tribunal Award was published, China conducted a 'massive island-building' project.[65] The Tribunal depicted, with supporting photographs, the transformation that had taken place on numerous features in the short period of time.[66]

Article 60 in the UNCLOS convention deals specifically with artificial islands – but as in other topics in the Convention, does not provide clear legal definitions of terms used. It clearly states that artificial islands do not have the status of 'islands,' and are not entitled to any maritime zones, including territorial sea, EEZ, or continental shelf.[67] The Tribunal reaffirmed that the status of a feature must be assessed on the basis of its 'natural condition.'[68] Nevertheless, States, especially China, continue to construct artificial structures and use them as justifications for their entitlements.[69]

5.4 Oil and Gas Activities

The South China Sea is a source of hydrocarbons (especially natural gas) and a crucial world trade route for energy supplies to the dynamic economies of China,

South Korea, Taiwan, and Japan. A third of global crude oil and half of global liquefied natural gas crosses the South China Sea, making it one of the most important global trade routes.

The US Energy Information Agency estimates that the basin contains approximately 11 billion bbls of oil and 190 Tcf of natural gas. Most of the proven reserves are in the relatively shallow nearshore uncontested coasts of Malaysia, Vietnam, Brunei, and China.[70] In addition to the proved and probable reserves, the US Geologic Survey (USGS) estimates that as much as 22 billion barrels of oil and 290 Tcf of gas are yet to be discovered in the South China Sea region.[71] A 2012 estimate by the Chinese National Offshore Oil Company (CNOOC) estimated the resources to be significantly higher – 125 billion bbls of oil and 500 Tcf of natural gas.[72]

Developing the region's offshore hydrocarbon resources is challenging. The geology is complex, the reservoirs are high-pressure and strong currents and regular typhoons require expensive equipment and infrastructure to develop. There are few trans-border or long-distance pipelines to efficiently transport hydrocarbons to the coastal markets.

Malaysia and Brunei began offshore oil production off the north coast of Borneo in the 1960s. In the early 1970s, both the Philippines and South Vietnam began exploration drilling off their respective coastlines. China has been independently exploring and producing from its nearshore fields, mainly adjacent to Hainan Island and Hong Kong, since the mid-1970s.

China has shown its willingness to resort to military action when other States embark on hydrocarbon activities within China's claimed area. States that have pushed the limits further have been Vietnam and the Philippines, both of which see high potential for hydrocarbons within their EEZs overlapping with China's claim areas.

5.4.1 Oil and Gas Activities in Disputed Areas between China and Vietnam

Since the 1980s, China and Vietnam have awarded licences in their overlapping claim areas. Both States have actively sought the assistance of, and investment by, foreign companies to provide capital, technologies, and managerial skills to assist in offshore exploration and production efforts. It is widely assumed that the award of concessions, especially to foreign entities, is, at least in part, to defend their respective maritime claims.[73]

Vietnam's 200-nm EEZ UNCLOS entitlement follows the shape of its mainland coast. The first 'dash' of China's nine-dash claim is just 50 nm from the mainland coast of Vietnam, well within Vietnam's 200-nm EEZ limit, creating a large, disputed overlapping claim area that covers 60–70% of Vietnam's total EEZ entitlement. This overlapping claim area encompasses proven, producing, and potential hydrocarbon resources.

In 1992, the Chinese government signed an oil exploration contract with Crestone Energy, an American private company, granting rights to explore a massive concession area located between Vietnam and Malaysia, inside both China's nine-dash line and Vietnam's 200-nm EEZ.[74] Vietnam 'harshly' protested the Crestone contract, claiming that the company's actions would be a violation of Vietnam's sovereignty.[75] Two years later, three Vietnamese vessels fired at Crestone's exploration ships. After a standoff, Crestone abandoned its work programme, complaining that despite protection promises, the Chinese navy did not intervene.[76]

After the Crestone incident, a drilling rig operating on behalf of VietSovPetro, a joint venture between Vietnam and Russia, began drilling in Vanguard Bank, inside the southwest corner in the same Chinese block awarded to Crestone earlier. China sent two warships to blockade the oil rig. The siege, which lasted for a few weeks, prompted diplomats to warn of potential armed conflict between the two countries.[77]

China continued to pressure foreign companies operating under licence from Vietnam in the overlapping claim area. In 2007, China's Ministry of Foreign Affairs complained to the Japanese government about the activities of a Japanese energy company consortium which had been planning seismic activities. The Japanese companies succumbed to Chinese pressure and suspended their Vietnam work programme.[78]

In 2011, PetroVietnam, the national energy company of Vietnam, signed exploration contracts with a consortium of Russian and Indian companies to allow exploration in the disputed zone. China protested the award of blocks and a few months later, Chinese surveillance boats cut cables being used by seismic exploration vessels operating on behalf of the consortium. At the time, the Vietnam Ministry of Foreign Affairs stated that China's claim is 'legally groundless and is contrary to the 1982 Law of the Sea Convention' to which China is a party and that China's 'claim encroaches the exclusive economic zones and the continental shelves of many regional countries, including Vietnam, and thus are rejected by many countries.'[79]

Two weeks after the 2011 incident, another seismic vessel, this time operating for a Canadian company, was intercepted in Block 136 in the southeast corner of Vietnam's EEZ, also overlapping Crestone's China concession. China's Fisheries Law Enforcement Command supported by a fleet of Chinese fishing vessels, sailed across the seismic sensor cables of the exploration ship, cutting them as the fishing nets became entangled in the cables.

China also began exploration efforts around the Paracels despite Vietnamese protests.[80] In 2014, CNOOC, a Chinese state-owned company, moved an exploration rig to a location 17 nm from the Paracel Islands. This move triggered boat ramming and anti-Chinese riots in Vietnam, which eventually led to violence against Chinese businesses and nationals in Vietnam.[81]

Aggressive actions by China have sporadically continued since then. Undoubtedly, actions by both Vietnam and China are frustrating the development of resources in the overlapping claim areas.[82] PetroVietnam has blamed maritime tensions with China for its declining offshore exploration and production activities.[83] The US Energy Information Agency (EIA) has observed that neither CNOOC nor the Chinese government has been able to attract international companies to participate in blocks located in overlapping territorial claims with Vietnam.[84]

5.4.2 Oil and Gas Activities in Disputed Areas between China and the Philippines

The declaration of *Kalayaan* as a part of the Philippines in 1971 was also, at least in part, motivated by the area's prospects for hydrocarbon resources.[85] *Kalayaan's* maritime features include the Reed Bank area where a test well discovered gas in 1976. However, the discovery was never developed.[86]

In 2002, the Philippines awarded a UK company the rights to explore a portion of Reed Bank.[87] This prompted China to send a *Note Verbale* to the UN which stated that the Philippines has 'seriously infringed upon China's sovereignty and sovereign rights and goes [sic] contrary to its commitments on the South China Sea issue and to the maintenance of peace and stability in the South China Sea. It is illegal, null and void.'[88]

The following year, in March 2011, a seismic exploration ship operating on behalf of the UK company was approached by Chinese Marine Surveillance vessels accompanied by a fleet of Chinese fishing vessels. The Philippines subsequently delivered a *Note Verbale* objecting to the incident, calling it a 'serious violation of Philippine sovereignty and marine jurisdiction.'[89] After the Chinese incident, the UK company stopped its exploration efforts.[90] Since then, despite the multiple rounds of exploration block offerings, the Philippines has not managed to attract international explorers to materially participate in further activities in its disputed waters.[91]

In contrast to its attitude towards Vietnam and the Philippines, China has been more tolerant of the activities of Malaysia and Brunei. Malaysia has developed fields within the Chinese nine-dash claim, and Malaysia and Brunei also have an agreement to jointly develop resources. A cited reason for the differences in China's more tolerant attitudes towards Malaysia and Brunei as opposed to the more aggressive stance against Vietnam and the Philippines could be the 'that Malaysia and Brunei downplay their differences with China, while Vietnam and the Philippines seek to rally international support.'[92]

5.5 JDA Status - Operational and Historical Proposals

Despite numerous incidents of confrontation in the South China Sea, there have also been some notable attempts at joint development. As early as 1980, Den Xiaoping, the Chinese leader at the time, promoted joint development as a peaceful method for dispute resolution of overlapping maritime claims.[93] This position has been reiterated on many occasions, even while China maintained its aggressive posture against Vietnam and the Philippines to thwart their efforts to unilaterally explore within the overlapping areas.

China has initiated joint development proposals separately to Vietnam, Malaysia, and the Philippines on multiple occasions. Though past overtures have largely been ignored, it seems clear that any State wanting to unilaterally develop resources within China's nine-dash claim line would either have to recognise China's territorial claims, or directly challenge Chinese presence and expect retaliation for its defiance. However, 'most other claimants ... see the presumption of the nine-dash line [as] the starting point of negotiations for joint development as fundamentally unfair,'[94] and that China's offers of joint development are just a 'symbolic gesture.'[95]

Vietnam, in particular, 'fears that joint development before agreeing on the disputed areas according to the UNCLOS would amount to legitimising the nine-dash line.'[96] A Vietnamese foreign ministry official is quoted as stating that,

> If a partner can't show me which area it claims with reasonable legal ground, we can't do joint development. We can't accept ambiguous claims without clarification. We can't just accept some dotted lines ... Vietnamese people and leaders see [EEZ] as our backyard. It is what we own. Someone comes in and say we want to do joint development in your backyard. It's not acceptable.[97]

There has been one instance of joint activity of limited success. In 2003, a group of Filipino politicians brokered direct negotiations between CNOOC and the Philippines National Oil Company (PNOC). The negotiators delineated an area of 143,000 km^2 north and west of Palawan, including Reed Bank, for joint seismic exploration. At the time, the politicians justified initiating the discussion as '30% of something was better than 100% of nothing.'[98]

In 2004, the resulting Joint Marine Seismic Undertaking (JMSU) for the Reed Bank area was signed during the Philippine President's state visit to China. The agreement called for a three-year seismic acquisition programme to be undertaken by CNOOC and PNOC and was presented as a 'marine scientific research project' under the auspices of the 2002 ASEAN – China *DoC*.[99]

Vietnam, which had initially condemned the JMSU, ultimately decided that it was better to be included in the survey than to be excluded.[100] An updated three-way JMSU was signed between PetroVietnam, PNOC, and CNOOC in 2005, and the JMSU contracted a Chinese survey ship that ultimately gathered 11,000 km^2 of seismic data. Though the survey yielded some promising results, the JMSU ended its three-year tenure in 2008 without completing its full study objectives, hampered by a growing corruption scandal and a change of government in the Philippines, and no clear path forward.[101] Though the success of JMSU was limited, it did allow the States to put aside their sovereignty claims for a short period, and 'demonstrated a model of joint development' that had been previously evaded.[102]

During the ensuing years, regional countries have embraced joint development agreements – albeit outside the disputed South China Sea areas.[103] Malaysia has signed agreements with Thailand (in 1990), Vietnam (in 1992), and Brunei (in 2009). The Malaysia-Thailand JDA is considered to be one of the more successful operating JDAs in the world, and its agreements, which are publicly available, could be used as a model for future JDAs globally.

Workshops and negotiations to define South China Sea JDA concepts have been held over the years, but difficulties with defining the JDA geographic limits, the complicated political situation, and the role of China have limited substantive progress.

5.6 Maritime Boundaries

5.6.1 China's Nine-Dash Claim

China's 'legally ambiguous'[104] 'U'-shaped nine-dash claim covers some 3 million km^2 out of the total estimated 3.5 million km^2 of the South China Sea.[105] The claim 'far exceeds' what is claimable as a Territorial Sea under UNCLOS, and, since it comes close to mainland coast of the other States, the Chinese claim area significantly overlaps the EEZ entitlements these States.[106] Though the maritime area covered is enormous, the total high-tide land area within the nine-dash line claim, excluding Taiwan, is less than 15 km^2.[107]

The nine-dash claim was first published in 1948 (and again in 2009) as a 'Map Showing the Location of the Various Islands in the South Sea' in the Republic of China (Taiwan) Atlas of Administrative Areas.[108] Initially, it was to be a claim of the maritime features located within the line, but, in the 1960s, the line took on a claim of maritime territory, including both sea and maritime features.[109] Some scholars have questioned whether it is possible to make a claim based on a 'dotted or broken line instead of an unbroken line,' arguing that a 'boundary line must be a continuous one.'[110]

The nature, scope, or even the geographic coordinates of the nine-dash 'U'-shaped claim line have never been clarified.[111] Instead, China has preferred to maintain legal ambiguity over whether the line indicates sovereign rights – or something less – over the entire area enclosed by the line. A 2007 report by the US government stated that

> maintaining this ambiguity can be viewed as an approach that preserves flexibility for China in pursuing its maritime claims in the South China Sea while making it more difficult for other parties to define specific objections or pursue legal challenges to those claims.[112]

China has maintained that its nine-dash line claimed area is 'confirmation of China's rights in the South China Sea formed throughout the … history ... [f]or a long time, no State questioned the legitimacy of the dotted line and it also appeared on the official maps of many States.'[113]

5.6.2 China–Taiwan (Unresolved)

Taiwan has maintained its independent position with respect to the South China Sea claims. Taiwan has cited 'history, geography, reality or international law' in justifying its claims over all the features in the South China Sea.[114] The status of Taiwan's maritime claims, and whether or not Taiwan should join China in rejecting maritime claims of other States, is unresolved.[115]

Though both support the nine-dash line claim area, Taiwan and China have conflicting claims on the Pratas Islands, where Taiwan currently occupies the main island and maintains a garrison. Taiwan also occupies the largest 'natural' island in the Spratlys, Itu Aba, occupied by the nationalists since 1946. China disputes

Taiwan's occupation of the island, but there have not been any military confrontations between the two States, and Taiwan has distanced itself from any Chinese action against other claimants.[116]

5.6.3 China–Vietnam (Unresolved in South China Sea/Resolved in Gulf of Tonkin)

Following the restoration of diplomatic relations between China and Vietnam in 1991, the two States signed an agreement on the principles to manage their land and maritime border in the Gulf of Tonkin, between the northern Vietnamese mainland and China's Hainan Island. The joint working group efforts culminated in the signing of the China–Vietnam *Gulf of Tonkin Delimitation Agreement*.[117] This agreement is notable as it was China's first maritime boundary agreement and also established the northern portion of the maritime boundary between Vietnam and China.[118] The remaining maritime boundary with Vietnam remains contested.

Following a number of incidents involving hydrocarbon exploration vessels operating in the overlapping EEZ claim areas, in 2000, China and Vietnam signed a declaration to ease tensions and encourage cooperation in the South China Sea, promising to seek a 'fundamental and everlasting solution acceptable to both sides through peaceful negotiations.'[119] However, the cooperative spirit was short lived and, as discussed previously, has been followed by more incidents involving each other's hydrocarbon exploration and fishing vessels and limited diplomatic progress.

5.6.4 China–Philippines (Unresolved)

Like the case of Vietnam, a large portion of the Philippines' 200 nm EEZ entitlement overlaps with China's 'U'-shaped nine-dash line claimed area. In contrast to the other claimants in the South China Sea, the Philippines has shown preference for involving other States, calling for the US as well as the UN to be involved. The decision by the Philippines to unilaterally submit the dispute to the Permanent Court of Arbitration under the auspices of UNCLOS Annex VII in 2013 was seen as a 'gambit by Manila to internationalize the problem.'[120]

In the *South China Sea Arbitration*, the Philippines' three main grievances were (1) China was not entitled to use historical rights to justify its nine-dash claim, (2) certain maritime features that China was using to assert its maritime rights did not have the ability to generate EEZ and continental shelf entitlements, and (3) China had unlawfully interfered with the rights of the Philippines under UNCLOS and other rules of international law.[121] The Tribunal was not asked to consider sovereignty or ownership of the maritime features because the *South China Sea Arbitration* was organised under UNCLOS Annex VII and thus restricted to covering interpretational aspects of UNCLOS only, not onshore sovereignty issues. Because China had made an Article 298 declaration exempting disputes involving marine delimitation from UNCLOS compulsory dispute resolution procedures, the Tribunal could also not adjudicate on China's maritime boundaries claims.[122]

The arbitration proceedings, in which China did not participate, took three years for the Tribunal to issue its Award on Jurisdiction, and another year to issue the Awards on Merit.[123] The Tribunal award ruled

> strongly in favour of the Philippines … ruling that China's nine-dash claim had no legal basis … that three of the Spratlys features that China occupies generate no entitlement to maritime zones; and that China did violate Philippines sovereign rights of the by interfering with … vessels and by damaging the maritime environment and engaging in reclamation works.[124]

With respect to China's claim being justified by historical rights, the Tribunal ruled that:

> If China had historic rights giving it a privileged position with respect to the resources of such waters, the acceptance of the exclusive economic zone as a matter of customary law and China's adherence to the Convention altered that situation. Through the Convention, China gained additional rights in the areas adjacent to its coasts that became part of its exclusive economic zone, including the areas adjacent to any island entitled to such a zone. It necessarily follows, however, that China also relinquished the rights it may have held in the waters allocated by the Convention to the exclusive economic zones of other States.[125]

As quoted above, the Tribunal ruled that China gave up historic rights when it accepted the Convention's EEZ. Because China's nine-dash 'U'-shaped claim is not compatible with UNCLOS and no maritime feature in the Spratlys is entitled to an EEZ, the Philippines would be entitled to its full 200-nm limit.[126] China would have no rights to exploit natural resources, including hydrocarbons or fisheries, in its claimed area, thus allowing other littoral States, including the Philippines, to enjoy exclusive rights within their EEZ entitlements.

Though the Award is 'final and without appeal' and should be compiled by the parties, there is no mechanism for enforcing the tribunal's award.[127] China firmly rejected the Award, calling it 'null and void' and having 'no binding force.'[128]

Since the Award, tensions and skirmishes have continued and China has largely ignored the Tribunal Award.

5.6.5 China–Malaysia and China–Brunei (Unresolved Maritime Boundaries)

China's nine-dash 'U'-shaped claim has an 80% overlap with the EEZ entitlements of both Malaysia and Brunei. Both of these States claim sovereignty over certain maritime features in the southern Spratlys. Malaysia claims 12 features and it occupies six of them. Brunei claims two features, one of which (Louisa Reef) is also claimed by Malaysia. Both Malaysia and Brunei justify their sovereignty claim on the basis of natural prolongation of the continental shelf, but this claim may be difficult to justify as extension of the continental shelf does not, by itself, give a State the right of sovereignty over maritime features in the extended zone.[129]

China has been less aggressive against the oil and gas activities of Malaysia and Brunei compared with the other claimants in the South China Sea.[130]

5.6.6 Malaysia–Indonesia and Malaysia–Philippines (Unresolved Maritime Boundaries)

Malaysia has two unresolved maritime borders on its eastern boundary, between its state of Sabah (in northern Borneo) and the Philippines and Indonesia.

The dispute with Indonesia is related to Indonesia's interpretation of its archipelagic status within UNCLOS allowing it to draw straight baselines between its major islands and extending its EEZ to 200 nm beyond the baseline. The ICJ, in 2002, ruled that two small islands in the area, Sipadan and Ligitan, belong to Malaysia on the basis of its effective control over them.[131] Indonesia has refused to accept Malaysia's assumption that the ICJ ruling should be extended to include an EEZ around the islands, entitling Malaysia to extend its EEZ using the islands as its baseline, and overlapping Indonesian claims based on archipelagic baselines.[132]

The dispute with the Philippines can be traced back to the Sulu Sultanate, an Islamic State in the 17th and 18th centuries that ruled the southern Philippines and northern Borneo, including the current Malaysian state of Sabah. In 1878, the North Borneo Chartered Company, a British colonial company, signed an agreement with the Sultanate for the North Borneo territory.[133] The Philippines claims that this agreement was a lease rather than a 'concession' and Sabah, and the maritime areas, including prolific oil and gas resources, should be returned to the Philippines. Islamic groups continue to operate in the region and though the three States, including Indonesia, have agreed to work together to resolve the terrorist issue, the maritime boundary remains unresolved, and the claims were, in 2022, raised in European courts.[134]

5.6.7 Cambodia–Vietnam and Cambodia–Thailand (Unresolved Maritime Boundaries)

Cambodia is not a party to UNCLOS, and it has unresolved maritime borders with both its immediate neighbours. Both disputes involve the interpretation of colonial treaties – the France–Thailand treaty of 1907 affecting the resolution of the border with Thailand, and different interpretations of the *Brevie* line defining the border with Vietnam.[135]

In 2001, Cambodia and Thailand signed the *Memorandum of Understanding regarding the Area of their Overlapping Claims to the Continental Shelf in the Gulf of Thailand* to delimit their continental shelf. The MOU provided for a JDA for the overlapping area with promising oil and gas prospects, as well as for the delimitation of maritime zones in a defined 'Area to be Delimited.'[136] Since the MOU was revoked by Thailand in 2009 after onshore border skirmishes and from the appointment of a former Thai prime minister by Cambodia, there has been limited progress on the JDA or maritime border resolution.

In 1982, Cambodia and Vietnam signed the *Cambodia–Vietnam Arrangement* that established a large Joint Historical Waters Area extending from the coastlines, specifying that delimitation agreements in this area should be concluded 'at a suitable time.'[137] The 1982 agreement envisioned joint development of resources in the area, and obliged each side to give up claims to certain disputed islands, endorsing the sovereignty situation of the islands in-place since the French colonial exit.[138] The legal validity of the agreement is now in question as it was agreed with the 'Vietnam-installed' regime in Cambodia at the time, and there has been no recent progress towards a maritime boundary delimitation.[139]

5.7 Proposed JDAs: Spratly Multilateral, China–Vietnam and Malaysia–Indonesia–Philippines

In an ideal world where bilateral tensions can be put aside, a multilateral JDA covering the central portion of the South China Sea, encompassing the main

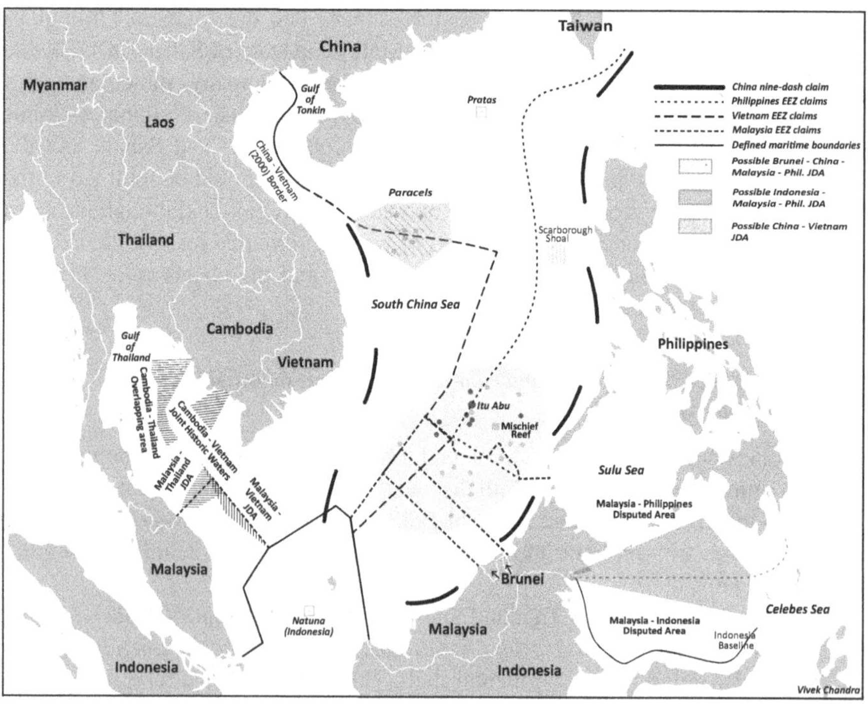

Figure 5.2 Proposed JDAs in the South China Sea

features of the Spratlys, would be the most efficient way to evaluate the hydrocarbon potential of the overlapping claim area. The Spratly JDA would be managed by a professional team and owned, in equal shares, by the littoral States. In return for funding a disproportionate share of JDA expenses, China would be the main market for any gas found by the JDA and could commit to building the export pipeline. All littoral States would have to agree to cease military activity and island building within the JDA and to abide by UNCLOS EEZ rules, including freedom of navigation.

Two smaller JDAs could also be negotiated in the region. A bilateral China–Vietnam JDA around the Paracel Islands, and a larger, tripartite JDA in the Celebes/Sulu Seas between Indonesia, Malaysia, and the Philippines.

These three proposed JDAs, shown in Figure 5.2, though difficult to negotiate, would ease tensions in the region, reduce the chance of military confrontation, and, importantly, confirm the hydrocarbon potential of the region with real data instead of unsupported estimates currently promoted.

5.8 Conclusions

The South China Sea can rightfully be described as the 'most contested maritime space in the world.'[140] Given that the disputed issues of the South China Sea are 'especially problematic,'[141] the prospects for the resolution of maritime boundary issues in the region are not promising. As Miyoshi observed in 2011, and remains true now:

> Only when the South China Sea players realize the urgent need to develop the natural resources of the area, can they possibly put aside the sovereignty issues and devise a method of sharing the resources in one way or another. Needless to say, all of this depends on the will of the States concerned: whether they can shelve, for the temporary purpose of exploiting the potential natural resources, the sensitive issue of sovereignty over the islands and islets enclosed by the dotted line in the South China Sea.[142]

Joint Development concepts have been promoted by all the claimant States, and many of the States, especially Malaysia, Vietnam, and Brunei, are presently partners in successful JDA arrangements.[143] The China–Philippines–Vietnam JMSU seismic study experience of 2004–2008 demonstrated that claimant States can work in a cooperative manner under defined guidelines, even if ultimately the effort was not successful. The multilateral Joint Development solution, as well as the two smaller JDAs, proposed in this chapter may be the most palatable option for the claimants to work together. Delimiting the joint development area and formulating an equitable profit-sharing mechanism will be difficult, but it is hard to see any other feasible option to develop hydrocarbon resources and diffuse tensions to settle maritime disputes.[144]

Notes

1 This chapter uses non-Chinese names for the maritime features of the South China Sea. For reference, the Pratas Islands are called Dongsha Qundao in Chinese, the Paracel Islands are called Xisha Qundao in Chinese, and the Spratlys are called Nansha Qundao in Chinese. Some lists also mention Macclesfield Bank and Scarborough Shoals in this list, but the three listed groups are more significant and contested.

2 Schematic map created by author based on various sources, including Nong Hong, *UNCLOS and Ocean Dispute Settlement: Law and Politics in the South China Sea* (Taylor & Francis Group, 2012) 15; US Energy Information Agency EIA, 'South China Sea' (Web page, 7 February 2013), https://www.eia.gov/international/analysis/regions-of-interest/South_China_Sea 12 'South China Sea'; Michael Bristow, 'China should respect South China Sea ruling, says Philippines' *BBC News* (14 July 2016); Sara Schonhardt and Saurabh Chaturvedi, 'South China Sea Ruling Increases Uncertainty for Shipping, Trade' *Wall Street Journal* (14 July 2016); Ralf Emmers, *Resource Management and Contested Territories in East Asia* (Palgrave Pivot, London, 2013) 91; David Ong, 'Implications of recent Southeast Asian State practice for the international law on offshore joint development' in Robert Beckman, et al. (eds), *Beyond Territorial Disputes in the South China Sea: Legal Frameworks for the Joint Development of Hydrocarbon Resources* (Edward Elgar, 2013) 181, 190; Meaghan Tobin, 'What's behind the revived dispute between Philippines and Malaysia over Sabah?' *South China Sea Morning Post* (Hong Kong, 9 September 2019).

3 M. T. Klare, *Resource Wars: The New Landscape of Global Conflict* (Henry Holt and Company, 2001) 119.

4 People's Republic of China, Ministry of Foreign Affairs, 'Historical Evidence To Support China's Sovereignty over Nansha Islands,' *The Issue of South China Sea* (Web Page, 1 November 2000) <https://www.fmprc.gov.cn/mfa_eng/topics_665678/3754_666060/t19231.shtml> ('Historical Evidence').

5 Katherine Morton, 'China's ambition in the South China Sea: is a legitimate maritime order possible?' (2016) 92(4) *International Affairs* 909, 909.

6 Sue Gronewald, 'The Ming Voyages,' *Asia For Educators – Columbia University* (Web Page, 2009) <http://afe.easia.columbia.edu/special/china_1000ce_mingvoyages.htm>.

7 Stein Tønnesson, 'The South China Sea in the Age of European Decline' (2006) 40(1) *Modern Asian Studies* 1, 3. ('SCS in the Age of European Decline').

8 Tønnesson, 'SCS in the Age of European Decline' (n 7) 3.

9 People's Republic of China, 'Historical Evidence' (n 4).

10 Stein Tønnesson, 'The South China Sea: Law Trumps Power' (2015) 55(3) *Asian Survey* 455, 466. ('SCS; Law Trumps Power').

11 Tønnesson, 'SCS in the Age of European Decline' (n 7) 29.

12 Tønnesson, 'SCS in the Age of European Decline' (n 7) 29.

13 *Treaty of Peace with Japan*, signed 8 September 1951 [1952] 136 UNTS 45 (entered into force 28 April 1952). Also known as *Treaty of San Francisco*.

14 *Treaty of Peace with Japan* (n 13) Article 2(f). In contrast, Article 2(a) lists territories, including the Quelpart Islands (Cheju in Korean) should be given to Korea.

15 Tønnesson, 'SCS in the Age of European Decline' (n 7) 41.

16 Hong (n 3) 12. Hong states that the *res nullius* claim was made by Tomas Cloma, one of the Cloma brothers who established the settlement on the Spratlys. Individuals may not be able to make *res nullius* claims; James Crawford, *Brownlie's Principles of Public International Law* (Oxford University Press, 9th edn, 2019) 245.

17 Sarah Raine and Christian Le Miere, *Regional Disorder: The South China Sea Disputes* (Taylor & Francis Group, 2013) 39.

18 *Continental Shelf Act* 1966, revised 1972 (Malaysia).

19 Tønnesson, 'SCS; Law Trumps Power' (n 10) 468.
20 Raine and Le Miere (n 17) 42.
21 *South China Sea Arbitration (The Republic of Philippines v. The People's Republic of China)* (Award) (2016) PCA Case 2013-19, 170 ILR 1, [175]. The Award excerpts the *Law on the Territorial Sea and the Contiguous Zone* (People's Republic of China) [2] which states: 'The territorial sea of the People's Republic of China is the sea belt adjacent to the land territory and the internal waters of the People's Republic of China. The land territory of the People's Republic of China includes the mainland of the People's Republic of China and its coastal islands; Taiwan and all islands appertaining thereto including the Diaoyu Islands; the Penghu Islands; the Dongsha Islands; the Xisha Islands; the Zhongsha Islands and the Nansha Islands; as well as all the other islands belonging to the People's Republic of China. The waters on the landward side of the baselines of the territorial sea of the People's Republic of China constitute the internal waters of the People's Republic of China.'
22 Carlyle A. Thayer, 'ASEAN'S Code of Conduct in the South China Sea: A Litmus Test for Community-Building?' (2012) 10(34) *The Asia-Pacific Journal: Japan Focus* 1.
23 *Declaration on the Conduct of Parties in the South China Sea*, Members States of ASEAN and People's Republic of China, signed 4 November 2002. Article 5 of the Declaration states, 'The Parties undertake to exercise self-restraint in the conduct of activities that would complicate or escalate disputes and affect peace and stability including, among others, refraining from action of inhabiting on the presently uninhabited islands, reefs, shoals, cays, and other features and to handle their differences in a constructive manner.' Article 6 of the Declaration states, 'Pending a comprehensive and durable settlement of the disputes, the Parties concerned may explore or undertake cooperative activities.'
24 Masahiro Miyoshi, 'China's "U-Shaped Line" Claim in the South China Sea: Any Validity Under International Law?' (2012) 43(1) *Ocean Development & International Law* 1, 8. Because Taiwan is not officially recognised by ASEAN, Taiwan was not invited to participate in the document.
25 Miyoshi (n 24) 11.
26 Hong (n 3) 20. After Malaysia and Vietnam submitted their claims to extend their continental shelves, China protested to the UN secretary-general, alleging that the submission 'seriously infringed China's sovereignty, sovereign rights, and jurisdiction' in the South China Sea.
27 *South China Sea Arbitration* (Award) (n 21) [182]. The Award references the *Note Verbale* from the Permanent Mission of the People's Republic of China to the United Nations to the Secretary-General of the United Nations, UN Doc CML/17/2009 (7 May 2009).
28 Mira Rapp-Hooper and Harry Krejsa, 'Reefs, Rocks, and the Rule of Law: After the Arbitration in the South China Sea' (CNAS Asia-Pacific Security Reports, April 2016) 2.
29 Tønnesson, 'SCS; Law Trumps Power' (n 10) 471. Hillary Clinton, the US Secretary of State at the time of the last request, stated: 'While we do not take sides on the competing sovereignty claims to land features in the South China Sea, as a Pacific power we have a national interest in freedom of navigation, the maintenance of peace and stability, respect for international law, and the unimpeded, lawful commerce across our sea lanes … We oppose the threat or use of force by any party to advance its claims.' The US continues to conduct Freedom of Navigation patrols in the region; Aileen S.P. Baveira, 'The Philippines and the South China Sea Dispute' and Mingjiang Li, 'China Debates the South China Sea Dispute' in Ian Storey and Lin Cheng-yi (eds), 'The South China Sea Dispute: Navigating Diplomatic and Strategic Tensions' (ISEAS Publishing, 2016) 7, 50, 172.
30 Department of Foreign Affairs of the Republic of the Philippines, 'Notification and Statement of Claim on the West Philippines Dispute' (22 January 2013).

31 Congressional Research Service Specialist in Naval Affairs (name redacted), 'Maritime Territorial and Exclusive Economic Zone (EEZ) Disputes Involving China: Issues for Congress' (Congressional Research Service Report No R42784, 12 December 2017) 21.

32 The State Council – The People's Republic of China, 'Summary of the Position Paper of the Government of the People's Republic of China on the Matter of Jurisdiction in the South China Sea Arbitration Initiated by the Republic of the Philippines' (7 December 2014).

33 Congressional Research Service (n 31) 21; Rapp-Hooper and Krejsa (n 28) 2.

34 *South China Sea Arbitration* (Award) (n 21).

35 Julian Ku, 'Assessing the South China Sea Arbitral Award after One Year: Why China Won and the U.S. is Losing,' *Lawfare* (Web Page, 12 July 2017) <https://www.lawfare-blog.com/assessing-south-china-sea-arbitral-award-after-one-year-why-china-won-and-us-losing>.

36 Edward Wong, 'U.S. Says Most of China's Claims in South China Sea Are Illegal' *New York Times* (13 July 2020).

37 Steven Lee Myers, 'China Fires Missiles Into South China Sea, Sending U.S. a Message,' *New York Times* (27 August 2020).

38 *United Nations Convention on the Law of the Sea*, opened for signature 10 December 1982, 1833 UNTS 3 (entered into force 16 November 1994) art 122. ('*UNCLOS*'). Article 122 defines a semi-enclosed sea as 'a gulf, basin or sea surrounded by two or more States and connected to another sea or the ocean by a narrow outlet or consisting entirely or primarily of the territorial seas and exclusive economic zones of two or more coastal States.'

39 Hong (n 3) 55.

40 Hong (n 3) 129. Taiwan does not qualify for membership to the Convention; UN, 'Chapter XXI: Law of the Sea,' *United Nations Treaty Collection* (Web Page, 5 October 2020) <https://treaties.un.org/Pages/ViewDetailsIII.aspx?src=TREATY&mtdsg_no=XXI-6&chapter=21&Temp=mtdsg3&clang=_en#EndDec>.

Vietnam became an UNCLOS party State on 24 July 1994, China became an UNCLOS party State on 7 June 1996, Malaysia became an UNCLOS party State on 14 October 1996, Philippines became an UNCLOS party State on 8 May 1984.

41 UN 'Chapter XXI: Law of the Sea' (n 40).

42 Chris Whomersley, 'The Award on the Merits in the Case Brought by the Philippines against China Relating to the South China Sea: A Critique' (2017) 16(3) *Chinese Journal of International Law* 387, 393; Hong (n 3) 61.

43 China is involved in seven unresolved disputes (against South Korea, Japan, Taiwan, Vietnam, the Philippines, Malaysia, and Brunei) and Malaysia in three disputes (against China, Indonesia, and the Philippines). Iran, which is grouped in the Persian Gulf region, is also involved in three unresolved disputes.

44 UN 'Chapter XXI: Law of the Sea' (n 40). The Philippines declared: 'The agreement of the Republic of the Philippines to the submission for peaceful resolution, under any of the procedures provided in the Convention, of disputes under Article 298 shall not be considered as a derogation of Philippine sovereignty.'

45 UN 'Chapter XXI: Law of the Sea' (n 40). Upon ratification of UNCLOS on 25 August 2006, China declared: 'The Government of the People's Republic of China does not accept any of the procedures provided for in Section 2 of Part XV of the Convention with respect to all the categories of disputes referred to in paragraph 1 (a), (b), and (c) of Article 298 of the Convention.' Article 298(1)(a)(i) allows a State to exclude itself from dispute resolution procedures for disputes concerning the interpretation or application of Articles 15 (Territorial Sea), 74 (EEZ) and 83 (Continental Shelf) boundary delimitations.

46 *South China Sea Arbitration (The Republic of Philippines v. The People's Republic of China)* (Award on Jurisdiction and Admissibility) (2015) PCA Case 2013-19, art 393. Paragraph 394 of 'The Award on Jurisdiction and Admissibility statement' states that, 'the Tribunal may not be able to reach the merits of certain of the Philippines' Submissions (Nos. 5, 8, and 9) without first delimiting the Parties' overlapping entitlements, a step that it cannot take in light of Article 298 and China's declaration.'
47 Hong (n 3) 70.
48 *South China Sea Arbitration* (Award) (n 21) [239].
49 *South China Sea Arbitration* (Award) (n 21) [271].
50 *South China Sea Arbitration* (Award) (n 21) [247].
51 *South China Sea Arbitration* (Award) (n 21) [256] [631].
52 *UNCLOS* (n 38) art 7. Article 7 restricts the usage of straight baselines, 'in localities where the coastline is deeply indented and cut into, or if there is a fringe of islands along the coast in its immediate vicinity.'
53 Robert Beckman, 'International law, UNCLOS and the South China Sea' in Robert Beckman, et al. (eds), *Beyond Territorial Disputes in the South China Sea: Legal Frameworks for the Joint Development of Hydrocarbon Resources* (Edward Elgar, 2013) 47, 59.
54 People's Republic of China, *Law on the Territorial Sea and the Contiguous Zone* (25 February 1992), art 3. This article states, 'The PRC's baseline of the territorial sea is designated with the method of straight baselines, formed by joining the various base points with straight lines.'
55 Maximo Paulino T. Sison III, 'Universalizing the Law of the sea in the South China Sea Dispute' (2018) 49(2) *Ocean Development and International Law* 157, 158.
56 *UNCLOS* (n 38) art 121. Article 121, Regime of islands, states that, '1. An island is a naturally formed area of land, surrounded by water, which is above water at high tide. 2. Except as provided for in paragraph 3, the territorial sea, the contiguous zone, the exclusive economic zone and the continental shelf of an island are determined in accordance with the provisions of this Convention applicable to other land territory. 3. Rocks which cannot sustain human habitation or economic life of their own shall have no exclusive economic zone or continental shelf.'
57 Davenport (n 4) 326. As discussed previously in this book, the implications for classification of maritime features are significant. An island is entitled to the same maritime zones as a mainland coastal State, including a 200 nm EEZ and continental shelf, while any lesser classification (i.e., as a 'rock') would reduce the entitlement to just a 12 nm territorial sea or, in case of low-tide features, no maritime entitlement at all.
58 *South China Sea Arbitration* (Award) (n 21) [615]; Rapp-Hooper and Krejsa (n 28) 7; M Van Dyke and Mark J. Valencia, 'How Valid are the South China Sea Claims under the Law of the Sea Convention?' (2000) *Southeast Asian Affairs* 47, 51.
59 *South China Sea Arbitration* (Award) (n 21) [618].
60 *South China Sea Arbitration* (Award) (n 21) [543].
61 *South China Sea Arbitration* (Award) (n 21) [543]. The award stated, 'Economic life, therefore, must be oriented around the feature itself and not focused solely on the waters or seabed of the surrounding territorial sea. Economic activity that is entirely dependent on external resources or devoted to using a feature as an object for extractive activities without the involvement of a local population would also fall inherently short with respect to this necessary link to the feature itself. Extractive economic activity to harvest the natural resources of a feature for the benefit of a population elsewhere certainly constitutes the exploitation of resources for economic gain, but it cannot reasonably be considered to constitute the economic life of an island as its own.'
62 *South China Sea Arbitration* (Award) (n 21) [543].
63 Van Dyke and Valencia (n 58) 51.

64 Elizabeth Mendenhall, 'Interpreting the law of the sea "regime of islands": An opportunity for productive US leadership' (2019) 99 *Marine Policy* 213, 213.
65 *South China Sea Arbitration* (Award) (n 21) [330].
66 Tara Davenport, 'Island-Building in the South China Sea: Legality and Limits' (2018) 8 (1) *Asian Journal of International Law* 76, 76.
67 *UNCLOS* (n 38) art 60(1). Article 60(1) states: 'In the exclusive economic zone, the coastal State shall have the exclusive right to construct and to authorise and regulate the construction, operation and use of: (a) artificial islands.' Article 60(8) states, 'Artificial islands, installations and structures do not possess the status of islands. They have no territorial sea of their own, and their presence does not affect the delimitation of the territorial sea, the exclusive economic zone or the continental shelf.'
68 *South China Sea Arbitration* (Award) (n 21) [508].
69 Mendenhall (n 64) 214, 215. Mendenhall questions if claimant States will further clarify the status of artificial installations that have destroyed natural reefs and required massive dredging campaigns to construct.
70 EIA, 'South China Sea' (n 3) 4.
71 EIA, 'South China Sea' (n 3) 2.
72 EIA, 'South China Sea' (n 3) 2.; Asia Maritime Transparency Initiative, A Blueprint for Cooperation on Oil and Gas Production in the South China Sea (Research Paper, The Center for Strategic and International Studies, 2018) 1. For comparison, China's daily consumption of oil is 12.8 million bbls, equating to 4.6 billion bbls of oil a year.
73 Morton (n 5) 923.
74 Sanqiang Jian, 'Multinational Oil Companies and the Spratly Dispute' (1997) 6(16) *Journal of Contemporary China* 591, 597.
75 Jian (n 74) 598.
76 Bill Hayton, *The South China Sea: the struggle for power in Asia* (Yale University Press, 2014) 130.
77 Philip Shenon, 'China Sends Warships to Vietnam Oil Site,' *New York Times* (21 July 1994).
78 Hayton (n 76) 138.
79 Ramses Amer, 'China, Vietnam, and the South China Sea: Disputes and Dispute Management' (2014) 45(1) *Ocean Development & International Law* 17, 23. Amer quotes the vice chairman of the National Border Committee.
80 Amer (n 79) 21.
81 Morton (n 5) 923.
82 Morton (n 5) 923.
83 James Pearson, 'As Rosneft's Vietnam unit drills in disputed area of South China Sea, Beijing issues warning,' *Reuters* (17 May 2018).
84 EIA, 'South China Sea' (n 3) 6.
85 Hong (n 3) 13.
86 Robert Beckman, 'Tribunal ruling a game changer,' *Straits Times* (Singapore, 14 July 2016) 5.
87 *South China Sea Arbitration* (Award) (n 21) [652] [653]. In 2010, the exploration permit was converted to a Service Contract that would allow production from the area.
88 *South China Sea Arbitration* (Award) (n 21) [654]. The Award references the *Note Verbale* from Embassy of People's Republic of China in Manila to the Department of Foreign Affairs, Republic of Philippines, No. (10) PG-047 (22 February 2010).
89 *South China Sea Arbitration* (Award) (n 21) [654]. The Award references the *Note Verbale* from the Department of Foreign Affairs, Republic of Philippines to Embassy of People's Republic of China in Manila No. (10) PG-047 (2 March 2011).
90 International Crisis Group, 'Stirring up the South China Sea (IV): Oil in Troubled Waters' (*Asia Report* No 275, 26 January 2016) 15.
91 International Crisis Group (n 90) 15.
92 International Crisis Group (n 90) 2.

93 Zou Keyuan, 'Joint Development in the South China Sea: A New Approach' (2006) 21(1) *Int'l J. Marine & Coastal L.* 83, 103.
94 International Crisis Group (n 90) 3.
95 International Crisis Group (n 90) 16.
96 International Crisis Group (n 90) 17.
97 International Crisis Group (n 90) 17.
98 Hayton (n 76) 132.
99 *Declaration on the Conduct of Partibes in the South China Sea* (n 23) art 6. Article 6 of the 2002 DoC states, 'Pending a comprehensive and durable settlement of the disputes, the Parties concerned may explore or undertake cooperative activities. These may include the following: a. marine environmental protection; b. marine scientific research'; Hong (n 3) 184.
100 Hayton (n 76) 134.
101 Hong (n 3)185; Hayton (n 76) 135.
102 The JMSU remains the only example of a three-State JDA identified by this book – but as it is no longer active, it is not included in the database.
103 EIA, 'South China Sea' (n 3) 3.
104 Morton (n 5) 918.
105 Sison (n 55) 158. As per estimates quoted by Sison, the line overlaps 60–70% of Vietnam's EEZ entitlement, 80% of both the Malaysian and Philippines South China EEZ entitlements, and 90% of Brunei's EEZ entitlement; US Department of State, 'China's Maritime Claims in the South China Sea' *Limits in the Seas* (Report No. 143, Office of Ocean and Polar Affairs, Bureau of Oceans and International Environmental and Scientific Affairs, 5 December 2014) 4. It should be noted that a 2014 US Department of State calculates the area covered by the 'U'-shaped nine-dash line claim to be 2 million km^2.
106 Congressional Research Service (n 31) 25.
107 US Dept of State (n 105) 4.
108 Sison (n 55) 158; China also submitted to the UN a map showing the nine dashes which encircled most of the maritime features of the South China Sea in 2009. This was prompted by Vietnam and Malaysia's joint submission to the UN Commission on the Limits of the Continental Shelf to extend their entitlements. Permanent Mission of the People's Republic of China, *Note Verbale dated 7 May 2009 from the Permanent Mission of the People's Republic of China to the Secretary-General*, UN Doc CML/17/2009 (7 May 2009). The Statement declared, 'China has indisputable sovereignty over the islands in the South China Sea and the adjacent waters and enjoys sovereign rights and jurisdiction over the relevant waters as well as the seabed and subsoil thereof … The above position is consistently held by the Chinese government and is widely known by the international community.'
109 Tønnesson, 'SCS; Law Trumps Power' (n 10) 463; Congressional Research Service (n 31) 25; US Dept of State (n 105) 4. Prior to 1953, the 'U'-shaped line had 11 dashes. After 1953, the dashes in the Gulf of Tonkin were dropped and the line thereafter has nine dashes. However, the exact positions of the dashes have changed over time and the dashes are not uniformly spaced.
110 Miyoshi (n 24) 3.
111 Sison (n 55) 158.
112 Congressional Research Service (n 31) 27.
113 *South China Sea Arbitration* (Award) (n 21) [200]. The Award quotes the Director-General of the Department of Treaty and Law at the Chinese Ministry of Foreign Affairs in 2016.
114 Ministry of Foreign Affairs of the Republic of China (Taiwan), 'Solemn declaration of the Ministry of Foreign Affairs of the Republic of China concerning the Philippine Senate Bill 2699 and House Bill 3216' (6 February 2009). The declaration stated, '[t]he Ministry of Foreign Affairs of the Republic of China solemnly declares as fol-

lows: 1. In terms of either history, geography, reality or international law, the Spratly Islands, Paracel Islands, Macclesfield Islands, Pratas Islands, as well as the surrounding waters, are the existent territories of the Republic of China. The fact that sovereignty of these areas belongs to our government is undeniable, Taiwan enjoys and deserves all rights accordingly. Any sovereignty claims over, or occupation of, these islands and their surrounding waters will not be recognised by the government of the Republic of China.'

115 Cheng-yi Lin, 'Taiwan's South China Sea Policy' (1997) 37(4) *Asian Survey* 323, 323.

116 Lin, C. (n 114) 334, 337.

117 China US Focus, 'Maritime Delimitation in the Gulf of Tonkin is Too Important to be Ignored,' *Security* (Web Page, 29 May 2015) <https://www.chinausfocus.com/peace-security/maritime-delimitation-in-the-gulf-of-tonkin-is-too-important-to-be-ignored#>.

118 China US Focus (n 116). The Gulf of Tonkin agreement also demonstrated Vietnam's preference for using a single line for both continental shelf and EEZ in areas with overlapping claims.

119 Amer (n 79) 20.

120 Ian Storey, 'Slipping Away? A South China Sea Code of Conduct Eludes Diplomatic Efforts' (2013) 11 *East and South China Seas Bulletin* 5.

121 Sison (n 55) 158.

122 *South China Sea Arbitration* (Award) (n 21) [395]. The Tribunal recognised China's UNCLOS Article 298 declaration in its Award, stating that 'the resulting overlap and the exclusion of boundary delimitation from the Tribunal's jurisdiction by Article 298, would prevent the Tribunal from addressing the Submissions.'

123 *South China Sea Arbitration* (Award) (n 21). The Award was issued on 12 July 2016.

124 Congressional Research Service (n 31) 21.

125 *South China Sea Arbitration* (Award) (n 21) [257].

126 Beckman (n 86) 5.

127 *UNCLOS* (n 38) annex VII, art 11; Congressional Research Service (n 31) 21.

128 Hao Duy Phan and Lan Ngoc Nguyen, 'The South China Sea arbitration: bindingness, finality, and compliance with UNCLOS dispute settlement decisions' (2018) 8(1) *Asian Journal of International Law* 36, 36.

129 Hong (n 3) 19.

130 International Crisis Group (n 90) 2.

131 *Sovereignty over Pulau Ligitan and Pulau Sipadan (Indonesia/Malaysia)* [2001] ICJ Reports 575.

132 Stephen Druce and Efri Baikoeni, 'Circumventing Conflict: The Indonesia–Malaysia Ambalat Block Dispute' in M. Oishi (ed.), *Contemporary Conflicts in Southeast Asia* (Springer Science + Business Media, 2016) 137, 139.

133 Tobin (n 3).

134 Tobin (n 3).

135 Nguyen Hong Thao, 'Joint Development in the Gulf of Thailand' (1999) Autumn 1999 *IBRU Boundary and Security Bulletin* 79,76. The *Temple of Preah Vihear (Cambodia v. Thailand)* (Judgment) (1961) ICJ Reports 52 also dealt with the same French-Thai treaty and dealt with the sovereignty of a temple located on the border between the two States.

136 Clive Schofield, 'Defining Areas for Joint Development in Disputed Waters' (Conference Paper, Recent Development of the South China Sea Dispute and Prospects of Joint Development Regime, 6–7 December 2012, Haikou, China) 4, 16.; Veasna Var, 'Cambodia–Thailand Sovereignty Disputes: Implications for Cambodia's Strategic Environment and Defence Organization' (2017) 41(2) *Strategic Analysis* 152, 153. According to Var, 'Cambodia remains highly optimistic that offshore natural resources will significantly boost its economy.'; Ong (n 3) 189; Ben Milligan, 'Legal and policy

options for the provisional joint management of maritime spaces subject to overlapping jurisdictional claims (PhD thesis, University of Wollongong, 2012) 172.
137 Milligan (n 136) 175 n 382. See Figure 5.1 for the location of this area.
138 Milligan (n 136).
139 Ong (n 3) 190–191.
140 Morton (n 5) 911.
141 Hong (n 3) 55.
142 Miyoshi (n 24) 12.
143 Keyuan (n 93) 109.
144 Keyuan (n 93) 109.

6 Maritime Borders

Persian Gulf

6.1 Introduction

The Persian Gulf[1] is arguably one of the most strategically and economically important bodies of water in the world. Though the Gulf is a relatively small body of water, with a total length of 900 km and maximum width of less than 300 km, it lies at the crossroads of ancient trade routes between Asia, Europe, and Africa. Bordering this enclosed body of water are two dominant States, Iran and Saudi Arabia, a collection of four relatively wealthy petro-States (Kuwait, Bahrain, Qatar, and the United Arab Emirates (UAE)), plus two larger States with limited Gulf coastlines, Iraq and Oman. The Persian Gulf has more littoral States than the larger Caspian and South China Seas.

Geographically, the Persian Gulf is known for its shallowness, with an average depth of only 50 m, its single connection to the open sea via the narrow Straits of Hormuz, and the presence of massive oil and gas deposits under and along its coasts. Many of the world's largest hydrocarbon resources are in the region, including both the world's largest offshore oil field (Al-Safaniya off the Saudi Arabian coast) and natural gas field (South Pars-North Field shared between Qatar and Iran).[2] Through the narrow 6-km-wide shipping channel in the Straits of Hormuz, nearly one-fifth of the global oil, and a quarter of global liquefied natural gas exports are transported.

The wider Middle East region, as well as the immediate area around the Persian Gulf, has been a perennial conflict zone. Prior to the mid-20th century, the region was ruled by tribal sheikhs and prominent families who did not prioritise concepts of sovereignty and territorial definition.[3] The concept of precise border delimitation in this region emerged after the British decision to withdraw from the region in the late 1960s.[4] This period coincided with discoveries of massive offshore and onshore oil reserves which further 'underlined the urgency of defining various states boundaries before the matter developed into a new series of conflicts.'[5]

Prior to the exploitation of hydrocarbons in the area, maritime boundaries were largely defined by fishing and pearling beds close to the shoreline. As the littoral States raced to explore the oil, and later, natural gas resources in their coastal waters by granting concessions to international companies, the need for maritime delimitation became increasingly important.[6] Iran, which has maritime boundaries with seven littoral States, recognised the need to delimit its boundaries as

DOI: 10.4324/9781003323051-6

a precursor to exploration and exploitation of hydrocarbons earlier than most of the other States.[7] As discussed in this chapter, only Iran's maritime borders in the northern reaches of the Gulf (between Iran and Iraq and Iran and Kuwait) and a portion of its border with the UAE in the southern Gulf remain unresolved and in dispute today.

Saudi Arabia, Iran's rival for dominance in the region, has asserted its political dominance in the region by fostering territorial and maritime claims.[8] Saudi Arabia has been involved in nine out of the 15 territorial and maritime border disputes in the Gulf since 1922.[9] Coincidently, many of the Saudi Arabian hydrocarbon fields are located close to onshore and offshore frontiers with the UAE, Oman, Qatar, Bahrain, Kuwait, and Iran.

Unlike other regions where multilateral organisations and other neutral third parties have been involved in resolving boundary disputes, the role of these entities in the Gulf region has been limited. Though most of the Gulf States (with the exception of Iran and Iraq) are members of the Gulf Cooperation Council (GCC), the Council's efforts to mediate border disputes between its members have been largely unsuccessful. This could be a result of Saudi Arabia's domination of the Council, thereby all but limiting its ability to be a neutral party in any inter-member disputes.[10] For example, both Saudi Arabia and the GCC were involved in attempts to resolve the long-running dispute between Qatar and Bahrain involving the Hawar Islands and the associated maritime boundary, but their efforts eventually failed and the dispute was finally resolved by the ICJ.

It is notable that only four maritime borders in the region remain unresolved – three involving Iran and the fourth being the long-running dispute between Iraq and Kuwait. All other maritime boundaries in the Gulf have been resolved by peaceful bilateral negotiations, notwithstanding the aforementioned ICJ-mandated Bahrain–Qatar settlement. Also notable is that most maritime boundary agreements in the region include specific articles about sharing or dividing hydrocarbon activities near maritime borders.

The Gulf region has been a pioneer in introducing, formulating, and operating the JDA concept to develop hydrocarbon fields that straddle maritime boundaries. The 1958 *Bahrain–Saudi Arabia Boundary Agreement* was the world's first hydrocarbon JDA agreement and still operating today.[11] This was followed by agreements which included JDA clauses between Kuwait and Saudi in 1965[12] and Qatar and the UAE in 1969.[13]

Six out of the eight littoral Gulf States are UNCLOS party States. Iran and the UAE have signed the Convention but have not completed the process to ratify it.[14] Various aspects of UNCLOS have been relevant for maritime delimitation in the Gulf. In particular, the rights of littoral States in semi-enclosed seas, the limited width of the Gulf resulting in overlapping EEZ claims, proportionality versus equity in determining maritime zones, the use of straight baselines and archipelagic baselines, historic claims to islands, and the rights of States to limit navigation in transit straits, have all contributed to the remaining unresolved maritime borders in the Gulf. Figure 6.1 shows the Gulf's maritime boundaries, EEZs, and location of select oil and gas fields relevant to these boundaries.

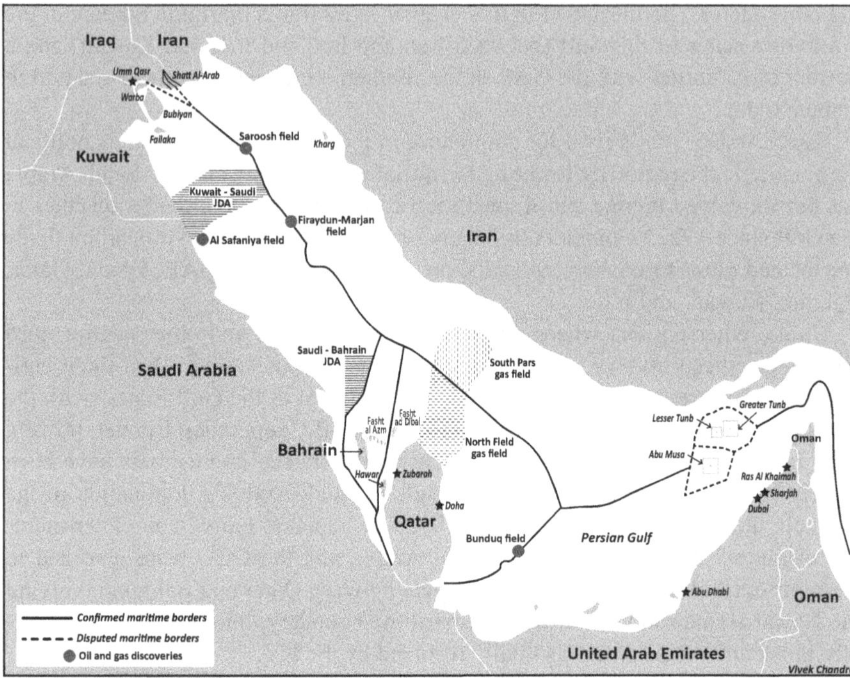

Figure 6.1 Schematic map showing the Persian Gulf, disputed areas, and certain oil and gas fields.[15]

6.2 Legal Background

From the 16th century until the 20th century, a sizeable portion of the Gulf region was under the effective control of the Ottoman Empire. In addition to the Ottomans, European powers, including the Portuguese, followed by the Dutch and the French, have also asserted their influence in the region. It was the British, however, who had the greatest impact in establishing relationships with tribal leaders and transforming their controlled territories into formal 'Western-model' States.[16]

In 1913, the British and Ottoman powers formally defined their respective 'spheres of influence' in the region with the execution of the *Anglo-Ottoman Convention of 1913*.[17] In the northern reaches of the Gulf, the British gained certain rights over the strategic Shatt al-Arab waterway between Iraq and Iran.[18] In the central and southern Gulf regions, beyond Ottoman-controlled areas, the British convinced local sheikhs to sign treaties of protection, whereby the British became responsible for their foreign affairs as well as defence.[19] Though the stated aim of the British was to maintain freedom of maritime trade and eradicate the slave trade in the Gulf region, they ultimately assumed responsibility for defence and foreign affairs matters for all the littoral States, except Saudi Arabia and Iran. For the local rulers, these agreements were their first experience with treaties that were binding not only on them, but also on their heirs and successors.[20]

As the Ottoman Empire collapsed in the aftermath of WW I, the British expanded their influence in the Gulf. British civil and military routes crossed the region on the way to India and beyond, prompting the building of communication infrastructure, airports, and emergency landing sites. To protect these assets, which were often in remote areas, from theft and destruction, the British negotiated protection agreements with local rulers obliging them to exercise greater control over their territories and citizens.[21] When oil was discovered in the region at the beginning of the 20th century, this influence allowed Britain's de-facto national oil company at the time, the Anglo-Persian Oil Company, to become the primary holder of the concessions to produce these resources, beating rivals from Europe and America.[22]

Prior to the discovery of oil, there was no perceived need to define the boundaries of each sheikh's territory. As interest in exploration expanded beyond coastal settlements, delimitation of territorial limits became imperative. Formerly imprecise boundaries, such as the infamous 'southernmost palm tree' marker used to define a section of the Iraq and Kuwait border, were deemed no longer sufficient.[23]

In the northern Gulf, at the confluence of Iran, Iraq, and Kuwait, precarious and shifting boundaries have resulted in wars extending since the 1980s. Though most of the onshore boundaries have now been defined, three maritime boundaries in the northern Gulf remain unresolved. Because of the presence of offshore oil and gas and strategic considerations dealing with waterways, the potential for serious conflict remains.

Iran, recognising in the 1960s that its Gulf coast was emerging as a major hydrocarbon resource region, began negotiations with other States to divide the Gulf. These efforts began in 1965, and by 1974, Iran had signed maritime border agreements with Saudi Arabia, Qatar, Bahrain, and Oman.[24] In 1966, Iran and Britain, on behalf of its protectorates in the Gulf, 'reaffirmed the principle of the median line of the Persian Gulf as the basis for dividing the continental shelf of that sea.'[25] The median line methodology was later adopted by subsequent maritime boundary agreements in the Gulf.[26]

In 1968, Britain announced its decision to withdraw from the Gulf. This action injected an urgency to the States to define their borders and sovereignty. Within a few years, all six Arab Gulf States, including Kuwait, Bahrain, Qatar, the UAE, Oman, and Saudi Arabia, became independent States dealing directly with each other instead of via British channels. In the early 1980s, the Arab Gulf States (with the exception of Iraq) formed the GCC. The GCC was created, in part, to resolve ongoing border and other disputes between member countries.[27]

The 1990s also began the period when the regional States accelerated efforts to develop their onshore and offshore hydrocarbon reserves. The settlement of previously undefined boundaries was a 'prerequisite' for exploration activities to proceed, and resulted in 'fixing, finalisation and (in most cases) demarcation of much more precise boundary delimitation.'[28]

At the 1994 GCC summit, the Supreme Council pledged to resolve outstanding bilateral border issues between its members.[29] At the time, the only remaining outstanding border issue between GCC States was the dispute over the Hawar Islands between Qatar and Bahrain.[30] Bahrain, which had hosted the 1994 GCC summit, initiated the year-long timeline to pressure Qatar to reach a bilateral settlement before the ICJ was to begin formal proceedings on the case in 1995.[31] The GCC efforts to resolve the dispute were not successful, and the dispute eventually went to the ICJ. The ICJ's *Qatar v. Bahrain* case is the only maritime border dispute between Arab States adjudicated by the ICJ and was the 'longest and most complex case brought to the Court.'[32]

The two decades following the *Qatar v. Bahrain* settlement have been punctuated by instability within Iraq, tensions between Iran and its Arab neighbours, and conflicts in the wider region (including Afghanistan, Yemen, and Syria). Since the UNCLOS in-force date of 1994, there has been no tangible progress towards resolution of the four outstanding maritime border disputes in the Gulf, three of which involve borders between northern Gulf States of Iraq, Kuwait, and Iran.[33]

6.3 Applicability of UNCLOS

Six of the eight littoral Gulf States are parties to UNCLOS. The remaining States, Iran and the UAE, have both signed the Convention but have not completed its ratification.[34]

As UNCLOS III was being debated, the categorisation of enclosed bodies of water became a relevant question for the Gulf States.[35] Iran, along with a handful of other States (including most of the Baltic States which saw the parallels between the Baltic Sea and the Gulf) wanted to separate the particular issues facing semi-enclosed seas from the general Convention.[36] The Iranian representatives promoted the view that the circumstances of enclosed and semi-enclosed seas raised problems which could only be solved by regional or bilateral agreements.[37] On the other side of this debate was Iraq (along with certain Mediterranean States) which wanted UNCLOS and its rules to regulate the rights of all States, including those surrounding semi-enclosed seas.[38]

Ultimately, the text of UNCLOS included a section on semi-enclosed seas. In Article 123, the Convention implores bordering States to cooperate with each other on matters of living resources, to protect the environment, and to coordinate scientific research.[39] Significantly, UNCLOS is silent on matters regarding cooperation for non-living resources, including hydrocarbons. This may have been a factor in encouraging the Gulf States, earlier than those in other regions with larger enclosed seas, to innovate their agreements to facilitate cooperation to jointly develop or amicably divide offshore hydrocarbon resources.

6.3.1 Maritime Delimitations

The development of maritime boundaries in the Gulf has been based primarily on the precedents set by the two dominant States, Iran and Saudi Arabia. In 1934, Iran claimed territorial waters of 6 nm measured from straight baselines. In 1949, Saudi Arabia followed identical principles. In 1958, Saudi Arabia expanded its territorial sea to 12 nm: This was followed by Iran, which made a similar declaration in 1959.[40]

Iran has proclaimed straight baselines along its entire coastline. As there are relatively few islands on the northern shore of the Gulf, this does not conform to UNCLOS Article 7(1).[41] The Iranian use of straight baselines has been disputed by the US and others as it affects the transit of ships through the Straits of Hormuz, as is discussed later in this chapter.[42]

6.3.2 Islands

In a majority of the regions discussed previously in this book, the status of islands and maritime features is a source of friction and is present in almost all maritime boundary disputes involving hydrocarbons.[43] Though the dominant Gulf countries, Iran and Saudi Arabia, do not have many coastal islands, the UAE (in particular, the emirate of Abu Dhabi) has over 200 islands and sandbanks along its coastline. Islands are also present off the coasts of Kuwait, Bahrain, Qatar, and Oman. As in the South China Sea, there have been efforts to classify low-level sand banks and shoals as 'islands' to gain maritime advantage.[44] This has been made more difficult because few of the islands in the Gulf are inhabited, and others have a history of only 'sporadic occupation.'[45]

Iran, with relatively few islands on its side of the Gulf, has stated its preference for islands not to influence baselines for all Gulf States.[46] However, in its ongoing maritime border dispute with Kuwait, both States have used their respective islands to establish their claim limits. The waters in the disputed area between these two States are considered to be among the richest oil reservoir areas in the Gulf.[47] Disputed islands between Iran and the UAE are also surrounded by oil- and gas-rich waters, and strategically located close to the Straits of Hormuz.[48]

One aspect of the Bahrain–Qatar dispute discussed below is the status of the Fasht ad Dibal shoal. This low-tide feature is located east (on the Qatari side) of the 1947 British-mandated equidistant borderline between Bahrain and Qatar. At that time, the British did not consider shoal features as islands that would be entitled to territorial waters.[49] However, in 1936, before the drawing of the borderline, the ruler of Bahrain granted offshore exploration rights around Fasht ad Dibal to the Bahrain Petroleum Company and a subsidiary of the Anglo–Iranian Oil Company.[50] The oil exploration partners subsequently converted the low-tide shoal into an artificial island to facilitate exploration efforts, further complicating the status of the feature.[51]

The status of Fasht ad Dibal was a subject of debate within the British Admiralty. Should the shoal be considered to be part of Qatar, as per the equidistance line principle, or should the British recognise the ruler of Bahrain's grant to the oil companies, which would benefit British commercial interests? In the latter case, the follow-on question was whether the artificial structure the oil companies built to facilitate their activities would generate a territorial sea zone for Bahrain.

In 1952, the British Admiralty closed the discussion by stating that 'artificial islands should not have territorial waters.' Bahrain subsequently declared that Fasht ad Dibal and adjacent Qit'at Jaradah as Bahraini 'islands' which remain dry at high tide and possess their own maritime zones. Qatar, on the other hand, protested that the features are not 'islands' and should belong to Qatar.[52] The issue, as discussed later in this chapter, was resolved by the ICJ in 2001.

UNCLOS Article 13 is clear that low-tide elevations cannot be used to claim territorial seas when located beyond the breadth of another territorial sea.[53] UNCLOS, however, is silent about the sovereignty or territorial status of low-tide elevation features. Although UNCLOS Article 60 grants the exclusive rights for States to build artificial islands within their maritime zones, the Convention is clear that artificial islands do not have the status of islands, and are not entitled to any maritime zones, including territorial sea.[54]

Of the four unresolved maritime border disputes in the Gulf, three involve the sovereignty and role of islands in maritime delimitation. The only ongoing dispute that does not involve the status of islands is the Iran–Iraq maritime boundary, although there are disputed sandbanks in the disputed Shatt al-Arab waterway. Three of the unresolved disputes are in the triangular marine area between Kuwait, Iraq, and Iran in the northern reaches of the Gulf. The last involves Iran and the UAE in the southern extent of the Gulf, near the mouth of the Straits of Hormuz. These unresolved disputes are detailed in later this chapter.

6.4 Oil and Gas Activities

The Persian Gulf is notable for two unique features: The relatively large number of coastal States around its periphery, and the massive oil and gas resources, both onshore and offshore, that have been discovered within the Gulf basin.

These two features make the Gulf one of the most strategically important regions in the world.[55] The presence of oil and gas in benign shallow water and coastal environments encouraged the littoral States to be among the first to extend their jurisdictions beyond their territorial sea limits.[56] Many of these jurisdictional extensions resulted in overlapping continental shelf and EEZ claims, creating 'obstacles towards delimitation' in the region.[57]

Oil was discovered in the region over a century ago. In other regions, the norm would be to define onshore borders prior to delimitation of maritime zones. In the Gulf, the dominant States, Iran and Saudi Arabia, pragmatically negotiated many of their offshore borders prior to resolution of all their onshore borders. This was a pragmatic solution to allow the development of offshore oil and gas resources while minimising conflicts between the newly defined States.

Iran, which occupies the entire north coast of the Gulf, realised earlier than other States that its continental shelf boundary would have to be defined as a 'first step in the exploration of the hydrocarbon resources in the seabed and the subsoil of the Persian Gulf.'[58] In 1949, a draft bill was submitted to the Iranian Parliament to define its continental shelf along its coast. The *Act of 18 June 1955 on the Exploration and Exploitation of the Natural Resources of the Continental*

Shelf of Iran[59] was the first to discuss subsea resources of the area.[60] In 1993, the Government of Iran passed the *Act on the Marine Areas of the Islamic Republic of Iran in the Persian Gulf and Oman Sea.*[61] The Act updated the *1955 Continental Shelf Act* and was criticised by the US in a 1994 Department of State report for non-compliance with UNCLOS in relation to Iran's use of straight baselines, right to suspend innocent passage in parts of its territorial sea, and rights to control the laying of cables and pipelines within its claimed EEZ.[62]

6.4.1 JDA Status

After passage of Iran's *1955 Continental Shelf Act*, all subsequent Iranian maritime border agreements included provisions to prevent unequal exploitation of reserves located near the maritime borders. The subsequent bilateral agreements prohibited the drilling of wells within 125 m of the maritime boundary (500 m in the case of the Iran–Saudi Arabia maritime boundary) without mutual agreement of the two States. They also included provisions obliging parties to coordinate activities or agree to divide a hydrocarbon resource which straddles the delimited boundary.[63] For example, the 1968 *Saudi Arabia–Iran Agreement* provided that the two States would divide oil fields equally based on 'the concept of an equitable division of the oil in the place.' A dedicated section of the agreement deals with oil exploration and production activities, including specifications on drilling protocols.[64]

Iranian encouragement for cooperative development is a precursor to the JDA concept, which was first formally adopted by Saudi Arabia and Bahrain. The region has three of the world's earliest negotiated JDAs (1958 Bahrain–Saudi Arabia, 1965 Kuwait–Saudi Arabia, and 1969 Abu Dhabi–Qatar). The fourth, between Iran and Sharjah (one of the Emirates in the UAE) was signed in 1971 but ongoing hostilities have prevented its implementation. Iran is not involved in any of the active JDAs in the Gulf (or in the Caspian where the active JDA is between Russia and Kazakhstan).[65]

6.4.2 Bahrain–Saudi Arabia JDA

The maritime area between the island of Bahrain and the Saudi Arabian mainland is shallow with low-tide elevation features. In 1941, Bahrain independently granted a concession to explore hydrocarbons in the area. Operations were stopped due to objections by the Saudi government.[66]

A 1949 Saudi Arabian Royal Pronouncement obliged Saudi Arabian maritime boundaries to be 'determined in accordance with equitable principles' and established in agreement with other States having jurisdiction.'[67] This philosophy led to the 1958 *Bahrain–Saudi Arabia Boundary Agreement.*[68] The JDA agreement allowed Bahrain to accept Saudi jurisdiction over the resources in return for half of the net revenue of the oil fields.[69] This revenue-sharing arrangement continues to the present day. The 1958 agreement evolved into a comprehensive maritime boundary agreement, which became the first maritime boundary agreement in the Gulf.[70]

6.4.3 Kuwait–Saudi Arabia JDA

The second JDA agreement in the world was also in the Gulf. After the establishment of their onshore borders in 1922, Kuwait and Saudi Arabia agreed to designate a large region along their coast as a 'neutral zone' under control of both States. Oil was discovered in this 5,700-km^2 area and produced cooperatively until the zone's eventual onshore partition in 1965.[71] The zone's offshore area, which included a number of islands, was left unsettled under the 1965 agreement.[72] The 1965 agreement specified that the States, 'shall exercise their equal rights in the submerged area beyond the aforesaid six-mile limit mentioned, by means of joint exploitation, unless the two Parties agree otherwise.'[73]

From 1965, hydrocarbon revenues were shared, and oil fields operated 'harmoniously.'[74] In 2000, Iran began drilling on an offshore gas field at the edge of the zone, in an area also claimed by both Saudi Arabia and Kuwait. This prompted Saudi Arabia and Kuwait to delimit their neutral zone offshore areas to prevent further encroachment by Iran. Their offshore JDA agreement, signed in 2000, granted the disputed islands to Kuwait, and stipulated that any oil or gas reserves were to be shared equally by the two States.[75]

6.4.4 Abu Dhabi (UAE)–Qatar JDA

The third JDA in the Gulf involves Abu Dhabi (one of the emirates in the UAE) and Qatar. Since the mid-19th century, the neighbours have been locked in a dispute over a number of small islands and associated maritime area.[76] In 1961, Britain dictated that the al-Ashat and Shara'iwa islands belonged to Qatar, but smaller islands in the group, including al-Dayyina belonged to Abu Dhabi. In 1969, Qatar and Abu Dhabi signed their maritime border agreement accepting the British decision.[77]

One of the geographical points on the boundary line defined by the 1969 agreement is the Bunduq oilfield. The 1969 agreement called for the field to be shared equally between Abu Dhabi and Qatar, and to be operated by the Abu Dhabi National Oil Company developing the field under a pre-existing concession from the Ruler of Abu Dhabi.[78] The settlement is seen as an example of the 'unity of deposit' concept in JDA agreements.[79] The Bunduq field continues to produce significant oil and gas today.

6.5 Maritime Borders

Most of the maritime borders in the Persian Gulf have been resolved by negotiation or by JDA agreements. The Bahrain–Qatar maritime border is the sole resolution via ICJ adjudication. Four maritime borders, three involving Iran, remain unresolved.

6.5.1 Bahrain–Qatar (Resolved by the ICJ)

Since 1936, Bahrain and Qatar have disputed sovereignty of the Hawar Islands, the shoals of Fasht ad Dibal (discussed above), Fasht al Jaradah shoal, Zubarah (an onshore district on the Qatar peninsula), and the maritime boundary between the two States. Though pearling and fishing were also discussed by the ICJ in the *Qatar v. Bahrain* case, the main prize was oil and gas resources whose ownership was determined by the sovereignty of the islands and the location of the maritime border.[80]

The main disputed island group was the Hawar Islands, located between the southeast coast of Bahrain and Qatar's southwestern coast. The largest island in the group is less than a mile off the coast of Qatar and, at low tide, can be reached on foot from the Qatari mainland.[81] Historically, the islands have been occupied by Assyrians, Romans, Persians, Macedonians, and Portuguese. The Al Khalifa tribe, which continues to rule Bahrain today, invaded and defeated the resident tribes on the island in 1783. In 1936, Bahrain granted oil exploration rights to the Bahrain Petroleum Company and Anglo-Persian Oil Company (later renamed Anglo-Iranian, and subsequently, British Petroleum, and more recently, BP) after erecting a military garrison on the island the previous year. This prompted protests by Qatar, and in 1939, the British Political Resident was asked to mediate between the two protectorate States. The official ruled in favour of Bahrain and the commercial interest of Anglo-Persian Oil Company.[82]

In 1976, Qatar reiterated that the islands were 'an integral part' of Qatar. This prompted military activities by Bahrain on the island and the detention of Qatari fisherman operating in the area.[83] During the ensuing years, there were several attempts to resolve the disputes through bilateral negotiations and mediation by Saudi Arabia and the GCC.[84] However, it was not until 1980, when Bahraini exploration efforts confirmed the potential of 'trillions of barrels' around the Hawar Islands, and Bahrain's realisation that without maritime border resolution, further drilling could not proceed without provoking Qatar, that resolution attempts began with 'immediate willingness.'[85]

In 1986, the dispute 'nearly escalated to war' after Bahrain constructed a coast guard station on Fasht ad Dibal, prompting the dispatch of 100 Qatari troops who seized the construction site. In response, Bahrain deployed its troops to the Hawar Islands. Qatar began building a bridge to Hawar Island from the Qatari mainland, declaring the Hawar Islands as a Qatari military zone.[86]

The ICJ was asked to adjudicate on the dispute by Qatar in 1991. It would be another five years before Bahrain consented to the ICJ involvement and gave up on regional mediation.[87] After ten years of deliberations, the ICJ gave its judgment in 2001.[88]

The Court accepted its mandate to draw a single maritime line for all maritime zones.[89] The decision awarded each State approximately half of the islands and shoals, and delimited an equidistance line adjusted for special circumstances, in accordance with UNCLOS Article 15.[90] The single maritime boundary line extends northward to the Iranian maritime boundary line.

Underscoring the role of oil and gas in the dispute, on the same day that the ICJ ruling was announced, Bahrain's ruler invited international oil companies to begin exploration and exploitation in the now delimited maritime zone.[91] Qatar granted exploration concessions in its awarded area in 2002.[92]

What was not fully appreciated at the time of the ICJ judgment was the enormous potential of the North Dome (also known as 'North Field') gas field. The North Dome gas field begins only 9 nm from Fasht ad Dibal and extends into Iran. Thanks to the ICJ ruling, the field is undisputedly not in Bahraini waters. The field is the world's largest offshore gas field and the source of natural gas for Qatar's massive liquefied natural gas (LNG) industry, enabling Qatar to be one of the richest countries in the world today. Without the resolution of the dispute, the development and resulting massive economic gains from the North Dome field may not have been realised.

6.5.2 Iran–Saudi Arabia (Resolved)

Saudi Arabia and Iran have the longest and most significant maritime boundary in the Gulf, with implications for all other maritime boundaries in the Gulf.[93] Between 1948 and the eventual signing of the maritime border agreement in 1968, both States independently granted oil and gas exploration concessions to international exploration companies in overlapping claim areas. This prompted each to claim infringement of their rights, creating 'serious obstacles to their orderly resource development.'[94]

In 1964, the two rivals agreed to resolve the status of two islands, Farsi and Al'Arabiyaha, as well as the rest of their maritime boundary.[95] The negotiations reached final agreement in 1968 (ratified in 1969), prompted by the announcement of British withdrawal from the Gulf. The desire to set an example to other Gulf States to also resolve their maritime boundaries may have been a motivation for both States to finalise the agreement.[96]

The Iran–Saudi Arabia maritime boundary follows the median line, except where it intercepts the giant Firaydun–Marjan oilfield.[97] The field was discovered by Saudi Arabia in 1964 after the maritime border negotiations had begun.[98] The two countries agreed to adopt an 'economic solution' which involved determining the reserve estimates in the field and agreeing to a proportional divided ownership, instead of a JDA solution. The maritime border was shifted to the agreed proportion, and the result is each State receiving 'a mutually-acceptable share of the oil and of the offshore area.'[99] Each State also received one of the disputed islands.[100]

6.5.2.1 Northern Gulf Region

In the crowded triangular area in the far northern reaches of the Gulf are three long-running converging maritime border disputes. The maritime border disputes can be traced back to two unresolved onshore borders, both of which have resulted in relatively recent wars (between Iran and Iraq and between Iraq and Kuwait). The maritime border disputes (between Iran and Iraq, Iraq and Kuwait, and Iran and Kuwait) are unlikely to be resolved prior to comprehensive onshore border agreements, even though the offshore area is known to be rich with hydrocarbon resources.[101]

6.5.3 Iran–Iraq (Unresolved)

Arguably, the most protracted border tension in the Gulf is the ancient dispute between Iran and Iraq. The core of the dispute is control over Shatt al-Arab, the 120-mile waterway that divides Iran and Iraq formed by the convergence of Iraq's Tigris and Euphrates rivers.[102] With the exception of Shatt al-Arab, and the more limited (but deeper water) western access via the Khor Abdullah waterway adjoining the Iraq–Kuwait border, Iraq is a landlocked country. With only 58 km of coastline, Iraq has the shortest Gulf coastline of any littoral State.[103]

During the Ottoman period, both banks of the Shatt al-Arab were under the control of the Ottomans. Following the end of WW I, the Kingdom of Iraq was established in 1921. Iraq assumed it had inherited, as a successor to the Ottoman Empire, the sovereignty rights over the Shatt al-Arab previously held by the Ottomans. This was disputed by Iran, whose access to its own ports on the waterway was restricted by Iraq. After debates at the League of Nations, the two States signed the 1937 *Border Agreement* that reasserted Iraq's control over the Shatt al-Arab, with the exception of a 4-mile anchorage where the border ran along the thalweg (deepest channel) line at the approaches to Abadan and Khorramshahr, the two main Iranian ports on the Shatt al-Arab.[104]

After the 1968 British withdrawal announcement from the Gulf, the Shah of Iran proclaimed Iran as the new 'guardian of the Gulf' and asserted its powers over the Straits of Hormuz, the islands of Abu Musa and the Tunbs (discussed in detail below), and the Shatt al-Arab.[105] Iran challenged the 1937 Border Agreement, demanding that the entire Shatt al-Arab waterway border should be thalweg boundary, along the deepest channel, not the median line.[106] Because the median line was not always the navigable channel, Iranian shipping was perceived to be at a disadvantage under the previous arrangement.

Skirmishes between the two States intensified in 1974–1975, with heavy casualties pushing the Iraqi army. The 1979 Iranian Revolution and subsequent creation of the Islamic Republic of Iran prompted Iraqi president Saddam Hussein to invade Iran, beginning an eight-year-long war between them. During the war, Iraq was effectively landlocked due to blockages in Shatt al-Arab.

In 1990, Iraq invaded Kuwait. Two weeks after its invasion, Iraq abandoned its territorial claims to Shatt al-Arab, accepting Iranian terms for a settlement reverting to the thalweg line.[107] This surprising move was seen as a way for Iraq to 'neutralise' the Iranian Republic from the Iraq's invasion of Kuwait taking place on Iraq's western coast. Iran took advantage of Iraq's overtures and registered the border settlement correspondence with the UN.[108] However, Iran and Iraq have yet to sign any formal document accepting the settlement.

The two States have long recognised that joint exploration of hydrocarbon resources located in the disputed maritime zone would be in the best interests of both parties. As early as 1963, Iran and Iraq announced that they had agreed on a basis for joint exploration for oil resources. However, this agreement was never signed.[109]

6.5.4 Iraq–Kuwait (Unresolved)

Iraq's only alternative access to the Gulf (other than via the Shatt al-Arab) is along its western border with Kuwait. Iraq's territorial ambitions in Kuwait and its coastal region can be traced back to the 1890s when Britain began taking an interest in the Sheikdom of Kuwait to stop a German plan to build a railway from Europe through Ottoman Iraq, to terminate in Kuwait.[110] In 1913, Britain and the Ottomans executed an agreement and Kuwait subsequently became a British protectorate.[111] In the aftermath of WW I, Britain gained control over the foreign policies of both Iraq and Kuwait, and in 1921, the British Colonial Office drew a line across southern Iraq 'in order to create Kuwait and prevent Iraq's access to the Gulf.'[112]

The 1932 Britain–Iraq agreement granted the islands of Warba and Bubiyan, at the mouth of the Khor Abdullah waterway, to Kuwait. The Khor Abdullah waterway provides the sole access to Iraq's two deepwater shipping ports of Umm Qasr and Khor Al Zubair.[113] The narrow waterway, which handles 80% of Iraq's imports, widens at its mouth, where it is 16.5 km across.[114] The islands and the waterway have long been the targets of Iraqi territorial ambitions.[115] Ownership of the islands would influence each country's Gulf access, baselines, and maritime zone limits, an area where oil deposits are likely to be found.[116]

Iraq never fully accepted the 1932 agreement granting the disputed islands to Kuwait.[117] The dispute culminated when, in 1990, Iraqi forces invaded Kuwait and quickly gained control of the country. In 1991, the US and its coalition forces attacked Iraq, pushing their forces out of Kuwait.

The following year, in 1992, a UN-sponsored commission began work on demarcation of the Iraq–Kuwait border, including partial delimitation of the maritime border. The furthest offshore point delimited by the UN was less than 3 nm from the coastlines, well short of the 12 nm territorial sea claims. Though the onshore borders were formally accepted by Kuwait in 1993 and, reluctantly, by Iraq in 1994 (and reaffirmed in 2013), the extent of the maritime limits of their respective territorial sea and EEZ remains undefined and disputed.

Iraqi claims over the islands and maritime areas continue, with some factions within Iraq continuing to believe that Iraq got a 'raw deal' from the UN commission.[118] Both sides have built artificial structures and port facilities along the waterway, accusing the other of encroaching on its maritime areas as well as promoting oil exploration activities in the disputed area.

6.5.5 Iran–Kuwait (Unresolved)

Though Iran and Kuwait do not share an onshore frontier, they have overlapping maritime claims in the northern Gulf.

In the late 1950s, Kuwait granted Kuwait Shell Company an offshore exploration permit for the area. In 1960, Iran objected to the concession, calling it 'incompatible and inconsistent with previous agreements.' A few years later, the National Iranian Oil Company offered two locations in the same area to international exploration companies. This was followed by meetings between the two governments to resolve demarcation of the maritime border and continental shelf.

The main points of disagreement were the median line base points around Kharg island (occupied by Iran) and Failaka Island (occupied by Kuwait). Kharg island is located 16 miles off the coast of Iran and is the world's largest oil loading terminal. The status of the Soroosh oil field, located in the middle of the Gulf, straddling the median line between Iran and Kuwait, also remains unresolved.

In 1970, both sides agreed to an equidistance boundary line generally measured from the coasts, adjusted for the two islands. Iran argued that since Kharg island was connected to the mainland by pipeline, its baseline should be drawn from Kharg, not the mainland. This would give Iran undisputed sovereignty over the Soroosh oil field.[119]

Kuwait countered with a similar treatment for Failaka island, allowing Kuwait to measure its Persian Gulf baselines from the island.[120] Though the two States have agreed to these baseline principles, their maritime border remains unresolved, and will likely remain until their mutual maritime boundaries with Iraq are resolved.

6.5.6 Iran–UAE (Unresolved)

The last unresolved maritime dispute in the Gulf involves three small islands strategically located near the southern entrance to the Gulf, close to the shipping channels of the Straits of Hormuz. The islands, with a collective size of 25 km^2, have been occupied by Iran since they were taken by force from Sharjah (in the case of Abu Musa Island) and Ras Al Khaimah (in the case of Greater and Lesser Tunb islands) at the time of the British withdrawal from the region in 1971. Sharjah and Ras Al Khaimah became a part of the UAE in the same year, and since then, the UAE and Iran have clashed over the sovereignty of the islands and the maritime zones around the islands.

The two Tunb islands lie 15 nm southwest of Iran's much larger Qeshm Island and 40 nm from the UAE coastline. Thus, they would lie on the Iranian side of a median line.[121] The larger Greater Tunb Island has a small settlement and is 4 km in diameter. In contrast, the smaller Lesser Tunb is uninhabited and devoid of water supplies.

Abu Musa is larger, with an area of 10 km^2, and has a permanent population of around 2,000 workers and Iranian settlers from the mainland. Abu Musa is only 33 nm from Sharjah, and thus on the UAE side of the median line. The Mubarak oil field is located to the east of Abu Musa.

The dispute can be traced back to the 18th century when the islands were held by the Qasimi family from Sharjah. Negotiations between the British, who operated on behalf of the Trucial States (predecessor to the UAE) and the Iranians, who claimed that the Qasimi family held the islands in tribute to the Iranians, floundered until Iran established a customs post in 1904. The British protested, and in 1913, retaliated by constructing a lighthouse on Greater Tunb. After the Qasimi family divided its residence between Sharjah and Ras Al Khaimah, the British recognised

Abu Musa as belonging to Sharjah and the Tunbs belonging to Ras Al Khaimah. Until the 1960s, little attention was paid to the islands. However, with the discovery of oil resources in the immediate region, increased awareness of their strategic importance to shipping lanes, and the announced withdrawal of the British in 1968, Iran reasserted its claims.[122]

In January 1968, Iran dispatched a navy frigate to Greater Tunb, provoking a British Royal Air Force response.[123] The British were 'deeply disturbed' and warned the Iranians of their 'commitments to the ruler [of Sharjah] under our treaty commitments.'[124]

The British wanted Iran to accept the median line of the Gulf as the boundary, thereby granting the Tunbs Islands to the Iranians and Abu Musa to Sharjah (UAE).[125] In August 1968, the Iranian Prime Minister offered the ruler of Ras Al Khaimah a share of any mineral wealth in return for Iranian sovereignty to the Tunbs. Ras Al Khaimah rejected the offer, and instead offered to lease the islands to Iran without relinquishing sovereignty. Iran rejected this offer. The standoff continued, and in early 1971, Iran dispatched a warship and landing party to Greater Tunb which occupied the islands for three days.[126]

As the date of British withdrawal, and independence of the UAE, grew closer, the British pressured Sharjah to accept sovereignty for Abu Musa. Under their proposed solution, Iran and Sharjah would each occupy a defined area of the island, and any oil revenues from the surrounding 12-nm territorial sea would be shared equally between Sharjah and Iran.[127] In late November 1971, a few days after the British proposal was accepted by the Iranians, Iran occupied the northern portion of Abu Musa. Iran also occupied the Tunbs, which were not a part of the shared proposal, provoking a skirmish in which both Ras Al Khaimah and Iran suffered fatalities. Because the British did not actively stop the Iranians from their actions in the Tunbs, several delegates to the UN Security Council accused the British of colluding with Iran.[128]

On 1 December 1971, the British officially exited from the Trucial States, and the UAE was born as an independent State. In the meantime, Iran continued to build infrastructure on the islands, including roads and schools. In 1992, Iran unilaterally claimed rights of control over exit and entry to Abu Musa.[129] All Arabs on the island were deported, and Iran refused to negotiate with the UAE on the grounds that its 1971 pact was with Sharjah, not the UAE. The GCC has regularly called on Iran to withdraw from all three islands. Though Iran and the UAE have signed a partial maritime boundary agreement, for areas north of the disputed islands, the agreement has not come into force.

Because of the location of the islands, especially the Tunbs, close to important shipping channels, the sovereignty of the islands also has geopolitical implications. The US and Iran have frequently clashed in the region, both accusing each other of overstepping their international rights. Iran has been accused of claiming 12-nm territorial seas around the islands, but then restricting navigation of ships, especially US warships, through the seas.[130] Article 19 of UNCLOS allows innocent passage of foreign ships, without exception for warships.[131] Iran claims that these rights are only reserved for parties of UNCLOS, and since the US is not a signatory, the US is not 'entitled to exercise transit passage in the Strait of Hormuz.'[132] However, Iran, though a signatory, never ratified the Convention and is also not party to UNCLOS.

The US maintains that the right of innocent passage has 'entered into customary law' (and predates UNCLOS) and is thus binding on all States. Clashes between Iran and the US continue, with recent incidents including the shooting down of an American drone in the area in June 2019.[133] It seems unlikely that the status of islands, their related maritime borders, and stranded hydrocarbons, will be resolved until there is a motivation by Iran to accept the terms of the 1971 agreement and withdraw from Abu Musa and from the Tunbs.

6.6 Proposed JDAs: Iran–Iraq–Kuwait and Iran–UAE

There are two distinct regions of maritime border disputes in the Persian Gulf: In the far north at the confluence of Iran, Iraq, and Kuwait, and in the south, near the Straits of Hormuz. Optimistically, they can both be resolved with two new JDA agreements, as shown in Figure 6.2.

The first proposed JDA would be a trilateral agreement over the disputed areas between Iran, Iraq, and Kuwait. As discussed earlier in this chapter, earlier efforts by Iran and Iraq to negotiate a JDA stalled as relations between them deteriorated. Adding Kuwait to the agreement could help to balance traditional rivalries between

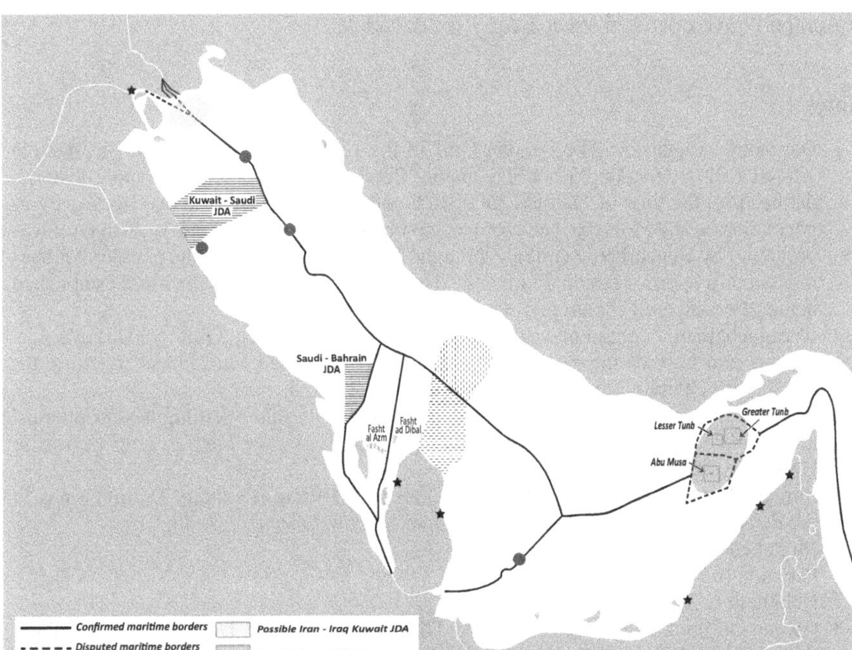

Figure 6.2 Proposed JDAs in the Persian Gulf

Iran and Iraq and bring valuable financial and technical resources that could be difficult for Iraq and Iran to mobilise themselves. The JDA would begin beyond the Kuwait–Iraq maritime border delimited by the 1992 UN-sponsored commission and extend over disputed Iran–Kuwait and Iran–Iraq maritime border areas. The area of the JDA would be relatively small, allowing for easier management and monitoring of the activities by all States.

Another potential JDA would be in the southern Gulf, around the Abu Musa and Tunbs islands. The JDA could include the producing Mubarak field. Though Iran and the UAE have tense diplomatic relations, they are relatively large trading partners. As a commercial arrangement, a JDA agreement could be more palatable than a political solution. The known gas resources in the area could be exported to the UAE, which currently imports pipeline and LNG.

6.7 Conclusions

The Persian Gulf represents, in a small geographic area, numerous issues related to offshore hydrocarbon production. The region's maritime boundary disputes involve historical justifications, the role of islands and low-tide features, inconsistent baselines, and delimitation principles. These disputes have led to skirmishes and to brutal wars. However, on a positive note, the region has shown that maritime disputes can be resolved by bilateral negotiations, intervention of outside bodies such as the ICJ, and, significantly, by JDA agreements that were pioneered in the region and have operated successfully for decades.

Notes

1 Dariusz R. Bugajski, 'The Persian Gulf in the Light of the Law of the Sea' (2016) XXXII *Prawo Morskie* 23 n 1. The name 'Persian Gulf' is considered more historic, dating from the time of Darius I (500 BC), and was the name used by Greek geographers, Strabo and Ptolemy. The more recent introduction of the name Arabian Gulf was promoted by General Nasser of Egypt in the 1950s as a result from the pan-Arab movement and to oppose Iranian dominance. However, this book uses the more established name, 'Persian Gulf' or simply, 'Gulf.'
2 Reza Dehghani, 'Continental Shelf Delimitation in the Persian Gulf' (PhD thesis, UN Oceans and Law of the Sea, The Nippon Foundation and Max Planck Institute for Comparative Public Law and International Law, 2009) 4.
3 J. E. Peterson, 'Sovereignty and Boundaries in the Gulf States Settling the Peripheries' in Mehran Kamrava (ed.), *The International Politics of the Persian Gulf* (Syracuse University Press, 2011) 21, 23.
4 Pirouz Mojtahed-Zadeh and BahadorIn Zarei, 'Maritime Boundary Delimitations in the Persian Gulf' (2017) 14(2) *International Studies Journal (ISJ)* 49, 51.
5 Mojtahed-Zadeh and Zarei (n 4) 53.
6 Peterson (n 3) 29.
7 Dehghani (n 2) 4.
8 Gwenn Okruhlik and Patrick J. Conge, 'The Politics of Border Disputes on the Arabian Peninsula' (1999) 54(2) *International Journal* 230, 248.
9 Krista E. Wiegand, 'Resolution of Border Disputes in the Arabian Gulf' (2014) 1(1) *The Journal of Territorial and Maritime Studies* 33, 35. ('Resolution of Border Disputes').

10 Wiegand, 'Resolution of Border Disputes' (n 9) 42.
11 *Bahrain–Saudi Arabia Boundary Agreement,* signed 22 February 1958 (entered into force 26 February 1958). The Second Clause of the Agreement simply states, 'The exploitation of the oil resources in this area will be carried out in the way chosen by His Majesty on the condition that he grants to the Government of Bahrain one half of the net revenue accruing to the Government of Saudi Arabia and arising from this exploitation, and on the understanding that this does not infringe the right of sovereignty of the Government of Saudi Arabia nor the right of administration over this above-mentioned area.'
12 *Agreement between the Kingdom of Saudi Arabia and the State of Kuwait concerning the submerged area adjacent to the divided zone,* signed 2 July 2000. The onshore agreement was signed in 1965. The offshore agreement, signed in 2001 states (in the Annex), 'The two countries have agreed that the natural resources in the submerged area adjacent to the divided zone shall be owned in common.'
13 *Agreement between Qatar and Abu Dhabi on the settlement of maritime boundaries and ownership of islands*, signed 20 March 1969 (entry into force 20 March 1969).
14 UN, 'Chapter XXI: Law of the Sea,' *United Nations Treaty Collection* (Web Page, 5 October 2020) <https://treaties.un.org/Pages/ViewDetailsIII.aspx?src=TREATY&mtdsg_no=XXI-6&chapter=21&Temp=mtdsg3&clang=_en#EndDec>. Iraq, Kuwait, Saudi Arabia, Bahrain, Qatar, and Oman are UNCLOS party States. Saudi Arabia is the only one to have made an Article 298(1) declaration rejecting compulsory dispute resolution procedures for border delimitation; *Vienna Convention on the Law of Treaties,* signed 23 May 1969 (entered into force 27 January 1980) 1115 UNTS 331 [18]. Article 18 states 'that a State is obliged to refrain from acts which would defeat the object and purpose of a treaty when: (a) It has signed the treaty or has exchanged instruments constituting the treaty subject to ratification, acceptance or approval, until it shall have made its intention clear not to become a party to the treaty.' Iran has chosen to accept certain aspects of UNCLOS, but has also chosen not to accept certain obligations, such as freedom of navigation in the Straits of Hormuz.
15 Will D. Swearingen, 'Sources of Conflict over Oil in the Persian/Arabian Gulf' (1981) 35(3) Middle East Journal 314, 325; Yoshifumi Tanaka, 'Reflections on Maritime Delimitation in the Qatar/Bahrain Case' (2003) 52(1) The International and Comparative Law Quarterly 53, 64; Sameer A. Marzoq, 'Northern Arabian Gulf A Critical Area For Maritime Safety and Security' (Msc thesis, World Maritime University, Malmo, Sweden, 2013) 41; Bugajski (n 1) 33.
16 Shahram Chubin and Charles Tripp, 'Domestic politics and territorial disputes in the Persian Gulf and the Arabian Peninsula' (1993) 35(4) *Survival* 3, 4.
17 *Anglo–Ottoman Convention of 1913*, signed 19 July 1913; S. H. Amin, 'The Iran-Iraq Conflict: Legal Implications' (1982) 31(1) *The International and Comparative Law Quarterly* 167, 169. ('Iran-Iraq Conflict').
18 Amin, 'Iran-Iraq Conflict' (n 17) 169–170.
19 Peterson (n 3) 24.
20 Peterson (n 3).
21 Peterson (n 3).
22 Marzoq (n 15) 4. Marzoq confirms that the formation of Anglo-Persian was to facilitate oil production in the region. The majority of the shares were acquired by the British Government in 1914, effectively nationalising the company. Anglo-Persian became Anglo-Iranian, and in 1954, the name was changed to British Petroleum. In 1998, the name was changed to BP.
23 Okruhlik and Conge (n 8) 233.
24 Greg Shapland, 'The maritime boundaries of the Arab Gulf states' *Arab Digest* (2018) 2, 3. Not all portions of the Iran–Oman period were completely defined by 1974. The remaining portion was delimited in 2015.
25 Mojtahed-Zadeh and Zarei (n 4) 53.

26 Mojtahed-Zadeh and Zarei (n 4) 53.
27 Krista E. Wiegand, 'Bahrain, Qatar, and the Hawar Islands: Resolution of a Gulf Territorial Dispute' (2012) 66(1) *Middle East Journal* 79, 88. ('Bahrain, Qatar, and Hawar Islands').
28 Richard Schofield, 'Finalising the Arabian territorial framework' (1997) 2(3) *Geopolitics and International Boundaries*, 90, 95.
29 Schofield, (n 28) 95.
30 Other maritime border disputes between GCC members and other littoral States continue to the present day. These include unresolved borders between Iran–Kuwait, Iran–Iraq, and Iraq–Kuwait.
31 Schofield, (n 28) 95.
32 Wiegand, 'Bahrain, Qatar, and Hawar Islands' (n 27) 80.
33 The fourth unresolved maritime dispute involves the seas around the three islands near the Straits of Hormuz claimed by both Iran and UAE.
34 Bugajski (n 1) 29.
35 *United Nations Convention on the Law of the Sea*, opened for signature 10 December 1982, 1833 UNTS 3 (entered into force 16 November 1994) art 122. UNCLOS article 122 defines 'enclosed and semi-enclosed seas' as '[a] gulf, basin or sea surrounded by two or more States and connected to another sea or the ocean by a narrow outlet or consisting entirely or primarily of the territorial seas and exclusive economic zones of two or more coastal States.'
36 Shapour S. Milan, 'The Legal Status of the Persian Gulf as a Semi-Enclosed Sea' (1987) 25(1) *Archiv des Völkerrechts – Japan and International Law* 92, 102.
37 *Enclosed and semi-enclosed seas*, Third United Nations Conference on the Law of the Sea, 1973–1982, volume II 2nd sess., 38th mtg, Agenda Item 17 (13 August 1974) A/CONF.62/C.2/SR.38 [1]; Milan, (n 36) 99.
38 Milan, (n 36) 99.
39 *UNCLOS* (n 35) art 123.
40 Bugajski (n 1) 30.
41 *UNCLOS* (n 35) art 7(1). UNCLOS allows straight baselines only 'in localities where the coastline is deeply indented and cut into, or if there is a fringe of islands along the coast in its immediate vicinity.'
42 Stuart Kaye, 'Indian Ocean maritime claims.' (2010) 6(1) *Journal of the Indian Ocean Region* 113, 119.
43 Clive Schofield and Richard Schofield, 'Testing the Waters: Charting the Evolution of Claims to and From Low-Tide Elevations and Artificial Islands' (2016) 1(1) *Asia-Pacific Journal of Ocean Law and Policy* 37, 38.
44 Swearingen (n 15) 319. Low-tide elevations were an important factor in the *Qatar v. Bahrain* case where both States pleaded to consider its claims on these features as islands with maritime zones.
45 Swearingen (n 15) 320.
46 Swearingen (n 15) 320.
47 Swearingen (n 15) 320. The contested Soroosh field is located in these disputed waters. See Figure 6.1.
48 James Kraska, 'Legal Vortex in the Strait of Hormuz' (2014) 54(2) *Virginia Journal of International Law* 323, 364.
49 Barbara Kwiatkowska, 'The Qatar v. Bahrain Maritime Delimitation and Territorial Questions Case' 33(3–4) *Ocean Development & International Law* 227, 237.
50 Wiegand, 'Bahrain, Qatar, and Hawar Islands' (n 27) 82.
51 Schofield, C. and Schofield, R. (n 43) 45.
52 Kwiatkowska (n 49) 237.
53 *UNCLOS* (n 35) art 13. Article 13 Low-tide elevations states, '1. A low-tide elevation is a naturally formed area of land which is surrounded by and above water at low tide but submerged at high tide. Where a low-tide elevation is situated wholly or partly

at a distance not exceeding the breadth of the territorial sea from the mainland or an island, the low-water line on that elevation may be used as the baseline for measuring the breadth of the territorial sea. 2. Where a low-tide elevation is wholly situated at a distance exceeding the breadth of the territorial sea from the mainland or an island, it has no territorial sea of its own.'

54 *UNCLOS* (n 35) art 60(1) and 60(8). Article 60(1) states: 'In the exclusive economic zone, the coastal State shall have the exclusive right to construct and to authorise and regulate the construction, operation and use of: (a) artificial islands.' Article 60(8) states, 'Artificial islands, installations and structures do not possess the status of islands. They have no territorial sea of their own, and their presence does not affect the delimitation of the territorial sea, the exclusive economic zone or the continental shelf.'

55 Bugajski (n 1) 33.

56 Dehghani (n 2) 151.

57 Dehghani (n 2) 151.

58 Dehghani (n 2) 121–122.

59 Dehghani (n 2) 119–122; *Act of 18 June 1955 on the Exploration and Exploitation of the Natural Resources of the Continental Shelf of Iran.* English translation referenced in United Nations Legislative Series, National Legislation and Treaties Relating to the Law of the Sea, UN Doc. ST/LEG/SER.B/16, 151 (1974). ('*1955 Iran Continental Shelf Act*').

60 Dehghani (n 2) 119.

61 US Department of State, 'Iran's Maritime Claims' (Working Paper, No 114 Limits in the Sea, Office of Ocean Affairs, Bureau of Oceans and International Environmental and Scientific Affairs). The Act is reproduced in this US Department of State report.

62 US Department of State (n 61). The report details all the US objections to the Iranian Act.

63 Mojtahed-Zadeh and Zarei (n 4) 54.

64 *Saudi Arabia–Iran Agreement*, signed 24 October 1968 (entry into force 29 January 1969). 696 UNTS 189.

65 Azamat Batyrov, 'Russia, Kazakhstan Push For Hydrocarbon Expansion With Kurmangazy Project,' *Caspian News* (9 December 2018). Russia and Kazakhstan jointly explore and develop the Kurmangazy field which straddles their non-disputed maritime boundary.

66 Swearingen (n 15) 328.

67 Charles G MacDonald, 'Regionalism and the Law of the Sea: The Persian Gulf Perspective' (1980) 33(5) *Naval War College Review* 73, 74.

68 *Bahrain-Saudi Arabia Boundary Agreement* (n 11).

69 *Bahrain-Saudi Arabia Boundary Agreement* (n 11). The Second Clause of the Agreement simply states, 'The exploitation of the oil resources in this area will be carried out in the way chosen by His Majesty on the condition that he grants to the Government of Bahrain one half of the net revenue accruing to the Government of Saudi Arabia and arising from this exploitation, and on the understanding that this does not infringe the right of sovereignty of the Government of Saudi Arabia nor the right of administration over this above-mentioned area.'

70 Swearingen (n 15) 328.

71 Wiegand, 'Resolution of Border Disputes' (n 9) 36.

72 Peterson (n 3) 36.

73 Dehghani (n 2) 108.

74 Peterson (n 3) 44.

75 *Agreement between the Kingdom of Saudi Arabia and the State of Kuwait concerning the submerged area adjacent to the divided zone,* signed 2 July 2000. Annex I of the agreement states, 'The two countries have agreed that the natural resources in the submerged area adjacent to the divided zone shall be owned in common.'

76 Peterson (n 3) 37.

77 *Agreement between Qatar and Abu Dhabi on the settlement of maritime boundaries and ownership of islands* (n 13).
78 *Agreement between Qatar and Abu Dhabi on the settlement of maritime boundaries and ownership of islands* (n 13). Paragraph 6 states, 'That ownership of al-Bunduq field shall be divided equally between the two Parties, which agree to consult periodically with respect to all matters relating to said field and its exploitation in order to exercise their rights thereto on the basis of equality.'
79 Dehghani (n 2) 111.
80 *Maritime Delimitation and Territorial Questions between Qatar and Bahrain* (*Qatar v. Bahrain*) [2001] ICJ Rep 40.[4]; Swearingen (n 15) 326.
81 Swearingen (n 15) 326.
82 Peterson (n 3) 31.
83 Swearingen (n 15) 326.
84 Wiegand, 'Bahrain, Qatar, and Hawar Islands' (n 27) 82.
85 Wiegand, 'Bahrain, Qatar, and Hawar Islands' (n 27) 89.
86 Wiegand, 'Bahrain, Qatar, and Hawar Islands' (n 27) 84.
87 Wiegand, 'Bahrain, Qatar, and Hawar Islands' (n 27) 86.
88 Wiegand, 'Bahrain, Qatar, and Hawar Islands' (n 27) 79; Glen Plant, 'Maritime Delimitation and Territorial Questions between Qatar and Bahrain (Qatar v. Bahrain)' ((2002) 96(1) *The American Journal of International Law* 198, 198. Libya is the only other Arab state to use the ICJ. However, its territorial dispute (with Chad) and maritime dispute over the continental shelf (with Malta) were against non-Arab States.
89 *Maritime Delimitation and Territorial Questions between Qatar and Bahrain* (*Qatar v. Bahrain*) (Merits Judgment of 16 March 2001) [2001] ICJ Rep 40 [168].
90 *Qatar v. Bahrain* (Merits) (n 89) [175] [176]; *UNCLOS* (n 35) art 15. Article 15 states, 'Where the coasts of two States are opposite or adjacent to each other, neither of the two States is entitled, failing agreement between them to the contrary, to extend its territorial sea beyond the median line every point of which is equidistant from the nearest point on the baselines from which the breadth of the territorial seas of each of the two States is measured. The above provision does not apply, however, where it is necessary by reason of historic title or other special circumstances.'
91 Wiegand, 'Bahrain, Qatar, and Hawar Islands' (n 27) 90.
92 Wiegand, 'Bahrain, Qatar, and Hawar Islands' (n 27) 91.
93 MacDonald (n 67) 75; S. H. Amin, 'Customary Rules of Delimitation of the Continental Shelf: The Gulf States Practice' (1980) 11(4) *Journal of Maritime Law and Commerce* 509, 513.
94 Amin (n 93) 514.
95 Dehghani (n 2) 122.
96 MacDonald (n 67) 76.
97 Swearingen (n 15) 328.
98 Offshore Technology, 'Marjan Oil Field Development' (Web Page). <https://www.offshore-technology.com/projects/marjan-oil-field-development/>.
99 Swearingen (n 15) 328–329.
100 MacDonald (n 67) 75.
101 Swearingen (n 15) 323.
102 Amin, 'Iran-Iraq Conflict' (n 17) 169.
103 The situation of Iraq and its access to the sea has similarities to the *Obligation to Negotiate Access to the Pacific Ocean (Bolivia v. Chile)* [2018] ICJ Rep 507 case, and, as stated earlier, to the situation of Germany in the *North Sea Cases* (*Ger. v. Den.; Ger. v. Neth.*).
104 Efraim Karsh, 'Geopolitical Determinism: The Origins of the Iran-Iraq War' (1990) 44(2) *Middle East Journal* 256, 261; Marzoq (n 15) 26.
105 Karsh (n 104) 264.

106 Randall Lesaffer, 'The Iran-Iraq Border: A Story of Too Many Treaties' *Oxford Public International Law* (Web Page, 11 August 2015) <https://opil.ouplaw.com/page/iran-iraq-border>.
107 Schofield, (n 28) 101.
108 Schofield, (n 28) 101.
109 Amin, 'Iran-Iraq Conflict' (n 17) 187.The situation has been summarised by Amin, who stated that, 'If Iran and Iraq settle their dispute over the Shatt al-Arab and Iranian territory, it is hoped that they will be more amenable to offshore boundary in the Gulf by mutual agreement. Both the customary rules of international law require States to enter negotiations, aiming at mutual agreement as regards any dispute boundaries. In the absence of agreement, and against a background conflict, Iran and Iraq are obliged under the provisions of the Peaceful Settlement of Disputes to submit their dispute to the Court of Justice.'
110 Schofield (n 28) 98. Britain's success in pushing out the Ottomans from the Gulf has certainly contributed to Iraq feeling 'squeezed out of the Persian Gulf.'
111 George Joffé, 'Arab frontier disputes: The consequences for Arab security' (1996) 1(2) *Geopolitics and International Boundaries* 159, 168; Peterson (n 3) 41.
112 Marzoq (n 15) 39.
113 Marzoq (n 15) 27. The Port of Umm Qasr handles 80% of Iraqi imports; Nazli Tarzi, 'This land is ours: Iraqi-Kuwait tensions rise in waterway row,' *Middle East Eye* (9 February 2017).
114 Marzoq (n 15) 27; Tarzi (n 113).
115 Dehghani (n 2) 111.
116 Swearingen (n 15) 323.
117 Marzoq (n 15) 40.
118 Shapland (n 24) 4.
119 Dehghani (n 2) 141.
120 Dehghani (n 2).
121 Richard A. Mobley, 'The Tunbs and Abu Musa Islands: Britain's Perspective' (2003) 57(4) *Middle East Journal* 627, 629.
122 Peterson (n 3) 35.
123 Mobley (n 121) 630.
124 Mobley (n 121) 631.
125 Mobley (n 121) 631.
126 Mobley (n 121) 634.
127 Mobley (n 121) 643.
128 Mobley (n 121) 644.
129 Joffé (n 111) 171.
130 Kraska (n 48) 365.
131 *UNCLOS* (n 35) art 19. Article 19 states: 'Passage is innocent so long as it is not prejudicial to the peace, good order or security of the coastal State. Such passage shall take place in conformity with this Convention and with other rules of international law'; Nilufer Oral, 'Transit Passage Rights in the Strait of Hormuz and Iran's Threats to Block the Passage of Oil Tankers' (2012) 16(16) *ASIL Insights* 1.
132 Kraska (n 48) 360.
133 Thomas Gibbons-Neff, 'Trump Says U.S. Shot Down Iranian Drone as Both Nations Dig In,' *New York Times* (18 June 2019).

7 Observations and Conclusions

7.1 Observations and Data Analysis

The achievements of UNCLOS are much heralded, but its shortcomings are neither trivial nor inconsequential. The absence of clear guidance for delimitation of maritime zones, especially when the overlapping claim areas have hydrocarbon resources, has, unsurprisingly, encouraged disputing States to maximise their claims resulting in rising tensions and impasse in some of the delimitation negotiations outlined in this study.

This study identified 108 bilateral maritime borders where the presence (or anticipated presence) of hydrocarbon resources influenced the delimitation process.[1] Three-quarters (81 out of 108) of these maritime borders have been resolved, with 34 resolutions before the UNCLOS in-force date of 1994 and 47 resolutions thereafter. However, 27 (25% of 108) disputes remain unresolved, many of them languishing, leading to rising tensions and, in some cases, 'gunboat' diplomacy between the disputing parties. Almost 90% of the unresolved borders are concentrated in the five semi-enclosed sea regions discussed in the preceding chapters of this book, including the eastern Mediterranean, Caspian Sea, northeast Asia, South China Sea, and Persian Gulf regions.[2]

As revealed in this conclusion chapter, many unresolved maritime boundary disputes share common characteristics, including the declaration of one or both disputing States to opt out of the Convention's compulsory resolution provisions for maritime delimitation disputes, and interpretation of ambiguous provisions related to the status of maritime features such as islands and rocks, and historical rights. This conclusion chapter also highlights the important, and often overlooked role, of JDA agreements in the resolution of maritime boundary disputes involving hydrocarbon resources.

7.1.1 Review of Resolution Methodology

The most adopted resolution methodology for resolving maritime border disputes involving hydrocarbon resources is not a negotiated delimited boundary agreement, as assumed to be generally the case for international borders,[3] but a negotiated JDA cooperative agreement which recognises and prescribes a sharing mechanism for hydrocarbon resources that straddle the boundary area.[4] The JDA cooperative

DOI: 10.4324/9781003323051-7

solution was used in 36 (44% of the 81) resolved disputes and was implemented successfully in cases where the bilateral boundary is delimited and also where it remains undefined.[5] Negotiated delimited boundary agreements resolved 26 (32%) of the disputes, nine before the UNCLOS in-force date and 17 since 1994. The ICJ adjudication process was used on four occasions before the UNCLOS in-force date, and seven occasions since then – a total of 11 judgments (14% of 81 resolved disputes).

Another important observation is that only six (7% of 81 resolved disputes) of the resolutions involved solutions that can be explicitly credited to methods created by UNCLOS: namely adjudicated by ITLOS or arbitration under UNCLOS-prescribed rules. The remaining 93% of disputes were resolved using JDA agreements, bilateral negotiated delimited boundaries, ICJ, and arbitration forums – all methods that were well established before UNCLOS and used extensively before and since the 1994 UNCLOS in-force date.[6]

7.1.2 Review of Rate of Resolution

In aggregate, the annual rate of hydrocarbon-related maritime dispute resolutions has doubled since the 1994 UNCLOS in-force date.[7] A decade-by-decade analysis of the rate of maritime border resolution shows a less optimistic trend. There were 11 resolutions in the 1970s, 8 in the 1980s, 12 in the 1990s, peaking at 26 resolutions in the period between 2000 and 2009. The rate has dropped to 11 in the decade between 2010 and 2019, a drop of 62% from the previous decade. At the 2010–2019 rate of 11 bilateral maritime borders per decade, it will take approximately 25 years to resolve the outstanding boundary disputes identified in this study.

7.2 Weaknesses of UNCLOS

UNCLOS is a monumental treaty that has introduced rules to the world's oceans. Its 320 articles have provided a framework for many aspects of ocean management, especially those related to shipping, fishing, and environmental conservation issues. It continues to be regarded as one of the UN's major achievements, and 'represents the culmination of thousands of years of international relations, conflict, and now nearly universal adherence to an enduring order for ocean space.'[8]

UNCLOS was a compromised 'package deal'[9] that granted 'generous'[10] maritime allocations and rights to exploit resources in return for a commitment from States to cooperate and to negotiate equitable solutions. However, the 'deliberately ambiguous'[11] language of many key articles has allowed States to interpret the provisions of UNCLOS to maximise their national interests.[12] This has allowed States to have the ability to 'pick what they like and disregard what they do not like.'[13]

This book's comprehensive review of global unresolved dispute 'hotspots' has highlighted several shortcomings of UNCLOS that are particularly consequential to the resolution and non-resolution of maritime disputes in areas of hydrocarbon deposits.

7.2.1 Review of Article 298(1)(a) Declaration

A closer examination of UNCLOS's dispute resolution procedures reveals its Achilles heel: The ability of a State to formally reject the dispute resolution procedures of the Convention for certain types of disputes, including 'disputes concerning the interpretation or application … relating to *sea boundary delimitations*, or those involving historic bays or titles.'[14]

Of the 81 resolved disputes identified in this book, 19 involve a State that is not party to UNCLOS. Thus, there are 62 resolved disputes where both disputing States are parties to UNCLOS.[15] Only nine of these resolved disputes (15% of 62) include a State that has made an Article 298(1)(a) declaration prior the resolution of the dispute.[16] The date of the declaration is important as it would not be relevant to the dispute if the declaration was made after the dispute was resolved. A State that is not party to UNCLOS would have no ability or need to make an Article 298(1)(a) declaration.

Analysing the list of unresolved disputes shows a contrasting result. Of the 27 unresolved disputes, 12 involve a State that is not a party to UNCLOS. Thus, there are 15 unresolved disputes in which both States are parties to UNCLOS. Crucially, 13 of these unresolved disputes (87% of 15) includes a State that has made an Article 298(1)(a) declaration.

In summary, when a hydrocarbon-related maritime boundary dispute involves only UNCLOS parties, 15% of resolved disputes versus 87% of unresolved disputes, include a State that had made an Article 298(1)(a) declaration. This contrast suggests that an unresolved hydrocarbon-related maritime boundary dispute is six times more likely to involve a State that has made an Article 298(1)(a) declaration than if neither State had made this declaration.

The proportion of unresolved hydrocarbon-related maritime disputes that include either a UNCLOS party that has made an Article 298(1) declaration or includes a State which is not a party to UNCLOS, is 93% (25 out of 27). The presence of one of these traits seems to be a very strong indicator of whether a hydrocarbon-related maritime dispute remains unresolved.

It is worth repeating that UNCLOS includes 168 State parties (out of 193 members of the UN)[17] and only 36 States have made Article 298(1)(a) declarations.[18] The data indicates that 19 States (10% of the total number of UN States), of which 10 are UNCLOS parties and have made Article 298(1)(a) declarations, are involved in over 93% of all unresolved maritime boundary disputes involving hydrocarbon resources.[19]

There are instances in which States have cited their Article 298(1)(a) declaration for refusal to resolve their maritime borders. For example, in the 2015 *South China Sea Arbitration* case,[20] China explicitly relied on its Article 298(1)(a) declaration, which it made in 2006 to justify its refusal to participate in the proceedings.[21] China is involved in seven (out of 27) unresolved disputes. In its negotiations with Timor-Leste, Australia referred to its Article 298(1)(a) declaration to reject the scope and timing of proceedings initiated by Timor-Leste.[22]

The above relationship may also have an alternative explanation. It is possible that States that have unresolved disputes are more likely to make an Article 298(1)

(a) declaration. Unresolved disputes may not be, as postulated by this book, a result of the declaration, but the other way around – the declaration is a result of the presence of unresolved disputes. It should also be noted that without the option of making the declaration, some States would have chosen not to participate in UNCLOS, thereby increasing the proportion of disputes involving States not party to UNCLOS.

The ability of States to make an Article 298(1)(a) declaration is not simply a manifestation of a compromise of UNCLOS's dispute resolution procedures as many have suggested – instead, it was likely a prerequisite for inclusion of compulsory dispute resolution clauses within UNCLOS.[23] However, as this analysis reveals, the use of the declaration 'loophole' has become an indicator of whether a maritime boundary dispute is likely to be resolved and stance of a disputing party towards eventual resolution.

7.2.2 Islands versus Rocks

Part VIII 'Regime of Islands' is one of the briefer parts of UNCLOS but 'perhaps no other provisions of the Convention have received as much attention and critical commentary,' as those in its single article (Article 121).[24]

Of the 27 unresolved disputes in the dataset, 22 (81%) involve the status of maritime features. All unresolved disputes in Asia (northeast Asia, South China Sea, and Southeast Asia) and the Persian Gulf include issues of island sovereignty, definitions of 'rocks' versus 'islands,' and associated maritime zone entitlements. Undoubtedly, UNCLOS has 'contributed to the intensification of the sovereignty disputes over [such] islands'[25] because, as has been discussed extensively in this book, the rights to exploit hydrocarbon resources in the maritime zones, especially in the EEZ, surrounding the feature, are determined by the characteristics of the feature.

The uncertainties and ambiguities in the Convention's definitions of 'islands' versus 'rocks' has led to inconsistent interpretations and disagreements.[26] This is 'intolerably imprecise.'[27] In some of the regions covered in this book, especially the South China Sea and Persian Gulf, the ambiguities surrounding natural as well as artificial islands have been leveraged for claiming extended maritime zones with no apparent recourse beyond rhetoric from other littoral (and non-littoral) States. The direct link between the wording of Article 121 and regional tensions was succinctly stated by Ramos-Mrosovsky:

> By enabling whichever country has sovereignty over the [islands] to claim exclusive rights over resources hundreds of miles offshore, the *law of the sea has inflamed the dispute* by vesting otherwise worthless islands with immense economic value.[28]

Attempts were made to amend the relevant clauses and limit the entitlements, but these were ultimately unsuccessful.[29] It is extremely unlikely that any amendments can be made to these, and other contentious articles in the foreseeable future. Any further clarification will likely originate from international court or arbitration judgments.

7.2.3 Balancing Historical Rights

The issue of historic rights and their relationship to maritime delimitation is present in all of the 27 unresolved disputes. Every disputing State has justified its maritime claims in whole or in part by invoking historical evidence dating back to WW II treaties, colonial actions, or in many cases, pre-colonial treaties and events. In the Asian disputes (northeast Asia, South China Sea, Southeast Asia), Persian Gulf, and West Africa, most of the unresolved disputes can be traced to purported historical navigation and fishing rights, colonial-era treaties between European powers, or peace treaties signed post WW II.

UNCLOS does not recognise historic rights in articles that pertain to EEZ or the continental shelf. The *South China Sea Arbitration* Tribunal's conclusion on this matter is clear:

> The Tribunal considers the text and context of the Convention to be clear in superseding any historic rights that a State may once have had in the areas that now form part of the exclusive economic zone and continental shelf of another State. There is no ambiguity here that would call for the Tribunal to have recourse to the supplementary means of interpretation.[30]

Several unresolved disputes can be traced to pre-UNCLOS treaties between colonial powers. In particular, the 1943 *Cairo Declaration*[31] and the 1951 Treaty of Peace[32] failed to resolve or clarify the sovereignty of certain maritime features, including the Senkaku, Dokdo, Spratly, and Itu Aba Islands, among others. Interpretation of colonial treaties has contributed to the current maritime claims made by littoral States. In the Caspian Sea region, successor States to the USSR have questioned the Iranian and Russian assertion that previous treaties between Iran and the USSR should be honoured by the successor States. Broader historical issues are also present in the eastern Mediterranean where tensions between Israel and its neighbours and between Cyprus (and its ally, Greece) and Turkey underlie many of the maritime border issues in the region.

7.3 Are JDA Agreements the Solution?

The benefits of JDA agreements to resolve maritime border disputes are multifaceted. These 'sovereignty neutral'[33] agreements offer disputing States a pragmatic solution to exploit resources, both living and non-living, from overlapping claim zones without prejudice to eventual maritime boundary delimitation or validity of the claims.[34] JDAs have become accepted as a practical option for disputing States to coordinate the exploration and exploitation of resources and, for oil and gas companies, fiscal and legal certainty to embark on their long and expensive journey from exploration to production. These resources, if proved to be commercially viable and enhance the domestic supply of energy resources which would have likely remained unexplored due to unresolved boundary disputes.[35] JDA agreements have successfully been operating where the maritime boundary has been delimited (as in the North Sea and in other regions) and where the boundary remains undefined (as in most cases in Asia and West Africa).

The JDA cooperative solution has been the most adopted resolution method for the 81 resolved disputes identified in the dataset, accounting for 36 (44%) of all resolutions, ahead of negotiated delimited boundary agreements, which accounted for 32% of all resolutions, and well ahead of all other adjudication methods such as the ICJ, ITLOS, and arbitration. JDA agreements have been executed by States that have previously gone to war, by States that have taken each other to the ICJ, and between States that were once part of the other State.[36]

All the JDA agreements identified are bilateral agreements between two adjacent or facing littoral States. Increasing the number of States in a regional cooperative agreement would increase the complexity of the agreement, but could also facilitate balanced and more neutral terms, especially in regions such as the South China Sea where China has used its dominance to pressure its smaller neighbours. In smaller semi-enclosed regions, such as the Persian Gulf, Caspian Sea, and eastern Mediterranean, many discovered fields are relatively close to each other but on different sides of claimed maritime boundaries and would benefit from joint operations. In these cases, multilateral JDAs, instead of the traditional bilateral model, could result in improved operational efficiencies, and potentially, even facilitate coordinated development of pipelines and other infrastructure. There are few precedents for JDAs involving more than two States, and none are currently active or actively negotiated.[37] The difficulties of increasing the number of parties in a JDA agreement would be challenging, but not insurmountable. Dominant States, such as China, would have to overcome their preference for negotiating the issues bilaterally with each party rather than on a multilateral basis.[38]

However, as this book has revealed, 25% of maritime disputes involving hydrocarbons remain unresolved. Many, including those in the South China Sea, East China Sea, Caspian Sea, and Persian Gulf regions, have had failed JDA attempts over the past four decades. And, because of the slowing rate of JDA agreements over the past decade (only four have been executed between 2010 and 2019, a drop of 63% compared to 11 executed agreements between 2000 and 2009),[39] there is a need to accelerate the negotiation process for these unresolved disputes.

This book introduced 'straw man' JDA proposals for each of the five highlighted regions. These simplistic geographic maps outline encompassing overlapping claims can serve as a starting point for negotiations, facilitating more refined solutions to be developed between disputing States. Many of the straw man proposals are regional solutions requiring multilateral acceptance. Past bilateral negotiations have resulted in impasse – it may be time to try creative multilateral solutions, especially if they can be coupled with model JDA terms discussed below.

7.3.1 Model JDA Terms

As stated previously, JDA agreements are difficult to negotiate and can take many years to reach agreement.[40] States that embark on JDA negotiations should be prepared to compromise,[41] and be willing to share resources which each 'believes it is exclusively entitled under international law.'[42] For negotiations to succeed, political will to overcome nationalistic sentiment and to break the impasse could be helpful. If the political landscape is 'charged,' tangible results are unlikely and, as a result, the dispute will remain unresolved and hydrocarbons remain unexploited.[43] If the need for access to the resources is more urgent because of domestic economic pressures, political and historical barriers could be overcome, and a 'face-saving' JDA agreement could be achievable.[44]

There have been previous efforts to create a 'model' agreement. The British Institute of International and Comparative Law (BIICL) model agreement provided some guidance on key terms and allowed for different JDA structures.[45] However, it is now over 30 years old and thus does not include lessons from recent JDA agreements. The BIICL document does not provide guidance on how the JDA should be geographically defined, does not differentiate between oil and gas development, and envisions the agreement between two States only.[46]

UNCLOS provides a model for operations of the JDA governing authority: Namely the existing framework rules for the 'Authority' for the exploitation of the 'Area,' the maritime zone beyond the continental shelf and defined in Part XI of the Convention. This part of the Convention, which includes 60 articles on management of resources in the Area, could, with sufficient incentives and motivations, be adapted to be the framework model for regional bilateral and multilateral JDA governing authorities.

An UNCLOS-recommended 'Model JDA Agreement' that defines key terms such as the areal extent (with clear rejection of historical rights and justifiable maritime feature claims), time limits to trigger JDA negotiations if other resolution methods such as negotiations fail, general governance structure and sharing mechanisms could be developed. The model agreement could take concepts from Part XI, prior studies on JDA agreements,[47] and successfully operating JDA agreements, and include options that parties can choose to tailor the agreement towards their circumstances. It should also call for disputing States to 'freeze' existing claims once the overlapping areas are defined and JDA negotiations begin.[48]

Determination of other terms, such as fiscal regulations, taxes, jurisdiction, and production arrangements are 'formidable – but not insurmountable' issues.[49] For these, the parties could begin with sharing profits equally and adjusted for equity if circumstances justify different proportions.[50] This could be a similar process to the ICJ three-step process for maritime border delimitation.[51]

As this book has demonstrated, States have, and will continue to interpret articles of the Convention to suit their self-interest. There is a balance between the level of ambiguity in the drafting of the articles and the degree of flexibility accorded to individual States. UNCLOS was drafted over 40 years ago, and since then, the JDA model has evolved and, in many ways, has converged towards a more common set of principles. There may be more acceptance of a prescriptive UNCLOS model agreement than in the past. The exercise of drafting such an agreement should not be seen as a weakness of the Convention, but rather a natural evolution and contemporary solution to solve many of the remaining unresolved maritime boundary disputes identified in this book. The author of this book is developing a JDA online resource (www.jdainstitute.com) with summaries, legislations, and pertinent articles for most of the JDAs discussed in this book.

7.4 Review of Significant Findings

Through a comprehensive analysis of global maritime boundary disputes involving hydrocarbon resources, a number of key findings that provide an insight into the role of UNCLOS have become evident.

The first finding is that the most widely adopted resolution methodology is not a negotiated boundary agreement, but a 'permanent' cooperative JDA agreement with resource prescriptive resource-sharing mechanisms. Other than a brief reference to 'provisional agreements' within UNCLOS, the Convention does not elaborate on this practical solution which was well established decades prior to UNCLOS.

The second finding is that only six out of 81 resolved disputes were settled by UNCLOS's unique dispute resolution methods, namely ITLOS or arbitration under UNCLOS-prescribed rules. Though UNCLOS devotes large sections of the Convention to these methods, States have largely chosen to settle their disputes through 'traditional' JDA agreements, bilateral negotiations, ICJ and arbitration solutions.

The third finding is the significance of the Article 298(1)(a) declaration 'loophole.' The data indicate that a maritime boundary dispute with hydrocarbon potential and which involves a State that has made an Article 298(1)(a) declaration is six times more likely to remain unresolved than if it did not involve a State that has made this declaration. There is also a 93% chance that a dispute remains unresolved if it involves a State that has made a 298(1)(a) declaration or involves a State that is not a party to UNCLOS.

The fourth finding is that there is a small number of States that are involved in a disproportionately large number of unresolved disputes. Just three of these (China, Iran, and Malaysia) are collectively responsible for 51% of all unresolved disputes.[52]

The fifth finding is that all 27 of the unresolved disputes involve at least one of the disputing States justifying their maritime zone claims based on historical evidence, and 81% of all unresolved disputes involve interpretations of UNCLOS's articles related to islands and rocks. Though subsequent judicial decisions, including the *South China Sea Arbitration*, have attempted to clarify these articles, their ambiguity has allowed States to interpret them to maximise their entitlements, thus contributing to the ongoing bilateral and regional tensions in these disputes.

UNCLOS granted generous rights to coastal States. Certain States have taken advantage of the ambiguities and shortcomings within the Convention to expand their influence, impede economic development that may result from oil and gas development, and contribute to rising tensions without any obvious recourse or liability.

7.5 Closing Remarks

> You set bounds to peoples, cities, great kingdoms: Without you, every field would be disputed.[53]
>
> [*Homage to Terminus, Roman God of Borders*]

Among the expectations of UNCLOS was that it would promote settlement of maritime border disputes.[54] Unfortunately, the delimitation of maritime boundaries, which is difficult when hydrocarbon resources are present, is made even more problematic when the ambiguities within UNCLOS are leveraged by disputing States.

The lack of any specific guidance for oil and gas activities within the Convention, in contrast to the extensive discussions on exploiting living resources, is an inexplicable shortcoming of the Convention.[55] The Convention draft was completed in 1982, well after the offshore oil and gas industry was established globally and the 'transformative potential of hydrocarbon resources to developing economies' was evident.[56] Many, if not all of the shortcomings identified in this book could be eliminated with modest revisions or addendums to the Convention. Recognising that UNCLOS was a major achievement that required decades of negotiation, revisions or clarifications would be extremely difficult to initiate but ultimately, beneficial to all.

The global landscape has changed in the past four decades – issues such as rising carbon emissions, global warming, advancing deepwater drilling and pipeline technology, recognition of the importance of energy security, dissolution of the Soviet-era bipolar world and the rise of China – were not present or as prevalent during the drafting of UNCLOS. Inclusion of these topics could be a catalyst for initiating revision discussions. The 2023 passing of the High Seas agreement is an example of an independent instrument of UNCLOS that further clarified the regulation of the world's High Seas. Optimistically, revisions of UNCLOS dealing with some of the issues discussed in this book could be negotiated in a similar manner.

The status quo is not sustainable. As certain States rise to regional and global superpower status, they will continue to exploit UNCLOS shortcomings to their advantage. And the age of oil and gas will inevitably be eclipsed by other energy sources which may not require these stranded maritime resources to be developed. At that point, the value of hydrocarbons that remain in place and unexploited could be lost without providing any economic benefit to States that have continued to resist resolving their maritime disputes.

Notes

1 To the knowledge of the author, this is the most comprehensive and systematic analysis of unresolved maritime border disputes involving hydrocarbon resources. The book database, which is summarised in the Appendices, excludes disputes in the Artic or

Antarctic regions and only includes bilateral maritime boundaries that have had oil and gas exploration or production activities, and in some regions, such as the North Sea, include multiple border agreements for the same 'pair' of States. For example, there are three separate JDA agreements between the UK and Norway and three between the UK and the Netherlands, each covering a different section of their maritime border. The database is current as of the date of book publication (mid-2023).

The disputes covered in the dataset are a small subset of the total number of global maritime boundary disputes. The British Institute of International and Comparative Law, *Report on the Obligations of States under Articles 74(3) and 83(3) of UNCLOS in respect of Undelimited Maritime Areas* (Report, 30 June 2016) n 32 quoting Anderson and van Logchem, 'Rights and Obligations in Areas of Overlapping Maritime Claims' in S. Jayakumar, T. Koh, and R. Beckman (eds), '*The South China Sea Disputes and the Law of the Sea*' (Edward Elgar, 2014) 198, stated, 'At the present time there are roughly 200 or so areas where the EEZs and continental shelves of opposite or adjacent States overlap where a definitive maritime boundary has not yet been established.'; Nguyen Hong Thao, 'Joint Development in the Gulf of Thailand' (1999) Autumn 1999 *IBRU Boundary and Security Bulletin* n 1. Quoting R. R. Churchill, 'Joint development zones: international legal issues,' in Hazel Fox, '*Joint development of offshore oil and gas, vol. II*' The British Institute of International and Comparative Law (1990) 56. 'More than 400 maritime boundaries must be defined, of which only one third have been settled by bilateral agreements or by jurisprudence.'

2 The three unresolved disputes not in the five selected regions include Guyana–Trinidad and Tobago, Costa Rica–Nicaragua, and Congo Brazzaville–Gabon.

3 Timothy J. Tyler, James L. Loftis, Emilie E. Hawker, Hana V. Vizcarra, and M. Imad Khan, 'Developing Arctic Hydrocarbon Resources' in Myron Nordquist, John Moore, Aldo Chircop, and Ronan Long (eds), *The Regulation of Continental Shelf Development: Rethinking International Standards* 319, 322. 'Under UNCLOS, the preferred method of delimitation is through bilateral agreement.'; Nugzar Dundua, *Delimitation of maritime boundaries between adjacent States*, United Nations–The Nippon Foundation (2006–2007). 16. 'The majority of bilateral treaties on maritime delimitation still use a line based on simplified or modified equidistance.'; Eddy Pratomo, 'Negotiating Maritime Boundaries' (2018) 21(3) *Journal of Legal, Ethical and Regulatory Issues* 1. 'Negotiation is a preferred method to delimit maritime boundaries.'

4 This book considers the execution of a JDA agreement as a 'resolution' of the boundary dispute, recognising that these arrangements, where there is no permanent border delimitation, are considered 'provisional agreements.' There are no cases identified where a JDA agreement has been replaced by permanent negotiated boundary agreement.

5 Of the 36 hydrocarbon-related resource-sharing JDA cooperative agreements, 23 of them were in areas with delimited borders and 13 of them where maritime borders remain undefined. Data is shown in Appendices A, B, and C.

6 Before the UNCLOS in-force date of November 1994, there were 34 dispute resolutions. These were resolved by JDA agreements (19), bilateral negotiated delimited boundary (9), ICJ (4) and Arbitration (2). Since the UNCLOS in-force date, there have been 47 resolutions. Of these, six were resolved by UNCLOS prescribed methods (two by ITLOS and four by UNCLOS arbitration rules). The remaining 41 disputes were resolved by JDA agreements (17), bilateral negotiated delimited boundary (17), and ICJ (7). Data shown in Appendix A.

7 Between 1958 and 1994, the rate of yearly resolutions was 0.94 resolutions per year. Since 1994, the rate has improved to 1.81 resolutions per year, with an increase in resolution rate of 91%. Data shown in Appendix A.

8 Peter Prows, 'Tough Love: The Dramatic Birth and Looming Demise of UNCLOS Property Law (and What Is to Be Done About It)' (2007) 42(2) *Texas International Law Journal* 241, 241.

9 Robert Beckman, 'Tribunal ruling a game changer,' *The Straits Times* (Singapore, 14 July 2016).

10 UN, 'The United Convention on the Law of the Sea (A historical perspective)' *United Nations Oceans & Law of the Seas* (Web Page 1998) <http://www.un.org/Depts/los/convention_agreements/convention_historical_perspective.htm>. 7.

11 Beckman (n 9); Jonathan I. Charney, 'Central East Asian Maritime Boundaries and the Law of the Sea' (1995) 89(4) *Am. J. Int'l L.* 724, 738. 'The delimitation articles of the Convention are ambiguous.'; Sam Bateman, 'UNCLOS and Its Limitations as the Foundation for a Regional Maritime Security Regime' (2006) 111 *Institute of Defence and Strategic Studies Singapore* 4. 'All the critical issues with resolving ambiguities in the law of the sea.'

12 Beckman (n 9) states: 'Also, the negotiators were aware that states would inevitably interpret the provisions in UNCLOS to maximise their national interests and in the light of their particular cultural and historical circumstances.'; Djibril Moudachirou, 'Ocean Resources' Ascendancy over African States Friendship Relations: Can UNCLOS Help Resolve Current or Future Maritime Boundary Delimitation Dispute Issues' (2016) 5(1) *Journal of Water Resources and Ocean Science,* 3. Moudachirou states that: 'And in order to fill the gaps left by UNCLOS, states interpret UNCLOS provisions according to their interests.'

13 Tommy T. B. Koh, 'A Constitution for the Oceans' (Statement at final session of the Conference at Montego Bay, 6 and 11 December 1982) stated: 'It is therefore not possible for States to pick what they like and disregard what they do not like. In International law, as in domestic law, rights and duties go hand in hand. It is therefore legally impermissible to claim rights under the Convention without being willing to assume the correlative duties.'

14 *United Nations Convention on the Law of the Sea*, opened for signature 10 December 1982, 1833 UNTS 3 (entered into force 16 November 1994) ('*UNCLOS*'). Article 298(1), 'Optional exceptions to applicability of Section 2,' states, '1. When signing, ratifying or acceding to this Convention or at any time thereafter, a State may, without prejudice to the obligations arising under Section 1, declare in writing that it does not accept any one or more of the procedures provided for in Section 2 with respect to one or more of the following categories of disputes: (a)(i) *disputes concerning the interpretation or application of Articles 15, 74 and 83 relating to sea boundary delimitations*, or those involving historic bays or titles, provided that a State having made such a declaration shall, when such a dispute arises subsequent to entry into force of this Convention and where no agreement within a reasonable period of time is reached in negotiations between the parties, at the request of any party to the dispute, accept submission of the matter to conciliation under Annex V, Section 2; and provide further that any dispute that necessarily involves the concurrent consideration of any unsettled dispute concerning sovereignty or other rights over continental or insular land territory shall be excluded from such submission.' Emphasis added.

15 Refer to Appendices A, B, and C for the underlying data used in the analysis.

16 In 29 of these disputes, the involved State (or States) made their declaration *after* the resolution of the dispute, thus not relevant to the resolution of the dispute.

17 UN, 'Growth in United Nations membership, 1945–present' (Web Page, September 2020) <https://www.un.org/en/sections/member-states/growth-united-nations-membership-1945-present/index.html>.

18 The list of the States that have made the Article 298(1)(a) declaration (and their date of the declaration) is in Appendix C.

19 This includes ten States that have made Article 298(1)(a) declarations (China, Egypt, Gabon, Greece, South Korea, Malaysia, Nicaragua, Philippines, Thailand, and Trinidad and Tobago) and nine States that are not party to UNCLOS (Cambodia, Iran, Israel, Palestine, Taiwan, Turkey, Turkmenistan, the UAE, and Venezuela). These 19 states

are involved in 25 out of 27 unresolved disputes. The two exceptions are the Cyprus–Lebanon dispute and the Iraq–Kuwait dispute.

20 *South China Sea Arbitration (The Republic of Philippines v. The People's Republic of China)* (2016) PCA Case 2013-19, 170 ILR 1.

21 *South China Sea Arbitration (The Republic of Philippines v. The People's Republic of China)* (Award on Jurisdiction and Admissibility) (2016) PCA Case 2013-19, 170 ILR 1, [366].

22 *Timor Sea Conciliation (Timor-Leste v. Australia)* (Decision on Australia's Objection to Competence) (2016) PCA Case 2016-10. This dispute is included in the study database.

23 Keyuan Zou and Qiang Ye, 'Interpretation and Application of Article 298 of the Law of the Sea Convention in Recent Annex VII Arbitrations: An Appraisal' (2017) 48(3–4) *Ocean Development & International Law* 331, 332. They suggest that the declaration 'strikes a well-designed compromise between state sovereignty and compulsory dispute settlement.'; Anne Sheehan, 'Dispute Settlement under UNCLOS: The Exclusion of Maritime Delimitation Disputes' (2005) 7 *University of Queensland Law Journal*, 166.

24 Clive Schofield and Richard Schofield, 'Testing the Waters: Charting the Evolution of Claims to and From Low-Tide Elevations and Artificial Islands' (2016) 1(1) *Asia-Pacific Journal of Ocean Law and Policy* 37, 38.

25 Sun Pyo Kim, Maritime Delimitation and Interim Arrangements in North East Asia (Martinus Nijhoff, 2004) 214.

26 Schofield and Schofield (n 24) 38.

27 Kim (n 25) 200 n 119.

28 Carlos Ramos-Mrosovsky, 'International law's unhelpful role in the Senkaku Islands' (2008) 29 *U. Pa. J. Int'l L.* 903, 906 (emphasis added).

29 Stefan Talmon, 'Part VII Regime of Islands' in Alexander Proelss (ed.) United Nations Convention on the Law of the Sea A Commentary (C. H. Beck Hart Nomos, 2017) 860–861.

30 *South China Sea Arbitration* (n 20) [247].

31 *The Cairo Declaration*, 26 November 1943. Published by Foreign Relations of the United States Diplomatic Papers, *The Conferences at Cairo and Tehran* (United States Government Printing Office History and Public Policy Program Digital Archive, 1961), 448–449. Declaration made by President Roosevelt, Generalissimo Chiang Kai-Shek, and Prime Minister Churchill.

32 *Treaty of Peace with Japan*, San Francisco, 8 September 1951 (entered into force 28 April 1952) 3 UST 3181, TIAS 2490, 136 UNTS 45.

33 Clive H. Schofield, 'Sharing Maritime Space: Options for Cooperative Management in Areas of Overlapping Maritime Claims' (2007) *Australian National Centre for Ocean Resources and Security* 2 ('Sharing Maritime Space'). Schofield cites the 'sovereign neutral' approach allowing joint activities.

34 *Agreement concerning joint development of the southern part of the continental shelf adjacent to the two countries*, Japan–Republic of Korea, signed 30 January 1974 (entry into force 22 June 1978). Many JDA agreements contain such clauses. For example, Article 28 of the Japan–Korea treaty states: 'Nothing in the Agreement shall be regarded as determining the question of sovereign rights over all or any portion of the Joint Development Zone or as prejudicing the positions of the respective Parties with respect to the delimitation of the continental shelf.'

35 Schofield, 'Sharing Maritime Space' (n 33) 2.

36 Argentina and UK have previously gone to war. Libya and Tunisia negotiated a JDA after ICJ proceedings regarding their maritime border. Kazakhstan was once a part of USSR and negotiated a JDA with Russia in in 2005 to unitise the Krumangazy field. Please refer to Appendices A, B, and C to view the data.

37 Nguyen (n 1) 86. In 1999, Thailand, Malaysia, and Vietnam negotiated 'an agreement in principle' for a JDA covering 800 km^2 of overlapping claims between Vietnam and the

pre-existing Malaysia–Thailand JDA. However, negotiations stalled on technical issues and cost-sharing terms.; Ben Milligan, 'Legal and policy options for the provisional joint management of maritime spaces subject to overlapping jurisdictional claims' (PhD thesis, University of Wollongong, 2012) 184. The 2005 tripartite agreement for joint seismic studies between the national oil companies of China, Philippines, and Vietnam, but this agreement was 'never meaningfully implemented' and expired in 2008.

38 Maximo Paulino T. Sison III, 'Universalizing the Law of the sea in the South China Sea Dispute' (2018) 49(2) *Ocean Development and International Law* 157, 161; Congressional Research Service Specialist in Naval Affairs (name redacted), *Maritime Territorial and Exclusive Economic Zone (EEZ) Disputes Involving China: Issues for Congress* (CRS Report Prepared for Members and Committees of Congress No R42784, 12 December 2017) 33.

39 The rate of JDA solutions peaked at 11 per decade between 2000 and 2009. However, since 2010, the total number of JDA agreement executions have dropped to a rate of four per decade. At the 2010–2019 JDA rate of four per decade, it could take almost 70 years to resolve the outstanding 27 disputes unless a more efficient process can be adopted by the disputing States. Please refer to Appendices A, B, and C to view the data.

40 Constantinos Yiallourides, *Maritime disputes and international law: disputed waters and seabed resources in Asia and Europe* (Routledge, 2019) 213.

41 *Guyana v. Suriname* (Awards) (2007) PCA Case 2004-04, 139 ILR 566 [461]. Article 461 of the Tribunal Award states, 'Indeed, the inclusion of the phrase "in a spirit of understanding and cooperation" indicates the drafters' intent to require of the parties a conciliatory approach to negotiations, pursuant to which they would be prepared to make concessions in the pursuit of a provisional arrangement.' Without the willingness to compromise, it is unlikely that a JDA agreement can be negotiated.

42 Yiallourides (n 40) 213 n 4. Yiallourides cites James C Hsiung, 'Sea Power, the Law of the Sea, and the Sino-Japanese East China Sea "Resource War"' (2005) 27(6) *American Foreign Policy Interests* 513, 523–5.

43 Yiallourides (n 40) 214–215.

44 Yiallourides (n 40) 247; Ian Townsend-Gault, 'Rationales for zones of co-operation' in Robert Beckman, et al (eds), *Beyond Territorial Disputes in the South China Sea: Legal Frameworks for the Joint Development of Hydrocarbon Resources* (Edward Elgar, 2013) 114, 133.

45 H. Fox et al., *Joint Development of Offshore Oil and Gas: A Model Agreement for States for Joint Development with Explanatory Commentary* (British Institute of International and Comparative Law, 1989).

46 Fox (n 45) 388–416. The final chapter of the book contains the Model Agreement. It should be noted that natural gas developments take longer to develop and are typically taxed at a different rate than oil resources. As discussed in this book, many of the disputed areas are areas of natural gas – rather than oil – potential.

47 Such as those done by the British Institute of International and Comparative Law. See Fox (n 45).

48 Ralf Emmers, '*Resource Management and Contested Territories in East Asia*' (Pelgrave Pivot, 2013) 82.

49 Valencia, Mark J., 'Regime-Building in East Asia: Recent Progress and Problems' (2006) 3 *Ocean Policy Studies* 672, 688.

50 JDA agreements that specify equal sharing of costs and benefits include the Malaysia–Thailand JDA, Malaysia–Vietnam JDA. The Guinea Bissau–Senegal JDA calls for 50/50 for fisheries, but 85/15% for other resources. Nigeria–Sao Tome calls for 60 Nigeria/40 Sao Tome and is valid for 45 years.

51 *Maritime Delimitation in the Black Sea (Romania v. Ukraine)* (Judgment) [2009] ICJ Rep 61, [115–122]. As per paragraphs 115–122, the ICJ adopted a three-stage process to delimit a single maritime boundary (for both EEZ and continental shelf) based on the

'equidistance/relevant circumstances' method. The first stage requires the construction of a provisional equidistance line. At the second stage, the court considers whether there are relevant circumstances that may call for an adjustment of the equidistance line in order to achieve an equitable result. At the third stage, the court conducts a disproportionality test to 'assess whether the effect of the line, as adjusted, is such that the parties' respective shares of the relevant area are markedly disproportionate to the lengths of their relevant coasts. If so, a further adjustment will be made.'

52 China is involved in seven unresolved disputes, Iran in five, and Malaysia in three unresolved disputes. Together, these three States are involved in 14 unresolved disputes (not 'double counting' the dispute between China and Malaysia). This equates to 51% of all unresolved disputes. States involved in two disputes are Azerbaijan, Cambodia, Cyprus, Greece, Guyana, Iraq, Israel, Japan, Korea, Kuwait, Lebanon, Philippines, Turkey, Turkmenistan, and Vietnam.

53 Homage to the Roman God of Borders, Terminus. Terminalia. <http://www.novaroma.org/nr/Terminalia>

54 Kim (n 25) 15.

55 *UNCLOS* (n 14). There are no discussions of oil and gas exploration and production within the Convention. Article 124 includes 'gas lines' in rights of access for land-locked states, Article 133 mentions 'gaseous mineral resources' in its definition of resources for the Area. The term 'drilling' is mentioned a few times, most notably in Article 81 discussing drilling on the continental shelf. However, whether the reference is for hydrocarbons or other minerals is not specified.

56 William Pentland, 'World's Five Largest Offshore Oil Fields' *Forbes* (7 September 2013). Three of the five largest offshore oil fields were discovered and producing before 1970; Tara Davenport, 'Southeast Asian Approaches to Maritime Boundaries' (2014) 4(2) *Asian Journal of International Law* 309, 344. Davenport states, 'In their quest for economic independence, Southeast Asian states have been well aware of the transformative potential of hydrocarbon resources to developing economies and have been eager to unlock the potential of such resources.'

Appendices

Appendix A

Resolved Disputes

Resolved Disputes		*Resolution Solution*	*Resolution Date*	*State Party A*		*State Party B*		*Does Dispute Involve …*		*Was 298(1)(a) declaration made prior to resolution date?*
				UNCLOS Status and 298(1)(a) Declaration Date		*UNCLOS Status and 298(1)(a) Declaration Date*		*A State not a UNCLOS party State?*	*298(1)(a) Declaration State?*	
1	Bahrain – Saudi Arabia	JDA [SM]	Feb 1958	Bahrain		*Saudi Arabia*	Jan 2018		Yes	
2	Norway – UK	Negotiated Delimited	Mar 1965	*Norway*	Jun 1996	UK			Yes	
3	Netherlands – UK	Negotiated Delimited	Oct 1965	Nether-lands		UK				
4	Qatar – Saudi Arabia	Negotiated Delimited	Dec 1965/ Jul 2008	Qatar		*Saudi Arabia*	Jan 2018		Yes	
5	Kuwait – Saudi Arabia	JDA [SM]	Jul 1965/ Jul 2000	Kuwait		*Saudi Arabia*	Jan 2018		Yes	
6	Abu Dhabi (UAE) – Qatar	JDA [SM]	Mar 1969	*UAE*	Not UNCLOS party	Qatar		Yes		
7	North Sea [Germany – Netherlands – Denmark]	ICJ	Feb 1969	Germany		Netherlands – Denmark	Nov 2004		Yes	
8	Iran – Saudi Arabia	Negotiated Delimited	Jan 1969	*Iran*	Not UNCLOS party	*Saudi Arabia*	Jan 2018	Yes	Yes	
9	Iran – Qatar	Negotiated Delimited	Sep 1969	*Iran*	Not UNCLOS party	Qatar		Yes		
10	Iran – Bahrain	Negotiated Delimited	Jun 1971	*Iran*	Not UNCLOS party	Bahrain		Yes		

(*Continued*)

Resolved Disputes		Resolution Solution	Resolution Date	*State Party A*		*State Party B*		*Does Dispute Involve …*		*Was 298(1)(a) declaration made prior to resolution date?*
				UNCLOS Status and 298(1)(a) Declaration Date		*UNCLOS Status and 298(1)(a) Declaration Date*		*A State not a UNCLOS party State?*	*298(1)(a) Declaration State?*	
11	Iran – Sharjah (UAE)	JDA [RS]	Nov 1971	*Iran*	Not UNCLOS party	*UAE*	Not UNCLOS party	Yes		
12	Canada–France (St Pierre et Miquelon)	Arbitration	Jun 1992	*Canada*	Nov 2003	*France*	Apr 1996		Yes	
13	Japan – Korea	JDA [JM]*	Jan 1974	Japan		*Korea*	Apr 2006		Yes	
14	Iran – Oman	Negotiated Delimited	Jul 1974	*Iran*	Not UNCLOS party	Oman		Yes		
15	France – Spain	JDA [RS]	Jan 1974	*France*	Apr 1996	*Spain*	Jul 2002		Yes	
16	Saudi Arabia – Sudan	JDA [JA]	Jun 1974	*Saudi Arabia*	Jan 2018	Sudan			Yes	
17	Norway – UK (Frigg field)	JDA [RS]	May 1976	*Norway*	Jun 1996	UK			Yes	
18	Mexico – USA	Negotiated Delimited	May 1978/ Jun 2000	*Mexico*	Jan 2003	*USA*	Not UNCLOS party	Yes	Yes	
19	Norway – UK (Statfjord field)	JDA [RS]	Oct 1979	*Norway*	Jun 1996	UK			Yes	
20	Norway – UK (Murchison field)	JDA [RS]	Oct 1979	*Norway*	Jun 1996	UK			Yes	
21	Iceland – Norway	JDA [RS]	Nov 1981	*Iceland*	Jun 1985	*Norway*	Jun 1996		Yes	

(Continued)

Resolved Disputes		*Resolution Solution*	*Resolution Date*	*State Party A*		*State Party B*		*Does Dispute Involve …*		*Was 298(1)(a) declaration made prior to resolution date?*
				UNCLOS Status and 298(1)(a) Declaration Date		*UNCLOS Status and 298(1)(a) Declaration Date*		*A State not a UNCLOS party State?*	*298(1)(a) Declaration State?*	
22	Cambodia – Vietnam	JDA [JM]*	Aug 1982	*Cambodia*	Not UNCLOS party	Vietnam		Yes		
23	Canada – USA (Gulf of Maine)	ICJ	Oct 1984	*Canada*	Nov 2003	*USA*	Not UNCLOS party	Yes	Yes	
24	Libya – Malta	ICJ	Jun 1985	Libya		Malta				
25	Guinea – Guinea-Bissau	Arbitration	Feb 1985	Guinea		Guinea-Bissau				
26	Libya – Tunisia	ICJ leading to JDA	May 1988	Libya		*Tunisia*	Apr 1985		Yes	
27	Libya – Tunisia	JDA	Aug 1988	Libya		*Tunisia*	Apr 1985		Yes	
28	Australia – Timor-Leste	JDA [JA]	Dec 1989	*Australia*	Mar 2002	Timor-Leste			Yes	
29	Trinidad & Tobago – Venezuela	Negotiated Delimited	Apr 1990	*Trinidad & Tobago*	Feb 2009	*Venezuela*	Not UNCLOS party	Yes	Yes	
30	Malaysia – Thailand	JDA [JA]*	May 1990	*Malaysia*	Aug 2019	*Thailand*	May 2011		Yes	
31	UK–Netherlands (Markham)	JDA [RS]	May 1992	UK		Netherlands				
32	Malaysia – Vietnam	JDA [JM]*	Aug 1993	*Malaysia*	Aug 2019	Vietnam			Yes	
33	Guinea-Bissau - Senegal	JDA [JA] via arbitration	Oct 1993	Guinea-Bissau		Senegal				

(*Continued*)

Resolved Disputes		Resolution Solution	Resolution Date	State Party A		State Party B		Does Dispute Involve ...		Was 298(1)(a) declaration made prior to resolution date?
				UNCLOS Status and 298(1)(a) Declaration Date		UNCLOS Status and 298(1)(a) Declaration Date		A State not a UNCLOS party State?	298(1)(a) Declaration State?	
34	Colombia – Jamaica	JDA [JA]	Dec 1993	*Colombia*	Not UNCLOS party	Jamaica		Yes		
35	Argentina – UK	JDA [JM]*	Sep 1995	*Argentina*	Dec 1995	UK			Yes	
36	Thailand – Vietnam	Negotiated Delimited	Aug 1997	*Thailand*	May 2011	Vietnam			Yes	
37	Kazakhstan – Russia	Negotiated Delimited	Aug 1998	Kazakhstan		Russia	Mar 1997		Yes	Yes
38	Equatorial Guinea – Sao Tome & Principe	Negotiated Delimited	Jun 1999	*Equatorial Guinea*	Feb 2002	Guinea			Yes	
39	Eritrea – Yemen	Arbitration	1998 / 1999	*Eritrea*	Not UNCLOS party	Yemen		Yes		
40	Denmark – UK (Faroe Islands)	Negotiated Delimited	May 1999	*Denmark*	Nov 2004	UK			Yes	
41	Equatorial Guinea – Nigeria	JDA [RS]	Sep 2000	*Equatorial Guinea*	Feb 2002	Nigeria			Yes	
42	Nigeria – Sao Tome & Principe	JDA [JA]*	Feb 2001	Nigeria		Sao Tome & Principe				
43	Bahrain – Qatar	ICJ	Jun 2001	Bahrain		Qatar				
44	Cambodia – Thailand	JDA [JA]*	Mar 2001	*Cambodia*	Not UNCLOS party	*Thailand*	May 2011	Yes	Yes	

(*Continued*)

Resolved Disputes		*Resolution Solution*	*Resolution Date*	*State Party A*		*State Party B*		*Does Dispute Involve …*		*Was 298(1)(a) declaration made prior to resolution date?*
				UNCLOS Status and 298(1)(a) Declaration Date		*UNCLOS Status and 298(1)(a) Declaration Date*		*A State not a UNCLOS party State?*	*298(1)(a) Declaration State?*	
45	Azerbaijan – Kazakhstan	Negotiated Delimited	Nov 2001	Azerbaijan		Kazakhstan				
46	Seychelles – Tanzania	Negotiated Delimited	Jan 2002	Seychelles		Tanzania				
47	Algeria – Tunisia	Negotiated Delimited	Mar 2002	*Algeria*	May 2018	*Tunisia*	Apr 1985		Yes	Yes
48	Angola – DR Congo	JDA [JM]*	Mar 2002	Angola		*DR Congo*	Apr 2014		Yes	
49	Angola – Namibia	Negotiated Delimited	Jun 2002	Angola		Namibia				
50	Azerbaijan – Russia	Negotiated Delimited	Sep 2002	Azerbaijan		*Russia*	Mar 1997		Yes	Yes
51	Cameroon – Nigeria	ICJ	Oct 2002	Cameroon		Nigeria				
52	Cyprus – Egypt	Negotiated Delimited	Feb 2003	Cyprus		*Egypt*	Feb 2017		Yes	
53	Indonesia – Vietnam	Negotiated Delimited	Jun 2003	Indonesia		Vietnam				
54	Barbados – Guyana	JDA [JM]*	Dec 2003	Barbados		Guyana				
55	UK–Netherlands (Blane field)	JDA [RS]	Jul 2005	UK		Netherlands				
56	Kazakhstan – Russia (Krumangazy)	JDA [RS]	Jul 2005	Kazakhstan		*Russia*	Mar 1997		Yes	Yes

(*Continued*)

	Resolved Disputes	Resolution Solution	Resolution Date	*State Party A*		*State Party B*		*Does Dispute Involve …*		*Was 298(1)(a) declaration made prior to resolution date?*
				UNCLOS Status and 298(1)(a) Declaration Date		*UNCLOS Status and 298(1)(a) Declaration Date*		*A State not a UNCLOS party State?*	*298(1)(a) Declaration State?*	
57	Benin – Nigeria	Negotiated Delimited	Aug 2005	Benin		Nigeria				
58	Barbados – Trinidad & Tobago	Arbitration UNCLOS	Apr 2006	Barbados		*Trinidad & Tobago*	Feb 2009		Yes	
59	Trinidad & Tobago – Venezuela (Loran-Manatee)	JDA [RS]	Mar 2007 & Aug 2010	*Trinidad & Tobago*	Feb 2009	*Venezuela*	Not UNCLOS party	Yes	Yes	
60	Guyana – Suriname	Arbitration UNCLOS	Sep 2007	Guyana		Suriname				
61	Honduras – Nicaragua	ICJ	Oct 2007	Honduras		Nicaragua				
62	Angola–Congo-Brazzaville	JDA [JM]*	Nov 2007	Angola		Congo-Brazzaville				
63	China – Japan (limited area)	JDA [JM]*	Jun 2008	*China*	Aug 2006	Japan			Yes	Yes
64	Romania – Ukraine	ICJ	Feb 2009	Romania		*Ukraine*	Jul 1999		Yes	Yes
65	Kenya – Tanzania	Negotiated Delimited	Jun 2009	*Kenya*	Jan 2017	Tanzania			Yes	
66	Brunei – Malaysia	JDA [SM]*	Apr 2009	Brunei		*Malaysia*	Aug 2019		Yes	

(*Continued*)

Resolved Disputes		Resolution Solution	Resolution Date	*State Party A*		*State Party B*		*Does Dispute Involve …*		*Was 298(1)(a) declaration made prior to resolution date?*
				UNCLOS Status and 298(1)(a) Declaration Date		*UNCLOS Status and 298(1)(a) Declaration Date*		*A State not a UNCLOS party State?*	*298(1)(a) Declaration State?*	
67	Cyprus – Israel	Negotiated Delimited	Dec 2010	Cyprus		*Israel*	Not UNCLOS party	Yes		
68	Bangladesh – Myanmar	ITLOS	Mar 2012	Bangladesh		Myanmar				
69	UK–Netherlands (ORCA field)	JDA [RS]	Jul 2012	UK		Netherlands				
70	Mexico – US	JDA [RS]	Nov 2013	*Mexico*	Jan 2003	*US*	Not UNCLOS party	Yes	Yes	
71	Bangladesh – India	Arbitration UNCLOS	Jul 2014	Bangladesh		India				
72	Kazakhstan – Turkmenistan	Negotiated Delimited	Nov 2014	Kazakhstan		*Turkmen-istan*	Not UNCLOS party	Yes		
73	Colombia – Nicaragua	ICJ	2012 and 2016	*Colombia*	Not UNCLOS party	Nicaragua		Yes		
74	Cote D'Ivoire – Ghana	ITLOS	Sep 2017	Cote D'Ivoire		Ghana				
75	Indonesia – Philippines	Negotiated Delimited	Apr 2017	Indonesia		*Philippines*	May 1984		Yes	
76	Senegal – Mauritania	JDA [JM]*	Feb 2018	Senegal		Mauritania				

(*Continued*)

	Resolved Disputes	*Resolution Solution*	*Resolution Date*	*State Party A*		*State Party B*		*Does Dispute Involve …*		*Was 298(1)(a) declaration made prior to resolution date?*
				UNCLOS Status and 298(1)(a) Declaration Date		*UNCLOS Status and 298(1)(a) Declaration Date*		*A State not a UNCLOS party State?*	*298(1)(a) Declaration State?*	
77	UK–Netherlands (Sillimanite field)	JDA [RS]*	Feb 2018	UK		Netherlands				
78	Equatorial Guinea – Gabon	ICJ (Mediation)	Jul 2018	*Equatorial Guinea*	Feb 2002	*Gabon*	Jan 2009		Yes	Yes
79	Equatorial Guinea – Sao Tome & Principe	JDA [JM]*	Mar 2020	*Equatorial Guinea*	Feb 2002	Sao Tome & Principe			Yes	Yes
80	Kenya – Somalia	ICJ	Oct 2021	*Kenya*	Jan 2017	Somalia			Yes	Yes
81	Israel – Lebanon	Negotiated	Oct 2022	*Israel*	Not UNCLOS party	Lebanon		Yes		
	JDA solution: 36 (44.4%) Negotiated: 26 (32.1%) ICJ: 11 (13.6%) ITLOS: 2 (2.5%) Pre-UNCLOS Arbitration.: 2 (2.5%) Post-UNCLOS Arbitration.: 4 (4.9%)					81 resolved disputes		**19**	**45**	**9**
								23.5 %	**55.6%**	**11.1%**
						62 resolved disputes involving only States party to UNCLOS			**38**	**9**
									61.3% of 62	**14.5%** of 62

(*Continued*)

JDA & other cooperative solution analysis
JDA (SM) = JDAs under Single Management Model (4)
JDA (RS) = JDAs under Revenue Sharing Model (14)
JDA (JM) = JDAs under Joint Management Model (11)
JDA (JA) = JDAs under Joint Authority Model (7)
(*) Indicates JDAs where maritime boundary defined (23). 13 JDAs are in undefined maritime boundary areas
States in Italics indicates that have either made UNCLOS Article 298(1)(a) declarations or are not UNCLOS parties

Appendix B

Unresolved Disputes

	Unresolved Disputes	*State Party A*	*UNCLOS Status and 298(1)(a) Declaration Date*	*State Party B*	*UNCLOS Status and 298(1)(a) Declaration Date*	*Does dispute Involve ... A State not a UNCLOS party State?*	*A State that has made 298(1)(a) declaration?*	*A non-UNCLOS party or a 298(1)(a) declaration State?*	*Island and rocks issue?*	*Histor-ical Rights issue?*
	Eastern Mediterranean									
1	Israel – Palestine	*Israel*	Not UNCLOS party	Palestine	UNCLOS observer	Yes		Yes		Yes
2	Cyprus – Lebanon	Cyprus		Lebanon						Yes
3	Greece – Turkey	*Greece*	Jan 2013	*Turkey*	Not UNCLOS party	Yes	Yes	Yes	Yes	Yes
4	Cyprus – Turkey	Cyprus		*Turkey*	Not UNCLOS party	Yes		Yes		Yes
5	Egypt – Greece	*Egypt*	Feb 2017	*Greece*	Jan 2013		Yes	Yes		Yes
	Caspian Sea									
6	Azerbaijan – Iran	Azerbaijan		*Iran*	Not UNCLOS party	Yes		Yes		Yes
7	Azerbaijan – Turkmenistan	Azerbaijan		*Turkmen-istan*	Not UNCLOS party	Yes		Yes	Yes	Yes

(*Continued*)

Unresolved Disputes		State Party A		State Party B		Does dispute Involve …				
		UNCLOS Status and 298(1)(a) Declaration Date		*UNCLOS Status and 298(1)(a) Declaration Date*		*A State not a UNCLOS party State?*	*A State that has made 298(1)(a) declaration?*	*A non-UNCLOS party or a 298(1)(a) declaration State?*	*Island and rocks issue?*	*Histor-ical Rights issue?*
8	Iran – Turkmenistan	*Iran*	Not UNCLOS party	*Turkmen-istan*	Not UNCLOS party	Yes		Yes	Yes	Yes
	Northeast Asia									
9	China – Japan	*China*	Jun 1996	Japan			Yes	Yes	Yes	Yes
10	Japan – Korea	Japan		*Korea*	Apr 2006		Yes	Yes	Yes	Yes
11	China – Korea	*China*	Jun 1996	*Korea*	Apr 2006		Yes	Yes	Yes	Yes
	South China Sea									
12	China – Taiwan	*China*	Jun 1996	*Taiwan*	Not UNCLOS party	Yes	Yes	Yes	Yes	Yes
13	China – Vietnam	*China*	Jun 1996	Vietnam			Yes	Yes	Yes	Yes
14	China – Philippines	*China*	Jun 1996	Philip-pines	May 1984		Yes	Yes	Yes	Yes
15	China – Malaysia	*China*	Jun 1996	*Malaysia*	Aug 2019		Yes	Yes	Yes	Yes
16	China – Brunei	*China*	Jun 1996	Brunei			Yes	Yes	Yes	Yes
	Southeast Asia									
17	Cambodia – Thailand	*Cambodia*	Not UNCLOS party	*Thailand*	May 2011	Yes	Yes	Yes	Yes	Yes
18	Philippines – Malaysia	*Philippines*		*Malaysia*	Aug 2019		Yes	Yes	Yes	Yes

(*Continued*)

Unresolved Disputes		*State Party A*		*State Party B*		*Does dispute Involve …*				
		UNCLOS Status and 298(1)(a) Declaration Date		*UNCLOS Status and 298(1)(a) Declaration Date*		*A State not a UNCLOS party State?*	*A State that has made 298(1)(a) declaration?*	*A non-UNCLOS party or a 298(1)(a) declaration State?*	*Island and rocks issue?*	*Histor-ical Rights issue?*
19	Cambodia – Vietnam	*Cambodia*	Not UNCLOS party	Vietnam		Yes		Yes	Yes	Yes
20	Indonesia – Malaysia	Indonesia		*Malaysia*	Aug 2019		Yes	Yes	Yes	Yes
	Persian Gulf									
21	Iran – UAE (Abu Musa & Tunbs)	*Iran*	Not UNCLOS party	*UAE*	Not UNCLOS party	Yes		Yes	Yes	Yes
22	Iran – Kuwait	*Iran*	Not UNCLOS party	Kuwait		Yes		Yes	Yes	Yes
23	Iraq – Kuwait	Iraq		Kuwait					Yes	Yes
24	Iran – Iraq	*Iran*	Not UNCLOS party	Iraq		Yes		Yes	Yes	Yes
	Other Regions									
25	Guyana – Trinidad & Tobago	Guyana		*Trinidad & Tobago*	Feb 2009		Yes	Yes	Yes	Yes
26	Costa Rica – Nicaragua	*Costa Rica*		*Nicaragua*	May 2000		Yes	Yes	Yes	Yes
27	Congo-Brazzaville – Gabon	*Congo-Brazzaville*		*Gabon*	Jan 2009		Yes	Yes	Yes	Yes

(*Continued*)

Unresolved Disputes	*State Party A*	*State Party B*	*Does dispute Involve …*				
	UNCLOS Status and 298(1)(a) Declaration Date	*UNCLOS Status and 298(1)(a) Declaration Date*	*A State not a UNCLOS party State?*	*A State that has made 298(1)(a) declaration?*	*A non-UNCLOS party or a 298(1)(a) declaration State?*	*Island and rocks issue?*	*Histor-ical Rights issue?*
		27 unresolved disputes	**12**	**16**	**25**	**22**	**27**
			44%	**59%**	**93%**	**73%**	**100%**
		15 unresolved disputes involving only States party to UNCLOS		**13**		**14**	**20**
				87%		**93%**	**100%**

States in Italics indicates that have either made UNCLOS Article 298(1)(a) declarations or are not UNCLOS parties

Appendix C

Article 298(1)(a) Declaration States

	Formal UNCLOS Confirmation, Accession, Succession, Ratification Date		*Article 298(1)(a) Declaration Date*	*Number of Resolved Disputes*	*Number of Unresolved Disputes Unresolved*
1	Algeria	Jun-96	May-18	One	
2	Argentina	Dec-95	Dec-95	One	
3	Australia	Dec-94	Mar-02	One	
4	Belarus	Aug-06	Jul-01		
5	Canada	Nov-03	Nov-03	Two	
6	Chile	Aug-97	Aug-97		
7	China	Jun-96	Aug-06	One	Seven
8	D R Congo	Feb-89	Apr-14	One	
9	Denmark	Nov-04	Nov-04	One	
10	Egypt	Aug-83	Feb-17	One	One
11	Equatorial Guinea	Jul-97	Feb-02	Two	
12	France	Apr-96	Apr-96	Two	
13	Gabon	Mar-98	Jan-09	One	One
14	Greece	Jul-95	Jan-13		
15	Iceland	Jun-85	Jun-85	One	One
16	Italy	Jan-95	Jan-95		
17	Kenya	Mar-89	Jan-17	Two	One
18	Korea	Jan-96	Apr-06	One	Two
19	Malaysia	Oct-96	Aug-19	Three	Three
20	Mexico	Mar-83	Jan-03	One	
21	Montenegro	Oct-06	May-11		
22	Nicaragua*	Dec-84	May-00		One
23	Norway	Jun-96	Jun-96	Five	
24	Palau	Nov-96	Apr-06		
25	Philippines *	May-84	May-84	One	Two
26	Portugal	Nov-97	Nov-97		
27	Russia	Mar-97	Mar-97	Three	
28	Saudi Arabia	Apr-96	Jan-18	Four	
29	Singapore	Nov-94	Dec-18		
30	Slovenia	Jun-95	Oct-01		
31	Spain	Jan-97	Jul-02	One	
32	Thailand	May-11	May-11	Two	One
33	Togo	Apr-85	Apr-19		
34	Trinidad & Tobago	May-11	Feb-09	Two	One
35	Tunisia	Apr-85	Apr-85	Two	
36	Ukraine	Jul-99	Jul-99	One	

(*) indicates declaration that were ambiguous and were interpretation by the author as shown above.

Bibliography

Articles / Books / Reports

ABC News, 'US concern Following China's Announcement of Air Defence Zone Over Disputed Islands' *ABC News* (Australia, November 25 2013). https://www.abc.net.au/news/2013-11-23/an-china-air-defence-zone/5112994.

Acer, Yücel, 'A Proposal for a Joint Maritime Development Regime in the Aegean Sea' (2006) 37(1) *Journal of Maritime Law & Commerce* 49.

Adede, A. O., *The System for Settlement of Disputes Under the United Nations Convention on the Law of the Sea* (Martinus Nijhoff, 1987).

Adede, A. O, 'Toward the Formulation of the Rule of Delimitation of Sea Boundaries Between States With Adjacent or Opposite Coasts' (1979) 19 *Virginia Journal of International Law* 207.

Adede, Andronico O., 'Book Review: The System for Settlement of Disputes Under the United Nations Convention on the Law of the Sea. By Andronico O. Adede Publications on Ocean Development, General Editor Shigeru Oda, Volume 10' (1989) 13 *Marine Policy* 81.

Adede, Andronico O., 'The System for Settlement of Disputes Under the United Nations Convention on the Law of the Sea' in Shigeru Oda (ed.), *Publications on Ocean Development*, Volume 10 (Martinus Nijhoff, 1987).

AFP, 'Seals, Caviar and Oil: Caspian Sea Faces Pollution Threat' *New Straits Times* (Malaysia, April 16, 2019). https://www.nst.com.my/world/2019/04/479891/seals-caviar-and-oil-caspian-sea-faces-pollution-threat.

Afshar, Houman, 'Caspian Dispute: Is a Doctrinal Analysis Too Late or Can We Turn Back the Hands of Time' (2003) 48(4) *New York Law School Law Review* 755.

Aguda, Henry Rhoel R.; Arellano-Aguda, Jesusa Loreto A., 'Philippine Claim Over the Spratly Group of Islands: An Application of Article 76 of the UNCLOS' (2008–2009) 83(3) *Philosphical* Law Journal 573.

Al Baharna, Husain M., 'Legal Implications of Maritime Boundary Disputes (With Special Reference to the Gulf)' (1994) 1 *Yearbook of Islamic and Middle Eastern Law* 68.

Al Mazrouei, Noura S., 'The Revival of the UAE–Saudi Arabia Border Dispute in the 21st Century' (2017) 32(2) *Journal of Borderlands Studies* 157. https://doi.org/10.1080/08865655.2015.1124242.

Alam, M. Shah Alam; Al Faruque, Abdulla, 'The Problem of Delimitation of Bangladesh's Maritime Boundaries With India and Myanmar: Prospects for a Solution' (2010) *The International Journal of Marine and Coastal Law* 406.

Al-Mughrabi, Nidal, 'Shell Gives Up on Gaza's Offshore Gas Field - Palestinians' *Reuters* (March 6 2018). https://www.reuters.com/article/israel-egypt-gas-idUSL5E8FM2XZ20120422.

Al-Nahyan, Khalid S. Z., *The Three Islands, Mapping the UAE-Iran Dispute* (Royal United Services Institute for Defence and Security Studies (RUSI), 2013). https://rusi.org/sites/default/files/201312_bk_the_three_islands_2.pdf.

Amer, Ramses, 'China, Vietnam, and the South China Sea: Disputes and Dispute Management' (2014) 45(1) *Ocean Development & International Law* 17.

Amin, S. H., 'Customary Rules of Delimitation of the Continental Shelf: The Gulf States Practice' (1980) 11(4) *Journal of Maritime Law and Commerce* 509.

Amin, S. H., 'The Iran-Iraq Conflict: Legal Implications' (1982) 31(1) *The International and Comparative Law Quarterly* 167. www.jstor.org/stable/759271.

Amin, S. H., 'The Law of Fisheries in the Persian/Arabian Gulf' (1983) 14(4) *Journal of Maritime Law and Commerce* 581.

Anadolu Agency, 'Turkey Welcomes Turkish Cypriot President's Proposal' *Hurriyet Daily News* (Turkey, July 13 2019). https://www.hurriyetdailynews.com/turkey-welcomes-turkish-cypriot-presidents-proposal-144950.

Anderson, D. H., 'Delimitation of the Maritime Boundary in the Bay of Bengal (Bangladesh/Myanmar) - Case No. 1' (2012) 106(4) *American Journal of International Law* 817.

Anderson, David, *'Article 283 of the United Nations Convention on the Law of the Sea'* (Brill, 2007).

Anderson, Sulome, 'Hezbollah Readies for Next War Against Israel' (September 2019) *Foreign Policy*. https://foreignpolicy.com/2019/09/04/hezbollah-readies-for-new-war-against-israel-lebanon-drone-strikes/#.

Antreasyan, Anaïs, 'Gas Finds in the Eastern Mediterranean Gaza, Israel, and Other Conflicts' (2013) 42(3) *Journal of Palestine Studies* 29.

Antrim, Caitlyn L., 'Ineral Resources of Stateless Space: Lessons From the Deep Seabed' (2005) 59(1) *Journal of International Affairs* 55.

Argus Media, 'Crescent Claims Victory in Iran Gas Arbitration' *Argus Media* (Dubai, August 11 2014). https://www.argusmedia.com/en/news/920913-crescent-claims-victory-in-iran-gas-arbitration.

Aronson, Geoffrey, 'Conflict expands in Eastern Mediterranean Over Gas Riches' *The Arab Weekly* (UK, January 19 2020). https://thearabweekly.com/conflict-expands-eastern-mediterranean-over-gas-riches.

Asia Maritime Transparency Initiative, 'A Blueprint for Cooperation on Oil and Gas Production in the South China Sea' (Research Update, South China Sea Expert Group, The Center for Strategic and International Studies, July 2018). https://amti.csis.org/a-blueprint-for-cooperation-on-oil-and-gas-production-in-the-south-china-sea/.

Asia Maritime Transparency Initiative, 'Failing or Incomplete Grading the South China Sea Arbitration' (Research Report, July 11 2019). https://amti.csis.org/failing-or-incomplete-grading-the-south-china-sea-arbitration/.

Asia Maritime Transparency Initiative, 'Who is Taking Sides After the South China Sea Ruling?' (Research Report Web, August 15 2016). https://amti.csis.org/sides-in-south-china-sea/.

Au, Kung-wing, 'Japan's Purchase of Disputed Islands: Fallout and Misperception' (2013) 30(3) *East Asia: An International Quarterly* 183.

Au, Kung-wing, 'The East China Sea Issue: Japan-China Talks for Oil and Gas' (2008) 25(3) *East Asia: An International Quarterly* 223.

Australia News Corp, 'South China Sea Ruling: UN-Backed Tribunal Says China Has No Rights Over Water, Resources' *Australia News Corp* (July 12 2016). https://www.news.com.au/world/south-china-sea-ruling-unbacked-tribunal-says-china-has-no-rights-over-water-resources/news-story/1550854ebc1b43078e3fab113b5f6f40.

Azernews, 'Turkmen Parliament Ratifies Convention on Legal Status of Caspian Sea' *Azernews* (Azerbaijan, December 3 2018). https://www.azernews.az/region/141946.html.

Baconi, Tareq, 'Pipelines and Pipedreams. How the EU Can Support a Regional Gas Hub in the Eastern Mediterranean' (Research Report, European Council on Foreign Relations Policy Brief, April 2017) 9. https://www.ecfr.eu/publications/summary/pipelines_and_pipedreams_how_the_eu_can_support_a_regional_gas_hub_in_7276.

Bagheri, Saeed, 'Iran's Attitude to Security in the Strait of Hormuz: An International Law Perspective' (2015) 13 *New Zealand Yearbook of International Law*. https://www.researchgate.net/profile/Saeed_Bagheri7/publication/317091037_Iran%27s_Attitude_to_Security_in_the_Strait_of_Hormuz_An_International_Law_Perspective/links/5930437daca272fc55e151c8/Irans-Attitude-to-Security-in-the-Strait-of-Hormuz-An-International-Law-Perspective.pdf.

Bahgat, Gawdat, 'Regional Report - The Caspian Sea: Potentials and Prospects' (2004) 17(1) *Governance*, 115.

Bahgat, Gawdat, 'Splitting Water: The Geopolitics of Resources in the Caspian Sea' (2002) 2 *SAIS Review* 273.

Bajrektarevic, Anis H.; Posega, Petra, 'The Caspian Basin: Territorial and Status-Related Disputes, Energy Transit Corridors, and Their Implications for EU Energy Security' (2014) 16(1) *Seton Hall Journal of Diplomacy and International Relations* 85.

Baker, Betsy, 'Filling an Arctic Gap: Legal and Regulatory Possibilities for Canadian-U.S. Cooperation in the Beaufort Sea' (2009) 34(1) *Vermont Law Review* 57.

Baker, James S.; Byers, Michael, 'Crossed Lines: The Curious Case of the Beaufort Sea Maritime Boundary Dispute' (2012) 43(1) *Ocean Development & International Law* 70.

Bandow, Doug, 'Don't Resurrect the Law of the Sea Treaty' (2005) 59(1) *Journal of International Affairs* 25.

Bantekas, Ilias, 'Bilateral Delimitation of the Caspian Sea and the Exclusion of Third Parties' (2011) 26(1) *The International Journal of Marine and Coastal Law* 47.

Baradari, Fatemeh; Asfaranjan, Y. S.; Nassimi, M., 'The Key Success Factors of Cooperation in Exploitation Gas Reserve in a Disputed Area: A Case of Malaysia Thailand Joint Authority (MTJA)' (2014) 6(3) *International Journal of Academic Research* 229.

Barnes, Richard A., 'Consolidating Governance Principles for Areas Beyond National Jurisdiction' (2012) 27(2) *International Journal of Marine & Coastal Law* 261.

Bastianelli, Fabrizio, 'Border Delimitation in the Mediterranean Sea' (1982) 17(4) *International Spectator* 319.

Bastida, Ana E.; Ifesi-Okoye, A.; Mahmud, S.; Ross, J., 'Cross-Border Unitization and Joint Development Agreements: An International Law Perspective' (2007) 29(2) *Houston Journal of International Law* 355.

Batongbacal, Jay, The Philippines-China MOU on Cooperation in Oil and Gas Development (Research Report, The Center for Strategic and International Studies, The Asia Maritime Transparency Initiative, December 5 2018). https://amti.csis.org/philippines-china-mou-cooperation-oil-gas-development/.

Batyrov, Azamat, 'Russia, Kazakhstan Push For Hydrocarbon Expansion With Kurmangazy Project' *Caspian News* (December 9 2018). https://caspiannews.com/news-detail/russia-kazakhstan-push-for-hydrocarbon-expansion-with-kurmangazy-project-2018-12-6-21/.

Bautista, Lowell, 'The Implications of Recent Decisions on the Territorial and Maritime Boundary Disputes in East and Southeast Asia' in C. Schofield (ed.), *Maritime Energy Resources in Asia - Legal Regimes and Cooperation* (The National Bureau of Asian Research, February 2012) 105.

Baveira, Aileen S. P., 'The Philippines and the South China Sea Dispute' in Ian Storey and Lin Cheng-yi (eds.), *The South China Sea Dispute: Navigating Diplomatic and Strategic Tensions* (ISEAS Publishing, 2016).

BBC, 'Iran Compromising Interests in New Caspian Sea Legal Regime - Commentary' *BBC Monitoring Middle East* (January 15 2008). https://monitoring.bbc.co.uk/.

BBC, 'Iran Should Have Taken Caspian Sea Rights Seriously - Commentary' *BBC Monitoring Middle East* (January 15 2008). https://monitoring.bbc.co.uk/.

BBC News, 'Murky Dividing Lines of Shatt al-Arab' *BBC News* (April 4 2007). http://news.bbc.co.uk/2/hi/uk_news/6496559.stm.

Beaugrand, Claire, 'Borders and Spatial Imaginaries in the Kuwaiti Identity' (2018) 23(3) *Geopolitics* 544. https://doi.org/10.1080/14650045.2017.1341407.

Becker-Weinberg, Vasco, *Joint Development of Hydrocarbon Deposits in the Law of the Sea* (Hamburg studies on Maritime Affairs, 2014)

Beckman, Robert, 'Factors Conducive to Joint Development in Asia - Lessons Learned for the South China Sea' (Research Papers - University of Wollongong Research Online, 2013). http://ro.uow.edu.au/cgi/viewcontent.cgi?article=2236&context=lhapapers.

Beckman, Robert, 'International Law, UNCLOS and the South China Sea' in Robert Beckman (ed.), *Beyond Territorial Disputes in the South China Sea: Legal Frameworks for the Joint Development of Hydrocarbon Resources* (Edward Elgar, 2013).

Beckman, Robert, 'Legal Framework for Joint Development in the South China Sea' (Conference Paper, Recent Development of the South China Sea Dispute and Prospects of Joint Development Regime, December 6–7 2012 Haikou, China). http://cil.nus.edu.sg/wp/wp-content/uploads/2012/12/Beckman-Paper-Hainan-Dec-6-7-submitted-Nov-22.pdf.

Beckman, Robert, 'The Establishment of a Cooperative Mechanism for the Straits of Malacca and Singapore Under Article 43 of the United Nations Convention on the Law of the Sea' in Aldo Chircop, Ted L. McDorman, and Susan Rolston (eds), *The Future of Ocean Regime-Building: Essays in Tribute to Douglas M. Johnston* (Martinus Nijhoff Publishers, 2009).

Beckman, Robert, 'Tribunal Ruling a Game Changer' *Straits Times* (Singapore, July 14 2016). https://www.straitstimes.com/opinion/tribunal-ruling-a-game-changer-south-china-sea.

Beckman, Robert; Bernard, Leonardo, 'Framework for the Joint Development of Hydrocarbon Resources' Centre for International Law (Report, National University of Singapore, 2013) 25. http://cil.nus.edu.sg/wp/wp-content/uploads/2010/08/BECKMAN-AND-BERNARD-FRAMEWORK-FOR-THE-JOINT-DEVELOPMENT-OF-HYDROCARBON-RESOURCES.pdf.

Beckman, Robert; Davenport, Tara, 'The EEZ Regime: Reflections After 30 Years (Conference Paper, LOSI-KIOST Conference on Securing the Ocean for the Next Generation, May 2012) 3. https://www.law.berkeley.edu/files/Beckman-Davenport-final.pdf.

Bederman, David J., 'Counterintuiting Countermeasures' (2002) 96(4) *American Journal of International Law* 817. www.jstor.org/stable/3070680.

Bederman, David J., 'The Old Isolationism and the New Law of the Sea: Reflections on Advice and Consent for UNCLOS' (2008) 49 *Harvard International Law Journal* 21. http://www.harvardilj.org/wp-content/uploads/2011/01/HILJ-Online_49_Bederman.pdf.

Beirut Star (The), 'Maritime Gas Feud Moves Toward Resolution' *The Beirut Star* (April 5 2012). http://www.dev.kataeb.org/news/2012/04/05/maritime-gas-feud-moves-toward-resolution.

Belding, Sean P., 'China's Island Building in the South China Sea: Collateral Effect on the UNCLOS and Potential Solutions' (2018) 40(3) *Houston Journal of International Law* 1003.

Bernard, Leonardo, 'Prospect-for-Joint-Development in the SCS' (Research, Centre for International Law, Singapore, National University of Singapore, June 2013). http://cil.nus.edu.sg/wp/wp-content/uploads/2013/06/Bernard-CSIS-Draft-1-June-2013-Prospect-for-Joint-Development-in-the-SCS.pdf.

Bhuiyan, Sharif, 'ITLOS Judgment: An Analysis' *The Daily Star* (Bangladesh, April 17 2012). https://www.thedailystar.net/news-detail-230381.

Biang, J. Tanga, 'The Joint Development Zone Between Nigeria and Sao Tome and Principe: A Case of Provisional Arrangement in the Gulf of Guinea. International Law, State Practice and Prospects for Regional Integration' (Research Paper, Division for Ocean Affairs and the Law of the Sea, United Nations New York, 2010). http://www.un.org/depts/los/nippon/unnff_programme_home/fellows_pages/fellows_papers/tanga_0910_cameroon.pdf.

Bilek, Büşra Nurç, 'Turkey Will Continue Its Activities in E. Med' Andalou Agency (Turkey, July 14 2019).

Blake, G. H., 'International Boundaries and Territorial Stability in the Middle East: An Assessment' (1992) 28(3) *GeoJournal* 365. www.jstor.org/stable/41145608.

Blanford, Nicholas, 'Oil and Gas Discoveries Produce Potential Israel-Lebanon Flash Points' *Christian Science Monitor* (November 1 2010).

Blyschak, P. M., 'Offshore Oil and Gas Projects Amid Maritime Border Disputes: Applicable Law' (2013) 6(3) *The Journal of World Energy Law & Business* 210.

Bolukbasi, Suha, 'The Controversy Over the Caspian Sea Mineral Resources: Conflicting Perceptions, Clashing Interests' (1998) 50(3) *Europe-Asia Studies* 397.

Borgergson, Scott, 'The National Interest and the Law of the Sea' (Research Paper, Council on Foreign Relations, 2009). www.cfr.org.

Bouchez, Leo J., 'North Sea Continental Shelf Cases,' (1969–1970) 1 Journal of Maritime Law and Commerce 113.

Bowlus, John, 'Eastern Mediterranean Gas: Testing the Field' *Energy Reporters* (May 27 2020). https://www.energy-reporters.com/opinion/eastern-mediterranean-gas-testing-the-field/.

Boyle, Alan, 'Dispute Settlement and the Law of the Sea Convention: Problems of Fragmentation and Jurisdiction' (1997) 46(1) *International and Comparative Law Quarterly* 37.

BP Statistical Review of World Energy 2018 (BP, 2018). https://www.bp.com/content/dam/bp/business-sites/en/global/corporate/pdfs/energy-economics/statistical-review/bp-stats-review-2018-full-report.pdf.

BP Statistical Review of World Energy 2020 (BP, 69th ed., 2020). https://www.bp.com/content/dam/bp/business-sites/en/global/corporate/pdfs/energy-economics/statistical-review/bp-stats-review-2020-full-report.pdf.

Bravender-Coyle, Paul, 'The Emerging Legal Principles and Equitable Criteria Governing the Delimitation of Maritime Boundaries Between States' (1988) 19(3) *Ocean Development & International Law* 171. https://doi.org/10.1080/00908328809545856.

Bristow, Michael, 'China Should Respect South China Sea Ruling, Says Philippines' *BBC News* (July 14 2016). https://www.bbc.com/news/world-asia-36791281.

British Institute of International and Comparative Law (The), *Report on the Obligations of States Under Articles 74(3) and 83(3) of UNCLOS in Respect of Undelimited Maritime Areas* (Report, June 30 2016). https://www.biicl.org/publications/report-on-the

-obligations-of-states-under-articles-743-and-833-of-unclos-in-respect-of-undelimited-maritime-areas.

Brown, E. D., 'Dispute Settlement and the Law of the Sea: The UN Convention Regime' (1997) 21(1) *Marine Policy* 17–18.

BRTK, 'New Proposal on Hydrocarbons' Bayrak Radio Television Corporation (TNRC, July 13 2019).

Bryza, Matthew J., 'Eastern Mediterranean Natural Gas: Potential for Historic Breakthroughs Among Israel, Turkey, and Cyprus' (2013) 12(3) *Turkish Policy Quarterly* 35.

Buga, Irina, 'Territorial Sovereignty Issues in Maritime Disputes: A Jurisdictional Dilemma for Law of the Sea Tribunals' (2012) 27(1) *International Journal of Marine & Coastal Law* 59.

Bugajski, Dariusz R., 'The Persian Gulf in the Light of the Law of the Sea' (2016) XXXII *Prawo Morskie* 23.

Burke, Naoimi, 'Annex VII Arbitral Tribunal Delimits Maritime Boundary Between Bangladesh and India in the Bay of Bengal' (2014) 18(20) *American Society of International Law Insights*. http://asil.org/insights/volume/18/issue/20/annex-vii-arbitral-tribunal-delimits-maritime-boundary-between.

Butt, Gerald, 'Turkey Pushes East Mediterranean Boundaries' *Petroleum Economist* (December 4 2019). https://www.petroleum-economist.com/articles/politics-economics/middle-east/2019/turkey-pushes-east-mediterranean-boundaries.

Byrne, James, 'Gazprom Walks Where BP Feared to Tread' *Interfax Global Energy* (January 29 2013). https://interfaxenergy.com/gasdaily/article/3933/gazprom-walks-where-bp-feared-to-tread.

Cameron, Peter D., 'The Rules of Engagement: Developing Cross-Border Petroleum Deposits in the North Sea and the Caribbean' (2006) 55(1) *International and Comparative Law Quarterly* 559. http://journals.cambridge.org/abstract_S0020589300069499.

Carpenter, Scott, 'New Pipeline Deal Gives Europe Access to Eastern Mediterranean Gas Reserves, Angering Turkey' *Forbes* (January 2 2020). https://www.forbes.com/sites/scottcarpenter/2020/01/02/new-gas-pipeline-deal-gives-europe-access-to-eastern-mediterranean-reserves-angering-turkey/#a976321c69d9.

Carroll, Oliver, 'Caspian Sea: After 22 Years of Wrangling, Deal Over Oil and Gas Rich Body of Water Reached – And It's Good News for Russia' *The Independent* (UK, August 10 2018).

Chandranegara, Ibnu; Hoesein, Zainal, 'Policy Concept and Designs of Oil and Gas Governance in Indonesia's Oil Companies' (2019) 9 *International Journal of Energy Economics and Policy* 121.

Charney, Jonathan, 'Entry into force of the 1982 Convention on the Law of the Sea' (1995) 35 *Virginia Journal of International Law* 381.

Charney, Jonathan I., 'Central East Asian Maritime Boundaries and the Law of the Sea' (1995) 89(4) *American Journal of International Law* 724.

Charney, Jonathan I., 'Law of the Sea: Breaking the Deadlock' (1977) 55(2) *Foreign Affairs* 598.

Charney, Jonathan I., 'Progress in International Maritime Boundary Delimitation Law' (1994) 88(2) *American Journal of International Law* 227.

Charney, Jonathan I., 'Rocks that Cannot Sustain Human Habitation' (1999) 93(4) *The American Journal of International Law* 863. www.jstor.org/stable/2555353.

Charney, Jonathan I., 'The Exclusive Economic Zone and Public International Law' (1985) 15(3–4) *Ocean Development and International Law* 233.

Charney, Jonathan I., 'The Implications of Expanding International Dispute Settlement Systems: The 1982 Convention on the Law of the Sea' (1996) 90(1) *The American Journal of International Law* 69.

Cherniavskii, Stanislav, 'Problems of the Caspian' (2002) 40(2) *Russian Politics and Law* 85.

China Daily, 'Provocative Japanese Test-Drilling Condemned' *China Daily* (July 16 2005). http://www.china.org.cn/english/2005/Jul/135134.htm.

China Daily, 'Production Begin at Chunxiao Gas Field' *China Daily* (August 8 2006). http://www.chinadaily.com.cn/china/2006-08/06/content_657939.htm.

China People's Daily, 'Oil Giants Pull Out of East China Sea Gas Fields Project' *China People's Daily* (September 30 2004).

China US Focus, 'Maritime Delimitation in the Gulf of Tonkin is Too Important to be Ignored' (Research Paper, May 29 2015). https://www.chinausfocus.com/peace-security/maritime-delimitation-in-the-gulf-of-tonkin-is-too-important-to-be-ignored#.

Chircop, Aldo E. (ed.), *The Regulation of International Shipping International and Comparative Perspectives: Essays in Honor of Edgar Gold* (Martinus Nijhoff Brill Academic Publisher, 2012).

Chiu, Hungdah, 'Some Problems Concerning the Application of the Maritime Boundary Delimitation Provisions of the 1982 United Nations Convention on the Law of the Sea Between Adjacent or Opposite States' (1985) 9(1) *Maryland Journal of International Law & Trade* 1.

Chubin, Shahram; Tripp, Charles, 'Domestic Politics and Territorial Disputes in the Persian Gulf and the Arabian Peninsula' (1993) 35(4) *Survival* 3. https://doi.org/10.1080/00396339308442709.

Chung, Chien-peng, 'The Diaoyu/Tiaoyutai/Senkaku Islands Dispute: Domestic Politics and the Limits of Diplomacy' (1998) 16(3) *American Asian Review* 135.

Churchill, R. R., 'Joint Development Zones: International Legal Issues' in Hazel Fox (ed.), *Joint Development of Offshore Oil and Gas*, Volume 2 (The British Institute of International and Comparative Law, 1990).

Churchill, Robin, 'The General Dispute Settlement System of the UN Convention on the Law of the Sea: Overview, Context, and Use' (2017) 48(3–4) *Ocean Development & International Law* 216. https://doi.org/10.1080/00908320.2017.1327287.

Churchill, Robin, 'The Persisting Problem of Non-Compliance With the Law of the Sea Convention: Disorder in the Oceans' (2012) 27(4) *International Journal of Marine & Coastal Law* 813.

Congressional Research Service Specialist in Naval Affairs (Name Redacted), *Maritime Territorial and Exclusive Economic Zone (EEZ) Disputes Involving China: Issues for Congress* (CRS Report Prepared for Members and Committees of Congress No R42784, December 12 2017) 33.

Connelly, Colby, 'Eastern Mediterranean Gas Discoveries, Progress, and What to Watch in 2023' (2023), *Middle East Institute.* https://www.mei.edu/publications/eastern-mediterranean-gas-discoveries-progress-and-what-watch-2023.

Constantinos, Taliotis, 'Energy Security Prospects in Cyprus and Israel: A Focus on Natural Gas' (2014) 3 *International Journal of Sustainable Energy Planning and Management* 5.

Corr, Anders, 'China's $60 Trillion Estimate of Oil and Gas in the South China Sea: Strategic Implications' (2018) *The Journal of Political Risk.* http://www.jpolrisk.com/chinas-60-trillion-estimate-of-oil-and-gas-in-the-south-china-sea-the-strategic-implications/.

Costa, Anna, *The China-Japan Conflict Over the Senkaku/Diaoyu Islands: Useful Rivalry* (Routledge, 2017)

Crawford, James, *Brownlie's Principles of Public International Law* (Oxford University Press, 9th ed., 2019).

Cruz, Enrico Dela, 'Philippines' Oil Still in Troubled Waters After South China Sea Ruling' *Reuters* (July 22 2016). https://www.reuters.com/article/us-southchinasea-ruling-philippines-ener/philippines-oil-still-in-troubled-waters-after-south-china-sea-ruling-idUSKCN1020HK.

Cusimano, Joseph J., 'An Analysis of Iran-Iraq Bilateral Border Treaties' (1992) 24 *Case Western Reserve Journal of International Law* 89.

Dagoumas, Athanasios; Flouros, Floros, 'Energy Policy Formulation in Israel Following Its Recent Gas Discoveries' (2017) 7(1) *International Journal of Energy Economics and Policy* 19. http://EconPapers.repec.org/RePEc:eco:journ2:2017-01-03.

Daiss, Tim, 'Why the South China Sea Has More Oil Than You Think' (2016) *Forbes* .https://www.forbes.com/sites/timdaiss/2016/05/22/why-the-south-china-sea-has-more-oil-than-you-think/#3a435871dd8f.

Dalay, Galip, 'Turkey, Europe, and the Eastern Mediterranean: Charting a Way Out of the Current Deadlock' (January 2021) *Brookings Doha Center Policy Briefing*. https://www.brookings.edu/research/turkey-europe-and-the-eastern-mediterranean-charting-a-way-out-of-the-current-deadlock/.

Davenport, Tara, 'Island-Building in the South China Sea: Legality and Limits' (2018) 8(1) *Asian Journal of International Law* 76.

Davenport, Tara, 'Joint Development in Asia: Lessons for Sustainable Peace in South China Sea' (Conference Paper, 8th Asian Law Institute Conference, Kyushu, Japan, 2011).

Davenport, Tara, 'Southeast Asian Approaches to Maritime Boundaries' (2014) 4(2) *Asian Journal of International Law* 309.

Davenport, Tara, 'Southeast-Asian Approaches to Maritime Delimitation' (Paper Presented at the 3rd NUS-AsianSIL Young Scholars Workshop, NUS Law School, Singapore, February 2012).

Davenport, Tara, 'The Exploration and Exploitation of Hydrocarbon Resources in Areas of Overlapping Claims' in Davenport, Tara (ed.), *Beyond Territorial Disputes in the South China Sea: Legal Frameworks for the Joint Development of Hydrocarbon Resources* (Edward Elgar, 2013).

Davenport, Tara, 'The Exploration and Exploitation of Hydrocarbon Resources in Areas of Overlapping Claims' in Robert Beckman (ed.), *Beyond Territorial Disputes in the South China Sea* (Edward Elgar Publishing, 2003) 100.

Davenport, Tara; Beckman, Robert, 'The EEZ Regime: Reflections After 30 Years' (Conference Paper, 2012 LOSI-KIOST Conference on Securing the Ocean for the Next Generation, Korea, May 2012). https://www.law.berkeley.edu/files/Beckman-Davenport-final.pdf.

Davis, Michael C., 'Can International Law Help Resolve the Conflicts Over Uninhibited Islands in the East China Sea?' (2015) 43(2) *Denver Journal of International Law and Policy* 119.

Dickinson, Edwin D., 'The Clipperton Island Case' (1933) 27(1) *The American Journal of International Law* 130. http://www.jstor.org.ezproxy-b.deakin.edu.au/stable/2189797.

Dobronravin, Nikolaj A.; Rubtsova, Alexandra, 'Contested States and Maritime Boundaries in the Contemporary Eastern Mediterranean' (2016) 100(3) *Nuova Rivista Storica* 1011.

Donaldson, John; Pratt, Martin, 'International Boundary Developments' (2004) 9(2) *Geopolitics* 501. https://doi.org/10.1080/14650040490460953.

Druce, Stephen; Baikoeni; Efri, 'Circumventing Conflict: The Indonesia–Malaysia Ambalat Block Dispute' in M. Oishi (ed.), *Contemporary Conflicts in Southeast Asia* (Springer

Science + Business Media, 2016) 137. https://www.researchgate.net/publication/287214343_Circumventing_Conflict_The_Indonesia-Malaysia_Ambalat_Block_Dispute.

Dubner, Barry Hart, 'The Caspian: Is It a Lake, a Sea or an Ocean and Does It Matter - The Danger of Utilizing Unilateral Approaches to Resolving Regional/International Issues' (2000) 18(2) *Dickinson Journal of International Law* 253.

Dudley, Dominic, 'The Race to Harness Gas Resources' (2014) 58(23) *MEED: Middle East Economic Digest* 40.

Duff, John A., 'A Note on the United States and the Law of the Sea: Looking Back and Moving Forward' (2004) 35(3) *Ocean Development & International Law* 195.

Dundua, Nugzar, 'Delimitation of Maritime Boundaries Between Adjacent States' (Research Report, United Nations – The Nippon Foundation (2006–2007)). http://www.un.org/depts/los/nippon/unnff_programme_home/fellows_pages/fellows_papers/dundua_0607_georgia.pdf.

Dunlap, Ben N., 'Divide and Conquer - The Russian Plan for Ownership of the Caspian Sea [Notes]' (2004) 27(1) *Boston College International and Comparative Law Review* 115.

Durden, Tyler, 'Japan Protests After Discovering Chinese Military Radar in Disputed Waters' *ZeroHedge*. https://www.zerohedge.com/news/2016-08-07/japan-protests-after-discovering-chinese-military-radar-disputed-waters-fleet-300-ch.

Dutton, Peter, 'Three Disputes and Three Objectives' (2011) 64(4) *Naval War College Review* 42.

Dutton, Peter, 'Viribus Mari Victoria? Power and Law in the South China Sea' (Conference Paper Managing Tensions in the South China Sea, June 5–6, 2013). http://csis.org/files/attachments/130606_Dutton_ConferencePaper.pdf.

Dyke, J. Van, 'Disputes Over Islands and Maritime Boundaries in East Asia' in Seoung-Yong Hong and Jon Van Dyke (eds.), M*aritime Boundary Disputes, Settlement Processes, and the Law of the Sea* (Martinus Nijhoff Publishers, 2009) 74.

Dyke, Jon Van, 'The Republic of Korea's Maritime Boundaries' (2003) 18(4) *The International Journal of Marine and Coastal Law* 509. http://www.hawaii.edu/elp/publications/faculty/TheRepublicofKorea.doc.

Economist (The), 'A Row Between Turkey and Greece Over Gas is Raising Tension in the Eastern Mediterranean' *The Economist* (UK, August 22 2020). https://www.economist.com/international/2020/08/22/a-row-between-turkey-and-greece-over-gas-is-raising-tension-in-the-eastern-mediterranean.

Economist (The), 'China is Resorting to New Forms of Bullying in the South China Sea' *The Economist* (UK, October 3 2019). https://www.economist.com/asia/2019/10/03/china-is-resorting-to-new-forms-of-bullying-in-the-south-china-seab.

Economist (The), 'Dealing With a Dangerous Dispute in the Eastern Med' *The Economist* (UK, August 22 2020). https://www.economist.com/leaders/2020/08/22/dealing-with-a-dangerous-dispute-in-the-eastern-med.

Economist (The), 'Might Turkey Seize a Tiny Greek Island?' *The Economist* (UK, January 12 2023). https://www.economist.com/europe/2023/01/12/might-turkey-seize-a-tiny-greek-island.

Economist (The), 'Persians Vs. Arabs. Same Old Sneers' (2012) 403(8783) *Economist* 46.

Economic Times (The), 'Krishna-Godavari Basin to Yield 160 Mt Oil' *The Economic Times* (India, November 1 2002). https://economictimes.indiatimes.com/krishna-godavari-basin-to-yield-160mt-oil-ril/articleshow/26900089.cms.

Eissler, Eric R.; Arasıl, Gözde, 'Maritime Boundary Delimitation in the Eastern Mediterranean' (2014) 159(2) *RUSI Journal: Royal United Services Institute for Defence Studies* 74.

Elferink, Alex G. Oude, 'The Regime of the Area: Delineating the Scope of Application of the Common Heritage Principle and Freedom of the High Seas' (2007) 22(1) *International Journal of Marine & Coastal Law* 143.

Elferink, Alex G. Oude; Johnson, Constance, 'Outer Limits of the Continental Shelf and "Disputed Areas": State Practice Concerning Article 76(10) of the LOS Convention' (2006) 21(4) *International Journal of Marine & Coastal Law* 461.

Elliott, Stuart, 'US' Noble to Adjust Work Schedule at Cyprus's Aphrodite Gas Project' *S&P Global Platts* (June 29 2020). https://www.spglobal.com/platts/en/market-insights/latest-news/natural-gas/062920-us-noble-to-adjust-work-schedule-at-cypruss-aphrodite-gas-project.

Ellis, Judy; Moore, John Norton; Nordquist, Myron H. (eds.), *Maritime Border Piplomacy* (Martinus Nijhoff Publishers, 2012).

Emary, K. O. 'Geological Structure and Some Water Characteristics of the East China Sea and the Yellow Sea' (1969) 2 Technical Bulletin (UN Economic Commission for Asia and the Far East Committee for Co-ordinating of Joint Prospecting for Mineral Resources in Asian Offshore Areas (C.C.O.P)) 41.

Emmers, Ralf, *Resource Management and Contested Territories in East Asia* (Palgrave Pivot, London, 2013).

Engel, Uggi, 'The Case of the Delimitation of the North Sea Continental Shelf Before the International Court of Justice' (1968) 38 *Nordisk Tidsskrift Int'l Ret* 18.

Englefield, Greg, 'A Spider's Web: Jurisdictional Problems in the Caspian Sea' (Autumn 1995) *IBRU Boundary and Security Bulletin*, 30.

Erdbrink, Thomas, 'A Tiny Island is Where Iran Makes a Stand 2012' *New York Times* (April 30 2012).

ET EnergyWorld, 'China Defends Gasfield Activity in East China Sea' *Energy News, ET EnergyWorld* (August 2 2017). https://energy.economictimes.indiatimes.com/news/oil-and-gas/china-defends-gasfield-activity-in-east-china-sea/59880351.

Evripidou, Stefanos, 'Cyprus and Egypt Sign Unitisation Deal on the Joint Exploitation' *Cyprus Mail* (Cyprus, December 13 2013). https://cyprus-mail.com/2013/12/13/cyprus-and-egypt-sign-unitisation-deal-on-the-joint-exploitation/.

Fackler, Martin, 'China and Japan in Deal Over Contested Gas Fields' *New York Times* (June 19 2008). https://www.nytimes.com/2008/06/19/world/asia/19sea.html.

Federal Republic of Germany, 'Official Documents--North Sea Continental Shelf' (1971) 65 *American Journal of International Law* 901.

Filis, Andrew; Leal-Arcas, Rafael, 'Legal Aspects of Inter-State Maritime Delimitation in the Eastern Mediterranean Basin' (2013) 11(3) *Oil, Gas & Energy Law Intelligence* 1.

Financial Tribune, 'Iran Reiterates Interest in Joint Gas Field With Kuwait' (2017). https://financialtribune.com/articles/energy/60124/iran-reiterates-interest-in-joint-gas-field-with-kuwait.

Fjærtoft, Daniel, 'Unitization of Petroleum Fields in the Barents Sea: Towards a Common Understanding?' 9 *Arctic Review on Law and Politics* 72. https://arcticreview.no/index.php/arctic/article/view/1083/2362.

Fleischhauer, Carl-August, 'The Relationship Between the International Court of Justice and the Newly Created International Tribunal for the Law of the Sea in Hamburg' (1997) 1(1) *Max Planck Yearbook of United Nations Law* 327.

Florida State Senate (The), 'Legal Issues and State Authority Related to Territorial Water' (Interim Project Report 2008-142, October 2007).

Folger, Julie M., 'A Proposal to End the Stalemate in the Caspian Sea Negotiations' (2003) 18(2) *Ohio State Journal on Dispute Resolution* 529.

Fox, Hazel, *Joint Development of Offshore Oil and Gas: A Model Agreement for States for Joint Development With Explanatory Commentary* (British Institute of International and Comparative Law, 1989).

Foy, Henry, 'Caspian Countries Ready to End Their Sea of Troubles Stand First' *Financial Times* (London, England, August 9 2018). https://www.ft.com/content/3d52c160-9af1-11e8-9702-5946bae86e6d.

Francks, Erik, 'Maritime Delimitation in the Caspian Sea: Legal Issues [Article]' (2006) 1 *China Oceans Law Review*, 1.

Franckx, E.; Benatar, M., 'Dots and Lines in South China Sea: Insights From Law of Map Evidence' (2012) 2(1) *Asian Journal of International Law* 89.

Franckx, Erik, 'Maritime Boundaries and Regional Co-Operation' (1990) 5(1) *International Journal of Estuarine & Coastal Law* 215.

Frashidi, Jamshid, *Palestine-Israel a Just Plan for Permanent Peace* (Xlibris US, 2009).

Freestone, David, 'The Law of the Sea Convention at 30: Successes, Challenges and New Agendas' (2012) 27(4) *International Journal of Marine & Coastal Law* 675.

Freestone, David, 'Twenty-Five Years of the Law of the Sea Convention, 1982–2007' (2007) 22(1) *International Journal of Marine & Coastal Law* 1.

Fu, Kuncheng (ed.), *Recent Developments in the Law of the Sea and CHINA* (Martinus Nijhoff Publishers, 2006).

Furuya, Kentaro, 'The Architecture of Japan's Maritime Security System in the East China Sea. The Dual-Layer Security System and the Role of the Japan Coast Guard' (2019) 72(4) *Naval War College Review* 26. www.jstor.org/stable/26775518.

Gamble, John; Watson, Ryan; Piera, Lauren, 'Ocean Regimes as Reflected in 500 Years of Multilateral Treaty-Making' in Aldo Chircop, Ted L. McDorman and Susan Rolston (eds.), *The Future of Ocean Regime-Building: Essays in Tribute to Douglas M. Johnston* (Martinus Nijhoff Publishers, 2009).

Ganjaliyev, Elchin, 'Building Azerbaijan's Legal Framework for Marine Operations on the Basis of UNCLOS' (Research Report, University of Southampton, 2012). https://www.un.org/depts/los/nippon/unnff_programme_home/fellows_pages/fellows_papers/ganjalyev_1112_azerbaijan.pdf.

Gao, Jianjun, 'The Obligation to Negotiate in the Philippines v. China Case: A Critique of the Award on Jurisdiction' (2016) 47 *Ocean Development & International Law* 272.

Gao, Zhiguo, 'China and the Law of the Sea' in Myron Nordquist, Tommy T. B. Koh, and John Norton Moore (eds.), *Freedom of Seas, Passage Rights and the 1982 Law of the Sea Convention* (Martin Nijhoff Publishers, 1999) 270.

Gau, Michael Sheng-Ti, 'The U-Shaped Line and a Categorization of the Ocean Disputes in the South China Sea' (2012) 43(1) *Ocean Development & International Law* 57.

Gautier, Phillipe, 'Some Reflections on the New Law of the Sea' (July 29 2022) 99 *International Law Studies* 1051.

Gibbons-Neff, Thomas, 'Trump Says U.S. Shot Down Iranian Drone as Both Nations Dig In' *New York Times* (June 18 2019). https://www.nytimes.com/2019/07/18/us/politics/iranian-drone-shot-down.html?auth=login-email&login=email.

Glaser, Bonnie S., 'Conflict in the South China Sea' (Report, Council of Foreign Relations, April 7 2015). https://www.cfr.org/report/conflict-south-china-sea.

Goble, Paul, 'Russia Tries to Work Around Iran's Failure to Ratify 2018 Caspian Convention' *Eurasia Review* (July 23 2022). https://www.eurasiareview.com/23072022-russia-tries-to-work-around-irans-failure-to-ratify-2018-caspian-convention-oped/.

Goldie, L. F. E., 'North Sea Continental Shelf Cases: A Postscript' (1972) 18 *New York Law Forum* 411.

Gotleib, Allan, 'Recent Developments Concerning the Exploration and Exploitation of the Ocean Floor Legislation' (1969) 15 *McGill Law Journal*.

Grau, Lester W., 'Hydrocarbons and a New Strategic Region: The Caspian Sea and Central Asia' (2001) 81(3) *Military Review* 17.

Grewlich, Klaus W., 'International Regulatory Governance of the Caspian Pipeline Policy Game' (2011) 29(1) *Journal of Energy & Natural Resources Law* 87.

Grigoriadis, Ioannis N., 'Energy Discoveries in the Eastern Mediterranean: Conflict or Cooperation?' (2014) XXI(3) *Middle East Policy* 124.

Grisel, Etienne, 'The Lateral Boundaries of the Continental Shelf and the Judgment of the International Court of Justice in the North Sea Continental Shelf Cases' (1970) 64(3) *The American Journal of International Law* 562. http://www.jstor.org/stable/2199204.

Grunstein, Miriam, 'Unitized We Stand, Divided We Fall: A Mexican Response to Karla Urdaneta's Analysis of Transboundary Petroleum Reservoirs in Deep Waters of the Gulf of Mexico' (2011) 33(2) *Houston Journal of International Law* 345.

Guernsey, Katherine N, 'The North Sea Continental Shelf Cases' (2000) 27(1) *Ohio Northern University Law Review* 141.

Guilfoyle, Douglas, 'The South China Sea Award. How Should We Read the UN Convention on the Law of the Sea?' (2018) 8(1) *Asian Journal of International Law* 51.

Guillaume, Gilbert, 'The Future of International Judicial Institutions' (1995) 44(4) *The International and Comparative Law Quarterly* 848. http://www.jstor.org/stable/760619.

Gurbanov, Ilgar, 'Caspian Convention and Perspective of Turkmenistan's Gas Export to Europe' (2018) 8(1) *Caucasus International* 159.

Gürel, Ayla; Le Cornu, Laura, 'Can Gas Catalyse Peace in the Eastern Mediterranean' (2014) 49(2) *International Spectator* 11.

Gürel, Ayla; Mullen, Fiona; Tzimitras; Harry, *The Cyprus Hydrocarbons Issue: Context, Positions and Future Scenarios* (PCC Report 1/2013). https://www.files.ethz.ch/isn/172873/Report%202013-1%20Hydrocarbons.pdf.

Halliday, Fred, 'The Empires Strike Back? Russia, Iran and the New Republics' (1995) 11 *The World Today* 220.

Hamd, Vida; Soha Frem; Karam , 'The Maritime Boundaries and Natural Resources of the Republic of Lebanon' (Research Report, UN Development Program - Common Space Initiative (CSI) Publications, December 2014). http://www.undp.org/content/dam/lebanon/docs/Governance/Publications/Legal%20section%201-6.pdf.

Hardwicke, Robert E., 'The Rule of Capture and Its Implications as Applied to Oil and Gas' (June 1935) 13(4) *Texas Law Review* 395.

Harold, Scott W., 'Ieodo as Metaphor? The Growing Importance of Sovereignty Disputes in South Korea-China Relations and the Role of the United States' (2012) 36(2) *Asian Perspective* 287.

Harris, Andrew, 'The Azerbaijan-Turkmenistan Dispute in the Caspian' (2018) 5(4) *Boundary & Security Bulletin*. https://www.dur.ac.uk/ibru/publications/view/?id=119.

Harrison, James, 'Defining Disputes and Characterizing Claims: Subject-Matter Jurisdiction in Law of the Sea Convention Litigation' (2017) 48(3–4) *Ocean*

Development & International Law 269. https://doi.org/10.1080/00908320.2017.1328924.

Harrison, S. S., 'China, Oil, and Asia: Conflict Ahead? A Study From the Carnegie Endowment for International Peace' (New York, Columbia Press, 1977).

Harrison, Selig S., 'Seabed Petroleum in Northeast Asia: Conflict or Cooperation?' (Research Report, Woodrow Wilson International Center for Scholars Asia Program, 2005).

Haruki, Wada, 'Resolving the China-Japan Conflict Over the Senkaku/Diaoyu Islands' (2010) 8(3) (Issue 43) *The Asia-Pacific Journal|Japan Focus*. https://apjjf.org/-Wada-Haruki/3433/article.pdf.

Hayom, Israel, 'Leviathan Offshore Natural Gas Field Goes Online' *Israel Hayom* (Israel, (December 31 2019).

Hayton, B., 'When Good Lawyers Write Bad History: Unreliable Evidence and the South China Sea Territorial Dispute' (2017) 48(1) *Ocean Development and International Law* 17.

Hayton, Bill, 'Beijing Shifts Strategy in South China Sea' (2017) *Nikkei Asian Review*. https://asia.nikkei.com/Politics/Beijing-shifts-strategy-in-South-China-Sea2.

Hayton, Bill, 'South China Sea: Vietnam 'Scraps New Oil Project' *BBC* (March 23 2018). https://www.bbc.com/news/world-asia-43507448.

Hayton, Bill, 'The Modern Creation of China's 'Historic Rights' Claim in the South China Sea' (2018) 49(3) *Asian Affairs* 370.

Hayton, Bill, *The South China Sea: The Struggle for Power in Asia* (Yale University Press, 2014).

Hong, N., 'The South China Sea Arbitration: A Test for the Efficacy of Compulsory Mechanism of UNCLOS and Implications for Dispute Management in the Region' (2018) 10(2) *Asian Politics and Policy* 219.

Hong, Nong, 'Law and Politics in the South China Sea - Assessing the Role of UNCLOS in Ocean Dispute Settlement' (PhD Thesis, University of Alberta, 2010). https://era.library.ualberta.ca/items/55e8d930-7fef-47e9-9863-b791b3930f85.

Hong, Nong, *UNCLOS and Ocean Dispute Settlement: Law and Politics in the South China Sea* (Taylor & Francis, 2012).

Hsiung, James C., 'Sea Power, Law of the Sea, and China-Japan East China Sea "Resource War"' (Conference Paper, Forum on China and the Sea - Institute of Sustainable Development, Macao, China, October 9-11, 2005) 2. http://www.nyu.edu/gsas/dept/politics/faculty/hsiung/sea_power.pdf.

Hwang, Kyung Moon, 'A Modest Proposal for Dokdo' in *Past Forward* (Anthem Press, 2019) 167. www.jstor.org/stable/j.ctvb1hts4.65.

Ian, Townsend-Gault; Stormont, William, 'Offshore Petroleum Joint Development Arrangements: Functional Instrument? Compromise? Obligation?' in Gerald Blake, William Hildesley, Martin Pratt, Rebecca Ridley, and Clive Schofield (eds.), *The Peaceful Management of Transboundary Resources* (1995).

IBRU, 'Israel Unilaterally Defines the Northern Limit of Its Maritime Space' (2011) *Boundary News*. https://www.dur.ac.uk/ibru/news/boundary_news/?itemno=12445.

ICJ, 'Qatar v. Bahrain - Maritime Delimitation' (1995) 2 *Yearbook of Islamic and Middle Eastern Law* 565.

Ikirodah, Barry B. Omo, 'The Legal Regime of the Continental Shelf, Its Economic Importance and the Vast Natural Resources of a Coastal State' (2005) 23(15) *Journal of Energy & Natural Resources Law*.

International Conference of Recent Development of the South China Sea Dispute and Prospects of Joint Development Regime 'Conference Notes' (Conference Paper,

International Conference of Recent Development of the South China Sea Dispute and Prospects of Joint Development Regime, Haikou, China, December 6–7, 2012).

International Crisis Group, 'Stirring Up the South China Sea (IV): Oil in Troubled Waters' (Research Asia Report No. 275, January 26 2016). https://www.refworld.org/pdfid/56a785c64.pdf.

Ioannidis, Nikolaos, 'The Continental Shelf Delimitation Agreement Between Turkey and "TRNC"' *EJIL: Talk! Blog of the European Journal of International Law* (May 2014). http://www.ejiltalk.org/the-continental-shelf-delimitation-agreement-between-turkey-and-trnc/#more-10927.

Ioannides, Nicholas A. *Maritime Claims and Boundary Delimitation: Tensions and Trends in the Eastern Mediterranean Sea* (Taylor & Francis Group, 2020).

Iran's Best Caspian Sea Prospects Are in Deepwater, and Rigs Are Scarce' *Offshore Magazine* (US, September 1 2000). https://www.offshore-mag.com/articles/print/volume-60/issue-9/news/general-interest/irans-best-caspian-sea-prospects-are-in-deepwater-and-rigs-are-scarce.html.

İŞErİ, Emre; Andrikopoulos, Panagiotis, 'Energy Geopolitics of the Eastern Mediterranean: Will Aphrodite's Lure Fuel Peace in Cyprus?' (2013) 5(51) *Doğu Akdeniz'in Enerji Jeopolitiği:Afrodit'in Cazibesi Kıbrıs'ta Barışı mı Teşvik Edecek?* 37.

Israel, Hayom, 'Leviathan Offshore Natural Gas Field Goes Online' *Israel Hayom* (Israel, December 31 2019). https://www.israelhayom.com/2019/12/31/leviathan-offshore-natural-gas-field-goes-online/.

Iwashita, Akihiro, *Japan's Border Issues: Pitfalls and Prospects* (Taylor & Francis Group, 2015).

Janusz, Barbara, 'The Caspian Sea: Legal Status and Regime Problems' (Briefing Paper BP 05/02, Chatham House, August 2005).

Janusz-Pawletta, Barbara, *The Legal Status of the Caspian Sea: Current Challenges and Prospects for Future Development* (Springer, 2015).

Jasnus, Barbara, 'Current Development of Negotiations on the Legal Status of the Caspian Sea: Sovereignty Issue' (2005) 2(3) *International Studies Journal* 95.

Jayakumar, S., 'UNCLOS--Two Decades On' (2005) 9 *Singapore Year Book of International Law* 1.

Jensen, Øystein; Bankes, Nigel, 'Compulsory and Binding Dispute Resolution Under the United Nations Convention on the Law of the Sea: Introduction' (2017) 48(3–4) *Ocean Development & International Law* 209. https://doi.org/10.1080/00908320.2017.1328927.

Jia, Bing, 'The Curious Case of Article 281: A 'Super' Provision Within UNCLOS?' (2015) 46(4) *Ocean Development & International Law* 266.

Jian, Sanqiang, 'Multinational Oil Companies and the Spratly Dispute' (1997) 6(16) *Journal of Contemporary China* 591. https://www.tandfonline.com/doi/pdf/10.1080/10670569708724298.

Jiao, Yiqiang, 'The Signing of the Convention on the Legal Status of the Caspian Sea and Its Implications' (2019) 75 *China International Studies* 178.

Jie, Shan, 'Harvesting Vegetables With 'Sand-to-Earth' Tech on S. China Sea Island Beach' *China Global Times* (May 19 2020). https://www.globaltimes.cn/content/1188873.shtml.

Joaquin, Matthew, 'Israel-Lebanon Maritime Dispute Explained' *Al Jazeera* (Qatar 2017) Audio.

Joffé, George, 'Arab Frontier Disputes: The Consequences for Arab Security' (1996) 1(2) *Geopolitics and International Boundaries* 159. https://doi.org/10.1080/13629379608407564.

Jonas, Ted, '"Parting the Sea": Caspian Littoral States Seek Boundary Disputes' Resolution' (2001) 99(22) *Oil & Gas Journal* 14.

Joyner, Christopher C.; Walters, Kelly Zack, 'The Caspian Conundrum: Reflections on the Interplay Between Law, the Environment and Geopolitics' (2006) 21 *International Journal of Marine and Coastal Law* 173.

Kalehsar, Omid Shokri, 'Iran and Azerbaijan Share Oil Fields, So What's Stopping Tehran From Drilling?' *The New Arab* (London, November 16 2018).

Karakasis, Vasileios P., 'Energy Security and the Cyprus Question: 'Securitization' of Energy in the Eastern Mediterranean' (2015) 27 *Politikon* 5.

Karam, Ewan; Jasem, Anderson, 'The Kuwait-Iraq Boundary: A Geopolitical Perspective' (1994) *IBRU Boundary and Security Bulletin.* https://www.dur.ac.uk/resources/ibru/publications/full/bsb1-4_anderson.pdf.

Karaman, Igor V., *Dispute Resolution in the Law of the Sea* (Martinus Nijhoff Publishers, 2012).

Karataeva, Elena, 'The Convention on the Legal Status of the Caspian Sea: The Final Answer or an Interim Solution to the Caspian Question?' (2020) 35(2) *International Journal of Marine & Coastal Law* 232.

Kariotis, Theodore C., 'A Greek Exclusive Economic Zone in the Aegean Sea' (2007) 18(3) *Mediterranean Quarterly* 56.

Kariotis, Theodore C., 'Hydrocarbons and the Law of the Sea in the Eastern Mediterranean: Implications for Cyprus, Greece, and Turkey' (Spring 2011) 2 *Mediterranean Quarterly* 45.

Karle, Prathamesh, 'Caspian Agreement: Many Issues Still to Be Settled' *Observer Research Foundation* (October 15 2018). https://www.orfonline.org/expert-speak/caspian-agreement-many-issues-still-to-be-settled-44871/.

Karsh, Efraim, 'Geopolitical Determinism: The Origins of the Iran-Iraq War' (1990) 44(2) *Middle East Journal* 256.

Kashani, Farshad M., 'Iran and the Incomplete Legal Regime of the Caspian Sea: More Than Two Decades After Fall of Soviet Union' (2014) 29(4) *Hemispheres* 89.

Kaye, Stuart, 'Indian Ocean Maritime Claims' (2010) 6(1) *Journal of the Indian Ocean Region* 113. https://doi.org/10.1080/19480881.2010.489674.

Kaye, Stuart, 'Lessons Learned From the Gulf of Maine Case: The Development of Maritime Boundary Delimitation Jurisprudence since UNCLOS III' (2008) 14(1) *Ocean & Coastal Law Journal* 73.

Kaye, Stuart, 'State Practice and Maritime Claims: Assessing the Normative Impact of the Law of the Sea Convention.' in Aldo Chircop, Ted L. McDorman, and Susan Rolston (eds.), *The Future of Ocean Regime-Building: Essays in Tribute to Douglas M. Johnston* (Martinus Nijhoff Publishers, 2009).

Kaye, Stuart, 'The Use of Multiple Boundaries in Maritime Boundary Delimitation: Law and Practice' (1998) 19 *Australian Year Book of International Law* 49.

Keating, Joshua E., 'The Island Dispute You Haven't Heard Of' (2012) 197 *Foreign Policy* 20.

Keating, Steven Geoffrey, 'Rock or Island? It Was an UNCLOS Call: The Legal Consequence of Geospatial Intelligence to the 2016 South China Sea Arbitration and Law of the Sea' (2018) 3 *Journal of National Security Law & Policy* 509.

Kesevan, K. V., 'Maritime Security in Asia Pacific Challenges and Prospects' (2006) 3 *Ocean Policy Studies - Nippon Foundation* 1. http://www.sof.or.jp/en/report/pdf/200607_ISSN_1880_0017_03.pdfh.

Keyuan, Zou, 'Can China Respect the Law of the Seas? An Assessment of Maritime Agreements Between China and Its Neighbors' (2010) 12(3/4) *Harvard Asia Quarterly* 39.

Keyuan, Zou, 'Joint Development in the South China Sea: A New Approach' (2006) 21(1) *International Journal of Marine & Coastal Law* 83.

Keyuan, Zou, 'The International Tribunal for the Law of the Sea: Procedures, Practices, and Asian States' (2010) 41(2) *Ocean Development & International Law* 131.

Khadduri, Walid, 'East Mediterranean Gas: Opportunities and Challenges' (2012) 17(1) *Mediterranean Politics* 111.

Khalfaoui, Anna; Yiallourides, Constantinos, 'Maritime Disputes and Disputed Seabed Resources in the African Continent' (2019) *Routledge Handbook of Energy Law*. https://ssrn.com/abstract=3330555.

Khalid, Nazery, 'All for One, One for All: Promoting Economic Activities in the South China Sea' (2011) 5(3) *IUP Journal of International Relations* 65.

Khanh, Vu; Pearson, James, 'Chinese Ship Back in Waters Off Vietnam Amid Coronavirus "Distraction"' *Reuters* (April 14 2020). https://www.reuters.com/article/us-vietnam-china-southchinasea/chinese-ship-back-in-waters-off-vietnam-amid-coronavirus-distraction-idUSKCN21W0CT.

Kim, Sun Pyo, *Maritime Delimitation and Interim Arrangements in North East Asia* (Brill Academic Publishers, 2004).

Kim, Sungbae, 'Understanding the Dokdo Issue: A Critical Review of the Liberalist Approach' (2010) 24(2) *The Journal of East Asian Affairs* 1. www.jstor.org/stable/23258212.

Kim, Young-Jin, 'Reef Vital to Protecting Korea's Economic Zone' *Korea Times* (September 18 2012). http://www.koreatimes.co.kr/www/news/nation/2012/09/117_120266.html.

Klare, M. T., *Resource Wars: The New Landscape of Global Conflict* (Henry Holt and Company, 2001). https://books.google.co.uk/books?id=4swk0glJuswC.

Klare, Michael T., 'The Growing Threat of Maritime Conflict' (2013) 112(750) *Current History* 26.

Klein, Natalie, *Dispute Settlement in the UN Convention on the Law of the Sea* (Cambridge University Press, 2005).

Klein, Natalie, 'The Timor Sea Conciliation and Lessons for Northeast Asia in Resolving Maritime Boundary Disputes' (2019) 6(1) *The Journal of Territorial and Maritime Studies* 30. www.jstor.org/stable/26664178.

Koch, Christian, 'Review of the Three Occupied UAE Islands: The Tunbs and Abu Musa, Thomas R. Mattair' (2009) 41(1) *International Journal of Middle East Studies* 158. www.jstor.org/stable/40206081.

Koh, Tommy T. B.; Moore, John Norton; Nordquist, Myron H. (eds.), *Freedom of Seas, Passage Rights and the 1982 Law of the Sea Convention* (Martinus Nijhoff Publishers, 2009).

Koh, Tommy T. B., 'Negotiating a New World Order for the Sea' (1984) 24(4) *Virginia Journal of International Law* 761.

Koh, Tommy T. B., 'The Exclusive Economic Zone' (1988) 30(1) *Malaya Law Review* 1.

Koh, Tommy T. B., 'The Origins of the 1982 Convention on the Law of the Sea' (1987) 29(1) *Malaya Law Review* 1.

Koh, Tommy T. B., 'The Territorial Sea, Contiguous Zone, Straits and Archipelagos Under the 1982 Convention on the Law of the Sea' (1987) 29(2) *Malaya Law Review* 197.

Koh, Tommy T. B., 'The Third United Nations Conference on the Law of the Sea: What Was Accomplished?' (1983) 46(2) *Law and Contemporary Problems* 5.

Kolmaš, Michal, 'Senkaku/Diaoyu Island Dispute and the Reconstruction of China as Japan's "Other"' (2017) 17(2) *Asia-Pacific Social Science Review* 267.

Koo, M. G., 'Belling the Chinese Dragon at Sea: Western Theories and Asian Realities' (2017) 48(1) *Ocean Development and International Law* 52.

Korea Herald, 'Dispute Bolsters Economic Profile of Dokdo Islands' *Korea Herald* (April 6 2010). http://www.koreaherald.com/view.php?ud=20050319000004.

Kramer, Andrew, 'In a Prize for Big Oil Firms, Caspian Deal Eases Access' *New York Times* (October 8 2018). https://www.nytimes.com/2018/10/08/business/energy-environment/caspian-sea-deal-eases-access.html?searchResultPosition=46.

Kramer, Andrew, 'Russia Agrees With Four Nations to Divide Resources Beneath Caspian Sea' *New York Times* (New York, August 13 2018). https://www.nytimes.com/2018/08/12/world/europe/caspian-sea-russia-iran.html.

Kramer, Andrew E., 'Russia and 4 Other Nations Settle Decades-Long Dispute Over Caspian Sea' *New York Times* (August 12 2018). https://www.nytimes.com/2018/08/12/world/europe/caspian-sea-russia-iran.html.

Kraska, James, 'Legal Vortex in the Strait of Hormuz' (2014) 54(2) *Virginia Journal of International Law* 323.

Kraska, James T., 'The Law of the Sea Convention: A National Security Success - Global Strategic Mobility Through the Rule of Law' (2007) 39 *George Washington International Law Review*. https://ssrn.com/abstract=1648629.

Krasna, Joshua, 'Politics, War and Eastern Mediterranean Gas' (March 2022) 16(4) *Tel Aviv Notes Moshe Dayan Center for Middle Eastern and African Studies at Tel-Aviv University*. https://dayan.org/content/politics-war-and-eastern-mediterranean-gas.

Kristof, Nicholas, 'Look Out for the Diaoyu Islands' *New York Times* (September 10 2010).

Ku, Julian, 'Assessing the South China Sea Arbitral Award After One Year: Why China Won and the U.S. is Losing' *Lawfare* (July 12 2017). https://www.lawfareblog.com/assessing-south-china-sea-arbitral-award-after-one-year-why-china-won-and-us-losing.

Kucera, Joshua, 'Iran Denies Compromise on Caspian Division' (2017) *Eurasia Net*. http://www.eurasianet.org/node/86566.

Kunoy, Bjorn, 'Establishment of the Outer Limits of the Continental Shelf: Is Crossing Boundaries Trespassing' (2011) 26(2) *International Journal of Marine & Coastal Law* 313.

Kuo, Lily, 'Will a Tiny, Submerged Rock Spark a New Crisis in the East China Sea?' (December 9 2013) *The Atlantic*. https://www.theatlantic.com/china/archive/2013/12/will-a-tiny-submerged-rock-spark-a-new-crisis-in-the-east-china-sea/282155/.

Kuo, Mercy A., 'The Geopolitics of Oil and Gas in the South China Sea' *The Diplomat* (December 12 2018). https://thediplomat.com/2018/12/the-geopolitics-of-oil-and-gas-in-the-south-china-sea/.

Kuok, Lynn, 'China is Winning in the South China Sea' *Wall Street Journal* (New York, July 17 2018). https://www.wsj.com/articles/china-is-winning-in-the-south-china-sea-1531868329.

Kwiakowska, Barbara, 'Equitable Maritime Boundary Delimitation - A Legal Perspective' (1988) 3(4) *International Journal of Estuarine and Coastal Law* 287. https://heinonline.org/HOL/P?h=hein.journals/ljmc3&i=317.

Kwiatkowska, Barbara, 'Equitable Maritime Delimitation – A Legal Perspective' (1988) 3(4) *International Journal of Estuarine and Coastal Law* 287.

Kwiatkowska, Barbara, 'The Qatar v. Bahrain Maritime Delimitation and Territorial Questions Case' 33(3–4) *Ocean Development & International Law* 227. https://heinonline.org/HOL/P?h=hein.journals/ljmc3&i=317.

Lagoni, Rainer, 'Interim Measures Pending Maritime Delimitation Agreements' (1984) 78(2) *The American Journal of International Law* 345. www.jstor.org/stable/2202280.

Lagoni, Ranier, 'Oil and Gas Deposits Across National Frontiers' (1979) 73(2) *The American Journal of International Law* 215. www.jstor.org/stable/2201608.

Lai, Christina, 'South Korea's and Taiwan's Territorial Disputes With Japan, 1990s to 2018' (2020) 60(3) *Asian Survey* 583.

Lavinson, Charles; Chazan, Guy, 'Big Gas Find Sparks a Frenzy in Israel' *Wall Street Journal* (December 30 2010). https://www.wsj.com/articles/SB10001424052970204204004576049842786766586.

Lee, Ivy; Ming, Fang, 'Deconstructing Japan's Claim of Sovereignty Over the Diaoyu/Senkaku Islands' (2012) 10(53) *The Asia-Pacific Journal|Japan Focus*. https://apjjf.org/2012/10/53/Ivy-Lee/3877/article.html.

Lee, Chang-Wee, 'China's Position on the Territorial Sea Regime in Terms of the South China Sea Disputes: Straight Baselines and Innocent Passage of Warships Around Disputed Islands' (2018) 30(4) *Korean Journal of Defense Analysis* 559.

Lee, Seokwoo, 'Territorial Disputes Among Japan, China, and Taiwan Concerning the Senkaku Islands' (2002) 3(7) *Boundary and Territory Briefing*. https://www.dur.ac.uk/ibru/publications/view/?id=222.

Lee, Seokwoo, 'The Resolution of the Territorial Dispute Between Korea and Japan Over the Liancourt Rocks' (2002) 3(8) *Boundary and Territory Briefing - International Boundaries Research Unit* 1. https://www.dur.ac.uk/ibru/publications/view/?id=223.

Lee, Seokwo; Young Kil, Park, 'Maritime Delimitation and Joint Resource Development in the East China Sea' (Conference Paper, Law of the Sea Institute, UC Berkeley–Korea Institute of Ocean Science and Technology Conference, Seoul, Korea, May 21–24 2012). https://www.law.berkeley.edu/files/Lee-Park-final.pdf.

Lee, Yusin, 'Toward a New International Regime for the Caspian Sea. Problems of Post-Communism' (2005) 52(3) *Problems of Post-Communism* 37.

Lee, Yusin; Kim, Sangjoon, 'Dividing Seabed Hydrocarbon Resources in East Asia: A Comparative Analysis of the East China Sea and the Caspian Sea' (2008) 48(5) *Asian Survey* 794.

Leitner, Peter M., 'A Bad Treaty Returns' (1998) 160(3) *World Affairs* 134.

Lelyveld, Michael, 'Iran/Azerbaijan: U.S. Rejects Military Involvement in Caspian Dispute' *Radio Free Europe/Radio Liberty* (March 15 2002). https://www.rferl.org/a/1099101.html.

Lesaffer, Randall, 'The Iran-Iraq Border: A Story of Too Many Treaties' *Oxford Public International Law* (August 11 2015). https://opil.ouplaw.com/page/iran-iraq-border.

Li, Lingqun, *China's Policy Towards the South China Sea: When Geopolitics Meets the Law of the Sea* (Routledge, 2018).

Liao, Tim F., *The China-Japan Border Dispute: Islands of Contention in Multidisciplinary Perspective* (Taylor and Francis, 2016).

Liao, Tim F.; Hara, Kimie; Wiegand, Krista (eds.), *The China-Japan Border Dispute: Islands of Contention in Multidisciplinary Perspective* (Taylor & Francis, 2016).

Lin, Cheng-yi, 'Taiwan's South China Sea Policy' (1997) 37(4) *Asian Survey* 323. http://www.jstor.org/stable/2645651.

Lin, Man-houng, 'US Diplomatic Note on the Diaoyutai Issue: Taiwan's Sovereignty Claim and the US Response' in Tim F. Liao, Kimie Hara, and Krista Wiegand (eds.), *The China-Japan Border Dispute: Islands of Contention in Multidisciplinary Perspective* (Taylor & Francis, 2016).

Lindsay, Maizland; Beina, Xu, The U.S.-Japan Security Alliance (Research Paper, Council of Foreign Relations, August 22 2019). https://www.cfr.org/backgrounder/us-japan-security-alliance.

Lloyd, Stephen, 'Natural Prolongation: Have the Rumours Its Demise Been Greatly Exaggerated' (1991) 3(3) *African Journal of International and Comparative Law.*

LNG World News, 'Iran Rejects Saudi Claims on Arash Gas Field' *LNG World News* (July 14 2014). https://www.lngworldnews.com/iran-rejects-saudi-claims-on-arash-gas-field/.

Lodge, Michael W., 'The Common Heritage of Mankind' (2012) 27(4) *International Journal of Marine & Coastal Law* 733.

Lowe, A. V., 'Reflections on the Waters Changing Conceptions of Property Rights in the Law of the Sea' (1986) 1 *International Journal* of *Estuarine & Coastal Law* 1.

Lowe, Vaughan, 'Was It Worth the Effort?' (2012) 27(4) *International Journal of Marine & Coastal Law* 875.

MacDonald, Charles G., 'Regional and the Law of the Sea: The Persian Gulf Perspective' (1980) 33(5) *Naval War College Review* 73. www.jstor.org/stable/44642106.

Macnab, Ron, 'The Case for Transparency in the Delimitation of the Outer Continental Shelf in Accordance With UNCLOS Article 76' (2004) 35(1) *Ocean Development & International Law* 1.

Maeier, Daniel, 'Lebanon's Maritime Boundaries - Between Economic Opportunities and Military Confrontation' (Research Paper, Center of Lebanese Studies - Papers on Lebanon, June 2013). https://lebanesestudies.com/wp-content/uploads/2019/09/maritime.pdf.

'Malaysia's Right to Stake Claim to Spratlys' *New Straits Times* (Malaysia, March 2 2019). https://www.nst.com.my/news/exclusive/2019/03/465397/malaysias-right-stake-claim-spratlys.

Manicom, James, 'Sino-Japanese Cooperation in the East China Sea: Limitations and Prospects' (2008) 30(3) *Contemporary Southeast Asia* 455. www.jstor.org/stable/41220523.

Manyin, Mark E., 'The Senkakus (Diaoyu/Diaoyutai) Dispute: U.S. Treaty Obligations' (CRS Report R42761 7-5700, US Congressional Research Service, October 14 2016).

Maritime Executive, 'Vietnam Halts South China Sea E&P After Chinese Threats' *Maritime Executive* (July 25 2017). https://www.maritime-executive.com/article/vietnam-halts-s-china-sea-ep-after-threat-from-china.

McCormack, Gavan, 'Much Ado Over Small Islands: The Sino-Japanese Confrontation Over Senkaku/Diaoyu' in Tim F. Liao, Kimie Hara, and Krista Wiegand (eds.), *The China-Japan Border Dispute: Islands of Contention in Multidisciplinary Perspective* (Taylor & Francis, 2016) 15.

McCurry, Justin, 'Japan to Spend Millions on Tiny Islands 1,000 Miles South of Tokyo' *The Guardian* (UK, February 3 2016). https://www.theguardian.com/world/2016/feb/03/japan-spend-billions-yen-tiny-okinotori-islands-1000-miles-south-of-tokyo.

McCurry, Justin, 'Japan: Teachers to Call Senkaku and Takeshima Islands Japanese Territory' *The Guardian* (UK, January 28 2014). https://www.theguardian.com/world/2014/jan/28/japan-teachers-call-senkaku-takeshima-island-japanese-territory.

McDorman, Ted L., 'The Canada-France Maritime Boundary Case: Drawing a Line Around St. Pierre and Miquelon' (1990) 84(1) *The American Journal of International Law* 157. www.jstor.org/stable/2203018.

McDorman, Ted L., 'The Continental Shelf Regime in the Law of the Sea Convention: A Reflection on the First Thirty Years' (2012) 27(4) *International Journal of Marine & Coastal Law* 743.

McDorman, Ted L., 'The Entry into Force of the 1982 LOS Convention and the Article 76 Outer Continental Shelf Regime' (1995) 10(2) *International Journal of Marine and Coastal Law* 165.

McLaughlin, Richard, 'Maritime Boundary Delimitation and Cooperative Management of Transboundary Hydrocarbons in the Ultra-Deepwaters of the Gulf of Mexico' in Seoung-Yong Hong and Jon Van Dyke (eds.), *Maritime Boundary Disputes, Settlement Processes, and the Law of the Sea* (Martinus Nijhoff Publishers, 2009) 231.

McLaughlin, Rob, *United Nations Naval Peace Operations in the Territorial Sea* (Martinus Nijhoff Publishers, 2009).

Mehdiyoun, Kamyar, 'Ownership of Oil and Gas Resources in the Caspian Sea' (2000) 94(1) *American Journal of International Law* 179.

Meier, Daniel, 'Introduction to the Special Issue: Bordering the Middle East' (2018) 23(3) *Geopolitics* 495. https://doi.org/10.1080/14650045.2018.1497375.

Mendelson, M. H.; Hulton, S. C., 'The Iraq-Kuwait Boundary: Legal Aspects' (1990) 23(2) *Revue Belge de Droit International/Belgian Review of International Law* 293.

Mendenhall, Elizabeth, 'Interpreting the Law of the Sea 'Regime of Islands': An Opportunity for Productive US Leadership' (2019) 99 *Marine Policy* 213.

Mensah, Thomas, 'The Dispute Settlement Regime of the 1982 United Nations Convention on the Law of the Sea' in Jochen Abr Frowein (ed.), *Max Planck Yearbook of United Nations Law* (Brill, 1998) 307.

Merrills, J. G., 'Images and Models in the World Court: The Individual Opinions in the North Sea Continental Shelf Cases' (1978) 41 *Modern Law Review* 638.

Metz, Helen Chapin, *Persian Gulf States: Country Studies* (Research Report, Federal Research Division, Library of Congress). https://lccn.loc.gov/93046476.

Mianabadi, Hojjat, 'Application of the Ordered Weighted Averaging (OWA) Method to the Caspian Sea Conflict' (2014) 28(6) *Stochastic Environmental Research & Risk Assessment* 1359.

Middle East Strategic Perspectives, 'Egypt: ENI's Zohr, a Boost for Political Stability' *Middle East Strategic Perspectives* (September 6 2015). http://www.mesp.me/2015/09/06/egypt-enis-zohr-a-boost-for-political-stability-in-egypt/.

Milan, Shapour S., 'The Legal Status of the Persian Gulf as a Semi-Enclosed Sea' (1987) 25(1) *Archiv des Völkerrechts - Japan and International Law* 92. www.jstor.org/stable/40798265.

Miller, J. Berkshire, 'The ICJ and the Dokdo/Takeshima Dispute' *The Diplomat* (May 2014). https://thediplomat.com/2014/05/the-icj-and-the-dokdotakeshima-dispute/.

Miller, Keith F., 'Implications of UNCLOS for Canada's Regulatory Jurisdiction in the Offshore - The 200-Mile Limit and the Continental Shell' (2007) 30 *Dalhousie Law Journal* 341.

Mills, Robin, 'Why Offshore Gas in the Eastern Mediterranean Has a Complicated Road Ahead' *The National* (UAE, June 15 2020). https://www.thenational.ae/business/comment/why-offshore-gas-in-the-eastern-mediterranean-has-a-complicated-road-ahead-1.1033237.

Minas, Stephen; Diamond, Jordan, *Stress Testing the Law of the Sea* (Brill, 2018).

Mingjiang, Li, 'China Debates the South China Sea Dispute' in Ian Storey and Lin Cheng-yi (eds.), *The South China Sea Dispute: Navigating Diplomatic and Strategic Tensions* (ISEAS Publishing, 2016).

Miyoshi, Masahiro, 'The Japan-South Korea Agreement on Joint Development of the Continental Shelf' (1985) 10 *Energy* 545.

Miyoshi, Masahiro, 'The Joint Development of Offshore Oil and Gas in Relation to Maritime Boundary Delimitation' (1999) 2(5) *Maritime Briefing International Boundaries Research Unit* 1. https://www.dur.ac.uk/ibru/publications/download/?id=236.

Miyoshi, Masahiro, 'China's 'U-Shaped Line' Claim in the South China Sea: Any Validity Under International Law?' (2012) 43(1) *Ocean Development & International Law* 1.

Miyoshi, Masahiro, 'Seabed Petroleum in the East China Sea: Law of the Sea Issues and the Prospects for Joint Development: Seabed Petroleum in Northeast Asia: Conflict or Cooperation' (Research Report, Wilson Center, 2005). http://usatoday30.usatoday.com/money/industries/energy/2008-06-15-china-japan_N.htm.

Mobley, Richard A., 'The Tunbs and Abu Musa Islands: Britain's Perspective' (2003) 57(4) *Middle East Journal* 627. www.jstor.org/stable/4329943.

Mojtahed-Zadeh, Pirouz, 'Border and Territorial Identity: Persian Identity Makes Iran an Empire of the Mind' (2012) 1 *International Studies Journal* 157.

Mojtahed-Zadeh, Pirouz; Amiri, Hashem; Salarian, Ramtin, 'Maritime Political Geography: Iran's Legal Dilemma in the Caspian Sea Ends up in Geographical Certainties for All' (2015) 12(1) *International Studies Journal* 67.

Mojtahed-Zadeh, Pirouz; Zarei, BahadorIn, 'Maritime Boundary Delimitations in the Persian Gulf' (2017) 14(2) *International Studies Journal (ISJ)* 49.

Morton, Katherine, 'China's Ambition in the South China Sea: Is a Legitimate Maritime Order Possible?' (2016) 92(4) *International Affairs* 909. https://onlinelibrary.wiley.com/doi/full/10.1111/1468-2346.12658.

Moudachirou, Djibril, 'Ocean Resources - Ascendancy Over African States Friendship Relations: Can UNCLOS Help Resolve Current or Future Maritime Boundary Delimitation Dispute Issues' (2016) 5(1) *Journal of Water Resources and Ocean Science* 1. http://www.wateroceanscience.org/article?journalid=166&doi=10.11648/j.wros.20160501.11.

Mroueh, Wassim 'Lebanon to Fight Israel at U.N.' *Daily Star* (Lebanon, July 11 2011). https://www.dailystar.com.lb//News/Lebanon-News/2011/Jul-11/143361-lebanon-to-fight-israel-at-un.ashx.

Muir, Richard, 'The Iraq–Kuwait Border Dispute: Still a Factor for Instability?' (2004) 35(2) *Asian Affairs* 147. https://doi.org/10.1080/0306837042000241037.

Müller, Daniel; Betaneli, Ketevan, 'The New Convention on the Legal Status of the Caspian Sea: New Opportunities and New Challenges' (Briefing Report, Freshfields Bruckhaus Deringer LLP, November 2018). http://knowledge.freshfields.com/en/Global/r/3848/the_new_convention_on_the_legal_status_of_the_caspian_sea.

Murat, Agdemir A., 'Israel and the Gas Resources of the Levant Basin' (2015) 6(2) *Ortadoğu Etütleri Turkmen Cooperation & Cultural Foundation Center for Middle Eastern Strategic Studies (ORSAM)* 136.

Murray, Bennett, 'Vietnam's Strange Ally in Its Fight With China' *Foreign Policy* (August 1 2019). https://foreignpolicy.com/2019/08/01/vietnams-strange-ally-in-its-fight-with-china/.

Murray, Lisa, 'The Four Main South China Sea Rulings Explained' *The Australian Financial Review* (Australia, July 13 2016). https://www.afr.com/world/the-four-main-south-china-sea-rulings-explained-20160713-gq4p8l.

Murray, Stephen J., 'Discussion of the World Court's North Sea Judgment, A' (1970) 19(3–4) *American University Law Review* 470.

Mustafayev, Nijat, 'Azerbaijan and Turkmenistan May Start Joint Development of Disputed Kepez Field in the Caspian' *Azeri-Press Agency* (Azerbaijan, April 27 2009). https://apa.az/en/azerbaijan_energy_and_industry/-101190.

Myers, Steven Lee, 'China Fires Missiles Into South China Sea, Sending U.S. a Message' *New York Times* (August 27 2020). https://www.nytimes.com/2020/08/27/world/asia/missiles-south-china-sea.html?searchResultPosition=1.

Myers, Steven Lee, 'Island or Rock? Taiwan Defends Its Claim in South China Sea' *New York Times* (May 20 2018). https://www.nytimes.com/2018/05/20/world/asia/china-taiwan-island-south-sea.html.

Nakauchi, Kiyofumi, 'Problems of Delimitation in the East China Sea and the Sea of Japan' (1979) 6 *Ocean Development & International Law* 305.

Nejat, Seyed Amin; Bavand, Davoud H.; Farshchi, Parvin, 'Formulation of the Caspian Sea's Legal Regime Using a Joint Zone Approach' (2016) 43(3) *Water Resources* 571.

Nelson, L. D. M, *The Jurisprudence of the International Tribunal for the Law of the Sea - Some Observations* (Brill, 2007).

Nelson, L. D. M., 'The Settlement of Disputes Arising From Conflicting Outer Continental Shelf Claims' (2009) 24(2) *International Journal of Marine & Coastal Law* 409.

Nemeth, Stephen C. 'Ruling the Sea: Managing Maritime Conflicts Through UNCLOS and Exclusive Economic Zones' (2014) 40(5) *International Interactions* 711.

Nemeth, Stephen C.; Mitchell, Sara McLaughlin; Nyman, Elizabeth A.; Hensel, Paul R., 'Ruling the Sea: Institutionalization and Privatization of the Global Ocean Commons' (Conference Paper, American Political Science Association, Chicago, USA, August 30–September 2 2007).

New Straits Times, 'Malaysia's Right to Stake Claim to Spratlys' *New Straits Times* (Malaysia, March 2 2019). https://www.nst.com.my/news/exclusive/2019/03/465397/malaysias-right-stake-claim-spratlys.

Ng, Teddy, 'Beijing Gives UN Baselines for Diaoyu Islands, Spurring Tension With Japan' *South China Morning Post* (Hong Kong, September 15 2012). https://www.scmp.com/news/china/article/1037254/beijing-gives-un-baselines-diaoyu-islands-spurring-tension-japan.

Nguyen, Hong Thao, 'Malaysia's New Game in the South China Sea' *The Diplomat* (December 21 2019). https://thediplomat.com/2019/12/malaysias-new-game-in-the-south-china-sea/.

Nguyen, Lan Ngoc, 'The UNCLOS Dispute Settlement System: What Role Can It Play in Resolving Maritime Disputes in Asia' (2018) 8(1) *Asian Journal of International Law* 91.

Noi, Gui Sui, 'South China Sea Ruling: About the Arbitral Tribunal' *The Straits Times* (Singapore, July 17 2016). https://www.straitstimes.com/asia/about-the-arbitral-tribunal.

Nordquist, Myron H., 'The Legal Status of Articles 1–3 of the Continental Shelf Convention According to the North Sea Cases' (1970) 1 *California Western International Law Journal* 60.

Nordquist, Myron H., *The Regulation of Continental Shelf Development: Rethinking International Standards* (Brill|Nijhoff, 2013).

Nordquist, Myron H.; Moore, John (eds.), *The Law of the Sea Convention US Accession and Globalization - Center for Oceans Law and Policy Volume 15* (Brill Academic Publishers and University of Virginia Martinus Nijhoff Publishers, 2012).

Nordquist, Myron H.; Rosenne, Shabtai; Sohn, Louis B. (eds.), *United Nations Convention on the Law of the Sea 1982: A Commentary* (Martinus Nijhoff, 1989).

Nossova, Irina, 'Cold Arctic and Hot Caspian Side by Side: New Legal Regimes Emerging Null' (2011) 18 *Juridica International* 113.

Noussia, Kyriaki, 'On International Arbitrations for the Settlement of Boundary Maritime Delimitation Disputes and Disputes From Joint Development Agreements for the Exploitation of Offshore Natural Resources' (2010) 25(1) *International Journal of Marine & Coastal Law* 63.

Noyes, John E., 'The Common Heritage of Mankind: Past, Present, and Future' (2011) 40 *Denver Journal of International Law & Policy* 447.

Noyes, John, 'The International Tribunal for the Law of the Sea' (1999) 32(1) *Cornell International Law Journal* 110.

Oda, Shigeru, 'Dispute Settlement Prospects in the Law of the Sea' (1995) 44(4) *The International and Comparative Law Quarterly* 863.

Odgaard, Liselotte, 'Maritime Security in East Asia: Peaceful Coexistence and Active Defense in China's Diaoyu/Senkaku Policy' (2017) 26(103) *Journal of Contemporary China* 118. https://doi.org/10.1080/10670564.2016.1206283.

Offshore Energy, 'Exxon's Cyprus Discovery 'Huge' But With Rocky Road Ahead, Analysts Say' *Offshore Energy* (March 4 2019). https://www.offshoreenergytoday.com/exxons-cyprus-discovery-huge-but-with-rocky-road-ahead-analysts-say/.

Okafor, Chidinma Bernadine, 'Joint Development: An Alternative Legal Approach to Oil and Gas Exploitation in the Nigeria-Cameroon Maritime Boundary Dispute?' (2006) 21(4) *International Journal of Marine and Coastal Law* 489.

Okafor, Chidinma Bernadine, 'Model Agreements for Joint Development: A Case Study' (2007) 25(1) *Journal of Energy & Natural Resources Law* 58.

Okafor-Yarwood, Ifesinachi, 'The Guinea-Bissau–Senegal Maritime Boundary Dispute' (2015) 61 *Marine Policy* 284.

Okruhlik, Gwenn; Conge, Patrick J., 'The Politics of Border Disputes - On the Arabian Peninsula' (1999) 54(2) *International Journal* 230.

Ong, David, 'Implications of Recent Southeast Asian State Practice for the International Law on Offshore Joint Development' in Beckman, Robert (ed.), *Beyond Territorial Disputes in the South China Sea: Legal Frameworks for the Joint Development of Hydrocarbon Resources* (Edward Elgar, 2013) 181.

Ong, David M., 'Joint Development of Common Offshore Oil and Gas Deposits: 'Mere' State Practice or Customary International Law?' (1999) 93(4) *American Journal of International Law* 771.

Ong, David M., 'The New Timor Sea Arrangement 2001: Is Joint Development of Common Offshore Oil and Gas Deposits Mandated Under International Law?' (2002) 17(1) *International Journal of Marine & Coastal Law* 79.

Oral, Nilufer, 'Non-Ratification of the 1982 LOS Convention: An Aegean Dilemma of Environmental and Global Consequence' (March 2009) *Publicist - An Online Publication of Berkeley Journal of International Law*. https://bjil.typepad.com/publicist/2009/03/publicist01-oral.html.

Oral, Nilufer, 'Transit Passage Rights in the Strait of Hormuz and Iran's Threats to Block the Passage of Oil Tankers' (2012) 16(16) *ASIL Insights*. https://www.asil.org/insights/volume/16/issue/16/transit-passage-rights-strait-hormuz-and-iran%E2%80%99s-threats-block-passage.

Orme, William A., Jr., 'Gas Deposits Off Israel and Gaza Opening Vision of Joint Ventures' *New York Times* (September 15 2000).

O'Rourke, Ronald, 'Maritime Territorial and Exclusive Economic Zone (EEZ) Disputes Involving China: Issues for Congress' (Research Report, US Congressional Research Service 2013). http://www.fas.org/sgp/crs/row/R42784.pdf.

Orttung, Robert W.; Wenger, Andreas, 'Explaining Cooperation and Conflict in Marine Boundary Disputes Involving Energy Deposits' (2016) 5(1) *Region* 75. www.jstor.org/stable/24896615.

Osborne, Simon, '"We Must Take Revenge" Chinese Call for War With Australia Over South China Sea Dispute' *Daily Express* (UK, August 3 2016). https://www.express.co.uk/news/world/695967/South-China-Sea-dispute-Australia.

Oude Elferink, Alex, 'The Establishment of Outer Limits of the Continental Shelf Beyond 200 Nautical Miles by the Coastal State: The Possibilities of Other States to Have an Impact on the Process' (2009) 24(3) *The International Journal of Marine and Coastal Law* 535.

Oude Elferink, Alex G., 'Article 76 of the LOSC on the Definition of the Continental Shelf: Questions Concerning Its Interpretation From a Legal Perspective' (2006) 21(3) *International Journal of Marine & Coastal Law* 269.

Oude Elferink, Alex G., 'Governance Principles for Areas Beyond National Jurisdiction' (2012) 27(2) *International Journal of Marine & Coastal Law* 205.

Oude Elferink, Alex G., '"Openness" and Article 76 of the Law of the Sea Convention: The Process Does Not Need to Be Adjusted' (2009) 40(1) *Ocean Development & International Law* 36.

Oude Elferink, Alex G., 'Third States in Maritime Delimitation Cases: Too Big a Role, Too Small a Role, or Both?' in Ted L. McDorman (ed.), *The Future of Ocean Regime-Building: Essays in Tribute to Douglas M. Johnston* (Martinus Nijhoff Publishers, 2009) 611.

Oude Elferink, Alex G.; Molenaar, Erik Jaap (eds.), *The International Legal Regime of Areas Beyond National Jurisdiction: Current and Future Developments* (Martinus Nijhoff Publishers, 2010).

Oxman, Bernard H., 'The Territorial Temptation: A Siren Song at Sea' (2006) 100(4) *The American Journal of International Law* 830.

Özertem, Hasan Selim, 'Turkish Foreign Policy and the Energy Bonanza in the Eastern Mediterranean' (2016) 18(4) *Journal of Balkan & Near Eastern Studies* 361.

Öztürk, Bayram; Ba!şren, Sertaç Hami, 'The Exclusive Economic Zone Debates and Fisheries in the Eastern Mediterranean Sea' (2008) 14(2) *Doğu Akdeniz'de ekonomik ölge tartışmaları ve bahkçilik* 77.

Paik, Jin-Hyun, 'The United Nations Convention on the Law of the Sea and Northeast Asian Maritime Practice' (1994) 22*Korean Journal of Computational Law* 107.

Pan, Junwu, 'Territorial Dispute Between China and Vietnam in the South China Sea: A Chinese Lawyer's Perspective' (2012) 5(1) *Journal of East Asia & International Law* 213.

Pan, Junwu, *Toward a New Framework for Peaceful Settlement of China's Territorial and Boundary Disputes* (Martinus Nijhoff Publishers, 2009).

Pannier, Bruce, 'Europe's Wait for Turkmen Natural Gas Continues' *Foreign Policy Research Institute* (September 13 2022). https://www.fpri.org/article/2022/09/europes-wait-for-turkmen-natural-gas-continues/.

Pannier, Bruce, 'Russia Says Caspian Legal Status Resolved, Agreement Ready for Signing' *Radio Free Europe/Radio Liberty* (2017). https://www.rferl.org/a/qishloq-ovozi-caspian-status-resolved-russia-says/28903729.html.

Papanicolopulu, Irini, 'The Law of the Sea Convention: No Place for Persons?' (2012) 27(4) *International Journal of Marine & Coastal Law* 867.

Parameswaran, Prashanth, 'Indonesia, Malaysia Pledge to Solve Maritime Dispute (Again)' (2016) *The Diplomat* (August 3 2016).

Paraschos, Peter E., 'Offshore Energy in the Levant Basin: Leaders, Laggards, and Spoilers' (2013) 24(1) *Mediterranean Quarterly* 38.

Pardo, Arvid, 'The Law of the Sea: Its Past and Its Future' (1984) 63(1) *Oregon Law Review* 7. https://heinonline.org/HOL/P?h=hein.journals/orglr63&i=17.

Park, Choon-Ho, 'Reviewed Work: Sharing the Resources of the South China Sea by Mark J. Valencia, Jon M. Van Dyke, Noel A. Ludwig' (1998) 92(2) *The American Journal of International Law* 354. http://www.jstor.org/stable/2998050.

Park, Choon-Ho, 'Seabed Boundary Issues in the East China Sea' (Research Report, *Wilson Center*, July 7 2011). https://www.wilsoncenter.org/sites/default/files/Choon-Ho_Park_1_.pdf.

Park, Seokwoo Lee; Kil, Young, 'Maritime Delimitation and Joint Resource Development in the East China Sea' (Conference Paper, Law of the Sea Institute, UC Berkeley–Korea Institute of Ocean Science and Technology Conference, Seoul, Korea, May 2012). https://www.law.berkeley.edu/files/Lee-Park-final.pdf.

Parliament of the Commonwealth of Australia - Joint Standing Committee on Treaties, Australia - Indonesia Maritime Delimitation Treaty - 12th Report (November 1997). https://www.aph.gov.au/Parliamentary_Business/Committees/House_of_Representatives_Committees?url=jsct/reports/report12/report12.pdf.

Patrick, Galey, 'Unifil Says It Cannot Intervene Over Maritime Border With Israel' *The Daily Star* (Lebanon, January 16 2011).

Pearson, James, 'As Rosneft's Vietnam Unit Drills in Disputed Area of South China Sea, Beijing Issues Warning' *Reuters* (May 17 2018). https://www.reuters.com/article/us-rosneft-vietnam-southchinasea-exclusv/exclusive-as-rosnefts-vietnam-unit-drills-in-disputed-area-of-south-china-sea-beijing-issues-warning-idUSKCN1II09H.

Pearson, James; Torode, Greg, 'Drilling Down: Risky Hunt for Oil in Vietnam's South China Sea Blocks' *Reuters* (2018). https://www.reuters.com/article/us-vietnam-oil-southchinasea/drilling-down-risky-hunt-for-oil-in-vietnams-south-china-sea-blocks-idUSKCN1IO0QV.

Pedrozo, Raul, 'A Response to Cartner's and Gold's Commentary on "Is It Time for the United States to Join the Law of the Sea Convention?"' (2011) 42(4) *Journal of Maritime Law & Commerce* 487.

Penick, F. V. W., 'Legal Character of the Right to Explore and Exploit the Natural Resources of the Continental Shelf,' (1985) 22(4) *San Diego Law Review* 765.

Peng, Nian; Ngeow, Chow Bing, 'Managing the South China Sea Dispute: Multilateral and Bilateral Approaches' (2022) 53(1) *Ocean Development & International Law* 37.

Pentland, William, 'World's Five Largest Offshore Oil Fields' *Forbes* (September 7 2013).

People's Daily Online, 'Oil Giants Pull Out of East China Sea Gas Fields Project' *People's Daily Online* (September 2004). http://en.people.cn/200409/30/eng20040930_158788.html.

Permanent Mission of Greece to the United Nations, 'Communication Dated 24 February 2005 From the Government of Greece Concerning Turkey's Objection to the Agreement Between the Republic of Cyprus and the Arab Republic of Egypt on the Delimitation of the Exclusive Economic Zone of 17 February 2003' (2005) 57 *Law of the Sea Bulletin* 129.

Peterson, J. E., 'Sovereignty and Boundaries in the Gulf States Settling the Peripheries' in Mehran Kamrava (ed.), *The International Politics of the Persian Gulf* (Syracuse University Press, 2011) 21. www.jstor.org/stable/j.ctt1j1ntkn.8.

Petty, Martin, 'Philippines' Duterte Says Xi Offering Gas Deal If Arbitration Case Ignored' *Reuters* (2019). https://www.reuters.com/article/us-philippines-china-southchinasea/philippines-duterte-says-xi-offering-gas-deal-if-arbitration-case-ignored-idUSKCN1VW07O.

Peuch, Jean-Christophe, 'Caspian Sea Oil: The Role of Private Corporations [Article]' (1998) 22(2) *Fletcher Forum of World Affairs* 27.

Phan, Hao Duy; Nguyen, Lan Ngoc, 'The South China Sea Arbitration: Bindingness, Finality, and Compliance With UNCLOS Dispute Settlement Decisions' (2018) 8(1) *Asian Journal of International Law* 36.

Pietrowski, Robert F., Jr., 'Guinea/Guinea-Bissau: Dispute Concerning Delimitation of the Maritime Boundary' (1986) 25(2) *International Legal Materials* 251.

Pifer, Ross H., 'The Rule of Capture in Pennsylvania Oil and Gas Law' (Research Paper, Agricultural Law Resource and Reference Center, Penn State University, 2009). https://pennstatelaw.psu.edu/_file/aglaw/Rule_of_Capture_in_Pennsylvania_Oil_and_Gas_Law.pdf.

Piscatori, James P., 'Saudi Arabia and the Law of the Sea' (1980) 61 *International Law Studies Series*. US Naval War College 633.

Plant, Glen, 'Maritime Delimitation and Territorial Questions Between Qatar and Bahrain (Qatar v. Bahrain)' (2002) 96(1) *The American Journal of International Law* 198. http://www.jstor.org.ezproxy-f.deakin.edu.au/stable/2686136.

Platts Oilgram News 'Turkmenis, Azeris Said Nearer to Resolving Kyapaz Dispute' (1999) 77(119) *Platts Oilgram News*.

Politakis, George P., 'The French-Canadian Arbitration Around St. Pierre and Miquelon: Unmasked Opportunism and the Triumph of the Unexpected' (1993) 1 *International Journal of Marine and Coastal Law* 105. https://heinonline.org/HOL/P?h=hein.journals/ljmc8&i=115.

Pradhan, S. D., 'ASEAN-China Single Draft Code of Conduct: Reflection of Continuing Differences' *The Times of India* (August 15 2018). https://timesofindia.indiatimes.com/blogs/ChanakyaCode/asean-china-single-draft-code-of-conduct-reflection-of-continuing-differences/.

Pratomo, Eddy, 'Negotiating Maritime Boundaries' (2018) 21(3) *Journal of Legal, Ethical and Regulatory Issues*. https://www.abacademies.org/articles/negotiating-maritime-boundaries-7357.html.

Pratt, Martin; Smith, Derek, 'How to Deal With Maritime Boundary Uncertainty in Oil and Gas Exploration and Production Areas' (Research Paper Prepared for Association of International Petroleum Negotiators, IBRU Durham University & Dewey & LeBoeuf, December 2007).

Prows, Peter, 'Tough Love: The Dramatic Birth and Looming Demise of UNCLOS Property Law (and What Is to Be Done About It)' (2007) 42(2) *Texas International Law Journal* 241.

Putz, Catherine, 'Caspian Sea Dispute Settled on the Surface' *The Diplomat* (August 13 2018). https://thediplomat.com/2018/08/caspian-sea-dispute-settled-on-the-surface/.

Quang, Nguyen Minh, 'Saving the China-ASEAN South China Sea Code of Conduct' *The Diplomat* (June 2019). https://thediplomat.com/2019/06/saving-the-china-asean-south-china-sea-code-of-conduct/.

Quismundo, Tarra, 'Itu Aba: PH Biggest Worry is Biggest Win' *Inquirer* (Philippines, July 18, 2016). https://globalnation.inquirer.net/141362/itu-aba-ph-biggest-worry-is-biggest-win.

Radio Free Europe/Radio Liberty, 'Iran Report: July 30, 2001' (2001) 4(28) *Radio Free Europe/Radio Liberty*. https://www.rferl.org/a/1342839.html.

Rahimov, Rahim, 'Azerbaijan, Iran Reach Breakthrough on Disputed Fields in the Caspian Sea' (2018) 15(52) *Eurasia Daily Monitor*. https://jamestown.org/program/azerbaijan-iran-reach-breakthrough-on-disputed-fields-in-the-caspian-sea/.

Rahman, Habibur, 'Kuwaiti Ownership of Warba and Bubiyan Islands' (1993) 29(2) *Middle Eastern Studies* 292. https://doi.org/10.1080/00263209308700949.

Raimbekova, Aliia, 'Littoral States Agree on Caspian Sea Status' *Anadolu Agency* (Turkey, August 12 2018). https://www.aa.com.tr/en/politics/littoral-states-agree-on-caspian-sea-status/1229011.

Raine, Sarah; Le Mière, Christian, *Regional Disorder: The South China Sea Disputes* (Routledge, 2013).

Ramos-Mrosovsky, Carlos, 'A Constructive Role for International Law in the Senkaku Islands?' in Tim F. Liao, Kimie Hara, and Krista Wiegand (eds.), *The China-Japan Border Dispute: Islands of Contention in Multidisciplinary Perspective* (Taylor & Francis, 2016) 115.

Ramos-Mrosovsky, Carlos, 'International Law's Unhelpful Role in the Senkaku Islands' (2008) 29(4) *University of Pennsylvania Journal of International Law* 903. https://scholarship.law.upenn.edu/jil/vol29/iss4/2.

Rapp-Hooper, Mira; Krejsa, Harry, 'Reefs, Rocks, and the Rule of Law: After the Arbitration in the South China Sea' (CNAS Asia-Pacific Security Reports, April 2016) 2. https://www.cnas.org/publications/reports/reefs-rocks-and-the-rule-of-law-after-the-arbitration-in-the-south-china-sea.

Rau, Moritz, Seufert, Günter; Westphal, Kirsten, 'The Eastern Mediterranean as a Focus for the EU's Energy Transition' (2022) *Stiftung Wissenschaft und Politik SVP Comments* (1) German Institute for International and Security Affairs. https://www.swp-berlin.org/publications/products/comments/2022C08_Mediterranean_EnergyTransition.pdf.

Rayfuse, Rosemary, 'The Future of Compulsory Dispute Settlement Under the Law of the Sea Convention' (2005) 36 *Victoria* University of *Wellington* Law *Rev*iew 683. http://www.nzlii.org/nz/journals/VUWLawRw/2005/30.html.

Reuters, 'Israel to Link Leviathan Gas Field to Egypt LNG Plants, Minister Says' *Reuters* (February 2021). https://www.reuters.com/article/israel-egypt-pipeline-int/israel-to-link-leviathan-gas-field-to-egypt-lng-plants-minister-says-idUSKBN2AL0FA.

RFE/RL, 'Iran Under Pressure by Russia to Accept a Small Share of the Caspian' *Radio Free Europe/Radio Liberty - Radio Farda* (December 17 2017). https://en.radiofarda.com/a/iran-russia-caspian-sea-rsources-borders/28922776.html.

RFE/RL, 'Russia Ratifies Caspian Convention With Iran Still Holding Out' *Radio Free Europe/Radio Farda* (October 2 2019). https://en.radiofarda.com/a/russia-ratifies-caspian-convention-with-iran-still-holding-out/30195078.html.

Riesenberg, David P., 'Recent Jurisprudence Addressing Maritime Delimitation Beyond 200 Nautical Miles From the Coast' (2014) 18(21) *ASIL*.

Ripley, Peter, 'Unlocking Oil and Gas Reserves in the Arctic Ocean: Is There a Conventional Solution to Delimitation of the Maritime Boundaries?' (2011) 29(2) *Journal of Energy & Natural Resources Law* 247.

Roach, J. Ashley, 'Arbitration Under the Law of the Sea Convention' in John Norton Moore (ed.), *International Arbitration: Contemporary Issues and Innovations* (Martinus Nijhoff Publishers, 2013).

Roach, J. Ashley; Smith, Robert W., 'Caspian Sea Boundaries' in Jonathan Charney (ed.), *International Maritime Boundaries* (M. Nijhoff, 1993) 3549.

Roach, J. Ashley; Smith, Robert W., *Excessive Maritime Claims* (Martins Nijhoff Publishers, 2012).

Robert, Beckman, 'International Law, UNCLOS and the South China Sea' in Robert Beckman (ed.), *Beyond Territorial Disputes in the South China Sea* (Edward Elgar Publishing, 2003) 55.

Rothwell, Donald (ed.), *Law of the Sea* (Edward Elgar, 2013).

Roughneen, Simon, 'How Beijing is Winning Control of the South China Sea' *Nikkei Asian Review* (June 13 2018). https://asia.nikkei.com/Spotlight/Cover-Story/How-Beijing-is-winning-control-of-the-South-China-Sea.

Roy, Denis, 'The Legal Continental Shelf: The Surprising Canadian Practice Regarding Oil and Gas Development in the Atlantic Coast Continental Shelf' (2012) 50(1) *Alberta Law Review* 65.

RSIS, 'The South China Sea - Towards a Cooperative Management Regime' (Conference Paper - The South China Sea: Towards a Cooperative Management Regime, 2007). http://www.rsis.edu.sg/publications/conference_reports/South_China_Sea_Report.pdf.

RSIS, 'UNCLOS and Its Limitations as the Foundation for a Regional Maritime Security Regime' (Research Report, Institute of Defence and Strategic Studies Singapore, 2006). https://www.rsis.edu.sg/wp-content/uploads/rsis-pubs/WP111.pdf.

Saeedi, Tariq, 'Turkmenistan-Azerbaijan Partnership Acquires Additional Features' *News Central Asia* (Turkmenistan, March 12 2020). http://www.newscentralasia.net/2020/03/12/turkmenistan-azerbaijan-partnership-acquires-additional-features/.

Sakran, Shadi, *The Legal Consequences of Limited Statehood: Palestine in Multilateral Frameworks* (Taylor & Francis Group, 2019).

Salcido, R., 'Law Applicable on the Outer Continental Shelf and in the Exclusive Economic Zone' (2010) 58 *American Journal of Comparative Law* 407. http://dx.doi.org/10.5131/ajcl.2009.0038.

Sam, Bateman, 'UNCLOS and Its Limitations as the Foundation for a Regional Maritime Security Regime' (2006) 111 *Institute of Defence and Strategic Studies Singapore* 4.

Sanei, Faraz, 'Caspian Sea Legal Regime, Pipeline Diplomacy, and the Prospects for Iran's Isolation From the Oil and Gas Frenzy' (2001) 34(3) *Vanderbilt Journal of Transnational Law* 681.

Sang-ho, Song, 'Ieodo Not Part of Territorial Dispute With China: Seoul' *Asia News Network* (March 13 2012).

Sato, Koichi, 'The Senkaku Islands Dispute: Four Reasons of the Chinese Offensive - A Japanese View' (2019) 8(1) *Journal of Contemporary East Asia Studies* 50.

Schmoll, Melanie Carina, 'Gas in the Maritime Exclusive Economic Zone of Israel and the Transformation of the Regional Security Complex Levant' (2017) 17(3) *Journal of Military and Strategic Studies* 73.

Schofield, Clive, 'Defining Areas for Joint Development in Disputed Waters' (Conference Paper, Recent Development of the South China Sea Dispute and Prospects of Joint Development Regime, December 6–7 2012, Haikou, China).

Schofield, Clive, 'Departures From the Coast: Trends in the Application of Territorial Sea Baselines Under the Law of the Sea Convention' (2012) 27(4) *International Journal of Marine & Coastal Law* 723.

Schofield, Clive, 'Island Disputes and the 'Oil Factor' in the South China Sea' (2012) 4(4) *Current Intelligence* 4. www.currentintelligence.net.

Schofield, Clive, 'Joint Development of the Continental Shelf Where Delimitation is Pending: Cooperative Opportunity or Complication in Oceans Governance' (Research Paper Slides). https://www.mofa.go.jp/files/000141429.pdf.

Schofield, Clive (ed.), *Maritime Energy Resources in Asia - Legal Regimes and Cooperation* (Research Report, The National Bureau of Asian Research, February 2012).

Schofield, Clive, 'Parting the Waves: Claims to Maritime Jurisdiction and the Division of Ocean Space' (2012) 1(1) *Penn State Journal of Law & International Affairs* 58.

Schofield, Clive, 'The Trouble With Islands: The Definition and Role of Islands and Rocks in Maritime Boundary Delimitation' in Jon M. Van Dyke and Seoung-Yong Hong (eds.), *Maritime Boundary Disputes, Settlement Processes, and the Law of the Sea* (2009, Martinus Nijhoff) 19.

Schofield, Clive; Schofield, Richard, 'Testing the Waters: Charting the Evolution of Claims to and From Low-Tide Elevations and Artificial Islands' (2016) 1(1) *Asia-Pacific Journal of Ocean Law and Policy* 37. https://heinonline.org/HOL/P?h=hein.journals/apjolp1&i=39.

Schofield, Clive; Townsend-Gault, Ian. 'Brokering Cooperation Amidst Competing Maritime Claims: Preventative Diplomacy in the Gulf of Thailand and South China Sea' in Aldo Chircop, Ted L. McDorman, and Susan Rolston (eds.), *The Future of Ocean Regime-Building: Essays in Tribute to Douglas M. Johnston* (Martinus Nijhoff Publishers, 2009) 643–670.

Schofield, Clive; Townsend-Gault, Ian, 'Time for the United States to Join the Party: Prospects for US Ratification of the United Nations Convention on the Law of the Sea' (2012) 6 *Int*ernational *Zeitschrift* 1.

Schofield, Clive H., 'Sharing Maritime Space: Options for Cooperative Management in Areas of Overlapping Maritime Claims' (2007) *Australian National Centre for Ocean Resources and Security* 2. https://documents.uow.edu.au/content/groups/public/@web/@law/@ancors/documents/doc/uow240631.pdf.

Schofield, Richard, 'Finalising the Arabian Territorial Framework' (1997) 2(3) *Geopolitics and International Boundaries* 90. https://doi.org/10.1080/13629379708407601.

Schofield, Richard, 'International Boundaries and Borderlands in the Middle East: Balancing Context, Exceptionalism and Representation' (2018) 23(3) *Geopolitics* 608.

Schofield, Richard, 'Regional Border Disputes' (2000) 51(1) *Whitehall Papers* 18. https://doi.org/10.1080/02681300009414848.

Schofield, Richard, 'The Crystallisation of a Complex Territorial Dispute: Britain and the Saudi-Abu Dhabi Borderland, 1966–71' (2011) 1(1) *Journal of Arabian Studies* 27. https://doi.org/10.1080/21534764.2011.576047.

Schofield, Richard, 'The United Nations settlement of the Iraq-Kuwait Border, 1991–1993' (1993) 1(2) *Boundary & Security Bulletin* 70. https://www.dur.ac.uk/ibru/publications/view/?id=15.

Schonhardt, Sara; Chaturvedi, Saurabh, 'South China Sea Ruling Increases Uncertainty for Shipping, Trade' *Wall Street Journal* (July 14 2016). https://www.wsj.com/articles/south-china-sea-ruling-increases-uncertainty-for-shipping-trade-1468487095.

School for Ethics 'The South China Sea Conflict' (Research, The School for Ethics and Global Leadership, June 26 2017). http://schoolforethics.org/wp-content/uploads/2017/07/The-South-China-Sea-Conflict.pdf.

Schultheiss, Christian, 'Charting a Peaceful Course for the Eastern Mediterranean Sea Disputes' *European Leadership Network* (May 21 2021). https://www.europeanleadershipnetwork.org/person/christian-schultheiss/.

Scovazzi, Tullio, 'Implications of the New Law of the Sea for the Mediterranean' (1981) 5(4) *Marine Policy* 302.

Scovazzi, Tullio, 'International Law of the Sea as Applied to the Mediterranean' (1994) 24(1) *Ocean & Coastal Management* 71. http://www.sciencedirect.com/science/article/pii/0964569194900531.

Scoville, Ryan M., 'Sovereignty Over the Senkaku/Diaoyu Islands: A Guide to the Legal Debate' in Tim F. Liao, Kimie Hara, and Krista Wiegand (eds.), *The China-Japan Border Dispute: Islands of Contention in Multidisciplinary Perspective* (Taylor & Francis, 2016) 85.

Seek, Andrew, 'Azerbaijan: Rediscovering Its Oil Potential - A Legal Perspective' (1995) 13(3) *Journal of Energy & Natural Resources Law* 147.

Segarra, Lisa Marie, 'These Are the Richest Countries in the World' *Fortune* (November 11, 2017). https://fortune.com/2017/11/17/richest-country-in-the-world/.

Sepulveda-Amor, Bernard, 'Contribution of the International Court of Justice to the Development of the International Law of the Sea' (2010) 1(6) *Aegean Review of the Law of the Sea and Maritime Law* 5. http://dx.doi.org/10.1007/s12180-009-0004-4.

Sepulveda-Amor, Bernardo, 'The International Court of Justice and the Law of the Sea' (2011) *Anuario Mexicano de Derecho, International Universidad Nacional Autonoma de Mexico - Insituto de Investigaciones Juridicas* 5.

Serdy, Andrew, 'Iran: What the Law of the Sea Says About Detaining Foreign Ships in Transit' *The Conversation* (July 23 2019). https://theconversation.com/iran-what-the-law-of-the-sea-says-about-detaining-foreign-ships-in-transit-120816.

Shaffer, Brenda, 'Israel—New Natural Gas Producer in the Mediterranean' (2011) 39 *Energy Policy* 5379.

Shaffer, Brenda, 'Natural Gas Supply Stability and Foreign Policy' (2013) 56 *Energy Policy* 114.

Shafiyev, Farid, 'The Legal Regime of the Caspian Sea: Views of the Littoral States' (2001) 7(6) *Jamestown Prism* 1. https://jamestown.org/program/the-legal-regime-of-the-caspian-sea-views-of-the-littoral-states/#.VaY7P_mqqko.

Shany, Yuval, 'International Law of the Sea Meets Israeli Constitutional Law: The New Israeli-Lebanese Maritime Border Agreement' (2023) *Lawfare* (January 9 2023). https://www.lawfareblog.com/international-law-sea-meets-israeli-constitutional-law-new-israeli-lebanese-maritime-border.

Shapland, Greg, 'The Maritime Boundaries of the Arab Gulf States' *Arab Digest* (2018) 2. https://arabdigest.org/visitors/sample-newsletters/maritime-boundaries-arab-gulf-states/.

Sharma, Surya P., 'The Single Maritime Boundary Regime and the Relationship Between the Continental Shelf and the Exclusive Economic Zone' (1987) 2(4) *International Journal of Estuarine and Coastal Law* 203.

Shaw, Malcolm, *International Law* (Cambridge University Press, 6th ed., 2008).

Shayan, Fatemeh, 'Geopolitical Subjectivity in Iran-GCC Relations: The Three Islands Issue Since 1979' (2013) 18(3) *Geopolitics* 633. https://doi.org/10.1080/14650045.2013.769961.

Sheehan, Anne, 'Dispute Settlement Under UNCLOS: The Exclusion of Maritime Delimitation Disputes' (2005) 7 *University of Queensland Law Journal* 175. http://www.austlii.edu.au/au/journals/UQLawJl/2005/7.html.

Sheikhmohammady, Majid; Kilgour, D. Marc; Hipel, Keith W. 'Modeling the Caspian Sea Negotiations' (2010) 19(2) *Group Decision & Negotiation* 149.

Shenon, Philip, 'China Sends Warships to Vietnam Oil Site' *New York Times* (July 21 1994). https://www.nytimes.com/1994/07/21/world/china-sends-warships-to-vietnam-oil-site.html.

Siddayao, Corazón Morales, 'Oil and Gas on the Continental Shelf: Potentials and Constraints in the Asia-Pacific Region' (1984) 9(1) *Ocean Management* 73. http://www.sciencedirect.com/science/article/pii/0302184X84900192.

Siddig, Khalid; Grethe, Harald, 'No More Gas From Egypt? The Israeli Gas Sector Between Offshore Discoveries and Import Uncertainty' (Conference Paper, Annual Conference on Economic Modeling, July 1 2013). http://EconPapers.repec.org/RePEc:ekd:004912:5446.

Sienho, Yee, 'Intervention in an Arbitral Proceeding Under Annex VII to the UNCLOS?' (2015) 14(1) *Chinese Journal of International Law* 79.

Siousiouras, Petros; Georgios, Chrysochou, 'The Aegean Dispute in the Context of Contemporary Judicial Decisions on Maritime Delimitation' (2014) 3(1) *Laws* 12.

Sison III, Maximo Paulino T., 'Universalizing the Law of the Sea in the South China Sea Dispute' (2018) 49(2) *Ocean Development and International Law* 157.

Smith, Helena, 'Huge Gas Discovery Off Cyprus Could Boost EU Energy Security' *The Guardian* (UK, 28 February 2019). https://www.theguardian.com/world/2019/feb/28/huge-gas-discovery-off-cyprus-could-boost-eu-energy-security.

Smith, Helena, 'Turkey Insists on Right to Drill for Energy Reserves Off Cyprus' *The Guardian* (UK, May 20 2019). https://www.theguardian.com/world/2019/may/20/turkey-insists-on-right-to-drill-for-energy-reserves-off-cyprus.

Smith, Mark A., 'Sovereignty Over Unoccupied Territories - The Western Sahara Decision' (1977) 9(9) *Case Western Reserve Journal of International Law* 135. https://scholarlycommons.law.case.edu/jil/vol9/iss1/8.

Socor, Vladimir, 'The Guns of Summer: Iran Prowls the Caspian' *Wall Street Journal* (US, August 3 2001). www.wsj.com/articles/SB996782868308580271.

Sofuoglu, Murat, 'How Turkey is Legally Entitled to Explore Gas in Eastern Mediterranean' *TRT World* (Turkey, July 12 2019). https://www.trtworld.com/turkey/how-turkey-is-legally-entitled-to-explore-gas-in-eastern-mediterranean-28199.

Sohn, Louis B., 'Settlement of Disputes Arising Out of the Law of the Sea Convention' (1974–1975) 12(3) *San Diego Law Review* 495.

Sohn, Louis B., 'Settlement of Law of the Sea Dispute' (1995) 10(2) *International Journal of Marine and Coastal Law* 205.

Song, Yann-hue, 'Conflicting Outer Continental Shelf Claims in the East and South China Seas: Proposals for Cooperation and Peaceful Resolution' (2013) 35(2) *University Haw Law Review* 485.

Song, Yann-huei, 'The July 2016 Arbitral Award, Interpretation of Article 121(3) of the UNCLOS, and Selecting Examples of Inconsistent State Practices' (2018) 49(3) *Ocean Development & International Law* 247. https://doi.org/10.1080/00908320.2018.1479355.

Squires, Nick, 'High Stakes in Cyprus as Turkish North Bids to Turn Bardot's Beloved Resort into New Las Vegas' *The Telegraph* (UK, October 6 2019). https://www.telegraph.co.uk/news/2019/10/06/turkish-cypriot-plan-revive-beach-ghost-town-could-kill-hopes/.

Stepek, Michael, 'Claims in Disputed Maritime Areas: Resolving International Disputes Arising From Activities Relating to Submarine Cables in Disputed Maritime Areas' (2022) *Global Arbitration Review*. https://globalarbitrationreview.com/guide/the-guide-telecoms-arbitrations/first-edition/article/claims-in-disputed-maritime-areas-resolving-international-disputes-arising-activities-relating-submarine-cables-in-disputed-maritime-areas.

Stephens, Tim; Rothwell, Donald R., 'The LOSC Framework for Maritime Jurisdiction and Enforcement 30 Years On' (2012) 27(4) *International Journal of Marine & Coastal Law* 701.

Stergiou, Andreas, 'Turkey–Cyprus–Israel Relations and the Cyprus Conflict' (2016) 18(4) *Journal of Balkan and Near Eastern Studies* 375. http://dx.doi.org/10.1080/19448953.2016.1195994.

Stocker, James, 'No EEZ Solution: The Politics of Oil and Gas in the Eastern Mediterranean' (2012) 4 *The Middle East Journal* 579.

Stone, Oliver L., 'Legal Aspects of Marine Oil and Gas Operations' (1969) 15 *Annual Institute of Mineral Law* 21.

Storey, Ian, 'Slipping Away? A South China Sea Code of Conduct Eludes Diplomatic Efforts' (2013) 11 *East and South China Seas Bulletin* 5. http://www.css.ethz.ch/en/services/digital-library/publications/publication.html/162591.

Storey, Ian, & Cheng-yi, Lin (eds.), *The South China Sea Dispute: Navigating Diplomatic and Strategic Tensions* (ISEAS Publishing, 2016).

Stratfor, 'Dokdo Island: A Case Study in Asia's Maritime Disputes' *Stratfor Worldview* (July 26 2015). https://worldview.stratfor.com/article/dokdo-island-case-study-asias-maritime-disputes.

Stratfor, 'What Does the New Caspian Sea Agreement Mean for the Energy Market?' *Stratfor Analysis* (August 17 2018). https://worldview.stratfor.com/article/what-does-new-caspian-sea-agreement-mean-energy-market.

Stratfor, 'What Iraq Has to Gain, and Lose, by Resurrecting a Border Deal With Iran' *Stratfor Worldview* (April 5 2019). https://worldview.stratfor.com/article/weighing-cost-iraq-iran-algiers-agreement-.

Strating, Bec, 'The Symbolic Politics of the Dokdo/Takeshima Dispute' (2017) *Lowy Institute - The Interpreter*. https://www.lowyinstitute.org/the-interpreter/symbolic-politics-dokdotakeshima-dispute.

Swearingen, Will D., 'Sources of Conflict Over Oil in the Persian/Arabian Gulf' (1981) 35(3) *Middle East Journal* 314. www.jstor.org/stable/4326248.

Szanto, Balazs, *China and the Senkaku/Diaoyu Islands Dispute: Escalation and De-Escalation* (Routledge, 2017).

Tae-Jin, Yi, 'Treaties Leading to Japan's Annexation of Korea' (2016) 56(4) *Korea Journal* 5. https://www.ekoreajournal.net/sysLib/down.php?file=..%2FUPLOAD%2FT_articles%2FKJ56-4%28Yi_Tae-Jin%29.pdf.

Takata, Toshihisa, 'The Conclusion by Japan of the United Nations Convention on the Law of the Sea (UNCLOS) and the Adjustment of Maritime Legal Regime' (1996) 39 *Japanese Annual International Law* 124.

Talmon, Stefan, 'The Chagos Marine Protected Area Arbitration: Expansion of the Jurisdiction of UNCLOS Part XV Courts and Tribunals' (2016) 65(4) *International & Comparative Law Quarterly* 927.

Tanaka, Hitoshi, 'Politicizing the Senkaku Islands: A Danger to Regional Stability' (2012) *East Asia Insight*. http://www.jcie.org/researchpdfs/EAI/7-3.pdf.

Tanaka, Yoshifumi, 'Reflections on Maritime Delimitation in the Qatar/Bahrain Case' (2003) 52(1) *The International and Comparative Law Quarterly* 53. www.jstor.org/stable/3663209.

Tang, Peter, 'China Confirms Record Wells in Several Areas' *Offshore Magazine* (September 1 1995). https://www.offshore-mag.com/regional-reports/article/16762345/asia-pacific.

Tanrıverdi, Abdullah, 'Eastern Mediterranean Natural Gas: Analyzing Turkey's Stance' (2013) 6(2) *European Journal of Economic & Political Studies* 83.

Tao, Long, 'Time to Teach Those Around South China Sea a Lesson' *China Global Times* (September 29 2011). http://www.globaltimes.cn/content/677717.shtml.

Tarzi, Nazli, 'Iraq and Kuwait Are at Loggerheads Over Conflicting Maritime Border Claims' *Middle East Monitor* (September 18 2019). https://www.middleeastmonitor.com/.

Tarzi, Nazli, 'This Land is Ours: Iraqi-Kuwait Tensions Rise in Waterway Row' *Middle East Eye* (February 9 2017). https://www.middleeasteye.net/news/land-ours-iraqi-kuwait-tensions-rise-waterway-row.

Tat, Tan Keng, 'South China Sea: Did the Ruling Sink the Rule of Law?' *The Straits Times* (Singapore, August 31 2016). https://www.straitstimes.com/opinion/did-the-ruling-sink-the-rule-of-law.

Tatsushi, Arai; Shihoko, Goto; Zheng, Wang (eds.), 'Clash of National Identities: China, Japan, and the East China Sea Territorial Dispute' (Research Report, Wilson Center, 2013). https://www.wilsoncenter.org/publication/clash-national-identities-china-japan-and-the-east-china-sea-territorial-dispute.

Tehran Times, 'Legal Framework of the Caspian Sea and the Interests of Iran' *Tehran Times* (Iran, November 6 2018).

Thang, Nguyen-Dang; Nguyen Hong Thao, 'China's Nine Dotted Lines in the South China Sea: The 2011 Exchange of Diplomatic Notes Between the Philippines and China' (2012) 43(1) *Ocean Development & International Law* 35.

Thao, Nguyen Hong, 'Joint Development in the Gulf of Thailand' (1999) *IBRU Boundary and Security Bulletin* 79.

Thao, Nguyen Hong; Amer, Ramses, 'Managing Vietnam's Maritime Boundary Disputes' (2007) 38(3) *Ocean Development & International Law* 305.

Thayer, Carlyle A., 'ASEAN'S Code of Conduct in the South China Sea: A Litmus Test for Community-Building?' (2012) 10(34) *The Asia-Pacific Journal: Japan Focus* 1. https://apjjf.org/2012/10/34/Carlyle-A.-Thayer/3813/article.html.

Thevenin, Pierre, 'The Caspian Sea Convention: New Status but Old Divisions' (2019) 44(4) *Review of Central and East European Law* 437.

Thomas, A. Mensah, 'Joint Development Zones as an Alternative Dispute Settlement Approach in Maritime Boundary Delimitation' in Rainer Lagoni and Daniel Vignes (eds.), *Maritime Delimitation* (Martin Nijhoff Publishers, 2006).

Thompson, Sarah; Macdonald, A.; Moullakis, Joyce, 'Woodside nears decision time on Korean exploration' *Australian Financial Review* (October 4 2016). www.afr.com/street-talk/woodside-nears-decision-time-on-korean-exploration-20161004-gru784.

Tobin, Meaghan, 'What's Behind the Revived Dispute Between Philippines and Malaysia Over Sabah?' *South China Sea Morning Post* (Hong Kong, September 9 2019). https://www.scmp.com/week-asia/explained/article/3026422/explained-whats-behind-revived-dispute-between-philippines-and.

Toktassynov, Temirtay, 'Caspian Sea Convention: The Settlement of the Long-Lasting Dispute and Its Implications' (2019) 6(3) *European Journal of Economics, Law and Politics (ELP)* 1.

Tønnesson, Stein, 'The South China Sea in the Age of European Decline' (2006) 40(1) *Modern Asian Studies* 1.

Tønnesson, Stein, 'The South China Sea: Law Trumps Power' (2015) 55(3) *Asian Survey* 455. https://www.prio.org/Publications/Publication/?x=8749.

Tønnesson, Stein, 'The South China Sea in the Age of European Decline' (2006) 40(1) *Modern Asian Studies* 1. https://www.cambridge.org/core/article/south-china-sea-in-the-age-of-european-decline/170B16B02C6B2C8922A0BD90D2A248DC.

Toumi, Habib, 'Kuwait, Iraq Embroiled in New Territorial Dispute' *Gulf News* (Bahrain, February 2 2017). https://gulfnews.com/world/gulf/kuwait/kuwait-iraq-embroiled-in-new-territorial-dispute-1.1971891.

Townsend-Gault, Ian, 'Rationales for Zones of Co-Operation' in Robert Beckman (ed.), *Beyond Territorial Disputes in the South China Sea: Legal Frameworks for the Joint Development of Hydrocarbon Resources* (Edward Elgar, 2013) 114.

Townsend Gault, Ian, 'The Frigg Gas Field' (1979) 3 *Marine Pol'y* 302.

TRT World, 'A Quick Look into the Eastern Mediterranean Gas Conundrum' *TRT World* (Turkey, December 10 2019). https://www.trtworld.com/turkey/a-quick-look-into-the-eastern-mediterranean-gas-conundrum-32062.

Tsakiris, Theodoros, 'Cyprus's Natural Gas Strategy: Geopolitical and Economic Preconditions' (2017) 28(1) *Mediterranean Quarterly* 29.

Tsamenyi, Martin; Herriman, Max, 'Ocean Energy and the Law of the Sea: The Need for a Protocol' (1998) 29(1) *Ocean Development & International Law* 3.

Tuerk, Helmut, *Reflections on the Contemporary Law of the Sea* (Martinus Nijhoff Publishers, 2012)

Tuerk, Helmut, 'The Contribution of the International Tribunal for the Law of the Sea to International Law' in Seoung-Yong Hong and Jon Van Dyke (eds.), *Maritime Boundary Disputes, Settlement Processes, and the Law of the Sea* (Martinus Nijhoff Publishers, 2009) 221.

Tunvir Shahriar, F. M., 'South China Sea Dispute: Asian Detonator to a Global Catastrophe?' (2013) 4(3) *Researchers World: Journal of Arts, Science & Commerce* 11.

Tyler, Timothy J.; Loftis, James L.; Hawker, Emilie E.; Vizcarra, Hana V.; Imad Khan, M., 'Developing Arctic Hydrocarbon Resources' in Myron Nordquist, John Moore, Aldo Chircop, and Ronan Long (eds.), *The Regulation of Continental Shelf Development: Rethinking International Standards* 319.

Tzeng, Peter, 'Jurisdiction and Applicable Law Under UNCLOS' (2016) 126(1) *Yale Law Journal* 242.

Ugwuanyi, Chijioke S., 'Does the Use of Joint Development Agreements Bar International Maritime Boundaries Delimitation' (2011) 1 *Dublin Legal Review* 28.

Uibopuu, Henn-Juri, 'The Caspian Sea: A Tangle of Legal Problems' (1995) 6 *The World Today* 119.

UN CCOP ECAFE, 'Geological Structure and Some Water Characteristics of the East China Sea and the Yellow Sea' (1969) Vol. 2 CCOP Technical Bulletin. https://www.gsj.jp/en/publications/ccop-bull/index.html.

United States - China Economic and Security Review Commission, 'Hearing Before the U.S. China Economic and Security Review Commission' (2013).

United States Congress and U.S.-China Economic and Security Review Commission. 'China's Maritime Disputes in the East and South China Seas. Hearing before the U.S.-China Economic and Security Review Commission' (2013) April 4, 2013. https://www.uscc.gov/Hearings/hearing-chinas-maritime-disputes-east-and-south-china-seas-webcast.

US Department of State. 'China's Maritime Claims in the South China Sea' *Limits in the Seas* (Report No. 143, Office of Ocean and Polar Affairs, Bureau of Oceans and International Environmental and Scientific Affairs, December 5 2014. https://www.state.gov/documents/organization/234936.pdf.

US Department of State, 'Iran's Maritime Claims' (Working Paper No 114 Limits in the Sea, Office of Ocean Affairs, Bureau of Oceans and International Environmental and Scientific Affairs). https://www.state.gov/wp-content/uploads/2020/01/LIS-114.pdf.

U.S. Geological Survey, 'Assessment of Undiscovered Oil and Gas Resources of Southeast Asia, 2010' (Report, June 2010). https://pubs.usgs.gov/fs/2010/3015/pdf/FS10-3015.pdf.

USA Today, 'Reports: Japan, China Agree on Gas Exploration in East China Sea' *USA Today* (June 15 2008). http://usatoday30.usatoday.com/money/industries/energy/2008-06-15-china-japan_N.htm.

USGS, 'Assessment of Undiscovered Oil and Gas Resources of Southeast Asia, 2010' Fact Sheet 2010–3015' *World Petroleum Resources Assessment Project.* https://pubs.usgs.gov/fs/2010/3015/pdf/FS10-3015.pdf.

Valencia, Mark J., 'Joint Jurisdiction and Development in Southeast Asian Seas: Factors and Candidate Areas' (1985) 10 *Energy* 573.

Valencia, Mark J., 'Regime-Building in East Asia: Recent Progress and Problems' (2006) 3 *Ocean Policy Studies* 672. http://www.sof.or.jp/en/report/pdf/200607_ISSN_1880_0017_03.pdf.

Valencia, Mark J., 'Regime-Building in East Asia: Recent Progress and Problems' (Research, Ocean Policy Studies - Nippon Foundation (2006) Vol. 3. http://www.sof.or.jp/en/report/pdf/200607_ISSN_1880_0017_03.pdfh.

Valencia, Mark J., 'Regional Maritime Regime Building: Prospects in Northeast and Southeast Asia' (2000) 31(3) *Ocean Development & International Law* 223.

Valencia, Mark J., 'The East China Sea Dispute: Context, Claims, Issues, and Possible Solutions' (2007) 31(1) *Asian Perspective* 127.

Valencia, Mark J.; Van Dyke, Jon M., 'Oil and the Lack of It in the South China Sea' (1999) 1 *Contemporary Southeast Asia* 153.

Valiyev, Anar, 'Azerbaijan-Turkmenistan Relations: Shattered Brotherhood' (2012) 9(122) *Eurasia Daily Monitor*. https://jamestown.org/program/azerbaijan-turkmenistan-relations-shattered-brotherhood/.

Van Der Meer, Sico, 'The Law and Politics of the Caspian Sea in the Twenty-First Century: The Positions and Views of Russia, Kazakhstan, Azerbaijan, Turkmenistan, With Special Reference to Iran' (2004) 5 *International Affairs* 1013.

Van Dyke, Jon 'Disputes Over Islands and Maritime Boundaries in East Asia' in Seoung-Yong Hong and Jon Van Dyke (eds.), *Maritime Boundary Disputes, Settlement Processes, and the Law of the Sea* (Martinus Nijhoff Publishers, 2009).

Van Dyke, Jon M.; Valencia, Mark J., 'How Valid Are the South China Sea Claims Under the Law of the Sea Convention?' (2000) *Southeast Asian Affairs* 47.

VanderZwaag, David L.; Vu, Hai Dang, 'Regional Cooperation in the South China Sea and the Arctic: Lessons to Be Learned?' in Aldo E. Chircop (ed.), *The Regulation of International Shipping International and Comparative Perspectives: Essays in Honor of Edgar Gold* (Martinus Nijhoff Publishers, 2012).

Var, Veasna, 'Cambodia–Thailand Sovereignty Disputes: Implications for Cambodia's Strategic Environment and Defence Organization' (2017) 41(2) *Strategic Analysis* 152.

Verani, Andre 'Dividing the Sea: The 1982 Law of the Sea Convention, Maritime Case Law, and the Current Dispute Between Guyana and Suriname' (2005–2006) 9 *Gonzaga Journal of International Law* 48.

Vida, Hamd; Frem, Soha; Karam, Karam, 'The Maritime Boundaries and Natural Resources of the Republic of Lebanon' (Report, UN Development Program - Common Space Initiative (CSI) Publications, December 2014). http://www.undp.org/content/dam/lebanon/docs/Governance/Publications/Legal%20section%201-6.pdf.

Vinogradov, Sergei; Wouters, Patricia, 'The Caspian Sea: Current Legal Problems' (1995) 55 *Zeitschrift für ausländisches öffentliches Recht und Völkerrecht* 604.

Vinogradov, Sergei; Wouters, Patricia, 'The Caspian Sea: Quest for a New Legal Regime' (2004) 9(1) *Leiden Journal of International Law* 87. https://www.cambridge.org/core/article/caspian-sea-quest-for-a-new-legal-regime/38C1D14FE3D9B6801BCAC67104457328.

von Hirschhausen, Christian; Engerer, Hella, 'Energy in the Caspian Sea Region in the Late 1990s: The End of the Boom?' (1999) 23(4) *OPEC Review: Energy Economics & Related Issues* 273.

Vu, Khanh; Pearson, James, 'Chinese Ship Back in Waters Off Vietnam Amid Coronavirus 'Distraction' *Reuters* (April 14 2020). https://www.reuters.com/article/us-vietnam-china-southchinasea/chinese-ship-back-in-waters-off-vietnam-amid-coronavirus-distraction-idUSKCN21W0CT.

Wang, Chao, 'International Arbitration of Maritime Delimitation: An Alternative for East Asia?' (2014) 7(2) *Journal of East Asia & International Law* 427.

Washington Report, 'Bahrain Retains Hawar Islands' (2001) 20(4) *Washington Report on Middle East Affairs*.

Watkins, Eric, 'A Mediterranean Hotbed' (2011) 109(2) *Oil & Gas Journal* 23.

Watkins, Eric, 'Japan, China Dispute Drilling in Area of E. China Sea' (2005) 103(17) *Oil & Gas Journal* 40.

Watkins, Eric, 'Japan, China in Stalemate Over Maritime Boundaries' (2004) 102(42) *Oil and Gas Journal* 28.

Watson, Sarah, 'The Bangladesh/Myanmar Maritime Dispute: Lessons for Peaceful Resolution' *Asia Maritime Transparency Initiative* (Report, October 19 2015). https://amti.csis.org/the-bangladeshmyanmar-maritime-dispute-lessons-for-peaceful-resolution/.

Watts, Robert C., 'Origins of a Ragged Edge U.S. Ambiguity on the Senkakus' Sovereignty' (2019) 72(3) *Naval War College Review* 101. www.jstor.org/stable/26654318.

Wei, Tan Dawn, 'Asean and China Should Aim to Conclude Talks on Maritime Code of Conduct in 3 Years: PM Lee' *Straits Times* (Singapore, November 14 2018). https://www.straitstimes.com/singapore/asean-and-china-should-aim-to-conclude-talks-on-maritime-code-of-conduct-in-3-years-pm-lee.

Weinstein, Michael, 'South Korea-Japan Dokdo/Takeshima Dispute: Toward Confrontation' (2006) 4(5) *The Asia-Pacific Journal Japan Focus*. https://apjjf.org/-Michael-Weinstein/1685/article.pdf.

Weissberg, Guenter, 'Maps as Evidence in International Boundary Disputes: A Reappraisal' (1963) 57(4) *The American Journal of International Law* 781.

Whitney, Charles, 'The Convention on the Legal Status of the Caspian Sea - A Sea or Not a Sea: That Is Still the Question' (Briefing Paper, Norton Rose Fulbright, September 2018). https://www.nortonrosefulbright.com/en-us/knowledge/publications/5f222b95/the-convention-on-the-legal-status-of-the-caspian-sea---a-sea-or-not-a-sea-that-is-still-the-question.

Whomersley, Chris, 'The Award on the Merits in the Case Brought by the Philippines Against China Relating to the South China Sea: A Critique' (2017) 16(3) *Chinese Journal of International Law* 387.

Wiegand, Krista E., 'Bahrain, Qatar, and the Hawar Islands: Resolution of a Gulf Territorial Dispute' (2012) 66(1) *Middle East Journal* 79.

Wiegand, Krista E., 'How Japan Benefits From the Senkaku/Diaoyu Islands Dispute' in Tim F. Liao, Kimie Hara, and Krista Wiegand (eds.), *The China-Japan Border Dispute: Islands of Contention in Multidisciplinary Perspective* (Taylor & Francis, 2016) 161.

Wiegand, Krista E., 'Resolution of Border Disputes in the Arabian Gulf (2014) 1(1) *The Journal of Territorial and Maritime Studies* 33. www.jstor.org/stable/26664097.

Wilder, Meagan P., 'Who Gets the Oil? Arctic Energy Exploration in Uncertain Waters and the Need for Universal Ratificatio of United Nations Convention on the Law of the Sea' (2010) 32(2) *Houston Journal of International Law* 505.

Winrow, Gareth M., 'The Anatomy of a Possible Pipeline: The Case of Turkey and Leviathan and Gas Politics in the Eastern Mediterranean' (2016) 18(5) *Journal of Balkan and Near Eastern Studies* 431. http://dx.doi.org/10.1080/19448953.2016.1196012.

Wolfrum, Rüdiger, 'Arbitration and the Law of the Sea - A Comparison of Dispute Resolution Procedures' in John Norton Moore (ed.), *International Arbitration: Contemporary Issues and Innovations* (Martinus Nijhoff Publishers, 2013).

Wong, Avril Lee, 'The North Seas Experience – An Analysis of Cross Border Unitisation – And Move Towards Establishing an International Legal Framework' (2008) 13(6) *CEPMLP Annual Review* 4.

Wong, Edward, 'U.S. Says Most of China's Claims in South China Sea Are Illegal' *New York Times* (July 13 2020). https://www.nytimes.com/2020/07/13/world/asia/south-china-sea-pompeo.html?searchResultPosition=4.

World Oil Review (Maribus, 2010). https://worldoceanreview.com/en/wor-1/energy/fossil-fuels/.

Yangwen, Zheng, *China on the Sea: How the Maritime World Shaped Modern China* (Brill, 1st ed., 2011).

Yann-Huei, Song; Blood-Patterson, N. Elias, 'Likelihood of U.S. Becoming a Party to the Law of the Sea Convention During the 112th Congress' (2012) 43(4) *Journal of Maritime Law & Commerce* 447.

Yayuz, Enex, 'The Eastern Mediterranean Dispute: Is There Light at the End of the Tunnel?' *TRT World* (Turkey, December 3 2019). https://www.trtworld.com/opinion/the-eastern-mediterranean-dispute-is-there-light-at-the-end-of-the-tunnel-31872.

Ye, Qiang; Jiang, Zongqiang, 'China's 'Nine-dash Line' Claim: US Misunderstands' (2015) No. 011 *RSIS Commentary*. https://www.rsis.edu.sg/wp-content/uploads/2015/01/CO15011.pdf.

Yefet, Nati, 'Israel, Lebanon on Gas Tender Collision Course' *Globes* (Israel, March 24 2017).

Yen, Ren, 'S. China Sea Verdict 'Null and Void' With No Binding Force: FM' *China Global* Times (July 7 2016). http://www.globaltimes.cn/content/993909.shtml.

Yiallourides, Constantinos, 'Joint Development of Seabed Resources in Areas of Overlapping Maritime Claims: An Analysis of Precedents in State Practice' (2019) 31(2) *University of San Francisco Maritime Law Journal*. https://ssrn.com/abstract=3258976; http://dx.doi.org/10.2139/ssrn.3258976.

Yiallourides, Constantinos, *Maritime Disputes and International Law: Disputed Waters and Seabed Resources in Asia and Europe* (Routledge, 2019).

Yiallourides, Constantinos, 'Senkaku/Diaoyu: Are They Islands?' (2017) 50(2) *International Lawyer* 347.

Yiallourides, Constantinos, 'Some Observations on the Agreement Between Greece and Egypt on the Delimitation of the Exclusive Economic Zone' (August 25, 2020) *European Journal of International Law EJIL: Talk!*https://www.ejiltalk.org/18969-2/.

Yingchun, Gong, 'Conflicts Over Rights in Disputed Sea Areas and Their Solutions' (2008) 2 *China Oceans Law Review* 307.

Yongming, Jin, 'The Contents of Japan's Submission on the Extended Continental Shelf and China's Position' (2009) 1 *China Oceans Law Review* 272.

Yoon, Mi Yung, 'European Colonialism and Territorial Disputes in Africa: The Gulf of Guinea and the Indian Ocean' (2009) 20(2) *Mediterranean Quarterly* 77.

Yoshifumi, T., 'Reflections on the Concept of Proportionality in the Law of Maritime Delimitation' (2001) 16(3) *International Journal of Marine & Coastal Law* 433.

Young, Margaret A., *Regime Interaction in International Law: Facing Fragmentation* (Cambridge University Press, 2012).

Young, Richard, 'Equitable Solutions for Offshore Boundaries: The 1968 Saudi Arabia-Iran Agreement' (1970) 64(1) *The American Journal of International Law* 152. http://www.jstor.org.ezproxy-b.deakin.edu.au/stable/2198622.

Yu, Jia; Ji-Lu, Wu, 'The Outer Continental Shelf of Coastal States and the Common Heritage of Mankind' (2011) 42(4) *Ocean Development & International Law* 317.

Yu, Yun; Kim, Ji Young, 'The Stability of Proximity: The Resilience of Sino-Japanese Relations Over the Senkaku/Diaoyu Dispute' (2019) 19(2) *International Relations of the Asia-Pacific* 327.

Zekos, Georgios, 'Arbitration as a Dispute Settlement Mechanism Under UNCLOS, the Hamburg Rules, and WTO' (2002) 19(5) *Journal of International Arbitration* 497.

Zhao, Li Guo, 'Seabed Petroleum in the East China Sea: Geological Prospects and Search for Hydrocarbons' in Selig S. Harrison (ed.), *Seabed Petroleum in Northeast Asia: Conflict or Cooperation?* (Research Report, Woodrow Wilson International Center for Scholars Asia Program, 2005).

Zhiltsov, Sergey, 'The International Legal Status of the Caspian Sea: Geopolitical Considerations of the Caspian States and Hydrocarbon Resources' (2017) 18(1) *Central Asia & the Caucasus* 50.

Zimmermann, Andreas; Baumler, Jelena, 'Navigating Through Narrow Jurisdictional Straits: The Philippines-PRC South China Sea Dispute and UNCLOS' (2013) 3 *The Law and Practice of International Courts and Tribunals* 431.

Zimnitskaya, Hanna; von Geldern, James, 'Is the Caspian Sea a Sea; And Why Does It Matter?' (2011) 2(1) *Journal of Eurasian Studies* 1. http://www.sciencedirect.com/science/article/pii/S1879366510000424.

Ziyadzade, Ziyad, 'Drilling for Black Gold: The Demarcation for Hydrocarbon Resources in the Caspian Sea' (2015) 16 *Chicago Journal of International Law* 312.

Zou, Keyuan; Qiang Ye, 'Interpretation and Application of Article 298 of the Law of the Sea Convention in Recent Annex VII Arbitrations: An Appraisal' (2017) 48(3–4) *Ocean Development & International Law* 331. https://doi.org/10.1080/00908320.2017.1320917.

Cases

Aegean Sea Continental Shelf Case, (Greece/Turkey) (Judgement) (1978) ICJ Reports 62. http://www.icj-cij.org/en/case/62.

Aegean Sea Continental Shelf Case, (Greece/Turkey) (Overview of the Case) (1978) ICJ Reports 62. http://www.icj-cij.org/en/case/62.

Aegean Sea Continental Shelf Case, (Greece/Turkey) (Reports of Judgments, Advisory Opinions and Orders) (1978) ICJ Reports 62. http://www.icj-cij.org/en/case/62.

Arbitral Award of 3 October 1899 (Guyana v. Venezuela) (Application Instituting Proceedings) (2018) ICJ Case 171. https://www.icj-cij.org/en/case/171.

Arbitral Award of 31 July 1989 (Guinea-Bissau v. Senegal) (Judgment) (1991) ICJ Rep 53. www.icj-cij.org/files/case-related/82/082-19911112-JUD-01-00-EN.pdf.

Arbitral Award of 31 July 1989 (Guinea-Bissau v. Senegal) (1991) ICJ Rep 53.

Barbados and the Republic of Trinidad and Tobago (Awards) (2006) PCA Case 2004–02. https://pca-cpa.org/en/cases/104/.

Barbados and the Republic of Trinidad and Tobago (Awards) (2006) PCA Case 2004-02. https://pca-cpa.org/en/cases/104/.

Bay of Bengal Maritime Boundary Arbitration between Bangladesh and India (Bangladesh v. India) (Awards) (2014) PCA Case 2010–16, 167 ILR 1. https://pca-cpa.org/en/cases/18/.

Bay of Bengal Maritime Boundary Arbitration between Bangladesh and India (Bangladesh v. India) (Awards) (2014) PCA Case 2010–16, 167 ILR 1, 53. https://pca-cpa.org/en/cases/18/.

Cameroon v. Nigeria (2002) *ICJ Rep* 303 [286].

Case of Cyprus v. Turkey (Judgment) (2001) European Court of Human Rights Application no. 25781/94. https://hudoc.echr.coe.int/eng#{%22documentcollectionid2%22:[%22GRANDCHAMBER%22,%22CHAMBER%22],%22itemid%22:[%22001-59454%22]}.

Clipperton Island Arbitration (France-Mexico)(1931) 2 R. Int'l Arb. Awards 1107.

Continental Shelf (Libya/Malta) (Judgment) (1985) ICJ Rep 13. www.icj-cij.org/files/case-related/68/068-19850603-JUD-01-00-EN.pdf.

Continental Shelf (Tunisia/Libya) (Diss. Op. Evensen) (1982) ICJ Rep 18. www.icj-cij.org/files/case-related/63/063-19820224-JUD-01-06-EN.pdf.

Continental Shelf (Tunisia/Libya) (Judgment) (1982) ICJ Rep 18. https://www.icj-cij.org/en/case/63.

Delimitation of Maritime Areas [St. Pierre and Miquelon] Between Canada and the French Republic (1992) Decision of Court of Arbitration 95 ILR 645. https://legal.un.org/riaa/cases/vol_XXI/265-341.pdf.

Delimitation of the Maritime Boundary Between Guinea and Guinea-Bissau (Judgment) (1985) 77 ILR 635. http://www.jstor.org/stable/20692951 (English).

Delimitation of the Maritime Boundary in the Gulf of Maine Area (Canada/United States of America) (Judgment) (1984) ICJ Rep 246. https://www.icj-cij.org/en/case/67.

Delimitation of Maritime Areas [St. Pierre and Miquelon] between Canada and the French Republic Decision of 10 June 1992, signed 10 June 1992. https://legal.un.org/riaa/cases/vol_XXI/265-341.pdf.

Dispute Concerning Delimitation of the Maritime Boundary Between Bangladesh and Myanmar in the Bay of Bengal (Bangladesh/Myanmar) (Judgment) (2012) ITLOS Case 16. https://www.itlos.org/fileadmin/itlos/documents/cases/case_no_16/C16_Judgment_14_03_2012_rev.pdf.

Dispute Concerning Delimitation of the Maritime Boundary Between Bangladesh and Myanmar in the Bay of Bengal (Bangladesh/Myanmar) (Notification Submitted by Bangladesh) (2009) ITLOS Case 16. https://www.itlos.org/fileadmin/itlos/documents/cases/case_no_16/Notification_Bangladesh_14.12.09.pdf.

Dispute Concerning Delimitation of the Maritime Boundary Between Ghana and Côte d'Ivoire in the Atlantic Ocean (Ghana/Côte d'Ivoire) (Judgment) (2017) ITLOS Case 23. https://www.itlos.org/en/cases/list-of-cases/case-no-23/.

Dispute Concerning Delimitation of the Maritime Boundary Between Ghana and Côte d'Ivoire in the Atlantic Ocean (Ghana/Côte d'Ivoire) (Request for the Prescription of Provisional Measures Submitted by the Republic of Côte d'Ivoire Under Article 290 of UNCLOS 27 February 2015) (2015) ITLOS Case 23. https://www.itlos.org/fileadmin/itlos/documents/cases/case_no.23_prov_meas/C23_Request_prov_measures_translation_Reg.pdf.

Dispute Concerning Delimitation of the Maritime Boundary Between Ghana and Côte d'Ivoire in the Atlantic Ocean (Ghana/Côte d'Ivoire) Special Chamber Prescribes

Provisional Measures, 27 April 2015 (2015) ITLOS Case 23. https://www.itlos.org/fileadmin/itlos/documents/press_releases_english/PR_229_EN.pdf.

Dispute Concerning Delimitation of the Maritime Boundary Between Mauritius and Maldives in the Indian Ocean (Mauritius/Maldives) (Judgment) (2019) ITLOS Case 28. https://www.itlos.org/en/cases/list-of-cases/case-no-28/.

Eritrea/Yemen - Sovereignty and Maritime Delimitation in the Red Sea (Phase Two Maritime Delimitation) (1999) PCA Case 1996–04, 91 ILR 543. https://pca-cpa.org/en/cases/81/.

Fisheries Case (UK/Norway) (Reports of Judgments, Advisory Opinions, and Orders) (1951) ICJ Rep 3, 129.

Frontier Dispute (Burkina Faso/Republic of Mali) (Judgment) (1986) ICJ Rep 1986, 554. https://www.icj-cij.org/en/case/69.

Gulf of Fonseca Case (El Salvador/Nicaragua), Central American Court of Justice, 1917, 11 *American Journal of International Law* 674 (1917). http://www.worldcourts.com/cacj/eng/decisions/1917.03.09_El_Salvador_v_Nicaragua.htm.

Guyana v. Suriname (Awards) (2007) PCA Case 2004-04, 139 ILR 566. https://pca-cpa.org/en/cases/9/.

Island of Palmas (or Miangas) (The Netherlands/The United States of America) (1928) PCA Case 1925–01 2 RIAA. https://pca-cpa.org/en/cases/94/.

Land and Maritime Boundary Between Cameroon and Nigeria (Cameroon v. Nigeria: Equatorial Guinea intervening) (Judgments) (2002) ICJ Rep 303. https://www.icj-cij.org/files/case-related/94/094-20021010-JUD-01-00-EN.pdf.

Legal Status of Eastern Greenland (1933) PCIJ Ser A/B No. 53.

Maritime Delimitation and Territorial Questions Between Qatar and Bahrain (*Qatar v. Bahrain*) (Merits Judgment of 16 March 2001) (2001) ICJ Rep 40. www.icj-cij.org/files/case-related/87/087-20010316-JUD-01-00-EN.pdf.

Maritime Delimitation and Territorial Questions Between Qatar and Bahrain (Qatar v. Bahrain) (Overview of Case) (2001) ICJ Rep 40. www.icj-cij.org/en/case/87.

Maritime Delimitation in the Black Sea (Romania v. Ukraine) *(Judgment)* (2009) ICJ Rep 61. https://www.icj-cij.org/files/case-related/132/132-20090203-JUD-01-00-EN.pdf.

Maritime Delimitation in the Indian Ocean (Somalia v. Kenya) (Application Instituting Proceedings) (2014) ICJ case 161. https://www.icj-cij.org/en/case/161.

North Sea Continental Shelf Cases (Ger. v. Den.; Ger. v. Neth.) (Sep. Op. Jessup) (1969) ICJ Rep 3. www.icj-cij.org/files/case-related/51/051-19690220-JUD-01-03-EN.pdf.

North Sea Continental Shelf Cases (Ger. v. Den.; Ger. v. Neth.) (Summaries of Judgment) (1969) ICJ Rep 3. www.icj-cij.org/files/case-related/52/5563.pdf.

North Sea Continental Shelf Cases (Ger. v. Den.; Ger. v. Neth.) (Judgment) (1969) ICJ Rep 3. www.icj-cij.org/files/case-related/52/052-19690220-JUD-01-00-EN.pdf.

Obligation to Negotiate Access to the Pacific Ocean (Bolivia v. Chile) (2018) ICJ Rep 507. https://www.icj-cij.org/en/case/153.

South China Sea Arbitration (The Republic of Philippines v. The People's Republic of China) (2016) PCA Case 2013–19, 170 ILR 1. https://pca-cpa.org/en/cases/7/.

South China Sea Arbitration (The Republic of Philippines v. The People's Republic of China) (Award on Jurisdiction and Admissibility) (2015) PCA Case 2013–19. https://pca-cpa.org/en/cases/7/.

Southern Bluefin Tuna Cases (New Zealand v Japan; Australia v Japan) (Provisional Measures) ITLOS Case Nos. 3 & 4, Order of 27 August 1999.

Sovereignty Over Pulau Ligitan and Pulau Sipadan (Indonesia/Malaysia) (2001) ICJ Reports 575. https://www.icj-cij.org/en/case/102.

Temple of Preah Vihear (Cambodia v. Thailand) (Judgment) (1961) ICJ Reports 52. https://www.icj-cij.org/en/case/45.

Territorial and Maritime Dispute (Nicaragua v. Colombia) (Judgment) (2012) ICJ Rep 624 [214]. https://www.icj-cij.org/files/case-related/124/124-20121119-JUD-01-00-EN.pdf.

Territorial and Maritime Dispute between Nicaragua and Honduras in the Caribbean Sea (Nicaragua v. Honduras) (Judgment) (2007) ICJ Rep 659. www.icj-cij.org/files/case-related/120/120-20071008-JUD-01-00-EN.pdf.

The "Volga" Case (Russian Federation v. Australia), Prompt Release (Declaration of Vice-President Vukas) (2002) ITLOS Case 21. https://www.itlos.org/cases/list-of-cases/case-no-11/.

The MOX Plant Case (Ireland v. United Kingdom) (Judgment) (2001) ITLOS Case 10. https://www.itlos.org/cases/list-of-cases/case-no-10/.

Timor Sea Conciliation (Timor-Leste v. Australia) (Decision on Australia's Objection to Competence) (2016) PCA Case 2016-10.

Western Sahara (1975) ICJ Rep 12. https://www.icj-cij.org/en/case/61.

Domestic Legislation

Cyprus: The Exclusive Economic Zone and the Continental Shelf Laws 2004 and *2014, Laws 64(I)/2004, 97(I)/2014)*. https://www.un.org/Depts/los/LEGISLATIONANDTREATIES/PDFFILES/CYP_EEZ-CS_Law_2014.pdf.

*Iran: A*ct of 18 June 1955 on the Exploration and Exploitation of the Natural Resources of the Continental Shelf of Iran. *English translation referenced in United Nations Legislative Series, National Legislation and Treaties Relating to the Law of the Sea, UN Doc. ST/LEG/SER.B/16, at 151* (1974). https://legal.un.org/legislativeseries/pdfs/volumes/book16.pdf.

*Iran: Act on the Marine Areas of the Islamic Republic of Iran in the Persian Gulf and the Oman Sea, 1993 1993.*https://www.un.org/Depts/los/LEGISLATIONANDTREATIES/PDFFILES/IRN_1993_Act.pdf.

*Malaysia: Continental Shelf Act 1966, Revised 1972.*http://www.agc.gov.my/agcportal/uploads/files/Publications/LOM/EN/Act%2083%20-%20Continental%20Shelf%20Act%201966%20Revised%201972.pdf.

People's Republic of China: Law on the Territorial Sea and the Contiguous Zone of 25 February 1992. https://www.un.org/Depts/los/LEGISLATIONANDTREATIES/PDFFILES/CHN_1992_Law.pdf.

US: Proclamation No. 2667 Policy of the United States With Respect to the Natural Resources of the Subsoil and Sea-Bed of the Continental Shelf, 10 Fed. Reg. 12305 (September 28 1945). https://www.gc.noaa.gov/documents/gcil_proc_2667.pdf.

US: Restatement of the Law (Third) The Foreign Relations Law of the United States §514 Cmt. A at 56, and Cmt. J.

Treaties and Declarations

Agreement 14 May 2003 on the Junction Point of Lines Delimiting Adjacent Zones of the Seabed and Subsoil of the Caspian Sea Between the Republic of Azerbaijan, Republic of Kazakhstan, and the Russian Federation, signed 14 May 2003, IMB 4056.

Agreement Between Qatar and Abu Dhabi on the Settlement of Maritime Boundaries and Ownership of Islands, signed 20 March 1969 (entry into force 20 March 1969). https://

www.un.org/Depts/los/LEGISLATIONANDTREATIES/PDFFILES/TREATIES/QAT-ARE1969MB.PDF.

Agreement Between the Government of Malaysia and the Government of the Kingdom of Thailand on the Constitution and Other Matters Relating to the Establishment of the Malaysia-Thailand Joint Authority, signed 13 May 1990.

Agreement Between the Government of Malaysia and the Government of the Kingdom of Thailand on the Constitution and Other Matters Relating to the Establishment of the Malaysia-Thailand Joint Authority, signed 13 May 1990. https://www.mtja.org/assets/pdf/en/agreement_en.pdf.

Agreement Between the Government of the Kingdom of Thailand and the Government of the Socialistic Republic of Vietnam on the Delimitation of the Maritime Boundary Between the Two Countries in the Gulf of Thailand, signed 9 August 1997, 39 *LOSB* 2000. 23 and 24.

Agreement Between *the Government of the Kingdom of the Netherlands and the Government of the United Kingdom of Great Britain and Northern Ireland Relating to the Delimitation of the Continental Shelf Under the North Sea Between the Two Countries*, 6 October 1965. http://www.marineregions.org/documents/NLD-GBR1965CS.PDF.

Agreement Between *the Government of the Kingdom of the Netherlands and the Government of the United Kingdom of Great Britain and Northern Ireland Relating to the Exploitation of Single Geological Structures Extending Across the Dividing Line on the Continental Shelf Under the North Sea*, 6 October 1965. https://www.un.org/Depts/los/LEGISLATIONANDTREATIES/PDFFILES/TREATIES/NLD-GBR1965GS.PDF.

Agreement Between *the Government of the State of Israel and the Government of the Republic of Cyprus on the Delimitation of the Exclusive Economic Zone*, signed on 17 December 2010 (entry into force on 25 February 2011). http://www.un.org/Depts/los/LEGISLATIONANDTREATIES/PDFFILES/TREATIES/cyp_isr_eez_2010.pdf.

Agreement Between the Government of the United Kingdom of Great Britain and Northern Ireland and the Government of Norway Relating to the Exploitation of the Statfjord Field Reservoirs and the Offtake of Petroleum therefrom, 16 October 1979. https://treaties.fco.gov.uk/.

Agreement Between the Government of the United Kingdom of Great Britain and Northern Ireland and the Government of the Kingdom of Norway Relating to the Delimitation of the Continental Shelf Between the Two Countries, 10 March 1965 (entry into force 29 June 1965). http://www.un.org/depts/los/LEGISLATIONANDTREATIES/PDFFILES/TREATIES/GBR-NOR1965CS.PDF.

Agreement Between *the Government of the United Kingdom of Great Britain and Northern Ireland and the Government of the Kingdom of Norway Relating to the Exploitation of the Murchison Field Reservoir and the Offtake of Petroleum Therefrom,* 16 October 1979, 39(1981) (entered into force 30 January 1981). https://treaties.fco.gov.uk/.

Agreement Between the Kingdom of Saudi Arabia and the State of Kuwait Concerning the Submerged Area Adjacent to the Divided Zone, signed 2 July 2000. https://www.un.org/Depts/los/LEGISLATIONANDTREATIES/PDFFILES/TREATIES/SAU-KWT2000SA.PDF.

Agreement Between *the Republic of Cyprus and the Arab Republic of Egypt on the Delimitation of the Exclusive Economic Zone*, signed 17 February 2003. http://www.marineregions.org/documents/EGY-CYP2003EZ.pdf.

Agreement Between *the Russian Federation and the Republic of Kazakhstan on the Delimitation of the Seabed of the Northern Part of the Caspian Sea for the Purposes of*

Exercising Their Sovereign Rights to the Exploitation of its Subsoil, IMB 4022–4033, signed 6 July 1998.

Agreement Between the United Kingdom of Great Britain and Northern Ireland and the Kingdom of the Netherlands Relating to the Exploitation of the Markham Field Reservoirs and the Offtake of Petroleum Therefrom, signed 26 May 1992, 38 (1993) (entered into force 3 March 1993). https://treaties.fco.gov.uk/.

Agreement Between *the United Kingdom of Great Britain and Northern Ireland and the Kingdom of the Netherlands relating to the Exploitation of the ORCA Field*, signed 27 November 2013. https://assets.publishing.service.gov.uk/government/uploads/system/uploads/attachment_data/file/281366/8802.pdf.

Agreement Between the United Kingdom of Great Britain and Northern Ireland and the Kingdom of The Netherlands Relating to the Exploitation of the Sillimanite Field, 19 July 2018.

Agreement Between the United Kingdom of Great Britain and Northern Ireland and the Kingdom of the Netherlands Relating to the Exploitation of the Sillimanite Field, 19 July 2018. https://assets.publishing.service.gov.uk/government/uploads/system/uploads/attachment_data/file/730574/TS_4.2018_UK_Netherlands_Sillimanite.pdf.

Agreement Between the United Republic of Tanzania and the Republic of Kenya on the Delimitation of the Maritime Boundary of the Exclusive Economic Zone and the Continental Shelf, signed 23 June 2009.

Agreement Concerning Delimitation of the Continental Shelf Between Iran and Oman, signed 25 July 1974.

Agreement Concerning Joint Development of the Southern Part of the Continental Shelf Adjacent to the Two Countries, Japan – Republic of Korea, signed 30 January 1974 (entry into force 22 June 1978).

Agreement Concerning Joint Development of the Southern Part of the Continental Shelf Adjacent to the Two Countries, Japan – Republic of Korea, signed 30 January 1974 (entry into force 22 June 1978). https://www.un.org/Depts/los/LEGISLATIONANDTREATIES/PDFFILES/TREATIES/jap-kor1974north.pdf.

Agreement on the Continental Shelf Between Iceland and Jan Mayen, Governments of Iceland and Norway, signed 22 October 1981. https://www.un.org/Depts/los/LEGISLATIONANDTREATIES/PDFFILES/TREATIES/ISL-NOR1981CS.PDF.

Agreement on the Delimitation of the Territorial Seas, Exclusive Economic Zones and Continental Shelves in the Beibu Gulf (Gulf of Tonkin) between the People's Republic of China and the Socialist Republic of Vietnam, 25 December 2000, IMB, 3755–3758.

Agreement Relating to the Joint Exploitation of the Natural Resources of the Seabed and Subsoil of the Red Sea in the Common Zone, Kingdom of Saudi Arabia and Sudan, signed 16 May 1974.

Alma-Ata Declaration, the Republic of Armenia, the Republic of Azerbaijan, the Republic of Belarus, the Republic of Kazakhstan, the Republic of Kyrgyzstan, the Republic of Moldova, the Russian Federation, the Republic of Tajikistan, the Republic of Turkmenistan, the Republic of Ukraine and the Republic of Uzbekistan, signed 21 December 1991. https://www.nytimes.com/1991/12/23/world/end-soviet-union-text-accords-former-soviet-republics-setting-up-commonwealth.html.

Anglo-Ottoman Convention of *1913*, signed 19 July 1913.

ASEAN, 'Joint Statement of the Meeting of Heads of State/Government of the Member States of ASEAN and the President of the People's Republic of China' (Presented at the Meeting of Heads of State/Government of the Member States of ASEAN and the President of the People's Republic of China, Kuala Lumpur, Malaysia, 16 December

1997). https://asean.org/?static_post=joint-statement-of-the-meeting-of-heads-of-stategovernment-of-the-member-states-of-asean-and-the-president-of-the-people-s-republic-of-china-kuala-lumpur-malaysia-16-december-1997.

ASEAN Declaration on the South China Sea, adopted 22 July 1992. https://cil.nus.edu.sg/wp-content/uploads/2017/07/1992-ASEAN-Declaration-on-the-South-China-Sea.pdf.

Bahrain-Saudi Arabia Boundary Agreement, signed 22 February 1958 (entered into force 26 February 1958). https://www.un.org/Depts/los/LEGISLATIONANDTREATIES/PDFFILES/TREATIES/BHR-SAU1958BA.PDF.

Blane Field Unitisation and Unit Operating Agreement, signed 6 July 2005. https://treaties.fco.gov.uk/.

Continental Shelf Delimitation Agreement in the Natuna Area of South China Sea, Indonesia-Vietnam, signed 26 June 2003, IMB. 3446.

Convention Between the Government of the French Republic and the Government of the Spanish State on the Delimitation of the Continental Shelves of the Two States in the Bay of Biscay (*Golfe de Gascogne/Golfo de Vizcaya*), signed 29 January 1974. https://www.un.org/Depts/los/LEGISLATIONANDTREATIES/PDFFILES/TREATIES/FRA-ESP1974CS.PDF.

Convention on Fishing and Conservation of the Living Resources of the High Seas, Opened for Signature 29 April 1958, 559 UNTS 285 (entered into force on 20 March 1966). https://treaties.un.org/pages/ViewDetails.aspx?src=TREATY&mtdsg_no=XXI-3&chapter=21.

Convention on the Continental Shelf, Opened for Signature 29 April 1958, 499 UNTS 311 (entered into force 10 June 1964) 1958 Optional Protocol of Signature concerning the Compulsory Settlement of Disputes.

Convention on the Continental Shelf, Opened for Signature 29 April 1958, 499 UNTS 311 (entered into force 10 June 1964). https://treaties.un.org/Pages/ViewDetails.aspx?src=TREATY&mtdsg_no=XXI-4&chapter=21&clang=_en.

Convention on the High Seas, Opened for Signature 29 April 1958, 450 UNTS 11 (entered into force 30 September 1962).

Convention on the High Seas, Opened for Signature 29 April 1958, 450 UNTS 11 (entered into force 30 September 1962). https://treaties.un.org/pages/ViewDetails.aspx?src=TREATY&mtdsg_no=XXI-2&chapter=21.

Convention on the Legal Status of the Caspian Sea, Republic of Azerbaijan, the Islamic Republic of Iran, the Republic of Kazakhstan, the Russian Federation and Turkmenistan), signed 12 August 2018 (not yet in-force). http://en.kremlin.ru/supplement/5328.

Convention on the Territorial Sea and the Contiguous Zone, Opened for Signature 29 April 1958, 516 UNTS 205 (entered into force 10 September 1964). https://treaties.un.org/pages/ViewDetails.aspx?src=TREATY&mtdsg_no=XXI-1&chapter=21.

Declaration on the Conduct of Parties in the South China Sea, Members States of ASEAN and People's Republic of China, signed 4 November 2002. https://asean.org/?static_post=declaration-on-the-conduct-of-parties-in-the-south-china-sea.

Exclusive Economic Zone Co-operation Treaty Between the State of Barbados and the Republic of Guyana Concerning the Exercise of Jurisdiction in Their Exclusive Economic Zones in the Area of Bilateral Overlap Within Each Of Their Outer Limits and Beyond the Outer Limits of the Exclusive Economic Zones of Other States, signed 2 December 2003 (entered into force 5 May 2004).

Joint Communique of the 29th ASEAN Ministerial Meeting, issued 20–21 July 1996. https://cil.nus.edu.sg/wp-content/uploads/formidable/18/1996-29th-AMMJC.pdf.

Joint Declaration of 27 September 1995 Cooperation Over Offshore Activities in the South West Atlantic, United Kingdom of Great Britain and Northern Ireland and the

Government of the Argentine Republic, signed 27 September 1995. https://www.fiassociation.com/key-documents.
Malaysia-Brunei Commercial Arrangement Area, signed April 2009.
Management and Cooperation Agreement Between the Government of the Republic of Senegal and the Government of the Republic of Guinea-Bissau, signed 14 October 1993 (entry into force 21 December 1995). https://www.un.org/Depts/los/LEGISLATIONANDTREATIES/PDFFILES/TREATIES/SEN-GNB1993MC.PDF.
Maritime Boundary Agreement Between the Government of the State of Israel and the Government of the Hashemite Kingdom of Jordan,signed 18 January 1996, 32 LOSB 1996. 97 and 98.
Maritime Delimitation Treaty Between Jamaica and the Republic of Colombia, signed 12 November 1993 (entry into force 14 March 1994). https://www.un.org/Depts/los/LEGISLATIONANDTREATIES/PDFFILES/TREATIES/JAM-COL1993MD.PDF.
Memorandum of Understanding Between Malaysia and the Socialist Republic of Vietnam for the Exploration and Exploitation of Petroleum in a Defined Area of the Continental Shelf Involving the Two Countries, signed 5 June 1992. https://cil.nus.edu.sg/wp-content/uploads/formidable/14/1992-MOU-between-Malaysia-and-Vietnam-for-the-Exploration-and-Exploitation-of-Petroleum.pdf.
Memorandum of Understanding Between the Kingdom of Thailand and Malaysia on the Establishment of a Joint Authority for the Exploitation the Resources of the Sea-Bed in the Defined Area of the Continental Shelf of the Two Countries in the Gulf of Thailand, signed 21 February 1979. https://www.mtja.org/assets/pdf/en/memorandum_en.pdf.
Memorandum of Understanding Between the Royal Government of Cambodia and the Royal Thai Government Regarding the Area of Their Overlapping Maritime Claims to the Continental Shelf, 18 June 2001, IMB. 3743 and 3744.
Plan of Action to Implement the Joint Declaration on ASEAN-China Strategic Partnership for Peace and Prosperity, ASEAN and People's Republic of China, signed 7 October 2003 (entered into force 1 November 2004). https://asean.org/plan-of-action-to-implement-the-joint-declaration-on-asean-china-strategic-partnership-for-peace-and-prosperity-2/.
Saudi Arabia – Iran Agreement, signed 24 October 1968,696 UNTS 189 (entry into force 29 January 1969). https://treaties.un.org/doc/Publication/UNTS/Volume%20696/volume-696-I-9976-English.pdf.
Seabed Boundary Agreement Between the Republic of Azerbaijan and the Republic of Kazakhstan, IMB 4048–4054, signed 29 November 2001. http://www.caspinfo.ru/library/doc/inter/inter_01.htm.
Seabed Boundary Agreement Between the Republic of Azerbaijan and the Republic of Kazakhstan, signed 29 November 2001, IMB 4048–4054. http://www.caspinfo.ru/library/doc/inter/inter_01.htm.
Seabed Boundary Agreement Between the Republic of Kazakhstan and the Russian Federation With Protocol, signed 6 July 1998.
Seabed Boundary Tripoint Agreement Between the Republic of Azerbaijan, the Republic of Kazakhstan, and the Russian Federation, 23 September 2002, IMB. 4039–4041.
Territorial Sea and Continental Shelf Boundary Between Guinea-Bissau and Senegal (Exchange of Letters Between Portugal and France), signed 25 May 1960. https://www.state.gov/wp-content/uploads/2019/11/LIS-68.pdf.
The Cairo Declaration, 26 November 1943. Published by Foreign Relations of the United States Diplomatic Papers, *The Conferences at Cairo and Tehran* (United States Government Printing Office History and Public Policy Program Digital Archive, 1961) 448–449. https://digitalarchive.wilsoncenter.org/document/122101.

The Eulsa Restriction Treaty, Japan-Korea, signed 17 November 1905. Also known as Japan-Korea Protectorate Treaty. http://dokdo.mofa.go.kr/eng/pds/pomflet_03.jsp.

The Framework Convention for the Sharing of Hydrocarbon Reservoirs Between the Republic of Cyprus and the Arab Republic of Egypt, signed 27 June 2012. http://www.marefa.org/images/5/54/The_Framework_Convention_for_the_sharing_of_hydrocarbon_reservoirs_between_Cyprus_and_Egypt.pdf.

The Government of the Kingdom of Norway Relating to the Exploitation of the Murchison Field Reservoir and the Offtake of Petroleum Therefrom, 16 October 1979, 39(1981) (entered into force 30 January 1981)

Timor Sea Treaty, Government of Australia and the Government of East Timor, signed 20 May 2002. https://www.un.org/Depts/los/LEGISLATIONANDTREATIES/PDFFILES/TREATIES/AUS-TLS2002TST.PDF.

Treaty Between Australia and the Democratic Republic of Timor-Leste Establishing Their Maritime Boundaries in the Timor Sea, signed 6 March 2018. https://www.dfat.gov.au/sites/default/files/treaty-maritime-arrangements-australia-timor-leste.pdf.

Treaty Between Equatorial Guinea and Nigeria on Joint Exploitation of Crude Oil, Especially at the Zafiro-Ekanga Oil Field Located at Maritime Boundary of Both Countries, signed 3 April 2002.

Treaty Between the Federal Republic of Nigeria and the Democratic Republic of Sao Tome and Principe on the Joint Development of Petroleum and Other Resources, in Respect of Areas of the Exclusive Economic Zone of the Two States, signed 21 February 2001. https://www.un.org/Depts/los/LEGISLATIONANDTREATIES/PDFFILES/TREATIES/STP-NGA2001.PDF.

Treaty Between the Federal Republic of Nigeria and the Republic of Equatorial Guinea Concerning Their Maritime Boundary, signed 23 September 2000 (entry into force 3 April 2002). https://www.un.org/Depts/los/LEGISLATIONANDTREATIES/STATEFILES/GNQ.htm.

Treaty Concerning the Establishment of the Republic of Cyprus, United Kingdom of Great Britain and Northern Ireland, the Kingdom of Greece and the Republic of Turkey, and the Republic of Cyprus, signed 16 August 1960. http://www.mfa.gr/images/docs/kypriako/treaty_of_establishment.pdf.

Treaty of Basic Relations, Japan – Republic of Korea, signed June 22, 1965 (1966) 583 UNTS 44 No. 8471. https://treaties.un.org/doc/Publication/UNTS/Volume%20583/volume-583-I-8471-English.pdf.

Treaty of Commerce and Navigation Between the Russian Socialist Federal Soviet Republic (RSFSR) and Persia, signed 25 March 1940, 144 British and Foreign State Papers 419.

Treaty of Friendship Between the Russian Socialist Federal Soviet Republic (RSFSR) and Persia, signed 26 February 1921, 9 LNTS 383.

Treaty of Golestan, Russia and Persia, signed 12 October 1813, British and Foreign State Papers vol 5 HMSO.

Treaty of Peace Between the Republic of China and Japan, signed 28 April 1952 (entered into force 5 August 1952). Also known as *Treaty of Taipei*. https://china.usc.edu/treaty-peace-between-republic-china-and-japan-treaty-taipei-1952.

Treaty of Peace With Japan, signed 8 September 1951 [1952] 136 UNTS 45 (entered into force April 28, 1952). Also known as Treaty of San Francisco. http://treaties.un.org/doc/Publication/UNTS/Volume%20136/volume-136-I-1832-English.pdf.

Treaty of Shimonoseki, Japan-China, signed April 17, 1895 (entered into force May 8 1895). https://china.usc.edu/treaty-shimonoseki-1895.

Treaty of Tordesillas Between the King of Portugal and the King and Queen of Castile, Aragon, signed June 7, 1494, (entered into force Sept. 5, 1494). A http://avalon.law.yale.edu/15th_century/mod001.asp.

Treaty of Turkomanchai, Persia-Russia, signed 22 February 1828, British and Foreign State Papers vol 15 HMSO.

Treaty on Relations of Co-Operation and Good Neighbourliness Between Romania and Ukraine, signed on 2 June 1997 (entered into force on 22 October 1997).

Treaty on Reversion to Japan of the Ryukyu and Daito Islands, signed 17 June 1971, 23 U.S.T. 446. https://www.nytimes.com/1971/06/18/archives/text-of-usjapanese-treaty-restoring-okinawa-and-nearby-islands-to.html.

Treaty Regarding Delimitation of the Maritime Boundary Between the Republic of Equatorial Guinea and the Democratic Republic of Sao Tome and Principe, signed 26 June 1999, IMB. 2654–2656

United Nations Convention on the Law of the Sea, Opened for Signature 10 December 1982, 1833 UNTS 3 (entered into force 16 November 1994). https://www.un.org/Depts/los/convention_agreements/texts/unclos/unclos_e.pdf.

United Kingdom of Great Britain and Northern Ireland and Norway Agreement Relating to the Exploitation of the Frigg Field Reservoir and the Transmission of Gas Therefrom to the United Kingdom, signed 10 May 1976 (entered into force 6 November 1996). https://treaties.un.org/doc/Publication/UNTS/Volume%201098/volume-1098-I-16878-English.pdf.

Vienna Convention on Succession of States in Respect of Treaties, Signed 23 August 1978, 1946 UNTS 3, 1115 UNTS 331 (entered into force 27 January 1980). https://legal.un.org/ilc/texts/instruments/english/conventions/3_2_1978.pdf.

UN Documents

Charter of Economic Rights and Duties of States, GA Res 3281(XXIX) UN GAOR, 29th Sess, Supp No. 31 (12 December 1974). https://www.aaas.org/sites/default/files/SRHRL/PDF/IHRDArticle15/Charter_of_Economic_Rights_and_Duties_of_States_Eng.pdf.

Charter of the United Nations

Government of Japan, Ministry of Foreign Affairs, 'The Senkaku Islands' https://www.mofa.go.jp/region/asia-paci/senkaku/pdfs/senkaku_en.pdf.

Koh, Tommy T. B., 'A Constitution for the Oceans' (1982) UN Conference. https://www.un.org/depts/los/convention_agreements/texts/koh_english.pdf.

Koh, Tommy T. B., 'A Constitution for the Oceans' Statement at Final Session of the Conference at Montego Bay (6 and 11 December 1982).

Lukoil, 'Lukoil Commissions Phase Three Facilities at Filanowsky Field' (Press Release, November 12 2019). https://www.lukoil.com/PressCenter/Pressreleases/Pressrelease?rid=441785.

Memorandum by the President of the Conference on Document UNCLOS Official Records Vols. I–XVII, NY: UN, 1973–1982, Vol. III, UN Doc A/CONF.62/WP.9/Add.1 (1976) 122 [6]. http://legal.un.org/diplomaticconferences/lawofthesea-1982/docs/vol_V/a_conf-62_wp-9_add-1.pdf.

Minster for Foreign Affairs and Emigrants, Lebanon letter to the Secretary-General of the United Nations, U.N. Doc. 3372.11D (3 September 2011).

Official Records of the Third United Nations Conference on the Law of the Sea, Volume VIII (Informal Composite Negotiating Text, Sixth Session), Explanatory Memorandum by the President of the Conference. UN Doc A/CONF.62/WP.10/REV.3/ADD.1 (28

August 1980). https://legal.un.org/docs/?path=../diplomaticconferences/1973_los/docs/english/vol_8/a_conf62_wp10_rev3.pdf&lang=E.

People's Republic of China, Ministry of Foreign Affairs, 'China's Oil and Gas Exploration in the East China Sea is Rightful and Legitimate' (Press Release, July 24 2015).

People's Republic of China, Ministry of Foreign Affairs, 'Foreign Ministry Spokesperson Jiang Yu's Remarks on China's Maritime Law Enforcement and Surveillance on the South China Sea' (May 28 2011). http://dm.china-embassy.org/eng/zt/wjbfyrth/t826601.htm.

People's Republic of China, Ministry of Foreign Affairs, 'Historical Evidence to Support China's Sovereignty Over Nansha Islands' (November 11 2000). https://www.fmprc.gov.cn/mfa_eng/topics_665678/3754_666060/t19231.shtml.

People's Republic of China, Ministry of Foreign Affairs, 'Position Paper of the Government of the People's Republic of China on the Matter of Jurisdiction in the South China Sea Arbitration Initiated by the Republic of the Philippines' (2014). https://www.fmprc.gov.cn/mfa_eng/zxxx_662805/t1217147.shtml.

People's Republic of China, Ministry of Foreign Affairs, 'Statement of the Government of the People's Republic of China on China's Territorial Sovereignty and Maritime Rights and Interests in the South China Sea' (December 7 2016). https://www.fmprc.gov.cn/nanhai/eng/snhwtlcwj_1/t1379493.htm.

People's Republic of China, Ministry of Foreign Affairs, 'The Statement of the Ministry of Foreign Affairs of the People's Republic of China on the Award of 12 July 2016 of the Arbitral Tribunal in the South China Sea Arbitration Established at the Request of the Republic of the Philippines' (2016) Home Position Paper. https://www.fmprc.gov.cn/nanhai/eng/snhwtlcwj_1/t1379492.htm.

People's Republic of China, Ministry of National Defence, 'Announcement of the Aircraft Identification Rules for the East China Sea Air Defense Identification Zone of the P.R.C.' (Press Release, November 23 2013).

People's Republic of China, The State Council, 'Summary of the Position Paper of the Government of the People's Republic of China on the Matter of Jurisdiction in the South China Sea Arbitration Initiated by the Republic of the Philippines' (December 7 2014).

People's Republic of China, The State Council, 'The Summary of the Position Paper of the Government of the People's Republic of China on the Matter of Jurisdiction in the South China Sea Arbitration Initiated by the Republic of the Philippines' (2013). http://english.www.gov.cn/archive/press_briefing/2014/12/07/content_281475020440060.htm.

Permanent Representative of Cyprus (Emilou, Nicholas), 'Letter Dated 15 June 2012 From the Permanent Representative of Cyprus to the United Nations Addressed to the Secretary-General, UNGA 66th Sess, Agenda Item 76, UN Doc A/66/851' (19 June 2012).

President of TRNC (Talat, Mehmet Ali) via Ambassador and Permanent Representation of Government of Turkey, 'Annex to the Letter Dated 2 February 2007 From the Permanent Representative of Turkey to the United Nations Addressed to the Secretary-General, Security Council 62nd Year, 61st Sess, Agenda Item 19, UN Doc A/61/727–S/2007/54' (2 February 2007). https://digitallibrary.un.org/record/592489?ln=en#record-files-collapse-header.

'Report of the International Law Commission on the Work of Its Eighth Session, Pt 1 Art 3 Territorial Sea, UN GAOR, 11th Sess, Supp No 9, UN Doc A/CN.4/104 (4 July 1956).

Republic of China (Taiwan), Ministry of Foreign Affairs, 'Solemn Declaration of the Ministry of Foreign Affairs of the Republic of China Concerning the Philippine Senate Bill 2699 and House Bill 3216' (February 6 2009). https://www.mofa.gov.tw

/en/News_Content.aspx?n=1EADDCFD4C6EC567&sms=5B9044CF1188EE23&s =585A1EF3AFBE9CFE.
Republic of China (Taiwan), Ministry of Foreign Affairs, 'South China Sea Issue' https:// www.mofa.gov.tw/en/theme.aspx?n=E5A0D5E2432C234D&s=83376F561B7165E6 &sms=BCDE19B435833080.
Republic of the Philippines, Department of Foreign Affairs, 'Notification and Statement of Claim on the West Philippines Dispute' (January 22 2013).
Republic of the Philippines, Department of Foreign Affairs, 'Notification and Statement of Claim on the West Philippines Dispute' (2013). https://www.dfa.gov.ph/images /UNCLOS/Notification%20and%20Statement%20of%20Claim%20on%20West %20Philippine%20Sea.pdf.
Republic of Turkey Ministry of Foreign Affairs, 'Press Release Regarding the New Cooperation Proposal of TRNC on Hydrocarbon Resources' (Press Release, July 13 2019). http://www.mfa.gov.tr/no_203_-kktc-nin-hidrokarbon-kaynaklarina-iliskin-yeni -isbirligi-onerisi-hk.en.mfa.
Republic of Turkey, Ministry of Foreign Affairs, 'Press Release Regarding the Efforts of the Greek Cypriot Administration of Southern Cyprus to Sign Bilateral Agreements Concerning Maritime Jurisdiction Areas With the Countries in the Eastern Mediterranean' (2007). http://www.mfa.gov.tr/_p_30-january-2007_-press-release -regarding-the-efforts-of-the-greek-cypriot-administration-of-southern-cyprus-to-sign -bilateral-agreements-concerning-maritime-jurisdiction-areas-with-the-countries-in-the -eastern-mediterranean_br___p_.en.mfa.
State of Palestine, Ministry of Foreign Affairs and Expatriates, 'Declaration of the State of Palestine Regarding Its Maritime Boundaries in Accordance With the United Nations Convention on Law of the Sea' (September 24 2019).
State of Palestine Ministry of Foreign Affairs and Expatriates, 'Declaration of the State of Palestine Regarding Its Maritime Boundaries in Accordance With the United Nations Convention on Law of the Sea' (September 24 2019). https://www.un.org/Depts/los/ LEGISLATIONANDTREATIES/PDFFILES/PSE_Deposit_09-2019.pdf.

Statute of the International Court of Justice

Submission from Permanent Mission of Lebanon to the United Nations pursuant to the UN Convention on the Law of the Sea (UNCLOS), 'Report on the Maritime Delimitation of Lebanon's Exclusive Economic Zone.' July 14 2010. http://www.un.org/depts/los/LEG ISLATIONANDTREATIES/PDFFILES/DEPOSIT/lbn_mzn79_2010.pdf.
Third United Nations Conference on the Law of the Sea, 'Enclosed and Semi-Enclosed Seas' 1973–82, Volume II, 2nd Sess, 38th Mtg, Agenda Item 17 A/CONF.62/C.2/SR.38 (13 August 1974).
UN, *Chapter XXI: Law of the Sea* (September 2 2020). https://treaties.un.org/Pages/ ViewDetailsIII.aspx?src=TREATY&mtdsg_no=XXI-6&chapter=21&Temp=mtdsg3 &clang=_en#EndDec.
UN, *Oceans: The Source of Life* (United Nations, 2002). https://www.un.org/depts/los/ convention_agreements/convention_20years/oceanssourceoflife.pdf.
UN, Official Records of the Third United Nations Conference on the Law of the Sea, Volume VIII (Informal Composite Negotiating Text, Sixth Session) Explanatory Memorandum by the President of the Conference. 28 August 1980, DOCUMENT A/CONF.62/WP.10/ REV.3/ADD.1, Ninth Session sess, UN Doc DOCUMENT A/CONF.62/WP.10/REV.3/

ADD.1 (28 July to 29 August 1980). https://legal.un.org/docs/?path=../diplomaticconferences/1973_los/docs/english/vol_8/a_conf62_wp10_rev3.pdf&lang=E.
UN, Twenty-Ninth Session Sess, Agenda Item Agenda Item 48 A/RES/29/3281. http://www.un-documents.net/a29r3281.htm.
UN CCOP ECAFE, 'Geological Structure and Some Water Characteristics of the East China Sea and the Yellow Sea' (1969) Vol. 2 CCOP Technical Bulletin. https://www.gsj.jp/en/publications/ccop-bull/index.html.
UN Convention on the Law of the Sea, 'Ad Hoc Meeting of States Parties, REPORT OF THE MEETING OF STATES PARTIES Prepared by the Secretariat, New York, 21 and 22 November 1994 mtg, UN Doc SPLOS/3' 28 February 1995.
UN General Assembly, 'H.E. Mr. Yoshihiko Noda, Prime Minister - Right of Reply (27 September 2012), General Assembly of the United Nations, Signed 26/27 September 2012 (67th Session)' https://gadebate.un.org/en/67/japan.
UN General Assembly, 'Letter Dated 15 June 2012 From the Permanent Representative of Cyprus to the United Nations Addressed to the Secretary-General Sixty-Sixth Session Sess, Agenda Item Agenda item 76, UN Doc A/66/851' (June 19 2012). https://undocs.org/A/66/851.
UN General Assembly, 'Status of Palestine in the United Nations, GA Res 67/19, 67th Sess, Agenda Item 37, UN Doc A/RES/67/19' (December 4 2012).
UN General Assembly GAOR, '22nd Sess, 1515th Mtg, Agenda Item 92, Paras 67 and 91'.
UN General Assembly GAOR, 'International Conference of Plenipotentiaries to Examine the Law of the Sea, UN GAOR, 11th Sess, 658th Plen Mtg, GA Res 1105 (XI)' (February 21 1957).
UN General Assembly GAOR, 'Report of the International Law Commission on the Work of its Eighth Session, 23 4 July 1956, Supplement No. 9 (A/3159), UN Doc A/CN.4/104' (July 4 1956). https://legal.un.org/docs/?path=../ilc/documentation/english/reports/a_cn4_104.pdf&lang=EFS.
UN General Assembly GAOR, First Committee Comm, 'Twenty-Second Session Sess, 1515th Meeting Mtg, Agenda Item Agenda Item 92' (November 1 1967). https://www.un.org/depts/los/convention_agreements/texts/pardo_ga1967.pdf.
UN General Assembly, Resolution 1105 (XI). 'International Conference of Plenipotentiaries to Examine the Law of the Sea, Resolution 1105 (XI, Official Records of the General Assembly, Eleventh Session Sess, 658th Plenary Meeting' (February 21 1957).
UN Permanent Mission of the People's Republic of China, 'Note Verbale Dated 7 May 2009 From the Permanent Mission of the People's Republic of China to the Secretary-General, UN Doc CML/17/2009' (May 7 2009). https://www.un.org/depts/los/clcs_new/submissions_files/mysvnm33_09/chn_2009re_mys_vnm_e.pdf.
UN Permanent Mission of the People's Republic of China, 'Note Verbale to the U.N. Secretary General From Permanent Mission of the People's Republic of China, UN Doc CML/8/2011' (April 14 2011).
UN Permanent Mission of the People's Republic of China, 'Note Verbale to the U.N. Secretary General from Permanent Mission of the People's Republic of China, UN Doc CML/8/2011b' (April 14 2011). https://www.un.org/Depts/los/clcs_new/submissions_files/mysvnm33_09/chn_2011_re_phl_e.pdf.
UN Permanent Representative of the Syrian Arab Republic, 'Letter Dated 29 April 2020 From the Permanent Representative of the Syrian Arab Republic to the United Nations Addressed to the Secretary-General, UN General Assembly 74th Sess, Agenda Item 74 (a) and 83, UN Doc A/74/831' (April 29 2020). https://undocs.org/en/a/74/831.

UN Permanent Representatives of Azerbaijan and Kazakhstan, 'Letter Dated 18 October 1996 From the Permanent Representatives of Azerbaijan and Kazakhstan to the United Nations Addressed to the Secretary-General, 51st Sess, Agenda Item 24, 64, 96, 97 and 98, UN Doc A/51/529 (October 21 1996).

UN Permanent Representatives of Kazakhstan and Turkmenistan to the United Nations, 'Letter Dated 14 March 1997 From the Permanent Representatives of Kazakhstan and Turkmenistan to the United Nations Addressed to the Secretary-General, 52nd Sess, Agenda Items 39, 99, 100 and 101, UN Doc A/52/93' (March 17 1997).

UN Permanent Representatives of the Islamic Republic of Iran and Turkmenistan, 'Letter dated 30 September 1998 from the Permanent Representatives of the Islamic Republic of Iran and Turkmenistan to the United Nations addressed to the Secretary-General, UN GAOR, 53rd sess, Agenda items 38, 93, and 94, UN DOC A/53/453' (October 2 1998). http://undocs.org/A/53/453.

United Arab Emirates, 'Ministry of Foreign Affairs Communication dated 17 November 2011 to UN' (2011). https://www.un.org/depts/los/LEGISLATIONANDTREATIES/PDFFILES/communications/are_note_re_sau_2011.pdf.

United Arab Emirates, 'Ministry of Foreign Affairs Communication Dated 17 November 2011 to United Nations' (2011). https://www.un.org/depts/los/LEGISLATIONANDTREATIES/PDFFILES/communications/are_note_re_sau_2011.pdf.

United Nations Convention on the Law of the Sea, 'Ad Hoc Meeting of States Parties', Statement by the Legal Counsel on behalf of the Secretary-General B Boutros-Ghali, SPLOS/3 (21 and 22 November 1994).

United Nations Convention on the Law of the Sea, Opened for Signature 10 December 1982, 1833 UNTS 3 (Entered into Force 16 November 1994).

Government/Corporate Documents

US Secretary of State Letter to the President, September 23, 1994. 'United States: President's Transmittal of the United Nations Convention on the Law of the Sea and the Agreement relating to the Implementation of Part XI to the U.S. Senate with Commentary' (1995) 34(5) *International Legal Materials* 1393.

US Senate, 'United States: President's Transmittal of the United Nations Convention on the Law of the Sea and the Agreement Relating to the Implementation of Part XI to the U.S. Senate With Commentary' (1995) 34(5) *International Legal Materials* 1393. www.jstor.org/stable/20698498.

Web Pages

Asia Maritime Transparency Initiative, 'A Blueprint for Cooperation on Oil and Gas Production in the South China Sea' (Research Paper, The Center for Strategic and International Studies, 2018).

Asia Maritime Transparency Initiative, 'Failing or Incomplete Grading the South China Sea Arbitration' (Web Page, July 11 2019). https://amti.csis.org/failing-or-incomplete-grading-the-south-china-sea-arbitration/.

Bowlus, John, 'Eastern Mediterranean Gas: Testing the Field' *Energy Reporters* (Web Page, May 27 2020). https://www.energy-reporters.com/opinion/eastern-mediterranean-gas-testing-the-field/.

China US Focus, 'Maritime Delimitation in the Gulf of Tonkin is Too Important to Be Ignored' *Security* (Web Page, May 29 2015). https://www.chinausfocus.com/peace-security/maritime-delimitation-in-the-gulf-of-tonkin-is-too-important-to-be-ignored#.

Congressional Research Service Specialist in Naval Affairs (Name Redacted). *Maritime Territorial and Exclusive Economic Zone (EEZ) Disputes Involving China: Issues for Congress* (CRS Report Prepared for Members and Committees of Congress No R42784, December 12, 2017) 33.

Durden, Tyler, 'Japan Protests After Discovering Chinese Military Radar in Disputed Waters' *Zero Hedge* (August 7 2018).

Gronewald, Sue, 'The Ming Voyages' *Asia For Educators - Columbia University* (Web Page, 2009). http://afe.easia.columbia.edu/special/china_1000ce_mingvoyages.htm.

Homage to the Roman God of Borders' Terminus. *Terminalia*.http://www.novaroma.org/nr/Terminalia.

Hydrocarbon Technology, 'Baku-Tbilisi-Ceyhan (BTC) Caspian Pipeline' (Web Page). https://www.hydrocarbons-technology.com/ projects/bp/.

IBRU, 'Israel Unilaterally Defines the Northern Limit of Its Maritime Space' *IBRU: Centre for Borders Research Boundary News* (Web Page, July 14, 2011). https://www.dur.ac.uk/ibru/news/boundary_news/?itemno=12445.

International Court of Justice, 'Cases' (Web Page). http://www.icj-cij.org/docket/index.php?p1=3&p2=2.

International Court of Justice, 'How the Court Works' (Web Page). https://www.icj-cij.org/en/how-the-court-works.

International Court of Justice, 'The Court' (Web Page). https://www.icj-cij.org/en/court.

International Tribunal for the Law of the Sea, 'History' (Web Page). https://www.itlos.org/the-tribunal/history/.

International Tribunal for the Law of the Sea, 'Members' (Web Page). https://www.itlos.org/en/the-tribunal/members/.

International Tribunal for the Law of the Sea, 'The Tribunal' (Web Page). https://www.itlos.org/the-tribunal/.

Karle, Prathamesh, 'Caspian Agreement: Many Issues Still to Be Settled' *Observer Research Foundation Raising Debates* (Web Page, October 15 2018). https://www.orfonline.org/expert-speak/caspian-agreement-many-issues-still-to-be-settled-44871/.

Kingsbury, Damien, 'Woodside Gas Deal Could Redraw Australia-East Timor Borders' (Web Page, Crickey.com, 2013). http://www.crikey.com.au/2013/02/12/woodside-gas-deal-could-redraw-australia-east-timor-borders/? wpmp_switcher=mobile.

Korea National Oil Corporation, 'Operations' (Web Page). https://www.knoc.co.kr/ENG/sub03/sub03_1_1_4.jsp.

Ku, Julian, 'Assessing the South China Sea Arbitral Award After One Year: Why China Won and the U.S. is Losing' *Lawfare* (Web Page, July 12 2017). https://www.lawfareblog.com/assessing-south-china-sea-arbitral-award-after-one-year-why-china-won-and-us-losing.

Lesaffer, Randall, 'The Iran-Iraq Border: A Story of Too Many Treaties' *Oxford Public International Law* (Web Page, August 11 2015). https://opil.ouplaw.com/page/iran-iraq-border.

Maizland, Lindsay; Xu, Beina, 'The U.S.-Japan Security Alliance' *Council on Foreign Relations* (Web Page, August 22 2019). https://www.cfr.org/backgrounder/us-japan-security-alliance.

Middle East Strategic Perspectives, 'Egypt: ENI's Zohr, a Boost for Political Stability' *Oil & Gas in Lebanon and the Eastern Mediterranean* (Web Page, September 6 2015). http://www.mesp.me/2015/09/06/egypt-enis-zohr-a-boost-for-political-stability-in-egypt/.

Ministry of Foreign Affairs of the Republic of China (Taiwan), 'Sustainable Governance and Enduring Peace in the South China Sea' *South China Sea Issue* (Web Page). https://www.mofa.gov.tw/en/theme.aspx?n=E5A0D5E2432C234D&s=83376F561B7165E6&sms=BCDE19B435833080.

Offshore Technology, 'Marjan Oil Field Development' (Web Page). https://www.offshore-technology.com/projects/marjan-oil-field-development/.

People's Republic of China, Ministry of Foreign Affairs, 'Historical Evidence to Support China's Sovereignty Over Nansha Islands' *The Issue of South China Sea* (Web Page, November 11 2000). https://www.fmprc.gov.cn/mfa_eng/topics_665678/3754_666060/t19231.shtml.

Rigzone, 'Shell Stops Production at Soroosh Field' *Rigzone* (Web Page, March 19 2003). https://www.rigzone.com/news/oil_gas/a/5974/shell_stops_production_at_soroosh_field_offshore_iran/.

Shell, 'Malampaya Phases 2 & 3' (Web Page). https://www.shell.com/about-us/major-projects/malampaya-phases-two-and-three.html.

Stratfor, 'Dokdo Island: A Case Study in Asia's Maritime Disputes' *On the Road - Stratfor* (Webpage, July 26 2015) 1. https://worldview.stratfor.com/article/dokdo-island-case-study-asias-maritime-disputes.

UN, 'Chapter XXI: Law of the Sea' *United Nations Treaty Collection* (Web Page, October 5 2020). https://treaties.un.org/Pages/ViewDetailsIII.aspx?src=TREATY&mtdsg_no=XXI-6&chapter=21&Temp=mtdsg3&clang=_en#EndDec.

UN, 'Chronological Lists of Ratifications of, Accessions and Successions to the Convention and the Related Agreements' *United Nations Oceans & Law of the Seas* (Web Page, October 3 2020). https://www.un.org/depts/los/reference_files/chronological_lists_of_ratifications.htm.

UN, 'Declaration and Statements' *United Nations Oceans and Law of the Sea Division of Ocean Affairs and Law of the Sea*. http://www.un.org/Depts/los/convention_agreements/convention_declarations.htm.

UN, 'Declarations Made Upon Signature, Ratification, Accession or Succession or Anytime Thereafter' *UN Oceans and Law of the Sea* (Web Page, updated February 13 2020). https://www.un.org/Depts/los/convention_agreements/convention_declarations.htm.

UN, 'Growth in United Nations Membership, 1945–Present' (Web Page, September 2020). https://www.un.org/en/sections/member-states/growth-united-nations-membership-1945-present/index.html.

UN, 'Oceans: The Source of Life, United Nations Convention on the Law of the Sea 20th Anniversary (1982–2002)' *United Nations Law of the Sea* (Web Page). https://www.un.org/depts/los/convention_agreements/convention_20years/oceanssourceoflife.pdf.

UN, 'Outer Limits of the Continental Shelf Beyond 200 Nautical Miles From the Baselines: Submissions to the Commission: Submission by the Republic of Korea' Oceans and Law of the Sea' *Commission on the Limits of the Continental Shelf (CLCS)* (Web Page, August 28 2013). https://www.un.org/Depts/los/clcs_new/submissions_files/submission_kor_65_2012.htm.

UN, 'Settlement of Disputes Mechanism' *UN Oceans and Law of the Sea* (Web Page, updated August 31 2019). https://www.un.org/depts/los/settlement_of_disputes/choice_procedure.htm#Choice_of_procedure.

UN, 'The United Convention on the Law of the Sea (A Historical Perspective)' *United Nations Oceans & Law of the Seas* (Web Page, 1998). http://www.un.org/Depts/los/convention_agreements/convention_historical_perspective.htm.

UN, 'The United Convention on the Law of the Sea (A Historical Perspective)' *United Nations Oceans & Law of the Seas* (Web Page, 1998). http://www.un.org/Depts/los/convention_agreements/convention_historical_perspective.htm at June 1 2014.

US Energy Information Agency EIA, 'Azerbaijan' (Web Page, January 7 2019). https://www.eia.gov/beta/international/analysis.cfm?iso=AZE.

US Energy Information Agency EIA, 'Caspian Sea Region' (Web Page, August 26 2013). https://www.eia.gov/international/analysis/regions-of-interest/Caspian_Sea.

US Energy Information Agency EIA, 'Contested Areas of South China Sea Likely Have Few Conventional Oil and Gas Resources' (Web Page, April 3 2013). https://www.eia.gov/todayinenergy/detail.php?id=10651.

US Energy Information Agency EIA, 'Country Analysis Brief: Malaysia' (2017). https://www.eia.gov/international/content/analysis/countries_long/Malaysia/malaysia.pdf.

US Energy Information Agency EIA, 'East China Sea' *Regions of Interest* (Web Page, September 17 2014). https://www.eia.gov/international/content/analysis/regions_of_interest/East_China_Sea/east_china_sea.pdf.

US Energy Information Agency EIA, 'More Than 30 Percent of Global Maritime Crude Oil Trade Moves Through the South China Sea' (Web Page, August 27 2018). https://www.eia.gov/todayinenergy/detail.php?id=36952.

US Energy Information Agency EIA, 'Oil and Natural Gas Production is Growing in Caspian Sea Region' (Web Page, September 11 2013). https://www.eia.gov/todayinenergy/detail.php?id=12911.

US Energy Information Agency EIA, 'Overview of Oil and Natural Gas in the Eastern Mediterranean Region' (Web Page, 2013). http://www.eia.gov/international/content/analysis/regions_of_interest/Eastern_Mediterranean/eastern-mediterranean.pdf.

US Energy Information Agency EIA, 'South China Sea' (Web Page, February 7 2013). https://www.eia.gov/international/analysis/regions-of-interest/South_China_Sea.

US Energy Information Agency EIA, 'Territorial Disputes Hamper Exploration and Production of Resources in the East China Sea' *Today in Energy* (Web Page, October 5 2012). https://www.eia.gov/todayinenergy/detail.php?id=8270.

US Energy Information Agency EIA, 'The Strait of Hormuz is the World's Most Important Oil Transit Chokepoint' *Today in Energy* (Web Page, June 20 2019). https://www.eia.gov/todayinenergy/detail.php?id=39932.

US Geological Survey, 'Fact Sheet: Assessment of Undiscovered Oil and Gas Reserves of the Levant Basin Province, Eastern Mediterranean' (Web Paage, World Petroleum Resources Project Fact Sheet 2010–3014, March 2010). http://pubs.usgs.gov/fs/2010/3014/pdf/FS10-3014.pdf.

US International Trade Administration, 'Oil and Gas - Kazakhstan: Recent Market Trends' (Web Page). https://www.export.gov/article?id=Kazakhstan-Oil-and-Gas-Equipment-and-Services.

US Library of Congress, 'China; Vietnam: South China Sea Agreement' (Web Page, October 17 2011). http://www.loc.gov/law/foreign-news/article/china-vietnam-south-china-sea-agreement/.

US Library of Congress, 'Vietnam: New National Law Intensifies International Dispute' (Web Page, July 19 2012). https://www.loc.gov/law/foreign-news/article/vietnam-new-national-law-intensifies-international-dispute/.

Wolfrum, Rüdiger; Pogies, Christian, 'With a Diplomatic Solution, There Would Be No Loser' *Völkerrechtsblog* (Web Page, August 30 2019). https://voelkerrechtsblog.org/with-a-diplomatic-solution-there-would-be-no-loser/.

Theses

Al Drazy, George, 'The Impact of Levant Basin Oil and Natural Gas Discoveries on Lebanese-Israeli Relations' (Master of Military Art and Science Thesis, U.S. Army Command and General Staff College, 2014).

Dehghani, Reza, 'Continental Shelf Delimitation in the Persian Gulf' (PhD Thesis, UN Oceans and Law of the Sea, The Nippon Foundation and Max Planck Institute for Comparative Public Law and International Law, 2009).

Dundua, Nugzar, 'Delimitation of maritime boundaries between adjacent States, United Nations – The Nippon Foundation (2006–2007)' www.un.org/depts/los/nippon/unnff_programme_home/fellows_pages/fellows_papers/dundua_0607_georgia.pdf.

Ganjaliyev, Elchin, 'Building Azerbaijan's Legal Framework for Marine Operations on the Basis of UNCLOS' (Thesis, University of Southampton, 2011–2012).

Huang, An-Hao, 'The Maritime Strategy of China in the Asia-Pacific Region - Origins, Development and Impact' (Doctor of Philosophy Thesis, University of Melbourne, 2009).

Long, Le Kim, 'The Potential for Cooperation in Shared Fisheries – Theory and Application to Vietnam's Fisheries Strategy in the South China Sea' (PhD Thesis, University of Tromso, 2009).

Marzoq, Sameer A., 'Northern Arabian Gulf a Critical Area for Maritime Safety and Security' (Msc Thesis, World Maritime University, Malmo, Sweden, 2013).

Miligan, Ben, 'Legal and Policy Options for the Provisional Joint Management of Maritime Spaces Subject to Overlapping Jurisdictional Claims' (PhD Thesis, University of Wollongong, 2012) 184.

Morton, Dirk Richard, 'Becoming a Good Neighbor in SEA - A Case for China's Territorial Disputes in the SCS, 1989–2006' (Doctor of Philosophy Thesis, Old Dominion University, 2007).

Nguyen, Lan Ngoc, 'The Contributions of UNCLOS Dispute Settlement Bodies to the Development of the Law of the Sea' (PhD Thesis, University of Cambridge, 2019).

Okafor, Chidinma Bernadine, 'Oil and Gas in the Nigeria - Cameroon Maritime Boundary Dispute: An Alternative Legal Approach' (University of Calgary, 2005).

Index